Date Due

JAN 2 7	2006		

Politics in
Southern Africa

Politics in Southern Africa

STATE AND SOCIETY IN TRANSITION

Gretchen Bauer
Scott D. Taylor

LYNNE
RIENNER
PUBLISHERS

BOULDER
LONDON

Published in the United States of America in 2005 by
Lynne Rienner Publishers, Inc.
1800 30th Street, Boulder, Colorado 80301
www.rienner.com

and in the United Kingdom by
Lynne Rienner Publishers, Inc.
3 Henrietta Street, Covent Garden, London WC2E 8LU

Library of Congress Cataloging-in-Publication Data
Bauer, Gretchen, 1959–
  Politics in southern Africa : state and society in transition /
  Gretchen Bauer and Scott D. Taylor.
  p. cm.
  Includes bibliographical references and index.
  ISBN 1-58826-332-0 (hardcover : alk. paper)
  ISBN 1-58826-308-8 (pbk. : alk. paper)
  1. Africa, Southern—Politics and government.
I. Taylor, Scott D., 1965– II. Title.
JQ2720.A58B38 2005
320.968—dc22

                           2004024451

British Cataloguing in Publication Data
A Cataloguing in Publication record for this book
is available from the British Library.

Printed and bound in the United States of America

5 4 3 2 1

Contents

Acknowledgments

We would like to acknowledge the important contributions of many people who helped make this volume possible. At the University of Delaware, two students, Atsuko Yokobori and Ann Kemp, provided helpful research assistance in the early stages of this project. Each of us was hosted by a research institution that facilitated portions of the research and writing process: Gretchen Bauer at the Institute for Public Policy Research in Windhoek, Namibia, and Scott Taylor at the Christian Michelsen Institute in Bergen, Norway. We are grateful for their support and for their hospitality. We would also like to thank our home institutions for financial and other support: the University of Delaware Department of Political Science and International Relations and the College of Arts and Sciences, as well as the School of Foreign Service of Georgetown University.

When we first glimpsed the "Regional Elections" mural now depicted on the cover of the paperback edition of this book, we immediately thought it would be ideal for the book. Although it depicts a South African scene, it perfectly captures the diversity of southern Africa as a whole, and its urban-rural and "modern"-"traditional" dichotomies. We are grateful to Ikem Okoye of the University of Delaware Art History Department for his help in locating and securing the photograph, as well as to the photographer, Sabine Marschall of the University of Durban–Westville. The mural, which is one of many community murals in South Africa, is located in Johannesburg and was painted by Apt Artworks, coordinated by Nicky Blumenfield.

The book benefited from the input of many individuals. We are indebted to many southern African friends, colleagues, and informants who have given generously of their time and insights during our numerous research trips to the region over the years. We would like to thank Lynne Rienner for persevering with this project and Shena Redmond, senior project editor at Lynne Rienner Publishers, for seeing it through the production phase. We owe particular thanks to Inge Tvedten and Gisela Geisler, who kindly read drafts of several chapters and offered valuable feedback. In addition, two anonymous reviewers provided useful comments and suggestions on the entire draft. Finally, we owe the greatest debt of gratitude to our families for their forbearance while we worked on this project. Without their support, we could not have brought this book to fruition.

Southern Africa

1

Introduction:
Southern Africa as Region

In a number of recent formulations, the African state has fared quite badly. It has been variously described as "criminal" (Bayart, Ellis, and Hibou 1999), as being "in chaos" (Ayittey 1998), or as having achieved a condition of "instrumentalized disorder" (Chabal and Daloz 1999). Further reports contend that the state has suffered so great a deterioration in Africa that anarchy and collapse prevail on the continent—a situation bordering on "statelessness" in which states are on the brink, at best, and societies exist without viable states, at worst (Kaplan 1994, 2000). Although a number of these analyses suggest that African states have failed due to a combination of internal corruption, depraved leadership, and a hostile external environment, but can be restored (Zartman 1995), one recent analysis suggests that the origin of African state dysfunction in the contemporary period is rooted in geography and dates to the *pre*colonial era, thus conforming to a centuries-old pattern of neglect of the countryside. According to Jeffrey Herbst (2000), precolonial political authorities lacked the incentive and capacity to project power beyond central cities; colonialism exacerbated the phenomenon, and hence the scope of the contemporary African state is limited geographically. As a result, sovereignty—indeed "stateness"—remains elusive. Another investigation attempts to portray Africa's predicament as normal (Chabal and Daloz 1999). In this view, the norm in Africa is a "vacuous and ineffectual" state, characterized by endemic corruption and neopatrimonialism; liberal democratic state models and forms of government are fundamentally incompatible with African culture, Western notions of civil society are inapplicable, and the state is merely an instrument for depraved elites.

We regard this Afropessimist literature as deeply problematic.[1] The danger of much of this work lies chiefly in the attempt to paint Africa with one brush, sweeping aside any empirical observations from this vast continent that might challenge Afropessimists' dismal assumptions and their equally dire conclusions. At the same time, it is hard to argue that pessimistic views of African state and society are not based at some level on observable realities, such as genocide in Rwanda, grisly civil war in Liberia and Sierra Leone, state collapse in Somalia, and embedded corruption in Nigeria. Rather, our point is that the writings of Kaplan, Chabal and Daloz, and Ayittey tend to obscure important regional and subregional distinctions and confirm Western preconceptions—and misconceptions—about the African continent.

Notably, much of the "evidence" for the dire assessments of Africa comes from West Africa, a region that has seen more than its share of tragedy and upheaval in four decades of independence. In that historically volatile region, there are today credible signs of stability and potential for renewal.[2] However, even while ignoring countervailing evidence from within West Africa itself, the message of these works is that what applies in West Africa obtains throughout the entire continent.[3] One of the goals of this book, then, is to challenge such assumptions and to illuminate Africa's political, economic, and social diversity by focusing on the distinct regional character of southern Africa.

The African continent represents a vast area of the globe. Africa is three times the size of the United States. Its population of 800 million people is nearly equal to that of the Americas, north and south. Its people reside in fifty-four countries and speak over a thousand different languages, many of which represent distinct cultures. African history—ancient and modern—is remarkably diverse, and its contemporary political and economic structures also vary widely. Quite simply, as Chris Allen (1995) has argued, "there are many Africas." Yet the impulse of both those unfamiliar with Africa and many scholars and practitioners is to treat Africa as a monolith. This use of "Africa" as convenient shorthand is particularly destructive and misleading, especially in the case of the Afropessimists, who attempt to extrapolate from a few countries a "theory" of African politics.

Even many African politics textbooks, which tend to be more evenhanded in their appraisal of Africa's problems and prospects, struggle to strike a balance between targeted analyses of specific countries and overgeneralizations of conditions on the continent (Tordoff 1996; Khapoya 1998; Chazan et al. 1999; Schraeder 2000; Gordon and Gordon 2001; Thompson 2001). Texts that examine Africa as a whole are quite useful in providing a broad introduction to a continent unfamiliar to many audiences. At the same time, certain common factors that do exist, such as the universality of colonialism and the preponderance of underdevelopment or maldevelopment, have led to a monolithic, undifferentiated approach to the study of African politics and society,[4] an approach that tends to obscure important regional distinctions.

■ Southern Africa as a Region

Southern Africa is one of the areas of the African continent that warrants systematic treatment as a region.[5] As Sandra MacLean observes, "regions are almost always more than geopolitical divisions; they are also 'social constructions,' i.e., processes based on shared interests and intersubjective understanding." And, although both political boundaries and identities can shift over time,

> it is well established that the region of southern Africa does exist empirically. As Vale states, "the notion of Southern Africa—like the notion of Europe—is a single and indivisible one." To be thus identified, a particular area or group of states must, over time, develop a sense of "regionness." There are various levels of this quality, determined largely by the degree to which the empirical and socially constructed attributes are entrenched and combined. (1999, 947)[6]

Building on this notion of regionness, it is possible to identify a number of common empirical and socially constructed attributes within and across states and societies in southern Africa. Indeed, given the many shared attributes and experiences, analysis of the countries as part of a regional bloc is a potentially fruitful and revealing exercise.

First, many of the contemporary states of southern Africa share a common colonial and early postcolonial history. The region was initially settled by the Portuguese on both coasts, in what is now Mozambique and Angola, and by the Dutch in South Africa. However, with the exceptions of Angola, Mozambique, and Namibia (which was under German rule), much of the territory had fallen under British imperial domination by the end of the nineteenth century. Although Portuguese, Afrikaner (Dutch), and German influences continue to play a role in one or more of the states of the region today, the Anglo linguistic, legal, political, and economic heritage remains a common feature for most.

Moreover, for nearly all of southern Africa, colonialism lasted far longer than elsewhere on the continent. In five countries—Angola, Mozambique, Zimbabwe, Namibia, and South Africa—liberation movements were forced to resort to armed struggle to attain independence. Each of these movements was marked by at least a rhetorical commitment to socialism. In the context of the Cold War, the stated commitment to socialist principles generated intense interest in the region among external actors. It also fueled apartheid South Africa's campaign of regional destabilization against neighboring countries, the effects of which were borne by all the countries in southern Africa. This extended colonialism—and the resort to war to obtain independence—have had profound and lasting effects on social, political, and economic developments in the region, which are elaborated in the country chapters of this book.

Second, the presence of large white settler populations, or at least settler interests, emerges directly from the region's unique history and represents a key feature of many of its states. Each of the five aforementioned states that underwent violent struggles for liberation had an expansive settler population. Although whites fled Angola and Mozambique on the eve of independence, their continued prominence in many countries, including South Africa, Zimbabwe, and Namibia, and to a considerably lesser extent in Botswana and Zambia, has been a double-edged sword. These states face severe and potentially destabilizing disparities of wealth and resources between rich and poor. Of course, there are wealthy black elites; however, a disproportionate share of wealth and productive capacity is owned and controlled by a "nonindigenous" white minority, a situation that has contributed to lingering tensions. There are also significant numbers of other "nonindigenous" groups, particularly Indians, who occupy important economic strata. How these countries incorporate racial and ethnic minorities affects their prospects for long-term stability.

At the same time, paradoxically, it can be argued that the white presence in southern Africa has improved the development prospects for the region. Whereas some settler regimes in Africa, such as in Kenya and Algeria, abandoned the continent in the 1960s, their southern African counterparts held on much longer. White-ruled regimes in Zimbabwe (until 1980), Namibia (until 1990), and South Africa (until 1994) used their tight control over resources and international access to provide a strong infrastructure and relatively sophisticated international economies that were inherited by black governments at independence.[7]

Third, southern Africa is politically and socially interconnected and interdependent. Although the region cannot be described as culturally homogeneous, the peoples of southern Africa are interrelated to a significant degree. The first inhabitants of the region were the Khoisan, whose descendants still live in parts of Namibia, South Africa, and Botswana. In the early centuries of the common era the Khoisan were joined, and substantially displaced, by successive waves of peoples from the north, as the Bantu migrations dispersed peoples throughout Africa. These Bantu-speaking peoples were agriculturalists, as well as pastoralists, who brought with them techniques of smelting iron and other metals. Their descendants are found today throughout southern Africa—for example, the Chewa in Malawi, the Bemba in Zambia, and the Xhosa and Zulu in South Africa, among many other groups. In the nineteenth century the accelerated arrival of Europeans and the formal onset of colonialism in southern Africa and

elsewhere meant the imposition of arbitrary boundaries that typically divided ethnic groups across colonial borders. With few exceptions, the colonial-
era map of Africa is unchanged, and therefore connections remain between
peoples across those same borders: there are Batswana in Botswana and
South Africa, Basotho in Lesotho and South Africa, Ovambo in Namibia
and Angola, Shona in Zimbabwe and Mozambique, and so on.

Connections among the peoples of southern Africa are also fostered by
a regionwide migrant labor system, which is another artifact of European
settlement and colonialism. With the discovery of diamonds and gold in the
future South Africa in the late 1800s, there emerged a migrant labor system
that brought workers from throughout the region to the mines in South
Africa. Before and after independence foreign migrant workers also
crossed borders to work in mines in Namibia, Botswana, Zambia, and
Zimbabwe. As they crisscrossed the region, mineworkers participated in a
cross-fertilization of ideas and experiences across national borders, leading
in some cases to an early organization of workers or the rise of nationalist
movements. Southern Africans also crossed regional borders in search of
educational opportunities. During the colonial period, for example, a number of southern African leaders (as well as other privileged elites) attended
Fort Hare College in South Africa, the first university for blacks in the
region. Much later, many black Namibians, with no tertiary-level educational opportunities in their own country, would flock to South African universities—and then return home imbued with tactics gleaned from South
Africa's liberation struggle.

Liberation struggles also fostered interconnectedness among peoples
and states of the region. Many of those fighting for independence in their
own countries were forced to spend long periods of exile in neighboring
countries. Countries like Angola, Mozambique, and Zambia, which gained
their independence first, became havens in the 1970s and 1980s for rebel
movements that were attempting to end minority rule in South West Africa
(Namibia), Rhodesia (Zimbabwe), and South Africa. Thus, tens of thousands of Namibians spent decades in Angola, many South Africans flocked
to Zambia, and Zimbabwean rebels established staging areas in
Mozambique, to cite but a few examples.[8] In the process, these young
exiles were also able to compare experiences from home and contemplate
a common southern African future. Moreover, throughout these same years
of struggle, the independent countries of the region were united in a political body known as the Frontline States (FLS), formed in an effort to iso-
late apartheid South Africa and bring an end to white minority rule in the
country.[9]

Fourth, as in much of the rest of Africa, countries in southern Africa
are currently undergoing processes of political and economic transition.
Although nearly every state in the region claims to be democratic, the

degree to which democracy exists varies widely, in part reflecting the varied experiences of transition and the difficulty of inculcating and consolidating democracy. Botswana, of course, is typically cited as one of the most democratic countries in Africa, with a history of peace and stability and democratic elections since independence in 1966. Namibia and South Africa, since their respective transitions in 1990 and 1994, have received widespread acclaim for their democratic constitutions and respect for the rule of law. Zambia and Malawi, following a pattern familiar to much of the rest of Africa, made transitions in the early 1990s from decades of single-party rule by presidents-for-life (de facto in Zambia, de jure in Malawi) to multiparty political systems. In Zimbabwe, the question of democratic rule hangs in the balance, as President Robert Mugabe, in office since 1980, has employed ruinous and often violent strategies to undermine a democratic opposition movement and continue his tenure in office by authoritarian means. Finally, the Lusophone states took divergent paths in the 1990s. In Mozambique, a successful transition from three decades of war to peace in 1992 made way for a vibrant period of reconstruction and development. In Angola, an end to decades of war was only accomplished after the death of rebel leader Jonas Savimbi in early 2002. An initially cautious cease-fire has since given way to a steady, if uncertain, movement toward economic and political transition in that country.

In addition to the nearly regionwide turn to democracy, the states of southern Africa share a unique feature in Africa: none has been the victim of a military coup. In fact, even coup *attempts* are rare, making southern Africa truly exceptional on the continent in this regard.[10] This may suggest a level of stability or at least a respect for and expectation of civilian rule that does not prevail throughout Africa. Moreover, the region is also characterized today by relative peace. With the exception of Zimbabwe, each of the other countries has, at the moment, manageable levels of social conflict and internal security and cohesion—again, a factor that differentiates the south from nearly every other zone in Africa. This peace and stability should bode well for future economic development and the sustainability of social and political movements attempting to achieve greater democracy.

Economically, there is considerable variation among southern African countries. That variation stems from a host of factors: population size (Botswana and Namibia have fewer than 2 million people, South Africa has more than 45 million); resource endowment (Botswana, Namibia, and South Africa have diamonds and other valuable minerals, Angola has diamonds and oil; by contrast, Malawi grows tobacco and Mozambique cashews and prawns); location (Botswana, Malawi, Zambia, and Zimbabwe are landlocked while the others have ample access to the sea); decades of war versus peace and stability; and so forth. In 2001, per capita gross domestic products (GDPs) (at purchasing power parity) in the region ranged from U.S.$11,290 in South Africa, whose industrialized economy dwarfs all of the others, to U.S.$570 in Malawi (United Nations Development Programme 2003). Taken together, however, the economies of southern Africa are among the strongest on the continent, and the potential for future collective growth and development is enormous.

Despite this relative economic strength, however, with the exception of Botswana and Namibia, all of the countries of southern Africa adopted some form of neoliberal economic reform, often referred to as structural adjustment programs (SAPs), in the 1980s and 1990s. Designed and implemented by the World Bank and International Monetary Fund,[11] these programs are intended to spur a process of fundamental economic transformation. SAPs were imposed across the continent beginning in the 1980s, when African states proved unable to recover from the collapse of global primary commodities prices, declining terms of trade, and rising debt levels. When they were introduced, however, adjustment programs were envisioned as a short-term series of measures that would restore Africa's economic health (World Bank 1981); in the third decade of adjustment, it is apparent how erroneous these rosy projections were. Moreover, although the programs themselves have been modified over the years in response to intense criticism, and lack of tangible and sustainable success (Mkandawire and Soludo 1999), they continue to adhere closely to an orthodox neoliberal economic model that regards state involvement in the economy negatively (World Bank 2000). Given the substantial economic role played historically by southern African states, this process of transformation has proved particularly unsettling and painful for many. The interconnectedness of this region has meant that economic difficulties in one country are keenly felt in neighboring states.

Indeed, regional proximity and economic interconnectedness have produced harmonies as well as tensions. A formal institution through which states attempt to mitigate conflict and promote economic and political cooperation is the Southern African Development Community (SADC). The SADC itself underwent a notable transition in the 1990s when it transformed itself from the Southern African Development Coordination Conference (itself made up of the members of the Frontline States grouping), into the Southern African Development Community, with South Africa at its core. Owing partly to South Africa's membership and its ability to play a hegemonic role given its far more developed economy, the SADC is today regarded by many as the most viable regional economic community in Africa (McCarthy 1999).[12] Although one of three (somewhat redundant) bodies concerned with regional trade relations, the SADC also represents a forum for regional cooperation on a large range of nontrade issues including politics, transport, gender, and health.

In sum, the histories, prevailing political, social, and economic conditions, as well as the fates of each of the countries of southern Africa are profoundly linked. This book attempts to regard them as such.

■ Theory and Southern Africa

Southern Africa has been examined through multiple theoretical lenses, each of which offers some insight on the politics of the region as a whole, or of its constituent parts. International relations theories are particularly suited to the former, and scholars have employed variations on realist, liberal, and Marxist approaches to the study of the region (Vale 2001). Operating at a lower level of abstraction, scholars of comparative politics have relied generally on related theoretical tools, such as the modernization, dependency, and statist approaches, as well as on pluralist models that emphasize societal actors (Chazan et al. 1999). Each of these theories and their various permutations have been employed to explain political and economic phenomena in independent Africa as a whole, though they have often come to conflicting conclusions about the nature of the politics in and of Africa.

Dependency and underdevelopment, for example, which have their intellectual origins in Marxism, were particularly helpful in conceptualizing the world as a system of states, in which the less-developed regions, including Africa, were unalterably relegated to the global periphery (Rodney 1974; Wallerstein 1974). Such perspectives, which elevate the notion of structure, had some validity: surely the marginal position from which African states entered the world stage—namely as economically backward, primary commodity exporters—helps to explain the contemporary African predicament (Leys 1994). These approaches, however, neglected too many factors. Like the structuralist theories within the international relations subfield, such as neorealism, which regarded the position of states as a result of power relations, the dependency tradition tended to ignore that power may also reside in states of the so-called periphery (as well as being vested in actors other than states).

In short, structural theories rely on material capacity and suggest that material attributes or endowments (whether wealth or power) determine political behavior (Finnemore and Sikkink 2001). In this view, African states are at the mercy of more powerful states in the developed north. Yet this is not consistently the case, and structuralist approaches are largely incapable of explaining the variation and change that defines political life, at both the international and national levels. An emphasis on *agency,* on the other hand, can help offset several of these shortcomings.

Depending on whether the level of analysis is international relations or at the state level, individual states or individual economic or political actors may be considered agents. If we examine first the role of the *state* as agent, the "power" that southern African states project in an international system is far more nuanced than structuralism allows. Structuralist theories are hard-pressed to explain, for example, how South Africa has used its "middlepowermanship" to effectively negotiate international accords to its benefit and at the expense of both its less-developed neighbors and *developed* countries (I. Taylor 2002). In a different way, Zimbabwe—and its neighbors—have resisted multiple forms of pressure from far more "powerful" developed states to remove President Robert Mugabe and to fashion a power-sharing arrangement between the ruling party and the embattled (but internationally appealing) opposition party (International Crisis Group 2003b). Throughout the 1990s, chronically poor Zambia was able to play its various donors and lenders off one another to its advantage (Rakner, van de Walle, and Mulaisho 2001). Botswana has defied many of the neoliberal tenets of "globalization" by successfully enacting and adhering to a state-centric, "developmentalist" model.

Moving more squarely into the realm of comparative politics, statist approaches reassert African (state) agency by proclaiming a greater role for the state, particularly concerning development questions and domestic affairs. They regard the state "as a primary motor force behind social and economic occurrences on the continent" (Chazan et al. 1999, 21). Of course, many African states lack bureaucratic capacity, or even legitimacy; yet whereas the state may be "weak by any conventional measure of institutional capacity . . . it remains the most prominent landmark on the African institutional landscape" (Bratton 1989, 410). In the statist view, African states are themselves actors, and their attributes, behaviors, and shortcomings help to explain problems of development and democracy.

Another theoretical framework frequently employed by Africanists is one that emphasizes the preeminent role of "one individual (the strongman, 'Big Man,' or 'supremo')" in African politics (Bratton and van de Walle 1997, 62). In this category, Robert Jackson and Carl Rosberg's *Personal Rule in Black Africa* (1982) was a prominent early example, and analyses that emphasize the ubiquity of neopatrimonial rule in Africa and the neopatrimonial nature of the state are certainly part of this tradition (Clapham 1982; Bratton and van de Walle 1997). Such "personalist" approaches are difficult to categorize using the agent-structure dichotomy introduced above, but their prominence in Africanist scholarship demands that we address them briefly here. In fact, such approaches fit rather uncomfortably in an agent-structure framework: on one hand, they *reduce* African politics and economy to the individual—the "big man"—claiming that he is responsible for political outcomes, attitudes, and behaviors. Hence they are in one sense the ultimate expression of agency. On the other hand, such approaches *deny* Africans in general any agency whatsoever, by suggesting that such neopatrimonial behaviors are immutable, deeply culturally embedded, and in effect *genetic,* thus giving them a structural quality. Such determinism is fundamentally at odds with our approach, which regards politics in southern Africa as dynamic rather than preordained.

The diversity of African politics demonstrates the necessity of utilizing different theoretical lenses to analyze political, economic, and social phenomena on the continent. We argue for balance, though, not for conceptual muddling. Neopatrimonialism, for example, may offer theoretical parsimony, but as Chazan and colleagues (1999, 23) point out, "politics in Africa (as elsewhere) cannot be reduced so easily to the activities of actors on the national scene." Quite simply, despite his significance, Mugabe does not *define* Zimbabwe, nor did Nelson Mandela, who practically embodied the first five postapartheid years, define South Africa. Thus, such reductionist emphasis on the "big man" (and arguably the culture of corruption he inspires) is inadequate to understanding contemporary Zimbabwe and President Robert Mugabe without reference to structural variables as well. Likewise, women's participation in southern African politics is constrained by what we might label *structural* biases against women, but reliance solely on structural factors denies women the agency they so obviously possess, evidenced by the gains of women politicians and activities of women's movements. As Alexander Wendt argues, "it is impossible for structures to have effects apart from the attributes and interactions of agents" (1999, 12). At bottom, the lesson to be drawn is that agency and structure, and how they interact, are important in the study of African politics.

Agents not only shape their environment, but they are shaped and constrained by domestic and international influences as well. Thus there are clear limits to exclusively agent-based approaches, which tend to treat "collective understandings as simply epiphenomena of individual action and deny that they have causal power or ontological status" (Finnemore and Sikkink 2001, 393). This is the basis of constructivist approaches, which may offer a corrective to prevailing theories (Ba and Hoffman 2003, 21); indeed, we find a number of helpful insights in this literature.[13] Among the most helpful contributions of the constructivist research program is its emphasis on learning.

Southern Africa has been shaped by agents and structural forces. External practices are not always simply imposed without adaptation on an African tabula rasa. Exogenous ideas are "endogenized" when they encounter "local" African norms and traditions (Magnusson 2002). Hence the influences on southern Africa are broadly international (for example, neoliberalism, globalization, democratization), domestic (local norms and traditions, including those of both democracy and authoritarianism), as well as regional (states, their leaders, and societies observe and are affected by one another in the regional context). Politics, economics, and society in the region are explained, therefore, as Bruce Magnusson (2002, 2) argues, "by the work (the practice) involved in the articulation of ideas, norms, and context among communities within the territorial state and across territorial lines." Martha Finnemore and Kathryn Sikkink (2001, 407) describe this practice as "learning": "The mechanisms that lead to learning include interaction (with domestic and international actors), comparison (with prior national experiences and with other countries' experiences), reflection (including internal debates and self-criticism) and personnel change."

The case study chapters reveal that in southern Africa, as elsewhere, there is learning across a range of social, political, and economic issues as regional norms and ideas shift in response to various exogenous—and endogenous—stimuli, continuing the process MacLean (1999), in the vernacular of constructivism, labels the "social construction" of southern Africa. Examples of such learning include emerging regional ideas about the symbolic and practical role of land, what it means to be African or southern African, and evolving norms of constitutionalism and presidentialism, to name a few. As Chazan and colleagues (1999, 23) suggest in endorsing their "political interaction framework," "by looking at the interaction of social forces, economic activities, formal institutions, and prevalent values, we may better grasp the meaning and direction of the diverse patterns that have evolved in Africa since independence."

Like Chazan and colleagues, we apply an eclectic theoretical approach in this book, and attempt to capture the diversity   and consistency—within the region. Indeed, whereas we employ a common framework for analyzing the countries, the research questions, and hence the emphases, in the chapters are varied. Nonetheless, each of the chapters explores the relationship between history, ideas, and institutions, broadly emphasizing economic development and democratization issues and seeking to identify the variables that enhance or retard the opportunities for their realization in the region. On the whole, the chapters serve to illuminate the tension between agent-based and structural explanations in Africa. Therefore, we draw on the theoretical literatures that privilege structure, state, and individual agents to inform the analysis of southern Africa's political, social, and economic transformations.

■ Country Case Studies

States of southern Africa could be analyzed in several possible ways. For example, on the basis of trade relations, such as those that are Southern African Customs Union members and those that are not. Or they could be divided by degree of democracy or level of economic development. They might also be categorized by European language and cultural influences:

predominantly Anglophone versus predominantly Lusophone. An alternative approach to analyzing the region might not privilege states at all, and instead weigh its *people* more heavily (Vale 2001, 28). Clearly, myriad other possibilities exist, and the choice of grouping or organization depends on which factors are emphasized. Thus, while recognizing the value of other possible criteria, this book divides the countries of southern Africa largely according to historical experience, with attention to recent political transitions. As such, we have grouped them in the following way.

Malawi and Zambia were the first states in the region to gain their independence from colonial rule and are distinct in the region for the way in which their economic and political trajectories, after independence, mirror closely those of the rest of sub-Saharan Africa rather than southern Africa. Like other countries in sub-Saharan Africa, Malawi and Zambia experienced significant political transitions in the early 1990s. Botswana also achieved independence in the 1960s from Britain and, like its counterparts, emerged under conditions that were both optimistic and uncertain. Yet in many ways, Botswana defies categorization, given its unique position in southern Africa and indeed in Africa as a whole. Botswana is one of the very few countries in Africa to have experienced both stable multiparty democracy and relative economic prosperity since independence.

The Lusophone countries, Mozambique and Angola, form a logical pairing based on historical criteria, although their paths have diverged in recent years. Each attained its independence in 1975, only to plunge immediately into protracted war. Mozambique and Angola struggled bitterly to achieve first their independence from Portugal and then, only recently, the peace that will allow them to develop and possibly catch up to some of their more developed neighbors. The postsettler societies of Zimbabwe, Namibia, and South Africa are the final grouping of states. These were the last countries in the region to attain their independence, and only after years of heightened struggle. All three countries contend today with the legacies of decades of oppressive white minority rule.

Malawi and Zambia are the subjects of Chapters 2 and 3. Both countries were colonized by the British, or British interests, in the late 1800s, were referred to as Nyasaland and Northern Rhodesia, respectively, and for the last ten years of colonial rule were part of the Central African Federation (together with Southern Rhodesia). Following the emergence of nationalist movements, the two countries gained their independence, largely peacefully, with the majority of other African countries in the early 1960s. Shortly after independence, moreover, both countries became one-party states led by presidents with a seemingly unbreakable hold on power: Malawi's Hastings Banda, as self-proclaimed president-for-life, and Kenneth Kaunda of Zambia, who faced no competition when he went to the polls every five years. While Malawi was clearly the more repressive of the two polities, Zambia was also intolerant of political dissent and permitted little autonomous societal organization. One significant difference between the two regimes was their stance toward apartheid South Africa and, by extension, the region. While President Kaunda in Zambia was one of the founders of the Frontline States organization, established to unite the region against South Africa, the Banda regime in Malawi was one of the very few friends of the apartheid state. Moreover, Zambia also allowed regional liberation movements fighting the South African regime to locate exile camps within its borders.

More recently, however, the two countries' political and economic paths have again converged. By the late 1980s both countries were experiencing economic crisis, though of somewhat different origins. Economic deprivation combined with the long-standing political repression led, in both countries, to calls for political liberalization. First in Zambia, and just a few years later in Malawi, the once all-powerful executives bowed to domestic and international pressure and agreed to an opening of their political systems. Transition elections were held first in Zambia in 1991 and then in Malawi in 1994, in both cases bringing new political parties and new leaders to power. In the decade or so since, however, the optimism and promise of those transitions have faded. Neither country has been able to effect major economic revival despite significant reform programs, and elected presidents Frederick Chiluba and Bakili Muluzi became increasingly inclined toward antidemocratic behaviors reminiscent of the tactics of their predecessors. In 2001, both considered using extraconstitutional measures to extend their terms of office, though neither was ultimately successful in that endeavor, in large part because of civil society's opposition.

Yet in a paradoxical way, Zambia and Malawi are in many respects further advanced along the democratic path than their southern African neighbors. Whereas all of the other countries profiled in this book are still led by first-generation liberation movements cum governments, Zambia and Malawi represent a noteworthy, if flawed, second generation. Their liberation governments were replaced a decade ago; while this has not resulted in flourishing democracies per se, it has seen the flourishing of opposition parties in these countries and the maturation of civil societies that have diminished tolerance for authoritarian politics. Thus, even though the immediate democratic future is uncertain, the longer-term political development of these states has much to commend it. In sum, these two countries form an important part of the region. Although their politics sometimes conforms to the rest of Africa, their experience may provide a blueprint—to be followed or avoided—for the rest of southern Africa.

Chapter 4 examines Botswana, considered by many observers to be an exceptional case in Africa. Like Zambia and Malawi, Botswana was also colonized by the British, though many argue that British colonial rule in

Botswana was particularly mild and allowed for a significant degree of continuity of traditional rule, in particular the institution known as *kgotla* (an assembly of all adult males in the community). Moreover, like Zambia and Malawi, Botswana achieved independence relatively peacefully under the leadership of the Botswana Democratic Party. That party has remained in power ever since, despite regular elections every five years. At the same time, Botswana has experienced smooth leadership transitions, with one president stepping down before his term of office expired. Botswana has also been a singular economic success story in Africa, experiencing among the world's highest economic growth rates after diamonds and other minerals were discovered in the late 1960s and early 1970s. Moreover, revenues generated from the country's mines and cattle ranches (the primary source of wealth accumulation before diamonds were discovered) have been used judiciously to invest in the country's infrastructure and human resource base, earning Botswana the distinction of being one of the few "developmental" states—or at least a state with developmental characteristics—in Africa. In one way, however, Botswana is all too much like its neighbors in the region, having the second highest HIV infection rate in the world in 2002 (UNAIDS 2004). Still, Botswana stands out for its progressive response to the HIV/AIDS crisis, among other things making antiretroviral drugs available to all Batswana who need them.

The two Lusophone countries, Mozambique and Angola, are analyzed in Chapters 5 and 6. Although much joins these two countries to their southern African neighbors, Mozambique and Angola are appropriately considered apart. Both were colonized by Portugal, a backward European power that imposed a particularly harsh colonial rule and refused to quit when other European powers were abandoning their colonial empires. Indeed, liberation movements in both countries fought for more than a decade until a military coup brought down the regime in Portugal and independence was finally granted to Portugal's African colonies. But the fighting continued in both countries, as rebel movements challenged new governments, in Mozambique until 1992 and in Angola until 2002. In both countries there was substantial sponsorship of hostilities and combatants by a host of external players, including Rhodesia (Zimbabwe) and South Africa, the United States, the Soviet Union, Cuba, and others. In a more constructive international role, the United Nations sought to broker peace agreements in the early 1990s and facilitate transitions to peace in both countries. In Mozambique they were successful. In Angola they were not; peace was only achieved in Angola a decade later.

Chapters 7, 8, and 9 address the postsettler societies of Zimbabwe, Namibia, and South Africa. These countries share one of the most significant features of the region, namely enduring and recalcitrant settler regimes; as a result, independence or black majority rule was only obtained decades after the rest of the sub-Saharan African countries had achieved it. In all three, liberation movements were forced to resort to armed struggle, even war, to gain independence. Namibia and South Africa are particularly closely related; indeed, Namibia was the de facto colony of South Africa for seventy-five years. Many of these linkages, economic and sociocultural, continue to the present. Zimbabwe, meanwhile, differs in some important ways from the rest of southern Africa, but it also shares many characteristics within this trio of states. The similar legacies include the ascension to power of the leader of the independence movement (who has proved intractable in the Zimbabwe case), gross and lasting disparities in land and resources, and the promotion of reconciliation without accountability. Each legacy has profound consequences for the future trajectories of these states. Zimbabwe's method of belatedly facing these challenges has proved aggressive, corrupt, and ultimately destructive. Nonetheless, Zimbabwe's decline serves as a warning, as all three countries face some common challenges in the twenty-first century, although Zimbabwe must also confront the challenge of reconstruction.

■ Organization of the Book

In order to facilitate comparison across cases, this book adheres to a similar format for each of the country chapters. First, the chapter identifies the key themes that help to define contemporary politics and society in the country. Then it provides some historical background, from the precolonial period, through colonialism and the struggle for independence, until final decolonization was achieved. What follows is an examination of enduring racial and ethnic cleavages, an important, often defining characteristic in a region where seven of eight states are multiethnic, and where six of eight experienced significant white settlement. Each chapter also offers a careful delineation of the different branches of government and the extent to which they act as a check on one another. After covering the realm of high politics and institutions, the chapter turns back to the role of civil society actors, before turning to the fundamentals of the political economy. Each country chapter concludes with an examination of the most pressing challenges to state and society in the twenty-first century.

Chapters 10, 11, and 12 treat issues that transcend state boundaries in southern Africa: the AIDS crisis, gender and politics, and southern Africa's international relations with Africa and the world. AIDS and gender are also subnational issues that relate to "deep politics." Although these are, or should be, of concern to states, these chapters offer at least a partial corrective to Peter Vale's indictment of approaches that neglect people (2001). Southern Africa's international relations, meanwhile, speak to supranational issues and also move beyond the limitations of the state and state-centric analyses.

Chapter 10 examines perhaps the most significant threat facing the region, namely the AIDS epidemic. Indeed, the countries with the highest HIV infection rates in the world are the countries of southern Africa. The rapid spread of HIV throughout the southern African region means that decades of development progress are being undone; already, life expectancy rates have plummeted to below preindependence levels. The HIV epidemic in the region threatens not just the social fabric, but also political stability and the prospects for economic growth and recovery.

Chapter 11 investigates gender and politics in the region. Gender intersects nearly every other issue, from political participation to social organization, and women fill much of the space created by weak state capacity in the region. Indeed, permeating gender relations in the region and enlisting the support of women will be essential to stemming the AIDS tide. More broadly, this chapter touches upon the way in which the role of women has been transformed over the decades in the region—from the precolonial period, through colonialism, and into the independence period. In particular the chapter focuses on the role of women in politics in contemporary southern Africa, where a number of countries have achieved among the highest representations of women in national political office in the world.

Chapter 12 explores southern Africa's international relations by analyzing economic and political linkages within the region, and strategic interactions between the region and the rest of Africa, and between the region and the world. Thus the chapter focuses on such regional institutions as the SADC, pan-African structures such as the African Union and the New Partnership for African Development initiative, and international relationships centered around trade, debt, and aid regimes. Southern Africa, principally through the efforts of South Africa, has taken a leadership role in these processes.

Chapter 13 concludes the book. Although the countries of southern Africa face entrenched problems and challenges—both individually and collectively—southern Africa is in many ways the most dynamic and most promising region on the African continent. In this concluding chapter we outline the lessons derived from explicit study of southern Africa, and we outline avenues for future research and analysis, which the region deserves, and social science demands.

■ Notes

1. Among the works cited, Ayittey 1998, Chabal and Daloz 1999, and Kaplan 1994 and 2000 are most readily identified as part of this Afropessimist genre.

2. West Africa's history of military coups and authoritarian rule is noteworthy, as was the destabilizing and largely unforeseen ethnomilitary conflict in Côte d'Ivoire, which began in September 2002. Although Nigeria remains fragile, worth noting are the "success stories" in West Africa: Senegal, Ghana, and perhaps Benin

and Mali as well as and the markedly improved prospects for Liberia beginning in 2003.

3. This is particularly the case with Robert Kaplan (1994). The Great Lakes region served as the basis for a similar continentwide condemnation in another journalist's account (Richburg 1997).

4. One text that does not take an explicitly regional approach, but nonetheless succeeds in capturing the diversity of the continent by categorizing African regime types, societies, and the like, is Chazan et al. 1999.

5. This book focuses exclusively on continental southern Africa, and therefore ignores the island states of Madagascar, Mauritius, and Seychelles. Neither do we engage in any systematic examination of Lesotho or Swaziland, although references occasionally are made to these states. Lesotho and Swaziland are surrounded by South Africa geographically, as well as politically and economically. Although the systems differ, these enclave states are unalterably tied to South Africa. Though Tanzania is a member of the Southern African Development Community, and is occasionally included among southern African countries, we regard its connection to East Africa as far more significant.

6. East Africa, North Africa, the Horn of Africa, West Africa, and arguably Central Africa also warrant attention on a regional basis. The specific countries one might include in any one of these regions, however, is to some degree a matter of interpretation, and overlapping affinities are clearly possible.

7. Ironically, in what some are describing as "the new white trek to the north," white South African farmers today are being offered land in neighboring countries in return for teaching agricultural and other skills to rural peasants (Legum 2000).

8. Wars in the region may have had a similar impact. As a result of Mozambique's civil war, nearly 1 million Mozambicans became refugees, for nearly a decade, in neighboring Malawi. Over the years, war in Angola similarly drove many Angolans to neighboring Namibia.

9. The Frontline States comprised Angola, Botswana, Mozambique, Zambia, and Zimbabwe, as well as Tanzania. Malawi, which supported the apartheid regime in South Africa, was not part of the Frontline coalition.

10. Africa has experienced more than ninety-five successful coups d'état (Howe 2001).

11. Zimbabwe's program was suspended in 1997 due to noncompliance. South Africa designed its program internally, albeit following substantially on the International Monetary Fund and World Bank model (Padayachee 1997).

12. The SADC is not without a number of problems, however, including South Africa's *reluctance* to play the role of regional hegemon (see Oden 2001 and Chapter 12 in this volume).

13. As Martha Finnemore and Kathryn Sikkink (2001, 393) maintain, constructivism is simply "a framework for thinking about the nature of social life and social interaction, but makes no claims about their specific content. . . . Agents and structures are mutually constituted in ways that explain why the political world is so and not otherwise." It does not provide "substantive explanations or predictions of political behavior until coupled with a more specific understanding" of structures and agents; thus we need to consider it alongside other approaches. See also Wendt 1999 for applications to international politics.

2

Malawi: Institutionalizing Multipartyism

In southern Africa, Malawi and Zambia stand out for being more like the countries in the rest of Africa. Both British colonies, Malawi and Zambia gained their independence in the mid-1960s. Within years, both were one-party states under the rule of self-declared presidents-for-life. Deteriorating economic conditions that made life unbearable by the end of the 1980s, coupled with a loss of international support for the single-party model, led to demands for greater political liberalization two and a half decades into independence. In the early 1990s both countries experienced democratic transitions, although the details were different. Both countries have since confronted the many challenges of simultaneous economic and political transition in a new world order in which Africa figures very marginally. In both countries the difficulties of democratic transition and consolidation have been compounded by the region's frightening AIDS epidemic.

Though Malawi and Zambia were both a part of the Central African Federation (with Zimbabwe) during the colonial period, Malawi has always been the poorer country. In 2001 Malawi had a per capita gross domestic product (at purchasing power parity) of only U.S.$570. Malawi's economic woes were made worse in the postindependence period by rule by an autocratic tyrant known in the region and beyond for his brutality and his predatory and corrupt rule. That tyrant, Hastings Kamuzu Banda, was finally challenged in the early 1990s by a combination of church groups, trade unionists, students, and political exiles who paved the way for the country's democratic transition.

Now, like other countries in the region, Malawi confronts the daunting challenges of democratic consolidation, including completing a peaceful presidential succession and institutionalizing a robust multiparty political system. In May 2004 Malawi held its third presidential and parliamentary elections since the transition to a multiparty political system. The elections,

Malawi: Country Data

Land area 94,080 km²
Capital Lilongwe
Date of independence July 6, 1964
Population 10.5 million, 15% urban
Languages English and Chichewa (official), other languages important regionally
Ethnic groups Chewa, Nyanja, Tumbuka, Yao, Lomwe, Sena, Tonga, Ngoni, Ngonde, Asian, European
Religions Protestant, 55%; Roman Catholic, 20%; Muslim, 20%; indigenous beliefs, 3%; other, 2%
Currency Malawian kwacha (MWK); Malawian kwachas per U.S. dollar: 88.84 (July 2003)

Literacy rate 61.0% (male, 75.0%; female, 47.6%)
Life expectancy 38.5 years (male, 37.9 years; female, 39.1 years)
Infant mortality 114 per 1,000 live births

GDP per capita U.S.$166
GDP per capita (PPP) U.S.$570
GDP per capita growth rate 1.5% (1990–2001)

Leaders since independence
- Hastings Kamuzu Banda, prime minister, 1964–1966
- Banda, president, 1966–1971
- Banda, "president for life," 1971–1994
- Bakili Muluzi, president, 1994–2004
- Bingu wa Mutharika, president, 2004–

Major political parties
Ruling party: United Democratic Front (UDF)
Other parties: Alliance for Democracy (AFORD)
Malawi Congress Party (MCP)
Malawi Democratic Party (MDP)

Women in parliament (lower/single house) 17% (2004)

Note: Data from 2001 unless otherwise indicated.

their outcome, and their aftermath illustrate well the many pitfalls on the path to more democratic rule after decades of authoritarian rule. While the country's two-term president, Bakili Muluzi of the United Democratic Front (UDF), did not run again in 2004, this was not for lack of trying. After Muluzi's attempts to change the constitution to allow for a third term failed, he anointed economist Bingu wa Mutharika as his successor. Mutharika then won the presidential race, though the ruling UDF did not win the parliamentary election, thus leaving the ruling party without enough votes to rule. Opposition parties, in particular the seven-party coalition Mgwirizano, cried foul, especially over the presidential election results. Foreign observers noted serious inadequacies at the polls, the Mgwirizano coalition promised a legal challenge to the results, and two days of rioting over the election in the city of Blantyre left several people dead. Within a month, however, Mgwirizano's leader and presidential candidate, Gwanda Chakuamba, in exchange for a post in the new government, threw his and his party's support to the UDF. With the backing of dozens more independent members of parliament (MPs), the UDF gained the majority in parliament it had failed to secure in the election. Patronage politics trumped electoral politics as a coalition of opposition parties was rendered meaningless and the ruling party and its presidential candidate retained power.

This chapter examines in greater detail Malawi's precolonial past, the colonial period, the postindependence period, and more recently, the post-transition period. The chapter highlights the ways by which a president-for-life was able to wield power for so long, the factors leading up to the country's democratic transition in the early 1990s, the meaning of ethnicity and region in Malawi politics, and the continuing power of patronage politics in the country.

■ Historical Origins of the Malawian State

As in so much of southern Africa, the original inhabitants of the area around Lake Malawi were "short-statured" peoples who resembled the Khoisan peoples of Botswana, Namibia, and South Africa. In Malawi these people were known as Akafula and they were also hunter-gatherers. These people were displaced or absorbed by later Bantu groups that moved into the region, leaving behind few distinctive traces beyond the cave wall paintings found in Malawi and elsewhere in southern Africa (Pachai 1973, 1–2). Around the ninth century, the Karanga moved into what is contemporary Malawi from the shores of Lake Tanganyika. These were agriculturalists and pastoralists who, as farmers, led a more settled existence. Between the thirteenth and sixteenth centuries most of central and southern Malawi was settled by Bantu-speakers. These Bantu-speakers were at first "a collective part of the vast and widely settled community of Maravi peoples" (Pachai 1973, 4). What started off as the Maravi, however, ended up as many of the ethnic groups in Malawi today, including the Chewa, Mang'anja, Nyanja, Chipeta, Nsenga, Chikunda, Mbo, Ntumba, and Zimba (Pachai 1973, 6). In the middle of this same period the Tumbuka came to inhabit northern Malawi, paying allegiance to the Maravi to the south. Two other groups, the Tonga and Kamanga, managed to remain independent of Maravi influence (Sindima 2002, 8). The nineteenth century witnessed a number of significant invasions into Malawi, of the Ngoni peoples from the south, and the Yao, affluent traders, from the southeast. The most recent African group to enter Malawi were the Lomwe, who fled into Malawi in the late nineteenth century, attempting to escape harsh treatment by the Portuguese in neighboring Mozambique (Sindima 2002, 9).

Most of the inhabitants of precolonial Malawi were farmers, although over time more specialized skills developed as people began to work with iron, make cotton cloth, and produce salt. Malawi was also well integrated into an extensive network of trade and commerce that linked central and eastern Africa. Ivory was a prized commodity and traded by the Maravi empire to European and Arab traders. In the eighteenth century, however, the coastal slave trade came to eclipse the trade in ivory, iron goods, and salt. This trade in slaves continued until the end of the nineteeth century. "The main slave capturers, buyers and traders in Malawi were the Yao who collaborated with the Arabs and the Portuguese," and before the slave trade ended at least two major slave stations had been established in the territory. The principal centers of the central African slave trade were Zanzibar and the "Portuguese" ports of Quelimane and Inhambane in Mozambique. The greatest demand for slaves at the time came from Arab enclaves on Africa's east coast and European-owned sugar and coffee plantations on the islands of Mauritius and Reunion (Williams 1978, 29–30).[1] According to Harvey Sindima (2002, 13) it was through ivory and slaves that Malawi was integrated into the world economy, but with clearly deleterious effect—displacing people, destroying villages, undermining the agrarian economy, and producing entrepreneurs who, when they became agents of foreign powers, weakened indigenous political authorities.

Three groups of Europeans—the Portuguese, Germans, and British—in addition to Arabs, were interested in Malawi before the territory eventually became a British colony. The Portuguese were the first to arrive, via Mozambique in the seventeenth century, followed by the Germans, who entered from the north from Tanganyika. When the British arrived they had to contend with both the Portuguese and the Germans, as well as Arabs still engaged in a lively trade in ivory and slaves in the middle to late nineteenth century (Sindima 2002, 15). During the mid-1800s significant missionary activity also commenced inside Malawi. In 1891 the British declared a protectorate over the region, calling it the British Central Africa Protectorate, and a year later began to establish the bureaucracy to administer it. In 1907 the name of the protectorate was changed to Nyasaland. In the same year executive and legislative councils were established, for European residents only. (African interests were represented by a Scottish missionary appointed by the governor.) In Malawi, as in their other colonies, the British followed a policy of indirect rule. This was implemented most concretely in 1933, when two ordinances were put into place. The Native Authority Ordinance recognized the place of traditional authorities, the chiefs, in the colonial administration and acknowledged their role in appointing "native authorities" in their jurisdiction. The Native Courts Ordinance did two things—it put into place a system of local government and it introduced a new court system that involved setting up "native courts" that would rely largely upon customary law (Sindima 2002, 35–36). But according to Sindima (2002, 36), as in all colonies, "the politics of the colonial administration in Malawi was that of exclusion. It was characterized by non-representation, centralized authority, hierarchical, and ruled by the bureaucratic elite—civil servants."

As in South Africa, the African population in Malawi organized itself very early in response to the imposition of colonial rule. Beginning in 1912 native associations were formed around the country, on a regional basis, usually with a twofold aim: first, to inform the colonial authorities of African opinion, and second, to inform the African populace of laws passed by the colonial state and provide forums for the discussion of those and other matters relevant to them. The native associations were largely formed from among the African elite: teachers, district clerks, and chiefs (Sindima 2002, 54). While the formation of the associations was initially sanctioned by the colonial state, by 1930 they were considered a nuisance that should be eliminated. Indeed, in 1933 when the above-mentioned ordinances were passed, district commissioners sought to abolish the native associations, but failed (Sindima 2002, 54). In 1944 the regional associations came together to form the Nyasaland African Congress (NAC). At the organization's inaugural meeting President Levi Mumba called for political representation and economic and social development for the African population as well as for racial equality in the territory (Sindima 2002, 37). One of the overriding goals of the new organization was to provide a unity that had been sorely lacking when the associations were local-level bodies dispersed throughout the colony. In 1946 the colonial government officially recognized the NAC as a body representing the native associations; moreover, the chiefs in the territory also endorsed the NAC as a body representing the African population.

Soon after its formation, the NAC confronted an issue long sought after by the European settlers in Malawi and nearby territories, namely the formation of a federation with neighboring Southern and Northern Rhodesia. Europeans in Nyasaland favored the creation of a Central African Federation, fearing otherwise that they and their needs would be overlooked by the larger British colonies around them.[2] Europeans in the Rhodesias favored such a federation as a way of ensuring access to Nyasaland's major labor reserves. Indeed, if such a federation were not formed, they worried that much of Malawi's migrant labor force would be lost to mines in South Africa (Sindima 2002, 44). The election of the Nationalist Party to power in 1948 in South Africa further spurred Europeans in the three territories toward closer union, as a means of forestalling any move north of Afrikaner influence and racist views (Sindima 2002, 46). The African population in Malawi, meanwhile, as represented by the NAC, vehemently opposed federation, predicting that it would benefit only the European population. As Sindima (2002, 61) notes: "Africans everywhere knew that the Federation was intended to secure the position of Europeans in the three countries." Moreover, African populations were more interested in pressing ahead for self-government than in a greater aggrandizement of European power in the region. In Nyasaland, African leaders were also fearful that some of the more racist policies followed in Southern Rhodesia would be transferred to Nyasaland. Indeed, missionaries in Nyasaland were opposed to federation for the same reason (Sindima 2002, 48–49, 61). Nyasaland chiefs traveled to Britain to express their strong opposition to the idea of federation and even sent a petition to the United Nations, but all to no avail. In 1953 the Central African Federation was formed from the three colonies and remained in place until 1963, when independence was imminent. In the end, the formation of the federation did much in Malawi to unite the African population and create the beginnings of a national consciousness.[3]

The failure to prevent the formation of the federation and the disputes that had emerged over strategies for doing so represented a temporary setback for Malawi's incipient nationalist movement. But nationalist sentiments were soon reinvigorated as a result of constitutional changes in 1955 that provided, for the first time, for elected (as opposed to appointed) African representation on the legislative council. The first elected members were a group of young, university educated, highly articulate, confident, and outspoken NAC members who very effectively represented African views and demands. At the same time, these "young militants" recognized that a more senior person was needed to lead the nationalist movement, in particular one who could "win the allegiance of senior members of Congress or . . . be accepted as national leader by the more conservative rural elders" (Williams 1978, 173). It is in this context that these same young men were successful in persuading Dr. Hastings Banda to return to Malawi from Ghana in 1958 to lead the nationalist struggle. Banda was both highly educated and "old" (in his fifties); therefore it was hoped that he would unite modern and traditional elements in the nationalist movement (Forster 1994, 488). According to Williams: "On 6 July 1958, Dr. Banda arrived at Chileka airport, Blantyre, to a tumultuous welcome. The young militants had done their job well; the nationalist movement had found not merely a leader but a Messiah, and it was soon to become apparent that Dr. Banda, intoxicated by the adulation, was delighted to be cast in that role" (1978, 176). One month later Banda was elected president-general of the NAC. Within the year, however, rioting broke out in Malawi over continued African resistance to federation, a state of emergency was declared, and Banda and other nationalist leaders were detained in early 1959. During 1959, while Banda was still in detention, the by then banned NAC was transformed into the Malawi Congress Party (MCP). When Banda and others were released from detention in 1960, Banda was made president of the MCP. By this time, the principal MCP demand was for self-government, and the British government began to take steps in that direction. In 1961 the first general elections were held in Malawi, won overwhelmingly by the MCP. In late 1962 a constitutional conference was held in London to discuss arrangements for granting complete self-government to Nyasaland, henceforth to be called Malawi (Williams 1978, 203). One immediate implication of the talks was the withdrawal of Malawi from the Central African Federation, announced in 1962 (prompting the demise of the federation). Plans for self-government proceeded apace. In 1963 the executive council was replaced by a cabinet and the legislative council transformed into a legislative assembly. Banda, meanwhile, was sworn in as prime minister. Formal political independence from British rule, under Banda, followed on July 6, 1964.

■ Society and Development: Regional and Ethnic Cleavages and the Politics of Pluralism

The system of political rule in Malawi under Hastings Kamuzu Banda has variously been described as authoritarian, repressive, tyrannical, neopatrimonial, predatory, and corrupt, among other monikers. Indeed, within months of independence the country was rocked by a "cabinet crisis" that set the tone for the years to come. In short, some of the founding members of the NAC—the "young militants" described above—were dismissed from the cabinet by Banda "for opposing his policy direction and his pretensions to absolute rule. Some fled the country, and some were pursued by MCP special branch officers who targeted them for assassination or abduction. This proved the first episode of what became a fixed feature of state politics: namely, the banning, detention, maiming, and murder of Banda's rivals within government and his critics outside it" (Kaspin 1995, 603).

Daniel Posner (1995, 134–135) has identified three broad trends that came to characterize politics in Malawi after the 1964 "cabinet crisis." The first was the centralization of political and economic power in the hands of President-for-Life Banda. On the political side, within two years of independence, Banda had taken over the Ministries of Agriculture, Foreign Affairs, Justice, and Public Works and established a one-party state. In 1971 he was designated president-for-life. "Parliament became a rubber stamp institution filled with Banda's sycophants. The British-model judiciary was emasculated by the creation of a parallel system of 'traditional courts,' controlled by the MCP, to which all political and serious criminal cases were referred." On the economic side, Banda wielded considerable power as well. "By virtue of his ownership—ostensibly 'in trust on behalf of the people of Malawi'—of Press Trust, a massive conglomerate of companies responsible for tobacco production, petroleum marketing, banking, insurance, and most of the country's manufacturing, Banda exerted a strong measure of personal control over more than 50 percent of the entire national economy." Banda used his economic power for patronage and to support a grandiose lifestyle.

The second trend of the Banda years was "the ruthless treatment of political opponents and the total control of public life by the MCP and its appendages. Political dissenters were routinely detained and tortured in Banda's notoriously horrific prisons" (Posner 1995, 134–135). Opponents who had fled Malawi to neighboring countries were abducted and tried for treason, as with the Chirwa brothers in 1981, or assassinated in exile, as with Attati Mpakati in 1983 and Mkwapatira Mhango in 1989. Dissident cabinet ministers and MPs were murdered, as happened in 1983 in the so-called Mwanza incident. Malawian poet Jack Mapanje, accused of seditious poetry, was detained in 1987 and imprisoned for five years (Kaspin 1995, 603; Posner 1995, 135). The cabinet was routinely reshuffled so as to prevent the emergence of any political rivals. The media were heavily censored and used for propaganda purposes. Civil society organizations were proscribed or co-opted by the ruling party. MCP appendages included the Malawi Young Pioneers, which became the armed wing of the MCP and the Women's League, "whose primary function seemed to be dancing for President Banda whenever he made public appearances" (Mchombo 1998, 24). According to Posner (1995, 135): "So pervasive was the system of informers in Malawi, so loose was the definition of disloyalty, and so draconian were the penalties for appearing to be at odds with the president that fear and suspicion came to permeate society."

The third trend of the postindependence period was "the crystallizing of regional identities." Though regional and ethnic allegiances were officially discouraged in independent Malawi, both had deep roots in the country (Chirwa 1994b, 96). Indeed, clear differences among regions—northern, central, and southern—were evident already from the colonial period. Less well endowed with resources and less well developed, the north was always more sparsely populated and during the colonial period functioned as a labor reserve for plantations in southern Malawi and mines and farms in South Africa and the two Rhodesias. At the same time, Scottish Presbyterian missionaries established a small number of "superior schools" in the north that provided important educational opportunities for some northerners. Together these two differences—"higher educational attainment and exposure to the outside world through migrant labor"—enabled northerners to take the lead in politics during the colonial period and also to move into good positions in the colonial and postcolonial civil service (Chirwa 1994b, 97).

The central region, by contrast, was an early center of smallholder tobacco production (from the early 1920s) and later became the center of plantation tobacco production (from the late 1960s). The region serves as the country's breadbasket, producing most of the maize, the staple food, as well as most of the tobacco, the major export crop and foreign exchange earner. The central region is more densely populated than the north, though relatively behind in terms of educational achievement. The south, meanwhile, was the center of the colonial economy. European settlers experimented with coffee, cotton, and tobacco in this region between 1890 and 1920, finally settling upon tobacco as the primary product until the 1930s, when they turned to tea. The south was also "the colonial commercial hub, partly to cater to the white settlers, and partly also because of its proximity to Mozambique, which provided access to the outside world" (Chirwa 1994b, 98). As the colonial commercial center, the south attracted people from throughout Malawi, as well as from Mozambique, who worked on the settler plantations and other establishments—and often remained permanently in the country. Among other things, this has meant that many southern Malawians are second- or third-generation Malawians and that the south is home to a significant mix of ethnolinguistic communities. The south is also Malawi's most populous and most urbanized region. Malawi's small manufacturing base is located in the south, as is a significant Asian business community (Chirwa 1994b, 98–99).

As in most of southern Africa, ethnic identities have figured prominently in postcolonial politics in Malawi. Continuing the colonial tradition after independence, all official documentation in Malawi contained information on one's ethnic group and region (Posner 1995, 136). While President Banda suggested in his speeches that the people of Malawi were Malawians and not members of individual ethnic groups, he usually went on to remind his listeners that he himself was a Chewa (the largest ethnic group in Malawi).[4] Deborah Kaspin (1995, 604) suggests that a process of "Chewa-ization" of Malawi was instituted under the Banda regime.

According to Posner:

> From the beginning of Banda's rule, Malawian culture was made synony-
> mous with Chewa culture. In 1968, the Chewa language was adopted as
> the sole national language; the use of other African languages in the press
> or on the radio was declared illegal. The relocation of the capital from
> Zomba in the south to Lilongwe in the central region was only the most
> notable instance of a broader pattern of shifting development expenditure
> and investment from the south and north to the Chewa heartland. (1995,
> 136)

Not only did President Banda privilege his own Chewa ethnic group—
pouring development money into the central region and new capital city,
imposing Chewa as the national language, and so on—but he also discriminated against others.[5] Kaspin (1995, 609) writes of a "politics of exclusion"
with regard to the north and the south. The north was allowed to stagnate
economically while its people, teachers, civil servants, and politicians were
vilified by the president and his ruling party. In the south, the situation was
not quite as bad: "Although southern politicians were also vulnerable to
Banda's relentless search for the enemy within, they were not subjected to
repeated accusations of tribalism nor to any other stereotype as southerners.
Nor was there a palpable lack of interest in the development potential of the
south. . . . Nevertheless, the regime did generate a pervasive experience of
cultural marginalization in the south." In the end, of course, these policies
served to ensure that both regions became significant sources of opposition
to the Banda regime.

Indeed, that opposition began to coalesce by the end of the 1980s and
beginning of the 1990s. Like so many other countries in sub-Saharan
Africa, Malawi experienced a democratic transition in the early 1990s.
Several factors have been cited as contributing to this transition, despite
President Banda's best efforts to avoid it, indeed to reject the clear global
trend in the direction of political liberalization (Ihonvbere 1997, 194–201).
First, a key factor in many political transitions in southern Africa, the
Malawian economy had deteriorated markedly by the early 1990s. In 1980
the country had entered into a structural adjustment program (SAP) sponsored by the International Monetary Fund; as with SAPs across the region,
the costs of adjustment were being borne by those who could least afford
them. More than a million refugees from neighboring war-torn
Mozambique further strained the Malawian economy. Drought in the early
1990s only exacerbated matters, driving many people from the rural to the
urban areas. By the end of 1993 inflation was running at more than 20 percent, and unemployment, crime, and hunger had reached unprecedented
levels. As living standards fell throughout the land, the Malawian people
held the government responsible for their worsening situation.

Second, and somewhat related, international donors played a role in Malawi's transition by refusing further economic assistance until human rights in Malawi were respected and a political liberalization was initiated. This included the World Bank and all of the major donors on whom Malawi had been heavily dependent for years. At a meeting of donors in Paris in 1992 Malawi received an "unprecedented shock" when the donors suspended "all new aid, except for drought and refugee relief, expressing deep concern about the lack of progress in the area of basic freedoms and human rights and linking new aid to 'good governance'" (Ihonvbere 1997, 196). Such conditionalities were encouraged by reports by Amnesty International and the Southern African Human Rights Foundation, which provided "chilling accounts of the brutality of Banda's government." While Western donor countries had supported Malawi and the Banda regime for years, due to its strongly anticommunist stance, once the Cold War ended in the early 1990s the rationale for such support was gone. Instead, Malawi and other African countries were suddenly called upon to demonstrate good governance and a host of other democratic attributes. Others have identified the key role played by the "demonstration effect," namely the effect on Malawi of the political liberalization process that unfolded in neighboring Zambia just before Malawi's commenced.

Third, again as in other countries in southern Africa, the church played a significant role in Malawi in forcing Banda to recognize the need for change. A pastoral letter released by the country's eight Catholic bishops in March 1992 "denounced corruption, indiscipline, repression and human rights abuses in the country, and noted that 'academic freedom is seriously restricted, exposing injustices can be considered a betrayal, revealing some evils of our society is seen as slandering the country, monopoly of mass media and censorship prevent the expression of dissenting views'" (Ihonvbere 1997, 196). The pastoral letter was the first of its kind in Malawi and is reported to have "stunned Banda." Moreover, it also unleashed a rash of protests across the country, one of which, in Zomba, was met with gunfire from the police. More important, however, the letter had the important effect of emboldening the people of Malawi. As Ihonvbere (1997, 197) writes: "People began to realize that Banda's regime was not God-ordained and once the religious leaders had condemned it, ordinary citizens had a spiritual responsibility to work for change."

Fourth, a foreign-based opposition also contributed to the political liberalization in Malawi in the early 1990s. This included a variety of groups that had varying agendas but that shared at least one common goal, namely "getting rid of Banda's dictatorship" (Ihonvbere 1997, 197). The Socialist League of Malawi operated first from Zambia and later Zimbabwe and even had intentions of creating a military wing to be trained in Cuba. In the United Kingdom the Malawi Support Committee had the active support of trade unionists and Labour Party parliamentarians. The Malawi Freedom Movement attempted a guerrilla attack in northern Malawi in the late 1980s but not much activity after that. Another group, the Congress for a Second Republic, frequently issued criticisms of the Banda government, calling attention to the crisis of governance in Malawi.

Finally, an opposition existed inside Malawi as well, and by the early 1990s it took to Malawi's streets. Opposition forces included students at the University of Zomba, who after the release of the pastoral letter demanded the introduction of multiparty politics in Malawi. In late 1993 civil servants and utility workers went on a strike in protest over worsening economic conditions; workers in the sugar cane plantations set the fields on fire in support of the strike. When striking civil servants won significant pay increases as a result of the strikes, workers throughout the country followed suit. While this activity did not lead immediately to the emergence of a strong labor movement, "the strikes reflected a new bold attempt at challenging Banda's dictatorship" (Ihonvbere 1997, 198). Most important, however, these two forces—external and internal—came together. At a meeting in March 1992 in Lusaka, Zambia, eighty opposition activists gathered and declared a renewed commitment to operating inside Malawi and "pushing the struggle for political liberalization to its maximum" (Ihonvbere 1997, 199). Called the Interim Committee for Democratic Alliance, the organization was also instructed to create a broad-based movement within the country to challenge the Banda regime. The first challenge came when exiled trade unionist and prodemocracy activist Chakufwa Chihana returned to Malawi in March 1992 to take on Banda. After reading a speech upon his arrival at the airport, Chihana was arrested and detained by the police. This prompted immediate riots and demonstrations that turned violent in many places. In response, Banda dissolved the parliament and held elections in June 1992 for 91 of the 141 parliamentary seats. These elections recorded the lowest voter turnout in the country's history and also the defeat of almost half the MPs, including those nominated and endorsed by Banda. The 1992 riots and demonstrations, clearly of a political nature, continued until President Banda finally capitulated in January 1993 and agreed to the holding of a referendum on March 15, 1993, on the introduction of multiparty democracy.

■ Organization of the State

The referendum was actually held in June 1993, in order to allow United Nations monitors to participate. President Banda was confident that he would prevail, citing the typical arguments against a multiparty political system in Africa—"that he was 'father' of the nation, that democracy would increase tribalism and regionalism and [that] it would lead to waste and intolerance" (Ihonvbere 1997, 200). In the event, an overwhelming majority of Malawians, 63.5 percent, voted in favor of multiparty politics. Within weeks of the referendum the constitution was amended to provide for a multiparty political system. Within a year, in May 1994, national elections were held for president and parliament. Eight political parties contested the parliamentary elections, though only three—the Alliance for Democracy (AFORD), the MCP, and the United Democratic Front—won seats. Five candidates contested the presidential race, though only three, AFORD's Chakufwa Chihana, the MCP's Banda, and the UDF's Bakili Muluzi, were serious contenders. In the parliamentary election, the UDF received the largest number of votes, 46.4 percent, followed by the MCP with 33.7 percent, and AFORD with 19.0 percent. The presidential results were remarkably consistent with those of the parliamentary election. Bakili Muluzi, a Muslim businessperson from the south, won the election with 47.2 percent of the vote. Former president-for-life Banda placed second with 33.4 percent of the vote, compared to northern trade unionist and former exile Chakufwa Chihana, who came in third with 18.9 percent of the vote (Wiseman 2000, 643–644).

Constitution

In February 1995 a national constitutional conference was held in Malawi for the purpose of recommending a permanent constitution to the National Assembly.[6] On May 17, 1995, a democratic constitution was adopted by the National Assembly (Mutharika 1996, 205). A major task of Malawi's constitution, according to Peter Mutharika (1996, 209), was "to address the excesses of the Banda regime while at the same time creating a document that gives a democratically elected government sufficient power to rebuild the country and to create a new political order." For example, the constitution provides that "state power is founded on the principles of accountability and transparency; require[s] the state to respect the fundamental human rights of all persons within the country; provide[s] that all persons are equal before the law; and provide[s] that no institutions or persons shall stand above the law." Moreover, the constitution also mandates that the state provide for the welfare and development of the people of Malawi. The constitution also provides for the creation of an independent electoral commission, and an office of ombudsman and a human rights commission, both of which are meant to protect individual Malawians against misconduct by public officials. Both bodies have extensive investigative powers (Mutharika 1996, 217).

The basic governmental structure of Malawi, as laid out in the constitution, "is neither parliamentary nor presidential." Mutharika (1996, 206) calls it a "hybrid system" that provides for a directly elected president able to appoint his/her own cabinet, while final legislative power is vested in a parliament. Moreover, after thirty years of one-man rule under President-for-Life Banda, the constitution also seeks to "structure a delicate system of checks and balances between the three branches of government." So, for example, under the new constitution, the power to appoint the chief justice is shared: the president makes the appointment, subject to a two-thirds affirmative vote by the National Assembly. There are other areas, as well, in which deliberate attempts have "been made to intersect the power of the executive and the legislative" (Mutharika 1996, 207).

■ Executive

The constitution provides for a president, first vice president, and second vice president; the second vice president may be appointed by the president if he decides it is in the national interest to do so, but may not be from the party of the president. According to the constitution, all three positions are limited to a maximum of two consecutive five-year terms, a direct response to Banda's life presidency (Mutharika 1996, 210). Like some other presidents in southern Africa, President Muluzi attempted to extend his term of office. First, he and the UDF tried to amend the constitution to remove the term limit altogether. When that effort failed, they moved to amend the constitution to extend the presidential term from two terms to three. That effort also failed, with the result that President Muluzi was not the UDF's candidate in the May 2004 presidential election (Economist Intelligence Unit [EIU] 2003i, 1; 2003e, 6).

As elsewhere in the region, the powers of the president in Malawi are quite extensive. They include the power to "convene and preside over meetings of the cabinet, confer honours, appoint ambassadors and other diplomatic representatives, negotiate, sign, enter into and accede to treaties, appoint commissions of inquiry, refer constitutional disputes to the High Court, and proclaim referenda and plebiscites as required by the Constitution or an Act of Parliament." At the same time, there are certain limitations on the president's powers—for example, the president is required to address the parliament on the state of the nation and may be called before the parliament to answer questions (Mutharika 1996, 212).

■ Judiciary

In Malawi the judiciary seems to have played a particularly significant— and positive—role in posttransition politics. Peter von Doepp (2001b, 235) suggests that since the transition, "the judiciary has emerged as a primary locus of political activity, deciding numerous cases relevant to the political and personal interests of the opposition." For example, opposition leaders have "turned to the courts for injunctions to halt government actions antithetical to their interests—whether state efforts to go ahead with poorly managed by-elections, extralegal state attempts to block opposition rallies, or plans to strip assets from MCP elites. They have also used the courts to challenge the results of electoral contests that they feel were rigged or inappropriately conducted" (2001b, 237).

According to Mutharika (1995, 215), since the judiciary was "subverted" under the Banda regime, the new constitution pays particular attention to it. In an effort to emphasize the independence of the judiciary, for example, "the constitution provides that all courts shall exercise their powers independent of any person or authority." Moreover, Malawi's High Court and Supreme Court of Appeal are empowered to "review any law, and any action or decision of the government, for conformity with the constitution" (von Doepp 2001b, 236). Further, the constitution abolishes the traditional courts established during the Banda era that were used to try (and invariably convict) political opponents of the Banda regime.[7] In keeping with legal systems throughout southern Africa, however, Malawi's new parliament is empowered by the constitution to establish new traditional courts "presided over by lay persons or chiefs with jurisdiction limited exclusively to civil cases at customary law and to such minor common law and statutory civil cases as prescribed by an Act of Parliament" (Mutharika 1996, 215).

Despite its important role in enabling a balance of power, the judicial system in Malawi, as in other countries in the region, remains "handicapped by serious weaknesses, including poor record keeping, a shortage of attorneys and trained personnel, a heavy caseload, and a lack of resources." In 2002, this same "inefficient, understaffed, and underfunded judicial system limited the ability of defendants to receive a timely, and in some cases, fair trial" (U.S. Department of State 2003c).

■ Military

Malawi has a relatively small military force, totaling 5,300 active personnel in 2002. This included an air force of 80 and a navy, which patrols Lake Malawi, of 220. The country also has a well-armed and well-trained mobile police force of 1,500, which is often deployed in internal security operations (EIU 2003e, 11). Malawi has not been involved in an external conflict since independence—remaining neutral in the regional conflicts of the past forty years.[8] Some Malawian armed forces were deployed in the Democratic Republic of Congo, but only as part of an African Union peacekeeping force, not as a party to the conflict (EIU 2003e, 10). Malawi has good relations with its immediate neighbors, none of which is involved in a military conflict.

■ Representation and Participation

▓ National Legislature

The new constitution originally provided for a bicameral parliament consisting of a directly elected national assembly and an indirectly elected senate. The primary function of the National Assembly was stated to be legislative and the Senate's was to be deliberative. Moreover, the Senate was to represent "special interest groups" such as chiefs, women's organizations, disabled groups, religious associations, and others.[9] Ultimately it was decided not to establish a senate in Malawi (in keeping with the majority of African countries, which have only unicameral legislatures), with cost being given as the reason (EIU 2003e, 7). The number of seats in the National Assembly is determined by the electoral commission before each general election. Malawi's first National Assembly, following the 1994 elections, had 177 members. Before the 1999 election, the number of seats was increased to 193 and remained the same for the 2004 election. Members of the National Assembly are elected for five-year terms that coincide with the term of the president. The new constitution confers more powers upon the National Assembly than under the Banda regime, including a role in approving certain high-level government appointments and certain financial management responsibilities (Mutharika 1996, 213–215). After six years with no local-level legislatures, elections for local authorities (mayor, city councils, and rural district councils) were finally held in 2000. "The local authorities have the power to levy taxes, spend money at their own discretion and run social services" (EIU 2003e, 7).

▓ Political Parties

The state of party politics in Malawi since the transition in the early 1990s reveals some of the many challenges of institutionalizing multiparty political systems wherein presidents-for-life and single parties have ruled for decades. Party politics in Malawi in the first posttransition decade have been marked by rivalry, factionalism, shifting alliances, changing coalitions, and complete U-turns by party leaders. A few larger parties exist alongside many smaller parties of lesser significance. Much of the public, meanwhile, has little trust and confidence in the country's political parties and leaders.

Even before the 1993 referendum was held in Malawi, new parties had emerged—for example, the UDF and AFORD launched in 1992. Since the transition, the UDF has been the ruling party in Malawi. The UDF has drawn most of its support from the populous south, home of former president and party leader Bakili Muluzi. AFORD's stronghold had been in the north, home to party leader Chakufwa Chihana. Shortly after the 1994 election, AFORD joined the UDF in a ruling coalition, receiving six positions in the cabinet for AFORD MPs. In 1996 Chihana decided to end AFORD's alliance with the UDF, though not all party members, including some of the AFORD cabinet members, left with him. For the 1999 elections AFORD joined the MCP in the presidential race, though in late 2001 Chihana renounced AFORD's alliance with the MCP and renewed his backing of the UDF. Indeed, AFORD contested the 2004 elections as the electoral partner of the UDF. In the run-up to the 2004 election, moreover, significant divisions emerged within the UDF over the issue of a third term for President Muluzi. In January 2001 some members of the UDF formed the National Democratic Alliance (NDA), intended as a pressure group opposed to President Muluzi's bid for a third presidential term. The NDA is led by Brown Mpinganjira, a former transport minister who was for many years the UDF's second in command. After forming the NDA in early 2001, Mpinganjira and others were expelled from the UDF and the NDA became a political party.

The largest opposition political party in Malawi has been the MCP, the ruling party for nearly thirty years under Hastings Banda. Historically, the MCP has drawn its greatest support from the central region of Malawi and continues to do so. The MCP came in second, after the UDF, in the 1994 and 1999 presidential and parliamentary elections and won the most votes in the 2004 parliamentary election.[10] After Banda's death in 1997, the MCP suffered a factional split between those aligned with John Tembo, a long-time associate of Banda, and those allied with Gwanda Chakuamba, the party's new president at the time. In the months before the 2004 elections Chakuamba left the MCP and formed a new party, the Republican Party, from among disaffected MCP members. The MCP still polled the most votes in the 2004 legislative election, leaving the UDF to scramble for legislative partners in order to remain the ruling party.

Numerous attempts were made to unite the country's fractured opposition in advance of the 2004 elections. Indeed, shortly before the election seven parties came together to form the Mgwirizano (Unity) Coalition, whose presidential candidate, Gwanda Chakuamba, placed third just behind the MCP's Tembo. Two larger parties, the MCP and the NDA, decided not to join the coalition, thereby weakening its prospects in the view of most Malawians. Malawi's churches, in particular the Central African Presbyterian Church, the Catholic Church, and the Anglican Church, were at the forefront of the effort to unite the opposition in a coalition to defeat the UDF. The inability of highly fragmented oppositions to come together to unseat incumbents has been a signpost of politics in the posttransition period in southern Africa.

The lure of a comfortable job in government is another marker of politics in posttransition southern Africa. As noted at the outset, in the aftermath of the election Gwanda Chakuamba abandoned the Mgwirizano coalition and joined forces with the UDF, in return for a post in government. In so doing Chakuamba "shocked" Malawians who had seen him as "the last principled politician" in the country for rejecting previous deals with the UDF. In so doing Chakuamba also signaled the end of the legal challenge to what many charged were blatantly manipulated election results. Many Malawians had hoped that Chakuamba and his seven-party coalition would hold the UDF government to account. Instead Chakuamba joined the government ("Did They Vote for This?" 2004).

▦ *Elections*

Since the democratic transition in the early 1990s, elections have been held every five years in Malawi. For the most part, the 1994 and 1999 elections were considered free and fair, although the 1999 election was somewhat problematic. John Wiseman (2000, 645) describes the 1999 election as having been "relatively free but not wholly fair" in that the ruling party had certain advantages over the other parties, namely "the UDF's control of radio broadcasting, use of state funds for campaigning, and the bias of the Electoral Commission's Chairman." In 2004 the UDF's advantage as the incumbent continued. Moreover, amid cries of vote rigging and fraud, even international observers conceded that the 2004 elections lacked transparency. At the same time, as Wiseman and others observe, "regional support patterns suggest that party allegiances are fairly entrenched" in Malawi. Moreover, according to Wiseman (2000, 641) and others, election campaigns in Malawi "are not conducted around serious debate over ideological or policy issues. Party manifestos and campaign speeches consist largely of extravagant promises of the enormous benefits from electing the party, and accusations of incompetence, corruption, narrow 'tribalism,' even deviant sexual practices, leveled against opponents."

A distinctive feature of all three elections (though less so for the 2004 election) has been the decisive impact of region upon the election outcome. Indeed, every analyst of the early elections observed the regional trend in the voting, namely that "people voted for candidates not because of the policies their parties stand for, but rather the region a party leader comes from" (Chirwa 1994a, 17).[11] The main political parties in the country have clear regional bases—north, central, and south—but if regional allegiances remain as strong as they have during the first posttransition elections, the UDF will always win. Indeed about 50 percent of the country's population lives in the south, the UDF stronghold; about 39 percent in the central region dominated by the MCP; and about 11 percent in the north, where AFORD has predominated (Chirwa 1994a, 17). In the 1994 and 1999 legislative elections the parties received almost the exact same percentages of the vote as the population percentages of the regions from which they hail. This was not the case in the 2004 election, in which the UDF and AFORD ran as electoral partners and numerous smaller parties and one large coalition also contested the presidential and parliamentary races.

In contrast to several other countries in southern Africa, no one party predominates completely in Malawi; none, for example, has attained a two-thirds majority or better in elections. Indeed, unlike in other countries in the region, election outcomes in Malawi are not necessarily predetermined. Thus, opposition parties in the country are potentially in a strategic position, theoretically able to engage in considerable power brokering. Indeed, shifting alliances over the past decade suggest that such power brokering is occurring, although the beneficiaries are often individual politicians rather than the people of Malawi.

■ Civil Society Organizations

Not surprisingly, after being "the most tightly controlled and highly personalized one-party state in Africa," Malawi cannot claim to have a very deeply rooted civil society (Wiseman 2000, 641; von Doepp 2001b, 232). Indeed, as in many countries in the region, most civil society organizations in Malawi (with the exception of the churches) have a very limited presence in the rural areas—where 85 percent of the population lives—being concentrated mainly in the major urban areas. Still, they are contributing to Malawi's new democracy, "voic[ing] important challenges against questionable government actions" (von Doepp 2001b, 233).

As noted earlier, the churches in Malawi were at the forefront of the democratization effort that began in Malawi in the early 1980s, and according to von Doepp (2001b, 233) they "have not wholly retreated from the political sphere." Indeed, "church leaders have been primary contributors to national political discourse—raising important issues such as the spread of corruption and the fractious behavior of political elites. They have also intervened to foster discussions among opposing elites whose disagreements have aggravated political tension in the country." And they were pivotal in trying to bring together the opposition in the months before the 2004 election. At the same time, von Doepp (2002, 42–43) also argues that at the local as opposed to the national level in Malawi, "most clergy have been disinclined to engage in extensive grassroots civil society activism." Reasons for this include "the kinds of religious ideas that inform their work and their relationships to other actors in communities who might frown on such activism." A third reason is the clergy's desire to enhance their class position in Malawi society. Von Doepp's work on local-level clergy in Malawi serves as a reminder of the many factors constraining the democratizing potential of civil society in Africa. Still, the churches in Malawi have a huge following and are considered to wield a significant influence over the population at large. They are more trusted than most politicians and for this reason may continue to play an important role in party politics in Malawi (EIU 2003i, 2).

In many countries in the region, youth or student organizations have been an important sector in an emerging civil society. In Malawi, university students also participated, through strikes and demonstrations, in the call for a democratic transition in the early 1990s. But youth organizations in Malawi in general have a more troubling heritage. Under the government of Hastings Banda and the MCP, youth organized as "the Malawi Young Pioneers and the MCP Youth League had the notorious task of safeguarding discipline and obedience, often resorting to physical violence if there was any reason to suspect dissidence." Unfortunately, in the new Malawi, according to Harri Englund (2002, 13), this pattern is being repeated, as "the UDF's youth wing, confidently referring to itself as 'Young Democrats,' has been implicated in acts that have been anything but democratic." Indeed, the fact alone that the ruling party has an official youth wing is a clear holdover from an earlier era. During the Muluzi years, the UDF's Young Democrats were implicated in acts of violence against those who have uttered public statements construed to be critical of the Muluzi/UDF government.

A new type of organization to emerge in posttransition Malawi is the voluntary association that promotes a particular language or ethnic identity. One in particular, the Chitumbuka Language and Culture Association, from previously marginalized northern Malawi, has been especially resilient, according to Englund (2002, 23). In Malawi, these language associations can fulfill some of the democratic functions attributed to civil society organizations, according to Gregory Kamwendo (2002, 149). For example, they can complement government efforts, hampered by lack of resources, to raise the status of languages marginalized during the years of Malawi's "Chewa-ization" under Hastings Banda. Further, according to Kamwendo, the language associations can help "in changing negative popular attitudes towards indigenous languages" (2002, 149). Finally, the language associations, like other civil society organizations, can act as watchdogs—in this case of language rights. The greatest danger with such associations, according to Kamwendo, is that they will be manipulated by politicians to attain their own political ends—for example, to mobilize communities around particular ethnocentric or parochial interests. And yet if language rights are to be understood as part and parcel of broader human rights, then their assertion and protection is potentially beneficial to a new democracy.

The media is potentially another important civil society actor in most southern African countries. Indeed, foreign media, in particular, played a significant role in Malawi's early 1990s transition. When Chakufwa Chihana returned from exile to challenge the Banda regime (and was arrested, upon arrival, at the airport), the British Broadcasting Corporation provided in-depth international coverage and "made Chihana a hero in the eyes of his countrymen" (Posner 1995, 139). But it was other media formats that really turned the tide in the struggle for political liberalization during those years. According to Posner, the fax machine, photocopier, and personal computer played crucial roles in turning the tide against the Banda regime:

> By the middle of 1992, Malawi was awash in a sea of anonymous faxes and photocopied leaflets containing leaked government documents supplied by disgruntled civil servants and parastatal employees, reports from foreign newspapers describing the country's economic and political difficulties, and other sorts of officially seditious material. Circulated in offices, passed among friends, or left in the night under stones in the markets and at bus stops, these fragments of uncensored communication played a critical role in demonstrating, both by their content and by their very existence, that the emperor had no clothes. (1995, 139–140)

Indeed, under the Banda regime the media was tightly controlled. Since the transition, however, this has changed. Malawi's new constitution provides for freedom of speech and of the press and this has generally been respected by the government. There are two daily newspapers in the country, three weekend papers, and more than a dozen smaller newspapers, representing a broad spectrum of political viewpoints. Most of them are privately owned, though several are owned by individuals and interests associated with particular political parties. Though there are several private radio stations, including a rural community radio station and six religious stations, radio service is dominated by the state-owned Malawi Broadcasting Corporation (MBC), which provides the main source for news in the rural areas. News coverage and editorial content of MBC programming was reported to be "clearly pro-government" in 2002. The only national television station, Television Malawi, was launched in 1999 and is, again, government owned and operated. Newspapers have been publicly condemned by government politicians for "irresponsible journalism" for reporting statements by citizens critical of government. In general, according to the EIU (2003e, 17), "low level repression of newspapers has increased as scrutiny of government policy and investigations into corruption allegations have grown." Meanwhile, in the 1999 election campaign and again during the 2000 local elections, the MBC "consistently denied opposition candidates equal access to the media. . . . In contrast slogans and songs of the ruling UDF party advertising upcoming political rallies were broadcast throughout the year" (U.S. Department of State 2003e). Clearly, the media in Malawi are still struggling to play their rightful role in politics and society.

■ Fundamentals of the Political Economy

Malawi is a slender, small, landlocked country, formed largely out of territory to the west and south of Lake Malawi, the third largest lake in Africa. Three more lakes are to be found in southern Malawi, as is the Shire River, which runs from Lake Malawi into the Zambezi River, which flows into the Indian Ocean. Malawi has fairly rich soils and grows cash crops such as tea, tobacco, and sugar, as well as some staple food crops, though it has very little in the way of valuable minerals. Despite being such a small country, Malawi had an estimated population of 11.6 million in 2001, 46 percent of which were under the age of fifteen. From 1975 to 2001 Malawi had one of the highest population growth rates in Africa, 3.1 percent. This, combined with the fact that more than 85 percent of the population remains in the rural areas, has put tremendous pressure on land in Malawi. The land problem is particularly acute in southern Malawi, where about half of the population lives (United Nations Development Programme 2003).

Most analyses of Malawi's postindependence economy divide it into two periods: the period before 1979, when nearly every sector of the economy experienced rapid growth, and the period after 1979, when almost every sector experienced rapid decline followed by erratic recovery trends (Chinsinga 2002, 29). Indeed, from independence until 1979 the country experienced annual economic growth rates of 6 percent, compared to annual population growth rates of about 3 percent. Exports rose nearly sixfold in the same period. A number of factors are cited as contributing to the country's early growth: "favourable world demand, favourable climatic conditions, rapid expansion of large-scale agriculture, high levels of gross domestic investment, and low and declining real wages and labour costs in the agricultural sector" (Chinsinga 2002, 29). By 1981, however, Malawi was registering a negative economic growth rate; while economic growth rates did subsequently increase somewhat, they have never returned to the pre-1979 levels. Again, a number of factors can be identified as contributing to the country's rapid economic downturn after 1979, some global and some quite specific to Malawi. These included the oil shock in the late 1970s, which affected the whole world, serious drought in the early 1980s, a sharp decline in terms of trade, the rise in interest rates on international financial markets, the closure of the Beira-Nacala trade corridor due to the war in Mozambique, the influx of refugees from war-torn Mozambique (ultimately totaling 1 million people), and declining levels of development assistance (Chinsinga 2002, 29–30). These factors were compounded by several "structural rigidities that underpinned the country's economy," such as a narrow export base and heavy reliance on tobacco, a reliance on imported fuel and declining stock of domestic fuel wood, and an inflexible system of government-administered prices and wages (Chinsinga 2002, 30).

Malawi's early sharp economic downturn meant that it was the first country in southern Africa to sign on to a structural adjustment program, which it did in 1981. And yet as Blessings Chinsinga notes, Malawi has gained very little from being the first country in the region to adopt an SAP:

> Despite being the pioneering country within the sub-region, Malawi is yet to show off the benefits for taking the lead in adopting the SAPs. The overall outcome has been disappointing. Several reviews emphasise that the SAPs have laid heavy social burdens on the vulnerable segments of the society, particularly women and children. The popular view in this regard is that the design of the SAPs did not take into account the potentially adverse effects on the poor in the short and medium terms. (2002, 30)

As a result of the economic hardships generated by the SAPs, the poor in Malawi have adopted certain coping strategies to survive (Chinsinga 2002, 31). For example, in the face of declining health services people have turned to traditional medicine and treatment at home. In the face of a falling and unaffordable housing stock, people have been forced to seek refuge in crowded and unsafe squatter settlements. Some people have resorted to selling off household goods and farm assets, or migrating to urban areas, even other countries. The negative impact of the SAPs on a wide swathe of vulnerable people (not a problem unique to Malawi) prompted the adoption in 1990 of a special program known as the Social Dimension of Adjustment. In Chinsinga's view (2002, 32), the adoption of this program led directly to the adoption, after the transition, of Malawi's poverty alleviation program in 1994.

That poverty is widespread in Malawi is indisputable according to Chinsinga (2002, 28). A number of socioeconomic indicators and trends reveal the depths of Malawi's challenges. For example, the country has a life expectancy of thirty-nine years, among the lowest in the world, attributable to the cumulative effects of poverty, the HIV/AIDS epidemic, chronic malnutrition, and substandard health services. Those substandard health services are marked by the lowest expenditure per head on health services in southern Africa in 2000 and the fewest physicians per head in the region in 2000.[12] As recently as 1998 just over half the population lacked access to clean drinking water. Poor health, moreover, has a direct, negative impact on a work force's labor productivity (EIU 2003e, 13–14). Labor productivity is also affected by education. Malawi continues to have a high illiteracy rate, even by African standards. In the late 1990s only about 15 percent of primary school leavers went on to secondary school. High failure and dropout rates are blamed on child malnutrition and long distances to schools. According to the EIU (2003e, 13), "Malawi's poor educational standards do not prepare people for jobs in industry and manufacturing, and surveys have found that the undereducated rural poor are not able to grow crops like tobacco which need intensive tending." There have been improvements since the democratic transition in 1994. After coming to power, the Muluzi government abolished fees for primary schools, contributing to an increase in enrollments of 50 percent. One impact of this, however, has been very high student-teacher ratios—the highest in southern Africa, about fifty-nine to one (EIU 2003e, 13).

As Chinsinga notes (2002, 38) "any tangible attempt at poverty alleviation [in Malawi] has to address the challenge of agrarian reform." This is because 85 percent of Malawi's population depends on agriculture for their livelihood. The staple crop, maize, is grown by most of Malawi's smallholders. Cash crops grown by smallholders include tobacco, groundnuts, rice, cotton, and maize. The country's large commercial estates also grow tobacco, the country's most important export earner, as well as tea, sugar, coffee, rubber, and nuts. During the Banda years, the land area occupied by the large estates expanded rapidly; indeed, the 1967 Land Act allowed only a "one-way transferability" of land—from the customary or smallholder sector to the estate sector. In 1990 this was halted, as a condition for further World Bank development assistance. In January 2002, meanwhile, the cabinet approved a new land policy for Malawi. Among other things, the policy protects customary land against conversion to public land, thereby providing some measure of land tenure security for smallholders. And yet the policy does not address the issue of the tremendous pressure on land in Malawi as a result of the extremely high population density in the country. Chinsinga (2002, 39) suggests that this is because of self-interest on the part of Malawi's elite: "Politicians, top policy-makers and prominent businessmen own vast tracts of land which they are not prepared to give up." Without a genuine redistribution of land, poverty alleviation will not be achieved, Chinsinga contends.

Malawi's poverty alleviation program is intended to address a number of features of poverty in the country, namely household food insecurity, low productivity among smallholders, a weak small business sector, limited access to essential social services, and more (Chinsinga 2002, 41). Indeed, the program aims to increase agricultural productivity at the subsistence level, assist in the development of small-scale enterprises, strengthen the delivery of social services, and develop management capacities. At the same time, according to Chinsinga (2002, 41), despite the poverty alleviation program, poverty—both rural and urban—is on the rise in Malawi. This can be attributed to a number of factors, including low productivity and high commodity prices due to market reforms and inflation, lack of access to farm inputs and credit, declining agricultural output, and falling employment opportunities. For the past several years, Malawi

has failed to achieved the 6 percent annual economic growth rate necessary to have a significant impact on poverty reduction in the country
(Chinsinga 2002, 41).

■ Challenges for the Twenty-First Century

The challenges for Malawi are many. After ousting one of Africa's most
tyrannical and predatory leaders, the people of Malawi have experienced a
multiparty political system for more than a decade. While one party, the
UDF, dominates, it is not a predominant party in the same way that ruling
parties elsewhere in the region are. Rather, it has frequently been forced to
rely upon allies or partners from other parties in order to accomplish its legislative goals. As elsewhere in the region, the multiparty political system in
Malawi is not yet fully matured, in the sense that the regional origins of the
main political parties appear more important to voters than any ideological
distinctions among the parties. Moreover, party politics in the country are
marked by frequent and radical shifts in alliances often to the benefit of
party leaders and the detriment of party bases. Thus the challenges of craft-
ing and consolidating democratic politics remain. Another challenge for
Malawi in the early 2000s is the AIDS scourge, which has ravaged Malawi
as well as neighboring countries in the region. By the end of 2001, 15 percent of the adult population was estimated to be living with HIV/AIDS,
with the same deleterious impact on economy and society as elsewhere in
the region. A national HIV/AIDS strategic framework has been put in
place, calling for building institutional capacity, promoting the use of condoms, increasing access to antiretroviral drugs, and improving education
and the reproductive health services available to the nation's young people.
Still, support from international donors is essential to finance the national
framework and to provide the health care necessary for those in need of
treatment (EIU 2003e, 14). Another immense challenge for Malawi is
addressing the poverty that has plagued the country for a generation.

■ Notes

1 As elsewhere in Africa, for the most part the slave trade had a devastating
impact upon those it touched, although there were some groups who benefited. As
David Williams (1978, 31) notes, "Vast areas were devastated and societies terror-
ized, and most people found themselves in a situation even worse than they had
been when the perennial threat of starvation and disease and the erratic, but ever
present, threat of war had put their lives constantly at risk. However, some individuals and some groups were able to seize advantage, sometimes very considerable
advantage, from the changed situation."

2. According to Williams (1978, 129): "The remoteness of Nyasaland, its lack
of mineral resources, the sparseness of its revenue, and the presence there of a small
but relatively powerful and articulate European community had all contributed in

their various ways to a belief among Europeans that considerable advantages would be gained from association with other territories."

3. Peter Forster (1994, 483) suggests that the emergence of a national identity in Malawi was aided by certain historical processes. For example, "the inhabitants had a long record of travelling outside the country as labour migrants or as soldiers: this had helped to create a collective identity because many came to be known as 'Nyasas' regardless of tribal origin."

4. As Wiseman Chirwa (1994b, 95) notes, there was a contradiction: on the one hand the Banda regime tried hard to forge a unified nation-state; on the other hand there were strong tendencies toward regionalism and ethnic discrimination.

5. According to Chirwa (1994b, 95), "We have ample evidence that Dr. Hastings Kamuzu Banda's regime 'pursued a policy of systematic exclusion of people from the Northern Region, as well as Yaos (and especially Lomwe) from the Southern Region, from political power.'"

6. One day before the 1994 election the National Assembly had adopted a provisional constitution, effective for a period of one year.

7. The judges in those traditional courts were traditional leaders who had no legal training. Moreover, in those courts "there was no right to legal representation and . . . the rules of evidence did not apply" (Mutharika 1996, 215).

8. Troops from Malawi's army were deployed in Mozambique from 1985 to 1993, on six-month rotations, to protect the Nacala rail line that provides Malawi with access to the sea. A clear result of that deployment, according to John Lwanda (2002, 158), was high death rates from HIV/AIDS among members of the Malawi military and their wives and girlfriends from 1989 onward.

9. According to Mutharika (1996, 214): "Second chambers have usually been adopted in countries with disparate regional, ethnic, linguistic or religious groups to ensure that the interests of small groups are adequately protected. Doubts were raised at the Constitutional Conference as to the need for a second chamber in Malawi and whether the country had enough resources to support such a chamber."

10. President Muluzi won the 1999 presidential election with 52.2 percent of the vote, compared to his main rival, Gwanda Chakuamba, the candidate for the MCP/AFORD alliance, who gained 45.2 percent of the vote. In the 1999 parliamentary election the UDF's vote was nearly unchanged, 47.3 percent, as was the MCP's with 33.8 percent. AFORD, by contrast, gained only 11 percent of the vote, with 6.7 percent going to independent candidates (Wiseman 2000, 643–644). In 2004 the UDF retained its hold on the presidency; with 35 percent of the vote Bingu wa Mutharika beat the MCP's John Tembo (27 percent), and Gwanda Chakuamba (26 percent) of the Mgwirizano coalition. In the parliamentary race the MCP won sixty seats, the UDF forty-nine seats, and the Mgwirizano twenty-seven seats, a considerable change from the 1999 electoral outcome ("Malawi President Gains Majority" 2004).

11. See, among others, Chirwa 1994b; Kaspin 1995; Van Donge 1995; Posner 1995; and Wiseman 2000.

12. In 2000 expenditure per head on health services in Malawi was U.S.$8.9 as compared to U.S.$155 in Botswana and U.S.$203 in South Africa. The number of physicians per 100,000 was 3 in Malawi compared to 30 in Namibia and 14 in Zimbabwe.

3

Zambia:
Civil Society Resurgent

Zambia gained its independence from Britain on October 24, 1964. In contrast to the protracted liberation struggles endured by many of its neighbors in the region, Zambia enjoyed a relatively peaceful transition to independence, although it was hardly without the tensions, machinations, and political protests that characterized the struggles of other states. Zambia's relatively rapid transition from British rule essentially was condensed into a three-year period, which itself followed three years of intensified nationalism that began in 1958. By the end of 1961, independence and majority rule—once distant aspirations—were irreversible. Free of much of the controversy of other southern African states, and free of the debilitating effects of war, Zambia embarked upon its independence under the leadership of its first president, Kenneth Kaunda, with great promise. Hence, shortly after independence it could be asserted that "the country starts . . . with a vision of whither it should go, a method of approach suitable to its circumstances and resources potentially sufficient to raise its standards. It is more favoured than most of its contemporaries" (Hall 1966, 299).

Indeed, in the early 1960s, Zambia was considered to have great potential for development. The country was blessed with mining infrastructure, bequeathed by the colonial regime; favorable international conditions for its principal export, copper; a viable foundation for industrial infrastructure; and a small but expandable base in commercial agriculture. Politically speaking, Zambia entered independence with a multiparty system, although one party, Kaunda's United National Independence Party (UNIP), predominated. Moreover, unlike in other states in the region, the small settler population that remained in Zambia following its transition adjusted to black rule and was largely committed to the development project of the country (Roberts 1976, 242).

Four decades after independence Zambia's initial promise has been squandered. Today, Zambia ranks as one of the poorest nations in the

Zambia: Country Data

Land area 752,612 km²
Capital Lusaka
Date of independence October 24, 1964
Population 10.3 million, 40% urban
Languages English (official), Bemba, Kaonda, Lozi, Lunda, Luvale, Nyanja, Tonga, and about 70 other African languages
Ethnic groups African, 98.7%; European, 1.1%; other, 0.2%
Religions Christian, 50–75%; Muslim and Hindu, 24–49%; indigenous beliefs, 1%
Currency Zambian kwacha (ZK); Zambian kwacha per U.S. dollar: 4,930.00 (July 2003)

Literacy rate 79.0% (male, 85.8%; female, 72.7%)
Life expectancy 33.4 years (male, 33.3 years; female, 33.4 years)
Infant mortality 112 per 1,000 live births

GDP per capita U.S.$354
GDP per capita (PPP) U.S.$780
GDP per capita growth rate –1.7% (1990–2001)

Leaders since independence
- Kenneth Kaunda, president, 1964–October 1991
- Frederik Chiluba, president, November 1991–2001
- Levy Mwanawasa, president, 2001–

Major political parties
    Ruling party: Movement for Multiparty Democracy (MMD)
    Other parties: United Party for National Development (UPND)
    United National Independence Party (UNIP)
    Forum for Democracy and Development (FDD)

Women in parliament (lower/single house) 12.0%

Note: Data from 2001 unless otherwise indicated.

world, and it is the fourth poorest of the twelve states in southern Africa as measured by gross domestic product (GDP) (Economist Intelligence Unit [EIU] 2003g). The economy has substantially collapsed in the wake of inappropriate and misspecified development strategies—both socialist and neoliberal—weak integration with the international marketplace, and a substantial decline in the global prices of Zambia's principal commodity export, copper. The impact of HIV, which infects some 19 percent of the adult population, reverberates throughout society and all sectors of the economy.

In the aggregate, Zambia's political trajectory since 1964 has been equally disheartening. Although Zambia began independence as a multiparty democracy, President Kaunda and UNIP gradually restricted political competition, culminating in a constitutional change that established a de jure one-party state in 1972. Kaunda was virtually impervious to challenge for the next two decades, despite ever-worsening standards of living and reports of political abuse. When, as a result of domestic and international pressures, Kaunda finally consented to multiparty elections in 1991, he was roundly defeated by the upstart Movement for Multiparty Democracy (MMD) and its presidential candidate, former trade union leader Frederick Chiluba.

Coming to office amid economic collapse but with enormous domestic and international goodwill, Chiluba in many ways turned out far worse than his predecessor (Bratton and Posner 1999; Chan 1999; Rakner 2001). If Kaunda had brought Zambia to the brink, politically and economically, then Chiluba can be (dis)credited with overseeing Zambia's descent into an antidemocratic kleptocracy in the 1990s. In many respects the country was in a much worse position at the end of Chiluba's rule than it had been a decade earlier, thus continuing the pattern of decline begun in the 1970s.

However, political developments since 2001—including the apparent zeal with which Chiluba's successor, Levy Mwanawasa, has attempted to attack corruption (including Chiluba and members of his cabinet)—provide some basis for cautious optimism regarding Zambia's democratic future. Given the interconnectedness of the political and economic spheres, these developments may also bode well for the country's economic prospects. Still, several caveats are also necessary.

First, it would be imprudent at this stage to offer more than contingent generalizations on Mwanawasa's presidency, whose positions thus far seem to alternate between democratic and autocratic, bold and status quo. Second, Zambia's problems are also structural in nature, and as such may defy "easy" policy solutions designed and imposed by political agents. These challenges include the way in which Zambia encounters the global economy and its continued dependence on primary commodity exports, namely copper; the country's location in a region of competing rather than complementary economies; and its geographic proximity to Zimbabwe and the Democratic Republic of Congo (and until recently, Angola), from whence refugees and instability have deeply and adversely impacted Zambia. In addition, the AIDS crisis threatens to further sap the country of human and material resources, as noted above. Nonetheless, the solutions to certain problems are in the purview of agents; individual actors and organizations, in the presidency, political parties, and civil society, are therefore vital to understanding Zambia's future trajectory.

Taking all these factors into consideration, this chapter addresses problems of both agency and structure in Zambia and examines the ability of the country's political and social institutions to confront its myriad development challenges. The case of Zambia, one of the first countries in the region to gain independence, undergo a democratic transition, attempt economic structural adjustment, and experience competitive party politics, provides a series of critical signposts for other countries in southern Africa.

■ Historical Origins of the Zambian State: Context, Key Actors, and Issues

The country known today as Zambia was established in 1890–1891, initially as a territory of the British South Africa Company (BSAC) under charter from the British crown. Shortly before, representatives of the same company had extracted concessions from African rulers in Southern Rhodesia, now Zimbabwe (Hall 1966). The name "Rhodesia," after BSAC head Cecil Rhodes, came into common use in 1895, initially to describe both territories. By 1897 the two regions, whose intertwined histories are well chronicled (Leys and Pratt 1960; Franklin 1963; Gann 1964), formally became known as Southern and Northern Rhodesia, respectively.

Although initial European incursions into the southern African region began with Portuguese trade, exploration, and limited settlement as far back as the early sixteenth century, the area occupied by contemporary Zambia did not garner much European attention until the 1850s, through the exploits of Scottish missionary and explorer David Livingstone, who visited the area as early as 1851 (Wills 1964). It was not until 1890 that measurable numbers of whites arrived in the region, mainly pushing out from South Africa in search of mineral wealth. Initially, those arriving in Northern Rhodesia were employed mainly by the BSAC, but within a decade other settlers began to trickle in (Hall 1966). Even so, when the period of BSAC "company rule" in the territory ended in 1923 and administration of Northern Rhodesia was formally ceded to the colonial office in London, the settler population numbered fewer than 5,000. Nonetheless, a legislative council, which asserted a high degree of autonomy from Britain, was established in the colony to provide Northern Rhodesia's small white population with representative government (Hall 1966, 182).

Given their common origins and dominant English-speaking settler populations, some combination of the two Rhodesias—either amalgamation into one territory or a form of federation—was long considered. The prospect was discussed between representatives of the Rhodesias and the colonial office in London as early as the 1930s. However, questions over sovereignty, "native policy," and other disputes prevented consensus for two decades (Leys and Pratt 1960). Finally, in 1953, Northern and Southern Rhodesia were linked, together with Nyasaland (modern-day Malawi), in the Central Africa Federation. Officials from Northern Rhodesia and Nyasaland believed that federation would allow them to immediately benefit from economic diversification by joining with the more industrialized southerners. They would also get the benefit of a larger white population, thus offering greater autonomy from London. For its part, Southern Rhodesia gained access to the human and natural resources of its two partners. The powers of the federal government centered on defense, trade, communications, industry, and finance, whereas national powers extended to local government, African education, health, agriculture, and land policy. This left the individual governments a considerable degree of autonomy in determining "native policy," always the most contentious issue.

As in Nyasaland, blacks in Northern Rhodesia had been the most resistant to federation, believing that racial policy would fall to the lowest common denominator: that of Southern Rhodesia, where blacks had been thoroughly dispossessed and pass laws were in effect. Despite the setback that federation signaled for blacks, it was nonetheless the case that by the mid-1950s, when the federation was at its peak, the colonial era had already begun to pass in Africa and elsewhere. In this period, fledgling African nationalist movements jelled. The nationalist movement in Northern Rhodesia was led by Harry Nkumbula and Kenneth Kaunda, first via the Northern Rhodesia African National Congress, which was renamed the African National Congress (ANC) in 1953. Nationalist activity began to reach peak levels of agitation in 1958, but a split emerged in the movement and Kaunda established a more radical faction, the Zambia African National Congress.[1] In 1959, the Zambia African National Congress was banned and Kaunda was imprisoned, but he emerged from incarceration in 1960 at the helm of the newly established United National Independence Party.

Despite the colonial government's reaction to African nationalism, Northern Rhodesia had always maintained a relatively more liberal set of social and political policies toward the African population, partly because of its smaller settler population, than had Southern Rhodesia—or, for that matter, than had the other settler states in the region. Thus, coupled with the retreat of empire internationally, domestic unrest in Zambia prompted constitutional negotiations rather than violence. These negotiations took place in 1961–1962, although an outright transfer to majority rule was not effected immediately (Northern Rhodesia Constitutional Conference 1961; Sklar 1975). Similarly, the federal government also began to make minor concessions to blacks at the same time.[2] However, the prospect of black rule was anathema to the larger and more autonomous settler population in Southern Rhodesia. Hence the dissolution of the federation became inevitable once an African majority was elected to the Northern Rhodesian legislative council in the 1962 elections.[3] This also paved the way for Northern Rhodesia's independence, which formally came in October 1964, and the country became known officially as the Republic of Zambia. Following an overwhelming electoral victory by UNIP (which occurred prior to official independence), Kenneth Kaunda became Zambia's first president.

The First Republic, which lasted from independence until 1972, was a multiparty, if not entirely democratic, system. In the early years of independence, the ANC provided a modicum of parliamentary competition, having won ten seats (to UNIP's fifty-five) in the sixty-five-seat assembly. Several other parties born in the First Republic arose out of internal conflicts within UNIP. One, the United Party, existed briefly between 1966 and 1968, but was then banned by the ruling party, which had grown increasingly sensitive to competition over time. The most significant UNIP splinter group, the United Progressive Party (UPP), was formed in August 1971 by Kaunda's former vice president, Simon Kapwepwe. The UPP posed potential problems for UNIP because it attracted support from traditional UNIP strongholds in Copperbelt and Northern provinces, particularly among ethnic Bemba (Zambia's most numerous group). When interparty violence emerged, it provided justification for UNIP to act on its calls for a one-party state in order to prevent future violence and curb "disunity" (Beveridge and Oberschall 1979; Gertzel 1984).

In February 1972, the UPP was banned, Kapwepwe and 123 leading members of the party were detained, and the UNIP cabinet announced its intention to establish a "one party participatory democracy" (Gertzel 1984). Subsequently, the leadership of the longtime opposition party, the ANC, was co-opted, and a constitutional amendment was passed in December 1972 making Zambia a de jure one-party state. Kaunda was then sworn in as president of Zambia's Second Republic,[4] which would endure for another eighteen years. Although fraught with problems, including systemic constraints on political competition,[5] the Second Republic in fact was fairly successful at restraining ethnic competition among Zambia's seventy-three ethnic groups.

■ Society and Development:
Zambia's Ethnic and Racial Cleavages

Racial and ethnic pluralism has profoundly, if differently, impacted development in all of the southern African countries. In marked contrast to Namibia, South Africa, and Zimbabwe, where race remained a major social cleavage, the centrality of race diminished in Zambia following its independence. Zambia's white population peaked at 73,000 in 1960, and the numbers declined thereafter.[6] Importantly, because Zambia was never completely a "settler state," it avoided a postcolonial crisis in which nationalists resorted to guerrilla warfare in order to bring about majority rule. Unlike in Zimbabwe, for example, the white settlers who remained in Zambia following independence were by and large those who demonstrated a willingness to live amicably under a black government (Roberts 1976, 249).

Besides the lower initial population and the low density of settler farmers and industrialists, several factors can be identified that have rendered race less significant and far less divisive in Zambia than in Zimbabwe and South Africa. The first two, the relatively better treatment of blacks throughout colonialism and the swiftness and relative tranquillity of the transition to majority rule, have been addressed above. The third factor is the predominance of multinational corporations (MNCs) present from the colonial era. These displaced or prevented the establishment of a sizable local white bourgeoisie that might compete directly with black economic interests after independence.[7] Nevertheless, certain latent racial hostilities persist, and it is inaccurate to suggest that racial discrimination against Africans (and a corresponding resentment on the part of Africans of whites and Indians)[8] has disappeared in Zambia. As in other countries in the region, whites are heavily represented in the light manufacturing and large-scale commercial farming sectors. In recent years, the government, seeking investment and agricultural expertise, has encouraged immigration of mostly white commercial farmers from South Africa and Zimbabwe. Although some analyses raise concerns that these migrants could import racial conflict to Zambia (EIU 2003g, 44), it is unlikely that they will reach sufficient numbers to incite great opposition.

More so than race, ethnicity might be expected to be a major fault line in contemporary Zambian society, given the sheer number of ethnolinguistic groups; among these, the Bemba, Tonga, Lozi, and Nyanja-speaking peoples are the most numerous and together account for over 50 percent of the population.[9] Various forms of ethnic management were practiced in the colonial era. Some ethnic groups were subjected to direct British interventions and others to forms of British "indirect rule." Examples of the former include the Bemba in Zambia's north and northeast, who provided much of the labor for the copper mining industry and saw their traditional political structures disrupted severely. Similarly, the Tonga people in the south were transformed into a "rural proletariat," as their rich farmland was appropriated by white settlers and the colonial state. Conversely, the Lozi, claimants of a precolonial kingdom concentrated in the western part of the country, were largely left alone and governed via indirect rule using traditional structures (Gertzel 1984).

One of the few arguable advantages conferred by direct rule was a semblance of "development." Populations subject to direct rule, particularly those proximate to settlement, gained access to a degree of modern infrastructure, a modicum of formal education, and a labor force more acquainted with a Western capitalist economy. Those groups in closest contact with the colonial enterprise frequently were its heirs following independence. Such uneven development precipitated lasting ethnic conflicts in other postcolonial states, such as Kenya and Nigeria. However, although Zambia's ethnic pluralism was a factor in a number of clashes, these tensions never erupted into wholesale ethnopolitical conflict. This resulted partly from demographics: given ethnic pluralism, no single group has the numerical superiority to allow it to dominate the others. President Kaunda helped to quell nascent ethnic tensions by balancing ethnic representation and support in his cabinet, particularly in the Second Republic.[10] Despite its antidemocratic character, Zambia achieved a semblance of unity through the one-party state; "One Zambia, One Nation," Kaunda's clarion call for national unity, was thus more than simply a political slogan.

The Third Republic administration of President Chiluba, himself of Bemba lineage, faced numerous accusations that the cabinet was increasingly dominated by the Bemba, although its actual composition did not appear disproportionately skewed toward that group. Nevertheless, this perception fostered resentment from some quarters and helped give rise to opposition parties in non-Bemba areas where MMD support was weakest. As early as 1992–1993, this was seen in Western province, a Lozi stronghold, and in Eastern province, where Kaunda and UNIP maintained their greatest support.[11] By the late 1990s, the phenomenon was perhaps most pronounced in Zambia's Southern province, where Tonga voters overwhelmingly flocked to the United Party for National Development (UPND), which was established in 1998 by Anderson Mazoka, a prominent businessman of Tonga descent. It is important to point out also that despite their own efforts to promote a national agenda with a national audience, most opposition parties have been unable to expand beyond regional and largely ethnic bases of support. Even the MMD, which was dominant virtually nationwide in the 1991 and 1996 elections, saw its support dwindle outside of Copperbelt, Northern, and Luapula provinces in the 2001 election.[12]

Nonetheless, though ethnic identity remains salient in contemporary Zambia, ethnic-based conflict is rare. In addition, notwithstanding sporadic accusations to the contrary, Zambia's cultural pluralism tends to be reflected in its government, and for the most part Chiluba and Mwanawasa have followed Kaunda's practice of ethnic balancing.

■ Organization of the State

▓ *The President and the Exercise of Executive Authority*

Zambia utilizes a presidential system, adopted at independence, in which the executive is the head of state and head of government. Much like his counterpart Hastings Banda in Malawi, President Kaunda was essentially a "president-for-life," although elections were held every five years from 1968 to 1988. After the 1972 declaration of the one-party state, candidates for parliament faced off against one another in what Michael Bratton and Nicolas van de Walle (1997) label a "competitive one-party system" under UNIP. Presidential elections, however, were merely a plebiscite on Kaunda's rule, since he was unopposed. Requiring all Zambians to unite under the UNIP banner seemed to fulfill Kaunda's credo, "One Zambia, One Nation." Rather than ushering in a new era of unity and tolerance, however, Zambia's Second Republic gave rise to new political restrictions and rising authoritarianism. UNIP hegemony was constitutionally guaranteed and Kaunda's authority was greatly enhanced. Proposals for a dual executive—with certain powers, such as ministerial appointments, vested in the prime minister—were rejected by UNIP officials; proposals to limit presidential terms were also rejected ("Chona Report" 1972). Thus, although power began to be concentrated in the person of the president as early as 1964, this phenomenon accelerated markedly in the Second Republic, as Kaunda increasingly conformed to the characteristics of the neopatrimonial "big man" in which "one individual . . . dominates the [bureaucratic] state apparatus and stands above its laws" (Bratton and van de Walle 1997, 62).

As with many other presidents of his generation, Kaunda, the independence leader, came to see himself as indispensable to his country; surrendering power was not considered. However, UNIP's constitutionally protected political hegemony from 1972 was accompanied by economic collapse, particularly following the oil crisis in 1973. By the 1980s, Zambia's economy was in free fall. Following disastrous experiences with economic structural adjustment programs in 1986 and 1990–1991, which led to sharp price hikes for staple foods, the UNIP regime faced substantial popular unrest. Although Kaunda suspended the programs in both cases, he failed to placate society, and once he lost the support of Zambia's crucial urban populations, Kaunda's demise was assured (Martin 1993). Coupled with international pressure and the spillover effects of the "third wave" of democracy in Africa and worldwide, Kaunda acquiesced to multipartyism in 1990 (Baylies and Szeftel 1992). A new constitution was enacted, clearing the way for multiparty elections in October 1991, the first since 1968.

The opposition coalesced into a broad movement, the Movement for Multiparty Democracy, which contested the 1991 elections as a political party. In spite of the considerable benefits of incumbency, the MMD routed UNIP, and former labor leader Chiluba was elected president with over 80 percent of the vote in a contest widely regarded as legitimate and fair. The 1991 constitution restricted the president to two terms of five years each. However, it failed to address many of the institutional perquisites of the president's position. Presidential power was undiminished under Chiluba, who wielded his authority sometimes ruthlessly.

In addition, the 1991 constitution left intact the presidential entitlement to appoint up to eight additional members of parliament (MPs). Common throughout the region, this provision gives the president power to add to his majority—or to create one where parliament reflects a closely divided electorate. Not surprisingly, these appointed seats increase *presidential* power because loyalty of these MPs lies as much with the president himself as with the ruling party (Bratton and van de Walle 1997). Cabinet appointments, which may include the eight appointed seats, also boost executive power by co-opting loyalties. "The government is made up of the President and cabinet ministers and other ministers and deputy ministers—a total number approaching 70—appointed by the President from members of the House" (Burnell 2002, 293).[13] The appointment of nearly 50 percent of sitting MPs to political positions provides an important patronage tool for the executive and helps to co-opt potential dissenting voices in the legislature. Prospective cabinet ministers are not vetted before parliament, and this lack of consultation has caused rifts between the president and the National Assembly.[14] Further, although the cabinet is collectively accountable to the parliament, the parliament has little means of enforcing that accountability and individual cabinet officials answer only to the president (Burnell 2002, 293).

Technically, the parliament can check executive authority by enacting (with a two-thirds majority) legislation to which the president withholds his assent, or by introducing an impeachment motion. However, neither of these avenues has seen success in Zambia. Another existing (but unused) leveling mechanism is that, whereas the president has the power to dissolve the parliament, the parliament can also dissolve itself, by two-thirds majority, thereby triggering elections for both parliament and the presidency. "Thus, unlike purely presidential systems, the two branches are not mutually independent" (Burnell 2002, 293). In practice, where the MMD controlled 125 and 131 of the elected seats following the 1991 and 1996 elections, the loyalty of the vast majority of the legislative body was to President Chiluba, as it was to Kaunda in the UNIP era. The MMD parliamentary monopoly was broken in 2001, but power continues to accrue to the executive, who not surprisingly "has monopolised the introduction of new legislation" (Burnell 2002, 293). The fact that the MMD has fashioned a strong party structure (in a universe of weak parties) also contributes to the president's control.[15] As leader of the party, as well as the state, the president can impose considerable discipline. Floor crossing is not permitted in Zambia, and therefore anyone expelled or resigning from his party loses his seat in parliament. Given this confluence of factors, it is clear that historically the Zambian parliament has been subordinate to the president.

In 2001, however, there was a major revolt that originated in the cabinet and spread to the wider parliament. Early that year, President Chiluba began to backtrack on earlier pledges to serve only two terms, and his supporters began to openly promote a constitutional change that would allow him to serve a third term in office, a maneuver requiring a two-thirds majority vote in parliament. The initial and most vociferous calls to block this cynical attempt to manipulate the constitution came from civil society, which appeared to lack the capacity to thwart the MMD ("Opposing Chiluba's Encore" 2001). However, by late April 2001, 22 ministers and deputy ministers, joined by a number of MMD and opposition MPs, *publicly* opposed their president; eventually, 74 of the 158 MPs signed a petition vowing to vote against a constitutional amendment bill.

The breakdown in party discipline and personal loyalty was as stark as it was unprecedented. Three factors explain this unlikely outcome. First, civic organization and protest reached its greatest level since 1991, as resistance to Chiluba spread nationwide. Civil society's clearest expression came through the Oasis Forum, which is addressed later in the chapter. Second, the security forces notified Chiluba that they would not intervene if protest turned violent. These two factors helped to shift many MMD insiders' perception of self-interest. Similarly, a third reason was that some senior members felt betrayed by the third-term bid, and that the advancement of their own political careers was being hijacked to accommodate Chiluba's. Hence, the notion that "it was our turn" appeared to figure prominently in the thinking of those who opposed Chiluba from within the MMD.[16] By July 2001, Chiluba recognized he could not win and announced he would not attempt to stand again for the presidency, although Levy Mwanawasa, who was selected by the MMD's forty-member national executive committee, was not announced as the party's candidate until August 2001 ("Presidential Candidate's Adoption" 2001).[17]

The December 2001 national elections signaled the possibility of unprecedented changes in legislative-executive relations. Mwanawasa, the former lawyer and onetime MMD and national vice president, narrowly won the presidential election with just under 29 percent of the vote. The MMD was unable to secure a majority of the elected seats in parliament, however, raising the possibility that henceforth laws would be passed through interparty negotiation, compromise, and coalition building, rather than simply by executive fiat as in the past. Instead, as president, Mwanawasa not only forced out many of the MMD old guard, but also moved to co-opt even opposition parties into his cabinet and engineered an alliance with UNIP, which by then held a small but majority-making thirteen seats in parliament.[18] In the process, Mwanawasa skillfully constructed a new base upon which to build loyalty—to him rather than to the office per se (EIU 2003k, 7).

One other important feature of presidential power in Zambia warrants mention. Historically, the president has had great discretion over financial resources, both through official and illicit transactions. Chiluba maintained a multimillion-dollar slush fund for use by his office (Rakner, van de Walle, and Mulaisho 2001).[19] For his part, President Mwanawasa reportedly has exercised particular control and influence over the Ministry of Finance (EIU 2003g). In itself, this is unsurprising, as the finance ministry is typically the most important in Africa, given its powerful fiscal role and its unparalleled international access and connections. However, as is the case elsewhere in Africa, institutional oversight of presidential accounting is weak, at best, and this raises concerns. Although Mwanawasa is regarded as an anticorruption reformer in some circles, Zambia's track record regarding financial rectitude is unambiguously poor. Mwanawasa has targeted his erstwhile benefactor, Chiluba, by prevailing on the parliament to lift his immunity from prosecution.[20] In 2003 Chiluba was formally charged with sixty-five counts of "public theft" totaling 19 billion Zambian kwacha, although the case may take years to complete (EIU 2003k, 15). In the meantime, Mwanawasa himself has faced accusations of both procedural and financial improprieties that resulted in a brief and unsuccessful impeachment attempt (EIU 2003k, 12).

■ **Constitutionalism**

The Zambian constitution has undergone several revisions since independence. The 1972 version established the one-party state; the 1991 constitution dissolved the one-party monopoly and introduced presidential term limits; and the 1996 constitution, which was highly controversial but remains in force, placed restrictions on citizenship and presidential candidates, among other things. As noted in the previous section, Chiluba attempted to change the constitution again in 2001 to allow himself to contest a third term. For his part, President Mwanawasa initiated a constitutional review process in August 2003 that was expected to last twelve months. This follows the model of each of the previous constitutional changes, which also were preceded by the establishment of a constitutional review commission (CRC), albeit with differing functions and mandates.

The 1996 constitution was derived in part from the input of the Mwanakatwe Commission, which solicited submissions and participated in town hall–type meetings throughout Zambia in 1993 and 1994. In theory, this is an admirable example of grassroots democracy, and the commission, named for its chairman, John Mwanakatwe, submitted its report in June 1995. However, the MMD-dominated parliament ignored numerous recommendations of the commission when the constitutional amendment bill was debated in 1996 (Bratton and Posner 1999, 393). The Economist Intelligence Unit (2003k, 15) claims that Chiluba's government rejected "70 percent of [the CRC's] submissions and instead authorise[d] a text custom-made in key respects for the president." Differing with this claim, but not with its consequences, Michael Bratton and Daniel Posner (1999, 393) note that the government actually agreed with many of the CRC's proposals, but that by cutting off intense public debate and ratifying the changes in parliament, the government committed a "gross violation of the spirit of democratic discourse that President Chiluba claimed to champion." Indeed, the government ignored a key recommendation of the Mwanakatwe Commission—and a civil society and donor demand—"that any new constitution should be ratified by a national referendum and a constituent assembly, rather than by parliament" (Bratton and Posner 1999, 393). Among the most controversial provisions of the 1996 constitution was a restriction—the "citizenship clause"—on who could contest the presidency; the new document barred any individual whose parents, like former president Kaunda's, were not also born in Zambia (*Constitution of Zambia 1996*, art. 34) This was a transparent attempt to bar Kaunda from rechallenging Chiluba for the presidency.[21]

In the end, parliament adopted the constitution "despite hostility from opposition parties, human rights groups, churches, trade unions, the free press, lawyers' associations and others," as well as international condemnation that put severe strain on Zambia's relations with the donor community (EIU 2003g, 16). CRC members argued that their efforts were wasted on what ultimately amounted to a public relations exercise.[22]

The most recent CRC, comprising forty-one members, was expected to address some of these inequities in the current constitution. Despite the widespread condemnation of the 1996 constitution and its method of adoption however, many Zambians, including commissioners themselves, are raising questions about the new effort. According to one CRC member, many commissioners question the utility of the exercise, but fear possible retribution from Mwanawasa if they do not participate; at the same time, the leadership of the commission is seen as too close to Mwanawasa to be considered impartial.[23] Moreover, despite the fact that President Mwanawasa picked all of its members, some commissioners are demanding a constituent assembly that would open the process to public scrutiny and debate (EIU 2003k, 15)—a demand reminiscent of 1996.

■ Court System

Zambia has a multitiered judicial system. The Supreme Court is the highest court and serves as the final court of appeal. It is headed by the chief justice and deputy chief justice and seven other judges who are nominated by the president and ratified by parliament. Below the Supreme Court is the High Court, which has "unlimited and original jurisdiction to hear and determine any civil or criminal proceedings under any law" (*Constitution of Zambia,* pt. 6, art. 94; para. 1), including, of course, appeals from lower courts. The High Court holds regular sessions in all nine provincial capitals. Judges on both the Supreme and High Courts serve until the mandatory retirement age sixty-five. At the next level are the magistrate courts, which have original jurisdiction in some civil and criminal cases. There is also an Industrial Relations Court, charged with hearing labor matters, and an extensive, if ill-defined system of local courts, which adjudicate principally customary and family law. "The local courts are today the busiest courts in Zambia. Some urban courts hear between 30 and 50 cases in a day." Yet these courts are without even the most basic facilities—paper, pens, transport—and are routinely neglected by higher courts and the country's political institutions (Afronet 1998, chap. 5). Indeed, at all levels, the twin problems of resource constraints and judicial independence have plagued Zambia's court system, as they have other countries in the region. A Freedom House survey (1999) noted that "some of Zambia's jurists retain a stubborn independence while others are subservient to Chiluba and the MMD." In addition, the survey decried the overburdened court system, detentions lasting years without trial in some cases, and arbitrary and often unconstitutional rulings in civil cases by customary courts of "variable quality."

While many of the systemic problems—insufficient resources, over-crowding, unrelieved dockets, and inadequate representation—continue to plague Zambia's judicial system, the more competitive politics prevailing since 2001 may have a salutary impact on judicial independence in Zambia's courts. As Jennifer Widner (2001, 100) notes, party competition gives "politicians a material incentive to check executive encroachment on judicial functions. Without competition, politicians' individual attitudes toward the courts mattered much more." Fortunately, President Kaunda's stance toward the courts was relatively benign.[24] According to Peter von Doepp (2001a), despite the lack of competition in Zambia's Second Republic, Kaunda generally eschewed interference in the judiciary and his government followed suit. However, Kaunda did intervene, indirectly, by appointing supportive jurists, and none were permitted to challenge the premise of one-partyism. On the other hand, judges occasionally issued politically unpopular decisions that challenged the ruling UNIP elites.

Ironically, pressure on the judiciary to conform with political interests may have increased under the ostensibly "democratic" rule of the MMD. Recall that genuine multiparty competition, though no longer illegal, was virtually nonexistent in the first decade of the Third Republic. Therefore, following Widner's logic (2001), MMD elites were little concerned with executive interference in the judiciary, demonstrating hostility toward legal rulings and jurists unfavorable to the ruling party (von Doepp 2001a). By 2003, political intimidation appeared to have waned, however, perhaps fostering an environment of increased judicial independence. The EIU (2003g, 17) suggests that "despite some questionable judgments in high-profile cases, the spirited judiciary has managed to preserve its independence from the executive and legislature." Paradoxically, some of the most politically sensitive cases on the docket involve President Mwanawasa and his government.

Mwanawasa has led a massive anticorruption campaign that targets a number of extremely powerful and high-profile former members of President Chiluba's cabinet, including Chiluba himself, whose trial began in August 2003. At the same time, however, Mwanawasa is also, in effect, a *defendant* before the High Court, where opposition parties filed a petition to invalidate the December 2001 election immediately after the new president was inaugurated in January 2002.[25] The case charges Mwanawasa with electoral fraud and illegal (and unconstitutional) use of state resources for his 2001 campaign (EIU 2003g, 14). It is not known whether Mwanawasa was aware of these alleged violations at the time they occurred, or whether he merely unwittingly benefited from the MMD's formidable political machine. If the court were to find against Mwanawasa, a new election would be required.

■ Representation and Participation

▨ *Legislative Branch*

The 158-member National Assembly, or parliament, is Zambia's unicameral legislative body. One hundred fifty MPs, representing single-member constituencies, are directly elected for five-year terms, and up to eight additional members are appointed by the president. Under both the UNIP and MMD governments, at least through the 1990s, the parliament served essentially as a rubber stamp for executive decisionmaking. As noted earlier, the executive exercises disproportionate authority, notwithstanding a constitutional nod to balance of power between branches, and his power is enhanced by control over spending, access to unbudgeted funds, and the ability to make ministerial appointments from among sitting MPs. Following the 2001 elections, however, the MMD lost its majority, creating the prospect of divided government in Zambia for the first time. And while divided government can lead to legislative gridlock, it also can also yield new alliances and unique compromises and cooperation. Indeed, the 2001 election presented a genuine opportunity for opposition parties, despite their diversity, to form an opposition alliance that would offset the executive power of the presidency.

But during 2002, "opposition parties failed to muster sufficient unity to disturb the government's legislative programme, and government soon managed to build itself a working majority in the assembly, thereby neutralising the potential threat the assembly had briefly posed" (EIU 2003g, 16). As a result, the lion's share of political power in Zambia remained vested in the president. Moreover, as an experienced governing party, the MMD took advantage of its ten-year tenure as the majority party, and the incumbency it still enjoyed in the presidency to woo both legislators and voters back into its camp. By-elections and defections thus helped MMD regain the parliamentary majority in 2002. By-elections are required within ninety days from the date a parliamentary seat becomes vacant, or whenever a sitting MP switches parties (including independents). By October 2003, the National Assembly's composition appeared as follows: the MMD, 74 seats; the UPND, 46; the Forum for Democracy and Development, 13; the Zambia Republican Party, 1; the Heritage Party, 2; UNIP, 13; plus 1 independent. This represented a five-seat increase for the ruling party over its 2001 election performance. Several of the new MMD members came at the expense of the UPND, which suffered a number of defections. However, the MMD's parliamentary supremacy is secured, ironically, by its old rival UNIP, with which it has formed a loose governing coalition. The advantage of this arrangement is that it is not necessary to put a seat at risk by holding a by-election.

In sum, whereas Zambia's parliament has become more competitive since 2001, it nonetheless continues to favor the ruling party. All parties produce dense manifestos, but tend to differ little on substance; personalities therefore emerge as central factors for voters, despite the fact that the system is highly centralized and constituency service is nearly nonexistent. Another hallmark of Zambian multipartyism is that party identities are incredibly fluid. Thus an MP's switch from the opposition to the ruling party is neither unexpected nor likely to lose him or her the seat.

▓ The Party System and Elections

In 1991, democratic, multiparty elections were a rarity in sub-Saharan Africa. Zambia's transition from authoritarian rule—whose critical elements included President Kaunda's willingness to allow multipartyism, the "free and fair" conduct of the election, and the peaceful transfer of power—was greeted with great enthusiasm both inside and outside the country. Indeed, because of this remarkably smooth process and apparently democratic outcome, Richard Joseph (1992) declared Zambia a "model for Africa," and other scholars were similarly impressed by the achievement (Baylies and Szeftel 1992; Bratton 1992). Zambia, therefore, was seen as something of a bellwether case, in that it was at the forefront of a democratic wave on the African continent.

To its credit, Zambia also held regular elections at the national level under the MMD, as it had under UNIP. Elections, of course, are only one part of democratic governance, albeit a critical part. After 1991 Chiluba was able to quickly consolidate his control over the party structure and the pliant parliament. The MMD's enormous parliamentary majority in 1991 (128 seats to UNIP's 22) left it in virtually the same position of UNIP in the First Republic: it achieved super majority status, with very few checks on political decisionmaking as a result. The MMD's overwhelming dominance fueled unchallenged policy choices, many of which proved disastrous, and growing authoritarianism in the 1990s. The party showed progressively less tolerance of opposition activities as the decade went on, a stance that was a reflection of its own growing insecurities.[26]

Notwithstanding the celebratory mood in 1991, Zambia was only nominally democratic throughout the decade. The propensity toward single-party dominance and the precarious nature of Zambian democracy was actually first signaled by President Chiluba's declaration of a state of emergency in March 1993 on spurious claims that UNIP was plotting to overthrow the government through a clandestine operation code named "Zero Option." Several UNIP leaders were detained and civil liberties were suspended for two months. When the charges turned out to be unsupportable and evidence of a coup conspiracy nonexistent, it became apparent that the MMD was merely attempting to consolidate power by undermining UNIP, then the only viable opposition party (Ihonvbere 1995; Bratton and Posner 1999). The hastily imposed state of emergency marked the beginning of Zambia's slide into renewed authoritarianism, although relative quiescence prevailed until 1996, the year MMD was required to go to the polls to renew its mandate.

In March 1996 the regime harassed and eventually incarcerated three independent journalists (employed by *The Post* newspaper), following controversy arising from their publication of articles critical of Chiluba (Bratton and Posner 1999). The arrests, officially on "contempt of parliament" charges, were spurious and were immediately condemned by international and local human rights groups, resulting in the reporters' eventual release. The crackdown on the press was followed in quick succession in

May 1996 by the promulgation of the widely criticized constitution, the explosion of a series of bombs, reportedly by a shadowy group called "Black Mamba," and the arrest of eight senior members of UNIP, again on specious charges of treason.[27] Finally, in November 1996 the MMD went ahead with the national elections under highly suspicious conditions, including allegations of voter registration fraud, a divisive constitution, and an atmosphere of intimidation. In response, UNIP and several other parties decided to boycott the elections, which the MMD then won in a landslide (Baylies and Szeftel 1997; Bratton and Posner 1999).

An actual coup attempt occurred in October 1997, although it was led by a small band of disgruntled soldiers, who were not only disorganized but also reportedly drunk at the time. The coup attempt, which amounted to little more than a half-day takeover of a broadcast station, led to a second state of emergency declaration two months later. Although their links to the coup attempt were tenuous at best, several opposition leaders, this time including former president Kaunda, were jailed along with seventy-eight soldiers. Most were held without charge for several months, and the trial did not begin until June 1998, reflecting the weakness of the government's case (particularly against the handful of accused civilians). Kaunda, whose ties to the coup were never supported by the evidence, was released just prior to the commencement of the trial. South African president Nelson Mandela and former Tanzanian president Julius Nyerere appealed to Chiluba for Kaunda's release; at the urging of his nationalist-era contemporaries, Kaunda agreed to give up active politics, thus diminishing the threat of a Kaunda resurgence long felt by Chiluba.

The failure to fulfill the political and economic promise of 1991 reflects the inability of the MMD and its leadership to even begin to address the Herculean problems facing the country in the 1990s. More broadly, however, this failure highlights the enormous difficulty of instituting genuine democracy after brief political openings that merely allow challengers to become incumbents and act like their predecessors. The rise of such "virtual democracies" has been an all too common occurrence following the democratic wave earlier in the decade (Joseph 1997). Zambia's virtual democracy was epitomized by the regime's authoritarian tendencies. But it was also aided by certain institutional features. The first-past-the-post, majoritarian electoral system favors large parties and particularly the incumbent party. Second, the Electoral Commission of Zambia (ECZ), which is charged with overseeing elections, voter registration, voter education, and the like, has little autonomy from the government (European Union [EU] 2001; Carter Center 2002). Although nominally independent, the ECZ is funded and influenced by the government, and its five commissioners are appointed by the president.

The political and institutional environment after 1991, therefore, was scarcely favorable to political opposition; yet paradoxically, opposition parties proliferated. One explanation for this surely lies in the desire for electoral alternatives. However, the requirements for party registration are minimal (just 200 signatures), so a number of the thirty or more parties that surfaced at any given time in the 1990s foundered quickly or existed almost entirely on paper, having little substance behind them. Since 1991, several parties were able to gain seats in parliament, although, as noted, most had only regional support: UNIP in the east; the National Party and, later, Agenda for Zambia, both predominantly supported by the Lozi community in Western province; and the UPND, with its strongest support in the south among the Tonga community. The Forum for Democracy and Development emerged mainly as an MMD spin-off in mid-2001, accommodating the MMD cabinet members and parliamentarians who refused to support Chiluba's third-term bid. However, the multiplicity of parties seldom translated into measurable parliamentary seats.[28] Indeed, of the seventeen parties that contested the 2001 parliamentary elections, only five gained more than a single seat.

The Zambian presidential, parliamentary, and local elections were held on December 27, 2001. Tables 3.1 and 3.2 illustrate the presidential and parliamentary results. These elections were also marred by allegations of voter fraud, intimidation, and harassment of opposition politicians and their supporters and errors by the ECZ (EU 2001). Unchastened by Chiluba's failed attempt to gain a third term, the ruling MMD used all the perks of incumbency to ensure victory for its candidates. Its overwhelming financial advantages, control of a politicized police force, and unfettered access to the public media made the party a formidable opponent. Moreover, the government postponed the elections until late December, ordinarily the height of the rainy season in Zambia, in an apparent attempt to depress turnout. Given these tactics, it was surprising that on election day nearly 70 percent of registered voters arrived at polling stations. People waited in line for hours on end—in some cases as many as twenty hours—usually without food, water, or shelter from the hot sun; fortunately, the rains held off until after the elections. Citizens expressed an unyielding resolve to voice their opinions, and many reported that they were "voting for change"—that is, an end to what they regarded as ten years of failed, corrupt MMD rule.[29] Many observers had predicted a win by presidential candidate Anderson Mazoka, a prominent businessman and head of the United Party for National Development. The UPND was perhaps the best organized party among the opposition, and had considerable momentum. In the end, although the UPND won forty-nine seats in the National Assembly, the MMD won sixty-nine and, of course, the presidency.[30] While the MMD clearly enjoyed continued support in many parts of the country, the questionable conduct of the election by it and the ECZ were important factors in securing the MMD's plurality of the parliamentary vote and Mwanawasa's narrow victory.

Table 3.1 Presidential Election, 2001

Candidate	Party	Number of Valid Votes	Percentage[a]
Tilyenji Kaunda	UNIP	175,898	9.96
Gwendoline Konie	SDP	10,253	0.58
Anderson Mazoka	UPND	472,697	26.76
Inonge Mbikusita-Lewanika	AZ	9,882	0.56
Godfrey Miyanda	HP	140,678	7.96
Nevers Mumba	NCC	38,860	2.20
Levy Mwanawasa	MMD	506,694	28.69
Benjamin Mwila	ZRP	85,472	4.84
Michael Sata	PF	59,172	3.35
Yobert Shampande	NLD	9,481	0.54
Christon Tembo	FDD	228,861	12.96
Total		1,737,948	98.39

Source: Electoral Commission of Zambia.
Notes: a. Percentage of total votes cast, including 28,408 invalid or spoiled ballots.
Registered voters: 2,604,838
Voter turnout: 66.72%

Table 3.2 Parliamentary Elections, 2001

Party	Number of Valid Votes	Percentage[a]	Number of Seats
MMD	490,680	27.48	69
UPND	416,236	23.31	49
FDD	272,817	15.28	13
UNIP	185,535	10.39	12
HP	132,311	7.41	4
ZRP	97,010	5.43	1
Independent	59,335	3.32	1
PF	49,362	2.76	1
NCC	35,632	2.00	0
ZAP	3,963	0.22	0
NLD	3,155	0.18	0
AZ	2,832	0.16	0
NP	1,228	0.07	0
SDP	809	0.05	0
LPF	175	0.01	0
ZUDP	138	0.01	0
DP	115	0.01	0
ZPP	19	0.00	0
Total	1,751,352	98.09	150

Source: Electoral Commission of Zambia.
Notes: a. Percentage of total votes cast, including 34,133 (1.91%) invalid or spoiled ballots.

Levy Mwanawasa's election, however tainted the process, has been followed by some potentially positive developments in Zambia. Although the economy remains extremely weak, and appropriate questions have been raised about governance—allegations behind the 2003 impeachment motion and the new CRC are but two examples—Mwanawasa has vigorously pursued the prosecution of Chiluba, and appeared initially to have little tolerance for kleptocratic behavior in his cabinet (EIU 2003k). Although the legitimacy of the process has been challenged on several fronts, Mwanawasa's very candidacy in 2001 would have been impossible without the critical role of civil society. In other words, had it not been for the tremendous opposition from civic groups, Frederick Chiluba certainly would have run for, and most assuredly captured, the presidency.

In February 2001, civil society organizations came together under the aegis of the Oasis Forum, whose principal mission was to prevent a Chiluba third term. The Oasis Forum, named after Lusaka's Oasis Restaurant, in which the first meeting was held, developed into a mass campaign that eventually forced Chiluba to capitulate. This was a prominent example of the vibrancy of civil society in Zambia and represents one of the three key junctures in state-society relations.

Civil Society

The first juncture that warrants examination centers on the role of civil society in the 1990–1991 transition. The Movement for Multiparty Democracy was established in July 1990 "as an umbrella committee of interest groups whose principal demand was, as its name suggested, the restoration of competitive politics. To form an opposition front, Frederick Chiluba led the trade union movement into a coalition with business, professional, student, and church groups. As well as bridging class and status divides, the urban-based MMD skillfully used the far-flung teachers' and civil servants' unions to mobilize support in the countryside" and drew in "a diverse set of ethnoregional groups as well" (Bratton and van de Walle 1997, 199). The interest groups that arrayed against Kaunda and the one-party state had depth as well as breadth. Thus the sheer number of actors involved and their national reach of their organizations—as represented in the MMD, which of course became a political party—brought considerable pressure to bear on President Kaunda to permit competitive elections.

The role of civil society in the transition has been the subject of considerable research (Baylies and Szeftel 1992; Bratton 1992; Ihonvbere 1995; Rakner 1998). This research is unanimous in its conclusion that civil society played an instrumental role in channeling popular discord into a formidable, organized social movement, and later into a party. Diverse and contradictory societal interest groups (for example, business and labor) engaged in a robust and cooperative effort, ultimately compelling Kenneth Kaunda to allow elections—and to stand down when he lost (Baylies and Szeftel 1992).

The second period, roughly from 1993 through the end of the decade, was nearly the converse of the first. It was characterized by the relative quiescence of civil society, which was in part a result of the authoritarian backlash of the Chiluba government. In the brief honeymoon period immediately following the 1991 election, associational life blossomed, particularly since the lawyers, churches, students, businesspeople, laborers, and the other actors who established MMD had reason to believe their interests would be well represented in the new government (Rakner 2001). Ironically, what transpired instead was a curtailment of civil liberties under the rubric of two hastily imposed (if short-lived) states of emergency, sustained harassment of the small independent press, and the marginalization of the labor, business, and nongovernmental organization (NGO) communities that aided the MMD's ascension to power (Rakner 2001; Bräutigam, Rakner, and Taylor 2002). Commenting on this period, Bratton and Posner (1999, 392) observed, "although rhetorically committed to openness and transparency, Chiluba's government has proven to be intolerant of criticism, slow to react to allegations of corruption within its ranks, and disturbingly willing to exploit its command over government resources and institutions (including the police and parliament) to undermine the opposition and favor its own party members."

During this time, far narrower segments of civil society played a watchdog role than might have been anticipated based on the 1991 transition. Only the independent print media, notably *The Post* newspaper, joined by a handful of NGOs, remained regular critics of the government. Other civic organizations, such as those representing the business community, offered more tailored criticism and attempted to attract donor support for their activities (Bräutigam, Rakner, and Taylor 2002). Local NGOs, like the Foundation for Democratic Process, the Zambia Independent Monitoring Team (ZIMT), and the Committee for a Clean Campaign (CCC) developed expertise in issues of voter education and election monitoring. However, the cost of speaking out against government abuse of power proved high after 1993. As Bratton and Posner (1999, 397) report, *The Post* "was the target of 20 separate acts of harassment by the government or its supporters between January 1994 and October 1996." Similarly, when ZIMT and the CCC "called press conferences to announce their opinion that the [1996] elections had been flawed, their offices were raided, their bank accounts were frozen, and their chairmen were detained by the police" (Bratton and Posner 1999, 401).

Such actions had a predictably chilling effect on societal discourse. Although public criticism of the government never stopped (*The Post,* for example, was unrelenting and occasionally over the top), interest groups were fearful of repercussions for speaking out. The Zambia National Farmers Union, for example, found itself ostracized by the government and was forced to conciliate.[31] The Chiluba government skillfully marginalized (or worse) those groups that showed it hostility. At the same time, it proved adept at cultivating new support bases in society through co-optation and patronage in the classical neopatrimonial pattern. Chiluba's multimillion-dollar slush fund was instrumental in this regard.

The quiescence of civil society at the end of the 1990s makes its resurgence in 2001 all the more noteworthy. Thus, at the third juncture is the Oasis Forum, the initially spontaneous consortium of interest groups that arose to challenge Chiluba's third term. The Oasis committee formally included the leaders of key groups in the legal, church, and NGO communities. Specifically, five organizations were represented: the Law Association of Zambia; three church umbrella bodies representing each of the major Christian faith traditions in the country, namely the Evangelical Federation of Zambia, the Christian Council of Zambia, and the Zambian Episcopal Conference; and finally the Nongovernmental Organizations Coordinating Committee, itself an umbrella of major NGOs operating in Zambia. Meeting in February 2001, the Oasis Forum wrote the Oasis Declaration, which was submitted to President Chiluba. The brief declaration recounted the Zambian peoples' desire, expressed repeatedly in constitutional review commissions in 1972, 1991, and 1996, to limit the president to two five-year terms. It specifically called on the president to respect the constitution and to resist calls for a third term, noting "that the ongoing debate is not only costly and counter-productive but is an ill considered attempt at legitimizing an ILLEGITIMATE or unlawful objective and desire to subvert the Constitution" (Oasis Forum, February 21, 2001, n. 7).

The Oasis Forum helped to focus a growing popular campaign to prevent Chiluba and the parliament from rewriting the constitution for narrow political gain. Moreover, the reach of the Oasis constituent groups, particularly the churches, was significant, thereby enabling opponents of the president's effort to reach a vast swath of Zambian society. Using Chiluba's own past statements, which condemned African leaders, including his predecessor, Kaunda, for clinging to power, critics throughout Zambian society became more vocal in their protest. In defiance of government efforts to block public protest against the third term, a popular "hooting" demonstration also emerged, in which those opposed to the third term sounded their car horns in unison. In this and more substantive ways, Zambian civil society united in the face of Chiluba's brazen grab for power. As discussed above, members of Chiluba's cabinet, though self-interested, also recognized the formidable resistance to the third term and abandoned Chiluba, who in turn was forced to abandon his bid.

Oasis's successful effort leads us to wonder where civil society was between 1991 and 2001. While at first glance, it would appear that Zambians' greatest expression occurs in decennial cycles, in fact the middle years of the 1990s did not find all Zambian civil society organizations in the doldrums. Indeed, a number of organizations, including some of those that participated directly and indirectly in the Oasis Forum, found a way to take advantage of the pluralist environment after 1991. Although access to the state was often limited or nonexistent (Rakner 2001), certain groups were able to build capacity and capabilities (almost invariably with donor assistance), notwithstanding the state's occasionally stark authoritarian methods. In the process, NGOs expanded indigenous capacity for everything from election monitoring to political and civic education to combating AIDS. This more "mature" civil society, prominently in evidence in the anti-third-term campaign of 2001, may provide a bulwark against future authoritarian impulses by the state.

■ Fundamentals of the Political Economy

The Chiluba government also came to power promising to reverse two decades of economic decline under Kaunda. In fact, Zambia's main economic engine remains little changed since independence in 1964. More worrying, the country's position in the global economy, as well as its ability to meet the needs of its own populace, have deteriorated badly in the intervening years. Indeed, the United Nation's 2003 *Human Development Report* ranked Zambia 163 out of the 175 poorest countries in the world; and Zambia has the dubious distinction of being "one of only three countries in the world with a worse development indicator index in 2001 than in 1975" (EIU 2003g, 36). At independence, Zambia was just emerging from ten years of federation in which the benefits flowed to Southern Rhodesia.[32] Yet despite the disadvantages of federation, the 1960s marked a period of great optimism for Zambia's future. Its small population of slightly over 3 million, low population density, fertile agricultural base, and existing copper resources held great development promise. Unlike Southern Rhodesia, Zambia at independence had few whites in industrial enterprises outside of the mining sector, and just 400 white commercial farmers (Hall 1966). But an indigenous African industrial or commercial agricultural base was practically nonexistent. Thus in terms of economic development, the country had to start virtually from scratch.

As in much of independent Africa, the state was regarded as the guarantor of economic security for the newly empowered black majority and it assumed a leading role; the private sector was dominated by MNCs, especially in the critical mining sector.[33] Zambia quickly adopted a program of import substitution industrialization (ISI), similar to other developing countries at that time, calling for local production of manufactured goods. The economic foundation of President Kaunda's policies was laid in the Mulungushi reforms, which were launched in 1967 and signaled the desire to put the economy in the hands of the black majority. Importantly, within Kaunda's worldview of "humanism," with its socialist undertones, Africanization meant a state-owned economy, not the development of an indigenous private sector. The Mulungushi initiative therefore called for massive acquisition by the state of locally and internationally owned enterprises. As in most African countries where nationalization took place, with the notable exception of Mozambique and more recently Zimbabwe, acquisition was part of a negotiated process for which firms were compensated; Zambia even borrowed internationally to fund the program, thereby adding to its debt burden (Kayizzi-Mugerwa 2003).

However, with the exception of the copper-mining firms Anglo-American Corporation and American Metal Climax Company, from which the state acquired a majority shareholding (subsequently consolidated under Zambia Consolidated Copper Mines [ZCCM]),[34] most of the nationalized firms produced solely for local markets.[35] Thus the key policy error by Kaunda and UNIP was not nationalization per se, but the fact that little effort was made to diversify the country's export revenue stream beyond copper, which accounted for approximately 90 percent of exports during the Kaunda regime and a similar percentage thereafter. Nationalization greatly hindered state flexibility, especially the ability to restructure the economy and bureaucracy, as the state became too dependent on the copper sector (Shafer 1994). Nevertheless, Zambia enjoyed relative prosperity for its first five years. World copper prices were high, enabling the government to pursue nationalization with vigor, and to grant cheap credit that fueled the growth of an emergent petty bourgeoisie (Gertzel 1984).

The dependence on copper revealed profound weaknesses in the economy, however, when prices began to soften by 1970 (Gertzel 1984). Even then, the Zambian government took few steps to diversify beyond the country's traditional copper export base. Cherry Gertzel (1984) suggests that a rebound in prices the following year may have contributed to the continued delusion that the copper boom was a permanent fixture of the international economy. It was not. The international oil crisis of 1973–1974, prompted by drastic cuts in production by the Organization of Petroleum-Exporting Countries cartel, sharply reduced global demand for copper. As a result, world copper prices fell sharply in 1974–1975, reducing Zambia's 1975 copper export revenues by over 43 percent.[36] The second international oil crisis, in 1979–1980, raised costs immeasurably for oil-dependent states like Zambia and precipitated a global recession that made matters worse. In the 1980s, Zambia was compelled to seek relief from the International Monetary Fund (IMF) and later the World Bank, marking the beginning of two decades—and counting—of dependence on loans from the international financial institution (IFIs) and the donor community.

■ Structural Adjustment and Donor Dependence: 1984–Present

Zambia actually had signed its first standby agreement with the IMF in 1973, availing itself of the IMF's Oil Facility (Ihonvbere 1995). However, the 1980s marked a sharp decline in the Zambian economy: copper prices did not recover, per capita GDP declined 3 percent per year, and the country faced a rising debt burden. As Julius Ihonvbere (1995, 78) observes, the government agreed to a 1983–1985 adjustment package with the Bank and the IMF to "restore financial stability," but by 1986 the Zambian government was over U.S.$100 million in arrears to the IMF and the program was suspended. Zambia briefly tried a "homegrown" structural adjustment strategy, but this too failed and neoliberal reforms were discontinued until the Chiluba government reinstated a structural adjustment program (SAP) under the auspices of the World Bank and the IMF in 1991 (Callaghy 1990; Martin 1993). Contrary to UNIP, the MMD had a popular mandate to implement SAPs, since the party made clear that fixing the economy would require austerity (Bratton 1992).

Encouraged to return to Zambia by the economic and political promises of the Chiluba government, with its professed commitment to governance, the donor community and the IFIs engaged the regime. Indeed, through much of the 1990s, more than 40 percent of the budget was donor-dependent, a level likely to continue throughout this decade (EIU 2003k, 8). In the 1990s the donors frequently praised the MMD's commitment to the SAP and Zambia's aggressive approach to privatization (Rakner, van de Walle, and Mulaisho 2001). Indeed, the EIU (2003g, 36) notes that the government "did go further than almost any other African administration in this period to retrench public-sector workers, privatise state assets, liberalise foreign-exchange dealings, control money-supply growth, reduce public expenditure and increase public revenue." But the conditions in Zambia continued to worsen in the 1990s, and analysts variously point to donors' lack of goals and government's lack of long-term strategy and waning commitment to reform (Rakner, van de Walle, and Mulaisho 2001) or the programs themselves (Mkandawire and Soludo 1999)—or all three (Bräutigam, Rakner, and Taylor 2002)—for the explanation. At bottom, Lise Rakner, Nicolas van de Walle, and Dominic Mulaisho (2001, 563) noted that "after almost a decade of uninterrupted policy reforms, the record in terms of economic growth, employment creation, investments, and poverty reduction remains weak."

In response, donor support has been withheld on multiple occasions. For example, reacting to the constitutional changes and the flawed elections in 1996, bilateral donors froze aid between 1996 and 1998. The delayed privatization of ZCCM after 1997 led to further suspensions by lenders. More recently, due to what the EIU (2003k, 16–17) reports as "fiscal laxity," the IMF withheld a U.S.$100 million poverty reduction and growth facility loan—the low-interest loan program launched by the IMF in 1999; a World Bank loan in the amount of U.S.$342 million was also on hold, as were bilateral commitments totaling some U.S.$38 million. Some donors may fear that Mwanawasa himself may become ensnared in the corruption prosecution of former president Chiluba. If Mwanawasa is implicated, "donors may have no choice but to stop funding the government" (EIU 2003k, 7). However, in the past, donor conditionalities proved difficult to enforce because, as Rakner, van de Walle, and Mulaisho (2001) point out, the IFIs and the bilateral donors were seldom in accord, particularly over political matters in the 1990s. This reduced the international leverage on the Chiluba government, and may have the same effect with Mwanawasa.

■ The Private Sector in Zambia: Past, Present—and What Future?

The Mulungushi reforms in the First Republic stifled much of the potential for an indigenous private sector. Even after the Mulungushi reforms, however, "foreign and state capital constituted overwhelmingly the dominant actor within the economy, holding virtually all of the large-scale private enterprises and dwarfing the participation of private Zambian capital. Indeed, even resident non-Zambian individuals probably remained more economically important than private Zambians" (Baylies and Szeftel 1984, 69). Under Kaunda, the state exercised hegemony in virtually every economic sector, forming a massive state holding company, the Zambia Industrial and Mining Corporation. The state invested heavily in manufacturing industries, including paint, chemicals, textiles, and sugar. In addition, the agricultural sector was controlled with a state monopsony on the marketing of many crops, particularly the national staple, maize. Government indirectly subsidized maize consumption by offering a low price ceiling to farmers, who had no other legal outlet for their produce. This was intended to placate potentially restive urban consumers by offering them the staple at low cost; however, such "urban bias" had the effect of driving producers out of the market, creating shortages and unsustainable economies (Bates 1981).

In those few sectors the state did not operate, some multinational firms, such as Colgate Palmolive, Reckitt and Coleman, and Dunlop, among others, stepped in to supply goods to the local market. Thus, outside the state and MNCs, there was limited space occupied by small and medium-scale manufacturers, commercial traders, and about 400 predominantly white commercial farmers; in short, the local private sector was small, weak, and vulnerable as a result of UNIP policies. Interestingly, it largely remained so in the 1990s, despite changes in the economic and political regime that accompanied the ascension of the promarket MMD (Bräutigam, Rakner, and Taylor 2002). In the 1990s, in place of a state antithetical to domestic private interests was an environment in which international firms, chiefly from South Africa, were able to swamp Zambian markets and overwhelm uncompetitive Zambian-owned enterprises. Zambia has undergone a significant deindustrialization as uncompetitive firms faced the regional and wider international marketplace following trade liberalization in 1992 (Bräutigam, Rakner, and Taylor 2002). The lack of competitiveness of most of the surviving local firms appears likely to continue (EIU 2003g).

Nonetheless, privatization, which has been a major feature of the Zambian economy after 1991, continues to be part of the agenda. In 1992, the Zambia Privatization Agency (ZPA) was set up, and by 1997 the professionally managed entity had sold 224 of the 275 formerly government-owned companies that had been listed for sale. International observers, including the World Bank, hailed Zambia's privatization, attributing the "success of the privatization program to the fact that the process through the [ZPA] was predominantly private sector-driven, with little interference from the government" (Rakner, van de Walle, and Mulaisho 2001, 562). Yet these cheerful assessments were clearly based on the *quantity* of Zambia's privatizations rather than the quality. For example, the 200-plus transactions (some of them suspect) yielded a relatively small sum—less than U.S.$100 million in proceeds. Moreover, the transaction that dwarfed all the others combined, the privatization of Zambia Consolidated Copper Mines, was botched, perhaps deliberately. Offers were made in 1997 and 1998 by an international consortium of mining companies and, quite inexplicably, were rejected by the government. "The view among the donors in Lusaka is that the negotiations failed because of a combination of incompetence and corruption on the part of the MMD government" (Rakner, van de Walle, and Mulaisho 2001, 563).

In 2000, the sale of ZCCM was finally completed—as an "unbundled" entity to a number of buyers, principally the longtime minority shareholder, the South Africa–based Anglo-American Corporation. However, the condition of the mines had declined in the intervening period, and the global price of copper had softened, resulting in a far lower final price for the ZCCM assets. Indeed, the delay alone may have cost Zambia hundreds of millions of dollars in forgone revenue (Rakner, van de Walle, and Mulaisho 2001). In an uncharacteristic display of parliamentary oversight, the National Assembly conducted a massive investigation into what went wrong. It discovered that the otherwise efficient ZPA was circumvented, and instead the sale was handled by political insiders without any transparency ("Report of the Committee on Economic Affairs and Labour"

2000). In addition, Peter Burnell (2002, 299) writes, the report found "evidence not simply of procrastination but illegal conduct, procedural irregularities and corruption, all of them costing the treasury and the country dearly in a number of ways." To make matters worse, in 2002, Anglo-American ceased its mining operation in Zambia, including two of the largest mines, writing off its investment because it could not make the enterprise financially viable. While negotiations with potential buyers eventually resulted in the acquisition of the largest mine, Konkola Deep, in 2004, the prospect that a revitalized mining sector will in turn revitalize the Zambian economy remains open to question.

As economic policy, privatization was always publicly defended by Chiluba's government, but behind the scenes it was contested; some elites had ideological objections to surrendering national assets and industries so dearly acquired (Rakner, van de Walle, and Mulaisho 2001). "National pride," coupled with corruption, surely explains much of the fiasco surrounding ZCCM. Mwanawasa reportedly is less interested in privatization than his predecessor (EIU 2003k). Moreover, the new finance minister, Ng'andu Magande, who was appointed in July 2003, is also resistant to further privatization, despite pressure from the donors and IFIs to privatize the national telephone company, Zamtel, the electrical utility, Zesco, and the Zambia State Insurance Company. Meanwhile, the Zambia National Commercial Bank (Zanaco) was being sold in late 2003, despite the earlier objections of Minister Magande (EIU 2003k, 18); thus it is unclear whether the resistance to privatization within the Mwanawasa government represents a genuine ideological stance or a bargaining chip.

In any event, the embrace of IFI- and donor-sponsored neoliberal reform, including privatization, will continue for the foreseeable future. Given its aid dependence, Zambia has little maneuvering room, although the recently completed poverty reduction strategy paper (PRSP) is intended to emphasize *country ownership* of reforms, rather than the sense of international imposition that was associated with SAPs. The PRSP process is seen as the critical step for countries to qualify for debt relief under the advanced highly indebted poor countries initiative. One of the principal goals of the PRSP exercise is diversification of the Zambian economy beyond copper by focusing on mining (Zambia's cobalt exports rose to about 10 percent of the export total in the 1990s) and agriculture, and facilitating development specifically aimed at poverty reduction (EIU 2003k, 8). As of this writing, substantial debt relief has not occurred because Zambia has not reached what is referred to as the completion point—that is, meeting certain targets in the PRSP regarding government spending, privatization, and so forth. Reaching the completion point, which had been expected originally in 2003, in turn also triggers new IMF loans under the IMF's Poverty Reduction and

Growth Facility (EIU 2003k). The effectiveness of the IFIs' newest approach to development, the poststructural adjustment model emphasizing poverty reduction, is not yet well known. However, Zambia's overhang of external public debt, U.S.$6.1 billion in 2003, has proved a substantial drain on the country's resources and policy flexibility. The ability of the PRSP process to eliminate some of that debt will be a boon to Zambia's economic picture.

Owing to the problems of loss-making state-owned enterprises and only partially successful privatization, ecological setbacks, and poor integration with the global economy, the Zambian economy shrank in real terms throughout the first half of the 1990s. As seen in Table 3.3, GDP declined precipitously from 1991 to 1995, partly as a result of debilitating droughts before rebounding in 1996. GDP has since rebounded to modestly positive levels, including 3.3 percent and 5.1 percent in 2002 and 2003, respectively, both of which exceeded population growth in real terms, (EIU 2003g, 2003k). Nonetheless, the EIU (2003g) estimates that the economy will have to experience real growth of 5 to 8 percent per year to meaningfully impact poverty levels. Complicating Zambia's economic growth potential, however, are its continuing susceptibility to climatological forces and structural imbalances. For instance, the region faced another drought from 2001 to early 2003 that forced the importation of relief maize and agricultural sector declines of 2.6 percent and 4.1 percent in 2001 and 2002, respectively (EIU 2003k,12). In addition, the economy remains substantially driven by the minerals sector, with copper and cobalt still constituting a combined 78 percent of exports in 2002. Moreover, its trade relations are similarly undiversified, and the country is particularly

Table 3.3 Real GDP Growth in Zambia, 1991–2003

	1991	1992	1993	1994	1995	1996	1997
Kwacha[a]	2,174	2,158	2,298	2,181	2,030	2,161	2,410
%	(1.8)	(3.8)	7.5	(5.1)	(6.9)	6.5	11.5

	1998	1999	2000	2001	2002	2003
Kwacha[a]	2,361	2,413	2,500	2,623	2,700	2,848
%	(2.0)	2.2	3.6	4.9	3.3	5.1[b]

Sources: Profit, July 1992; Central Statistics Office 1996; Economist Intelligence Unit 2004.

Note: Parentheses indicate negative growth.
a. Kwacha (millions) in constant 1997 prices.
b. EIU (2004) estimate.

vulnerable on the import side: two-thirds of Zambia's imports come from South Africa—some 64 percent in 2002 (EIU 2003k). These trends show little sign of ebbing.

■ Challenges for the Twenty-First Century

By the late 1990s, it was clear to all that Chiluba and the MMD had overseen the unraveling of a once-promising democratic experiment. The MMD leaders were just as authoritarian as their predecessors, and fantastically more corrupt. Leading intellectuals and technocrats, people who had been essential to the MMD's foundation, had either bolted the party or been dismissed (Rakner, van de Walle, and Mulaisho 2001). The economic renewal that many expected to accompany the MMD's tenure was not forthcoming as a result of exogenous shocks, lack of adequate planning by both the Zambians and the donors, an inability to attract trade and investment due to global competition, and outright corruption. Against this backdrop, the ten-year anniversary of the first multiparty elections marked a clear opportunity to reclaim Zambia's democratic promise, reinvigorate civil society, and renew international interest and attention on Zambia.

Mwanawasa's 2001 election was tainted to be certain, although it remains to be determined to what degree, if any, he was personally involved in the alleged violations by his party of electoral law.[37] Moreover, it was widely assumed that Mwanawasa would merely be a stooge for Chiluba, who would pull the strings behind the scenes. To the surprise of many, as president, Mwanawasa quickly demonstrated his independence, in part by pursuing criminal investigations against Chiluba and his cohorts. Having endured a decade of democratic disintegration and kleptocracy under Chiluba's rule, initial public skepticism about Mwanawasa declined rapidly. Restoring a trademark characteristic of the MMD's first year in 1991, he appointed individuals who were well regarded for their competence, rather than their loyalty to the party. However, not long after this quite unexpected honeymoon period, Mwanawasa's image was tarnished by his renewed political alliances with some of the Chiluba cabinet members who were facing charges, including those he had accused (EIU 2003k). He also has been accused of corruption by his former vice president, Enock Kavindele, and has shown an antidemocratic streak in several decisions, such as his defiant recess appointment of Nevers Mumba as vice president and the obsessive push for the constitutional review commission.

Zambia has an unambiguously strong presidential system. Unlike his predecessors, however, Mwanawasa was constrained by parliamentary opposition. But the fact that he was able to coax UNIP into a loose alliance, and co-opt members of other parties into either switching to the MMD or joining his cabinet (ostensibly as opposition), indicates that at the very least, the president is an adroit political operator whom many had earlier discounted; slightly more than a year after taking office, Mwanawasa was no longer constrained. Whether he continues his reformist path, or slides into the authoritarian pattern of his two predecessors, may determine whether Zambia can enjoy the growth and economic stability that characterize many of its southern African neighbors.

Zambia faces many other severe challenges ahead, including drought, food shortages, economic collapse, a halting relationship with donors and IFIs, and of course the devastating impact of the AIDS epidemic. These problems would present enormous obstacles for even the most committed of governments. President Mwanawasa must not only commit to the difficult process of addressing these crises, but also resist the authoritarian impulse to which his predecessor quite quickly succumbed. With a reinvigorated civil society and a credible opposition, it is unlikely that he will be able to rule as freely or arbitrarily as his predecessors. Thus, although daunting challenges remain, Zambia's political prospects, at least, appeared brighter in 2004 than at any time in a decade.

■ Notes

1. Nkumbula wanted to participate in the Northern Rhodesian elections, whereas Kaunda believed the process to be antithetical to black interests (Roberts 1976, 220).

2. At the federal level, pressure from London, and rising African nationalism in both northern territories, prompted the governing United Federal Party to make at least superficial steps toward African representation. For example, in 1961 a new federal constitution was adopted that offered blacks fifteen out of sixty-five seats in the federal legislature and a "Bill of Rights" (Sklar 1975).

3. As a result of the negotiations, African representatives were permitted to form a majority, "provided some of them were also supported by a minimum percentage of white voters." This allowed whites to control, to a degree, the *type* of African elected. Additional constitutional changes in 1963 allowed for universal adult suffrage. UNIP won fifty-five seats and the ANC ten; an additional ten seats were reserved for whites until formal independence in October 1964 (Sklar 1975, 17).

4. The Second Republic constitution was passed in August 1973. The first elections under the one-party constitution were held in December 1973 (Gertzel 1984).

5. Zambia's one-party state was characterized by participation and competition, though the latter, limited to a choice between two candidates of the same party, was a source of rising frustration among the electorate (Bratton and van de Walle 1997, 141–142).

6. The European population was 3,000 in 1920, 36,000 in 1950, and 73,000 by 1960 (Sklar 1975, 9, 16). The 1995 census revealed a total population of 10.2 million, of whom 30,000 were of European descent and 20,000 of Asian (primarily Indian) descent.

7. Since many MNCs were nationalized or forced into joint ventures with the

state, "Africanization" generally did not come at the expense of *local* private sector actors. Refer to the section on political economy later in this chapter.

8. For example, Indian merchants in the southern city of Livingstone were the targets of well-publicized violence in 1997, and several prominent businessmen and politicians of Indian descent were the targets of racist statements from several black politicians in the run-up to the 2001 elections.

9. Twenty-five percent of the population speaks Bemba as its first language, followed by Nyanja (11.7 percent), Tonga (11.7 percent), and Lozi (5.6 percent), based on the 1990 census. However, since these tongues serve as regional lingua francas, actual ethnic identification is lower (http://www.ethnologue.com).

10. Interestingly, shortly after independence, UNIP was regarded, particularly by the ANC, as a "Bemba party," despite its representation from all over Zambia (Roberts 1976, 242). Kaunda himself is not Bemba; his parents were Nyasa missionaries from Malawi to Zambia's northern province, where the younger Kaunda was raised among Bemba-speakers (Hall 1966, 124). In the First Republic, Nkumbula's ANC had strong support among the Tonga (Hall 1996, 227). See also Sklar 1975, 9.

11. In the west, Lozis predominate, and Chiluba's treatment of Lozi officials fostered considerable resentment.

12. Although these three provinces have the largest Bemba populations, they were also long-standing MMD strongholds. Mwanawasa himself is from the Lenje ethnic group, a minority indigenous to Central province. Thus the 2001 result may reflect other groups' abandonment of the MMD.

13. In 2003 the government briefly debated reducing the number of ministries from twenty-one to fourteen, but President Mwanawasa rejected the idea in early 2004.

14. In May 2003, President Mwanawasa unexpectedly dismissed his vice president, Enock Kavindele, whom he accused of corruption. Kavindele was replaced by Nevers Mumba, an evangelical Christian pastor and a minor-party presidential candidate in 2001. The appointment was controversial, and apparently unconstitutional, since Mumba was not an MP at the time of his promotion, and as a candidate for office in the prior election he should have been disqualified under Article 68. This helped motivate opposition MPs to launch an unsuccessful impeachment motion against Mwanawasa (EIU 2003k, 13).

15. Peter Burnell (2001, 241) labels Zambia a dominant-party system "where one party commands, alone and over time, the absolute majority of seats." The possibility of alternation exists, even if it is unlikely.

16. Author interview with Ackson Sejani, Forum for Democracy and Development party secretary and former MMD minister, Lusaka, October 26, 2001. It is worth noting, however, that despite this rather remarkable revolt, President Chiluba and his cohorts were able nonetheless to cajole the vast majority of MMD members into changing the *party* constitution to allow Chiluba a third term as party leader ("Zambia's Ruling Party" 2001). The MMD party rules then stipulated that the leader of the party stand as the MMD presidential candidate in the general election.

17. Chiluba briefly retained his role as MMD party president after leaving national office in 2001, but was forced to relinquish the party post in 2002 in order to access certain retirement benefits from the state.

18. In addition to bringing in cabinet members from opposition parties UNIP, the Zambia Republican Party, and the Forum for Democracy and Development in February 2003, the MMD eventually gained a majority through by-elections and

defections and "further strengthened its position by agreeing to an ill-defined alliance with UNIP in May 2003" (EIU 2003g).

19. "In 1998 the Zambian Parliament approved a discretionary fund of approximately US $5 million for the president of the republic, and in 1999 the government refused to announce the amount allocated to the presidential fund," which had no "system of accountability in place to ensure it is used for legitimate purposes" (Rakner, van de Walle, and Mulaisho 2001, 570).

20. Under the law, former presidents are entitled to immunity from prosecution for alleged crimes committed in office. However, Mwanawasa persuaded the parliament to lift Chiluba's immunity in July 2002 (EIU 2003g). Some human rights and anticorruption advocates applauded; however, other observers regard it as a dangerous precedent that will backfire because authoritarians will refuse to relinquish office rather than risk prosecution.

21. By 1995, Kaunda had begun to make a political comeback and Chiluba was clearly threatened by Kaunda's ascendancy. The new document also imposed the two-term limit retroactively, a move that was also aimed at Kaunda (Bratton and Posner 1999, 393–394).

22. Author interview with CRC member, Lusaka, May 22, 1996.

23. Author telephone interview with CRC member, October 13, 2003.

24. President Kaunda clashed with some members of the then all-white higher courts early in the Second Republic, leading several jurists to resign from the bench (Roberts 1976).

25. Zambia's electoral laws require that the president be sworn in within forty-eight hours following the certification of election results. Thereafter, any challenge to the poll results must be done through the legal system.

26. Although only UNIP, the MMD, and a handful of insignificant parties contested the 1991 elections, opposition parties multiplied thereafter: some forty-one were registered by late 1997.

27. The "UNIP eight" were jailed on suspicion of their involvement with the bombings, despite the fact that there was no evidence linking them to the explosions or to the "Black Mamba" organization. Most observers suspect that the bombings were actually orchestrated by the MMD as a pretext to marginalize UNIP by paralyzing its leadership. The UNIP leaders were freed after nearly six months in prison (Bratton and Posner 1999; Rakner, van de Walle, and Mulaisho 2001).

28. There was also a growing tendency in the 1996 election and after for individuals to be elected to parliament as independents, some of whom had previous party affiliations. Ten won seats in 1996. However, only one independent was elected in 2001.

29. Reflected in author interviews with voters, Lusaka and Chongwe district, December 27, 2001.

30. International and domestic observers alike criticized the conduct of the election and electoral process. Opposition parties used the statements of delegations from the Carter Center, the European Union, the Southern African Development Community Parliamentary Forum, and others, which pointed out numerous irregularities. Armed with the international evaluations and comprehensive reports from domestic monitors, Mazoka and the other losing candidates lodged the court challenge to have Mwanawasa's victory overturned.

31. Author interview with Songwayo Zyambo, ZNFU executive director, June 25, 1999.

32. According to Richard Sklar (1975, 16), it "is generally thought that as a result of the redistribution of revenues following the establishment of the federa-

tion, Northern Rhodesia lost about £7 million per year to Southern Rhodesia—a total of £70 million during the federation's ten-year life span." Moreover, there can be no question that the [Zambian] Copperbelt [was] the financial backbone of the federal fiscal structure." Indeed, William Tordoff (1980, 2) argues that "for a period of almost 10 years Northern Rhodesia became the milch cow of predominantly Southern Rhodesian white interests."

33. This was not appreciably different from the role the state had played for whites in the colonial era, in which subsidies were made available for white commercial enterprises, especially farming (Roberts 1976).

34. The two foreign firms retained minority shareholding of just over 34 percent after nationalization.

35. Import substitution industrialization was expensive and inefficient to maintain: most of the finished goods produced required the importation of expensive raw material and intermediate good inputs, which Zambia did not produce.

36. Although prices rebounded somewhat by the end of the decade, production peaked in 1976 at 745,700 tons and has generally declined in the years since (Mulemba 1992). By way of contrast, 336,700 tons were produced in 2002 (EIU 2003k).

37. Even if Mwanawasa was an unwitting participant, a new election is required if the charges are proved.

4

Botswana:
Dominant Party Democracy

By all accounts Botswana is a remarkable exception in southern Africa, indeed in Africa as a whole. Of little interest to European settlers, Botswana experienced an apparently mild colonization by the British, one that relied more heavily than most on indigenous leaders and long standing political practices. The territory experienced a peaceful transfer of power from British to indigenous rule in 1966, avoiding any resort to arms to gain its independence, or any hint of civil strife or war afterward. Since that independence in 1966, Botswana has been a stable, multiparty democracy (though clearly a party system in which one party dominates) with a military that has largely eschewed involvement in the regional conflicts that have entangled neighboring countries over the years. National elections have been held every five years beginning with the first preindependence elections in 1965 and all have been considered free and fair. Though there has been no alternation of power, in terms of a change in ruling party, there have been two successful leadership transitions, including one president who retired while still in office. While Botswana does not boast a thriving civil society, organizational activity increased considerably in the 1990s and a political opposition has grown, both of which indicate a maturing political culture.

Landlocked, with a harsh arid climate and small population (under 2 million in 2004), at its independence Botswana was one of the poorest countries in the world. With a per capita gross national income of U.S.$3,630 (U.S.$8,810 at purchasing power parity) in 2001, the country is designated an "upper middle income country" by the World Bank (2003b, 234). Indeed, since diamonds and other minerals were discovered in the 1960s and 1970s, Botswana has experienced enviable economic growth rates—its sustained real gross domestic product (GDP) growth rate averaging 6.1 percent from 1966 to 1991 was among the highest in the world—matched only by the East Asian newly industrialized countries in the same

---

Botswana: Country Data

Land area 585,370 km²
Capital Gaborone
Date of independence September 30, 1966
Population 1.6 million, 49% urban
Languages English (official), Setswana
Ethnic groups Tswana, 79%; Kalanga, 11%; Basarwa, 3%; other,
    including Kgalagadi and European, 7%
Religions indigenous beliefs, 85%; Christian, 15%
Currency pula (BWP); pulas per U.S. dollar: 4.87 (July 2003)

Literacy rate 78.1% (male, 75.3%; female, 80.6%)
Life expectancy 44.7 years (male, 43.3 years; female, 46.0 years)
Infant mortality 80 per 1,000 live births

GDP per capita U.S.$3,066
GDP per capita (PPP) U.S.$7,820
GDP per capita growth rate 2.5% (1990–2001)

Leaders since independence
   • Seretse Khama, president, September 1966–July 1980
   • Quett Masire, president, July 1980–April 1998
   • Festus Gontebanye Mogae, president, April 1998–

Major political parties
   Ruling party: Botswana Democratic Party (BDP)
   Other parties: Botswana National Front (BNF)
   Botswana Congress Party (BCP)
   Botswana Alliance Movement (BAM)

Women in parliament (lower/single house) 7.0% (2004)

Note: Data from 2001 unless otherwise indicated.

---

period. While much of this growth is attributable to the postindependence exploitation of diamonds, Botswana has also sought to diversify its economy, moving, among other things, to attract foreign investment to the Selebi-Phikwe regional development project and to cultivate its tourism industry. Many in the country continue to rely upon the long-standing source of wealth accumulation—cattle raising—while many more are subsistence farmers in the rural areas. Although income disparities remain great in the country, ordinary Batswana[1] have benefited from the postindependence economic growth, especially in terms of access to social services and infrastructure.

Indeed, Botswana has been described as the only clear example of a "developmental state" in Africa (Wiseman 1998). And like the developmental states of East Asia, Botswana has been labeled an African "miracle" by some observers (Samatar 1999). It is consistently rated the least-corrupt country in Africa by Transparency International and was recently ranked the most competitive economy in Africa by the World Economic Forum. The gains from Botswana's considerable economic growth have been used to invest in the country's infrastructure and human resource base. Where once there were dirt roads, there are now high-quality tarred roads. Free universal education has been provided for all, and Botswana has one of the highest literacy rates in Africa. Botswana has also experienced one of the fastest rates of urbanization in the world since independence. As of 2002, however, Botswana also had the second highest HIV infection rate of any country in the world (after Swaziland as of 2002), just shy of 40 percent of the adult population. This is a devastating development that threatens to undo the impressive accomplishments of the postindependence period. (Fortunately, Botswana is also a leader in the region in terms of confronting the AIDS crisis.) Other challenges to Botswana's future include potential spillover effects of Zimbabwe's rapid economic and political downward spiral and, as in all the countries in southern Africa, the need to diversify its politics away from the current pattern of dominant-party rule. Growing poverty, income inequalities, and unemployment, especially in the rural areas, also threaten Botswana's future.

With such a distinctive position on the African continent, Botswana has attracted widespread attention from academics and others eager to understand the sources of its apparent success. Explanations for Botswana's accomplishments are varied and focus on a range of factors both structural and agent-based, including the colonial practice of "parallel rule" and retention of the *kgotla* and other traditional legal institutions after independence, a relative ethnic homogeneity, remarkable leadership skills on the part of founding president Seretse Khama, in particular, the discovery of diamonds *after* independence, and the wise and judicious use of diamond revenues by a developmental state.

■ Historical Origins of the Botswana State: Context, Key Actors, and Issues

One of the factors that distinguishes Botswana enormously from other African countries is its relative ethnic homogeneity. Indeed, 85 percent of the population is Tswana, although the Tswana people are further divided into eight important subgroups, often referred to as separate "tribes." These eight subgroups hail from eight Tswana chiefdoms that emerged in the late eighteenth and early nineteenth centuries from a number of smaller groups in what is today eastern Botswana and northern South Africa (Holm 1988, 181).[2] Of the eight groups, the Bamangwato are the largest, composing 35 percent of the population. Three other groups—the Bakwena, Bangwaketse, and Bakgatla—once rivaled the Bamangwato, though today each represents a much smaller percentage of the population. The four other groups—the Barolong, Batlokwa, Bamalete, and Batawana—were, and remain, quite small, totaling 12 percent of the population all together (Holm 1988, 181).

According to John Holm (1988, 181–183), three factors accounted for the growth of the four larger chiefdoms during the late precolonial period: war, trade, and strong leadership by chiefs. In order to withstand attacks by Zulu armies coming from the southeast in the early 1800s,[3] and later incursions by Afrikaner trekkers seeking to escape British rule in the Cape colony, the four groups were forced to become strong militarily. This need to defend against outside attack also promoted development of a more autocratic leadership style within these groups (Holm 1988). Second, during the same period the Tswana chiefdoms were a locus for regional trade, "strategically placed to control movements of goods to African peoples north and east of their area." These Tswana chiefdoms also became heavily involved with European traders once they moved into the area—"granting licenses and otherwise manipulating the transit of goods for their profit" (Holm 1988, 181).

The Tswana chiefs' successes in war and trade, which enabled their expansion during this period, were attributable in part to the fact that the chiefs were already powerful rulers (Holm 1988, 181). These were hereditary rulers who had little need to rely upon "public support" in making their decisions. The chiefs played key roles in local economies, allocating all land within their chiefdoms and controlling or owning all the cattle, the primary form of wealth. Chiefs were also the religious leaders, not only practicing various forms of traditional healing, but also supervising others in the community who "worked with the world of the spirits" (Holm 1988, 182). Not surprisingly, chiefs dominated decisionmaking as well. However, in so doing they relied upon a mechanism that exists to this day in Botswana, the *kgotla,* an assembly of all adult males in the community. The *kgotla,* which was convened when pressing matters needed to be discussed, provided a measure of popular discussion and consultation. Moreover, though chiefs theoretically had the authority to make laws unilaterally, the *kgotla* served as a check on chiefly authority, since its principal goal was to gain approval of the members of the chiefdom for a given course of action

(Samatar 1999, 42). There were more direct constraints on chiefly power as well. For example, "immediate relatives might usurp his authority by deserting to another tribe with followers, refusing to follow orders in a military campaign, assassinating him, or in the last resort, establishing a new chiefdom" (Holm 1988, 182). In addition, the chiefs had to abide by the dictates of traditional law. This law was largely determined by a group of elder advisers who, under threat of insurrection, expected the chief, like everyone else, to comply with its dictates.

Cattle provided the primary form of wealth accumulation in precolonial Botswana—not surprising in an arid country, a good part of which is taken up by the Kalahari.[4] As such, the potential for agriculture was not a significant draw for European settlers in the colonial period; nor were minerals, which were only discovered after independence. Still, as in other parts of southern Africa, European traders and Christian missionaries arrived in the territory in the early nineteenth century. According to Christiaan Keulder (1998, 98), by 1870 "relatively permanent trading and missionary settlements had been developed," as well as the beginnings of a migrant labor system that would send Batswana men to the newly established diamond and gold mines in South Africa. Among other things, the early traders and missionaries facilitated the granting of concessions to European companies during this period, so much so that "colonialism in Botswana, unlike in most other parts of Africa, occurred almost entirely through concessions" (Keulder 1998, 98).

Indeed, the colonization of Botswana was fairly unique in Africa in that the indigenous population, the Tswana chiefs, invited a European power, the British, to declare a protectorate over their territory, which the British called Bechuanaland (Holm 1988; Keulder 1998). The chiefs did this out of fear of a worse subjugation by the Afrikaners, who continued to make incursions into their territory from the Transvaal, and rumblings from the Germans in Namibia about linking that territory with German Tanganyika (never mind the Germans' brutal suppression of the indigenous population). Thus in 1880 an informal protectorate relationship was secured between the Tswana chiefs and the British government in Cape Town, and in 1885 this agreement was formalized and Bechuanaland made a "crown colony of the British" (du Toit 1995, 22). The British agreed, in part out of concern to protect road links with its Rhodesian colonies to the north, but also to avoid the territory's incorporation into what were then the Boer republics in South Africa. As such, the colonization of Botswana was much less violent than that of Namibia, South Africa, or Zimbabwe, "with fewer clashes between the indigenous people and the newcomers" (Keulder 1998, 99). There were significant consequences of Botswana's route to colonization—first by concession and then by invitation. According to Keulder:

First, fewer Europeans settled in the Bechuanaland Protectorate than in South Africa, Namibia or Zimbabwe. This meant that less pressure was placed on the colonial government to protect European interests at the cost of indigenous ones, and that racism was not so institutionalized as in the other colonies mentioned. Second, the colonial government could leave much of the day-to-day administration to the traditional leaders. Traditional power configurations were less distorted, and the leaders retained much of their legitimacy as they were allowed far more freedom to perform their functions to the benefit of their subjects. Traditional leaders thus remained prominent during the colonial period (even though their powers were substantially reduced). (1998, 99)

Thus colonial rule in Botswana has been described as "so mild that even the term 'indirect rule' [used elsewhere in Africa by the British] would be an exaggeration" (Holm 1988, 183). Most refer instead to a system of "parallel rule" that emerged in the colony, whereby "the colonial government regulated the affairs of the European population while the tribal authorities managed tribal affairs with very little interference" (Keulder 1998, 100). Magistrates acted as a link between the colonial authorities and the traditional leaders. By and large, the chiefs continued to rule with only a few constraints: "they could no longer make war; they were supposed to collect a small hut tax to support the colonial administration; and they had to curb certain practices that offended British sensibilities, like slavery and polygamy" (Holm 1988, 183). British administrative headquarters, meanwhile, were not even set up in the Bechuanaland protectorate, but rather across the border in South Africa.

Nonetheless, for much of the colonial period, the Bechuanaland protectorate faced an uncertain future. For some time after the formation of the Union of South Africa in 1910, South Africa sought to incorporate Botswana, an effort it only abandoned when South Africa became a republic and left the Commonwealth in 1961. During much of the same period until the 1950s, Southern Rhodesia (Zimbabwe) also sought to incorporate Bechuanaland into its territory (du Toit 1995, 23). This uncertainty provides a "partial explanation (as well as an excuse) for the lack of a British commitment to the educational, social and physical infrastructure development of the territory" (Picard 1985, 11).

Meanwhile, events in neighboring South Africa prompted the emergence of a nationalist movement in Botswana, although much later than in other parts of Africa.[5] Following the Sharpeville massacre and the banning of the African National Congress (ANC) and the Pan-Africanist Congress (PAC) in 1960, an estimated 1,400 South Africans fled into Bechuanaland over a four-year period. As Holm (1988, 185) argues, this "infusion of the politically aware" South Africans led directly to the founding of the first nationalist party in Botswana, the urban-based Botswana People's Party (BPP). Indeed, so great was the South African connection that five of the party's twenty-two branches in 1961 were located in Johannesburg (serving Batswana migrant workers there). While the BPP did not last for long, its attacks on colonial rule sent a clear message to colonial authorities that independence would soon have to be granted. Eventually this group split into two and the Bechuanaland Democratic Party (BDP) emerged to carry the nationalist torch more successfully.

The BDP was organized by a number of activists—Seretse Khama, Quett Masire, and others—based in the rural areas. As Holm (1988, 185) writes, Seretse Khama himself embodied the powerful social groups that came to form the support base for the BDP.[6] He was the first-born son of a Bamangwato chief and should have become Bamangwato chief himself when he returned home from his university studies in the United Kingdom in the late 1940s. He was prevented from doing so, however, by pressure from the Nationalist Party government in South Africa, which was greatly displeased by his example of racial mixing—he had married a white woman while in Britain and was returning with her to Botswana.[7] The Bamangwato people were outraged that they were being denied their rightful chief and quickly rallied around Khama's nascent organization, the BDP. Indeed, it has been suggested that in not becoming Bamangwato chief, Khama was ultimately able to broaden his appeal as a truly national leader and to avoid the encumbrances of the day-to-day duties of chieftancy (Wiseman 1998). Upon his return from the UK, Khama had also taken up cattle ranching—the only major productive sector of the Botswana economy before independence. In so doing, Khama carefully cultivated relations with commercial farmers in the country—both black and white—and was able to ensure a reliable financial base for his party. To the colonial authorities, meanwhile, the BDP was a much more attractive group than the more radical BPP. In 1961 Khama was named as one of two Africans to serve on the territory's executive council, thereby gaining valuable administrative experience. Thus, within a relatively short period of time, Khama secured the support of four influential groups who helped propel the BDP into power: traditional authorities, the educated elite, cattle ranchers, and the colonial civil service (Holm 1988, 186). When the first elections were held in Botswana in March 1965, the BDP won 80 percent of the vote. On September 30, 1966, Botswana gained its independence and Seretse Khama became the new country's first president.

■ Organization of the State

▒ *Constitution*

Botswana is described in its constitution as a unitary state and a parliamentary republic. The constitution created an executive presidency in which the president is both head of state and head of government. The constitution also provides for a unicameral legislature, a National Assembly based on the Westminster parliamentary system. The National Assembly consists of fifty-seven elected members, the president, the speaker, the attorney general, and four members appointed by the president.[8] The constitution further provides for a fifteen-member (nonelected) House of Chiefs, which advises government on traditional and customary issues. Finally, the constitution provides for an independent judiciary that is able to enforce the code of human rights contained in the constitution and may also interpret the constitution (Economist Intelligence Unit [EIU] 2003b; du Toit 1995, 30–31; Lekorwe et al. 2001, 2).

According to the U.S. Department of State (2003c), the government of Botswana has generally abided by its 1966 constitution, respecting the human rights and freedoms of its citizens. However, there have been some infractions. During 2002, for example, there were reports that criminal suspects were beaten or mistreated by the police, and that the judicial system was unable to provide timely and fair trials because of a serious and increasing backlog of cases. Moreover, there were reports in the same period that the government attempted to limit the freedom of the press, and it continued to dominate domestic broadcasting. The government has been accused of human rights abuse with respect to the already marginalized Basarwa (or San) people living in Central Kalahari Game Reserve, forcing many of them to leave the reserve in the course of 2002. These actions put the lives and livelihoods of Botswana's original inhabitants in danger. Finally, trade unions in Botswana continued to face some legal restrictions in 2002, including those against the right to strike, and the government failed to ensure that existing labor laws were always respected.

Executive

The president of Botswana is not popularly elected by the people; rather he or she is selected by the elected members of the National Assembly and serves a five-year term, concurrent with the term of the National Assembly. This indirect method of presidential election is also used in South Africa. The president heads the cabinet, which is appointed from among members of the ruling party in the National Assembly. The president is required only to consult with the cabinet, which acts in an advisory capacity to him. In a cabinet reshuffle in September 2002 the number of cabinet members was increased from sixteen to twenty, the largest number in Botswana's history. As in Namibia then, the cabinet completely dominates the country's National Assembly and effectively blunts any trend toward parliamentary autonomy.

By 2004 there had been three presidents of Botswana, all members of the BDP. Seretse Khama, who led the country to independence, was the first, and was reelected as president in 1969, 1974, and 1979 before dying in office in 1980. He was succeeded by his vice president and BDP cofounder Quett Masire, who was reelected in 1984, 1989, and 1994 before retiring from the presidency in 1998.[9] Masire was succeeded by his vice president, Festus Mogae, who was then reelected by parliament in 1999 and 2004. President Mogae chose Ian Khama, the son of Seretse Khama and previously head of the armed forces, as his vice president. Botswana's experience with presidentialism is unlike that of other countries in southern Africa. Botswana has avoided the kind of divisive constitutional maneuvers orchestrated by some regional presidents and their parties—such as those contemplated or achieved in Namibia, Zambia, and Malawi—to extend presidential terms. Indeed, following Khama's death, presidents left office voluntarily—in Masire's case, even before the expiration of his term. After being reelected in 2004, Festus Mogae announced that he would step down in 2008, one year before the next scheduled election. In short, unlike many of its counterparts in the region, Botswana has an established tradition of executive turnover marked by a smooth transfer of power between presidents.

■ Judiciary

As in other countries in the region, Botswana retained a dual legal system at independence in which customary law, albeit in a clearly subordinate position, was institutionalized alongside a judicial system based on Roman Dutch law. The dual legal system consists of modern courts, which apply Roman Dutch common and statutory law in the country, and customary courts. The modern courts are composed of magistrate courts at the lowest level, a high court, and a court of appeals. Alongside these, more than 200 customary courts deal with the civil and penal laws of the country. These customary or traditional courts are presided over by local chiefs and their representatives and headmen (du Toit 1995, 28–29). There are four categories of customary courts, with the category determining the powers of the court (for example, whether they may engage in reconciliation only, or may impose punitive rulings).

As in most of southern Africa, most people in Botswana first encounter the legal system through the traditional or customary courts. Most civil cases are tried in customary courts, under the authority of a traditional leader. These courts handle matters such as land, marital, and property disputes. In such courts, defendants have no legal counsel and there are no precise rules of evidence. However, rulings may be appealed through the civil court system. Perhaps not surprisingly, the quality of decisions reached within the traditional courts tends to vary considerably (U.S. Department of State 2003c). At the same time, as Pierre du Toit (1995, 59–60) argues, Botswana's dual legal system is a source of strength to the

Botswana state: "By protecting the customary courts of the lekgotla assemblies after independence, the state effectively merged the established rules of social control with those of the modern constitutional system. This merging has had the effect of making traditional, established, indigenous survival strategies largely compatible and congruent with those prescribed by the modern legal state."

▪ Military

As Mpho Molomo (2001) notes, Botswana's security and defense situation is determined in large part by its location—it shares long borders with Namibia, South Africa, and Zimbabwe and just touches upon Zambia. In the past, Botswana suffered the spillover effects of armed liberation struggles in neighboring countries and of South African–sponsored regional destabilization. During the early 1970s, for example, Botswana experienced frequent incursions by Rhodesian security forces, allegedly in pursuit of Zimbabwean liberation fighters. These forces "wreaked havoc in Botswana by carrying out acts of kidnapping, abduction, arson, and murder of innocent civilians" (Molomo 2001). Indeed the entire Botswana-Zimbabwe border became a war zone from which residents were forced to flee, leaving behind homes and fields.

Botswana experienced similar destabilization from South Africa during the same period. Following the Soweto uprising in 1976 many South African youth sought political asylum in Botswana, prompting still more raids by the South African Defense Force (SADF). South Africa's "total strategy," deployed from 1977 onward, had clear regional implications, among them repeated incursions by the SADF into Botswana throughout the remainder of the 1970s and into the 1980s, allegedly in pursuit of ANC combatants.[10] In that period Botswana was defended only by the Police Mobile Unit (PMU), a group of paramilitary police responsible for internal security. With the PMU overwhelmed by the task and calls for greater defense by the opposition, the government established the Botswana Defense Force (BDF) in 1977 (Molomo 2001). Despite this, raids and incursions continued from across both borders until those respective internal conflicts were settled.

Since 1986 the military budget in Botswana has increased annually and, according to Thomas Ohlson and Stephen John Stedman (1994, 220), "the military has tried to exempt itself from the bureaucratic openness that characterizes other sectors of the state." This was particularly evident in the early 1990s, when the Botswana military refused to discuss plans to build an extensive air base in the country, reportedly also to be used by the U.S. Air Force. Those plans were later abandoned, but the military buildup has continued, raising many questions about why Botswana is doing this, now that relative peace and stability have been achieved in southern Africa. In 1996, Ian Khama, then lieutenant-general of the BDF, was quoted by the South African Press Agency as saying: "The BDF needed to prepare itself in order to deal with instability that might spill over into Botswana from South Africa" (Molomo 2001). In particular, Khama cited rising crime rates in South Africa, political conflict in KwaZulu-Natal, and an influx of illegal weapons to the country and the region.

By the early 2000s the BDF consisted of 10,500 troops: 8,500 in the army, 500 in an air force, and 1,500 in the police mobile unit. Despite the fact that the country faced no military threat, total expenditure on the military was as high as 8 percent. According to the EIU (2001a, 9), "such high spending is justified by the need for a strong regional peacekeeping force, but is probably more a result of national pride and a perceived need to keep Botswana's more volatile neighbours on their guard."

Others have been concerned that "if you build up a large military without a purpose, it becomes a threat to the country" (Molomo 2001). Indeed, there has been strong reaction to the buildup of the BDF inside and outside the country. Some have suggested that expanding Botswana's military could have something to do with the country's internal politics—for example, as a response to the growth of a more significant political opposition.[11] Moreover, the military has been called upon to assist the police in fighting increased criminal activity in the country, including carjackings, armed bank robberies, cattle rustling, and illegal immigration. Botswana's neighbors have also objected to the expansion of the military as well, in particular Namibia, with which Botswana has experienced some conflict over border issues and the repatriation of refugees. At the same time, the military remains firmly under civilian control in Botswana, reporting to the minister of presidential affairs and public administration, and accountable to parliament on budget matters. When the BDF joined the South African National Defense Force to intervene in an uprising in Lesotho in September 1998, the decision to do so was taken by the executive (Molomo 2001; U.S. Department of State 2003c).

■ The Bureaucracy

At independence in 1966 Botswana was woefully unprepared for the challenges that lay ahead. As a colony, Bechuanaland, along with the other two "High Commission territories" of Swaziland and Basotholand, had been drawn into the economic ambit of South Africa, utilizing the South African currency, belonging to a single customs union, and sharing road, rail, and communications networks. The benefits from this arrangement accrued to South Africa but worked to the disadvantage of the other three, since industry and investment were most attracted to South Africa as the most developed of the areas. Investment in social and economic infrastructure was meager during the colonial period in Bechuanaland, with the combined result that at independence "Botswana showed a distinctive profile of underdevelopment" (du Toit 1995, 26–27). In a huge country, only twenty-five kilometers of road were tarred, only one government secondary school existed (opened in 1965), and only a handful of Batswana had attended university. Moreover, most of the retail trade in the territory was controlled by foreigners, and most of the population were subsistence cattle farmers, with a significant minority of men traveling to the mines of South Africa as migrant laborers.

Not surprisingly, Botswana was also bequeathed an underdeveloped public bureaucracy at independence. That bureaucracy was rapidly transformed in the years after independence, however, and many credit the bureaucracy with helping to achieve Botswana's multiple postindependence gains (Samatar 1999). One characteristic of this transformation was the rapid expansion of the central government service in the years after independence, leading to a significantly increased public sector employment. Moreover, "a striking feature of this institutional expansion," according to du Toit (1995, 33), was "the extent to which the colonial pattern of expatriates holding crucial public service positions endured." Thus, rather than proceed with a rapid indigenization of the public service, Botswana opted for a gradual replacement of expatriates.[12] (At the same time, training of Batswana "in significant numbers at home and abroad" to join the bureaucracy was an integral part of this strategy, and may have helped diffuse any pressures for more rapid, politically driven Africanization [Samatar 1999, 95].) Du Toit (1995, 35) argues that "this expatriate sector of the public work force contributed a vital ingredient to the quality of the statehood that evolved in post-independence Botswana"—adding not only to the strength of the state but also to its autonomy. That autonomous bureaucracy, according to du Toit (1995, 47), "in coalition with the BDP, has succeeded, through its technocratic priorities of growth and stability (at the expense of participation and equity), in establishing a solvent state that can deliver public goods (roads, schools, watering facilities, clinics, etc.) on a nontribal, nonregional basis. . . . Consequently the state is seen as neutral, not as an ethnic body, and the legitimacy of the state, the regime, the constitution, and the parliamentary system is enhanced."

Indeed, this is one of the explanations often put forward for Botswana's political and economic successes since independence—that Botswana is one of the few African states with the characteristics of a developmental state (Tsie 1996, 601; Hwedie 2001b). According to Balefi Tsie (1996, 601), "since independence Botswana's bureaucratic and political elites have pursued a series of policies calculated to promote economic growth and development. In the process, both elites acquired a developmental orientation. The bureaucratic elite in Botswana is powerful and generally effective in formulating and executing development policy." The epicenter of the development process is the Ministry of Finance and Development Planning, which Abdi Ismail Samatar (1999, 96) likens to the Japanese Ministry of Trade and Industry, the centralized, meritorious, and autonomous agency that oversaw Japanese industrial development. As evidenced by the ministry's bureaucratic capacity, "much of the development in Botswana has been state-sponsored and directed. It is in this sense that one can speak of a developmental state in Botswana" (Tsie 1996, 601). It is important to note the degree of Botswana's exceptionalism in this regard. Whereas Botswana's strong, *centralized* state has been instrumental in its ability to transform the economy, its counterparts in the region have experienced enormous pressure from the international financial institutions for more than a decade to decentralize their states (Samatar 1999, 96).

■ Representation and Participation

▨ *Legislative Bodies*

There are only two tiers of government in Botswana—national and local. At the national level, the legislature consists of an elected national assembly and unelected house of chiefs. In the National Assembly, members of parliament (MPs) are elected to five-year terms on the basis of a first-past-the-post or winner-take-all electoral system. Mogopodi Lekorwe and colleagues (2001, 2) assert that the first-past-the-post electoral system in Botswana "has produced a predominant party system in which the ruling Botswana Democratic Party has won each and every election by a landslide victory (at least in terms of legislative seats)." So, for example, with 65 percent of the vote in the 1989 election the BDP won thirty-one of thirty-four seats in the National Assembly (91 percent), in 1999 with only 54 percent of the popular vote the BDP won thirty-three of forty seats (82 percent), and in 2004 with only 51 percent of the vote, the BDP won forty-four of fifty-seven seats (77 percent) (see Tables 4.1 and 4.2). The ruling party's numbers in the National Assembly are further enhanced by the appointment, by the president, of four "specially" elected members of parliament. These four additional MPs also help to cement the president's control over the National Assembly. According to John Holm and Staffan Darnolf (2000, 127–128): "These persons are usually former civil servants or defeated BDP MP candidates. They owe a special loyalty to the president for their appointment given the limitations of their mass political base. With a few exceptions, this group of MPs have been among the most articulate in pushing the president's position with fellow legislators." More recently, women's organizations have demanded that the president nominate

Table 4.1 Number of Seats in Parliament, 1965–2004

Party	1965	1969	1974	1979	1984	1989	1994	1999	2004
BDP	28	24	27	29	28	31	27	33	44
BNF	—	3	2	2	5	3	13	6	12
BPP	3	3	2	1	1	0	0	—	0
BIP/IFP	0	1	1	0	0	0	0	—	—
BCP	—	—	—	—	—	—	—	1	1
BAM	—	—	—	—	—	—	—	0	0
MELS	—	—	—	—	—	—	0	0	0
Total seats	31	31	32	32	34	34	40	40	57

Sources: Lekorwe et al. 2001, 3; personal communication with Jacob Ncapedi, IT manager, Independent Electoral Commission, November 16, 2004.

Table 4.2 Party Support, 1965–2004 (percentage of popular vote)

Party	1965	1969	1974	1979	1984	1989	1994	1999	2004
BDP	80	68	77	75	68	65	55	54	51
BNF	—	14	12	13	20	27	37	25	25
BPP	14	12	6	8	7	4	4	—	2
BIP/IFP	5	6	4	4	3	2	4	—	—
BCP		—	—	—	—	—	—	11	16
BAM	—	—	—	—	—	—	—	5	3
Other	1	0	1	0	2	2	0	0	1
Rejected	—	—	—	—	—	—	—	5	2
Total	100	100	100	100	100	100	100	100	100

Sources: Lekorwe et al. 2001, 3; personal communication with Jacob Ncapedi, IT manager, Independent Electoral Commission, November 16, 2004.

women to all four of the specially elected seats in the National Assembly. In 1994 two of the four were women (Machangana 1998, 125).

In general, executive influence over the legislature runs deep in Botswana, as it does throughout southern Africa. Candidates for National Assembly elections are nominated by their parties. Moreover, candidates must pledge themselves to the party's presidential candidate in advance of the election. Further, in appointing cabinet members the president is not required to consult with parliament. At the same time, it is suggested that most MPs would like to become cabinet ministers and therefore "work hard to remain in the president's good graces" (Holm and Darnolf 2000, 127). Moreover, just as in Namibia, the small size of the national legislature ensures that more than a majority of MPs from the ruling party are either ministers or deputy ministers. Thus, "once the president secures cabinet approval for a policy, the cabinet members are easily able through sheer numbers to determine the BDP parliamentary delegation's position on any vote" (Holm and Darnolf 2000, 127).

At the local level a variety of institutions constitute local government. These include district (rural) councils and town (urban) councils that are elected every five years, at the same time that members of the National Assembly are elected and using the same electoral system. Other institutions of local government include land boards that are responsible for the allocation and administration of land under the jurisdiction of district councils, district administration that is "a high profile agency representing the central government in a local authority area," and tribal administration, the oldest local government institution that today has jurisdiction primarily over the administration of justice through customary law and practice (Mogotsi 1995, 55). The most significant contribution of the tribal administration is the provision of the *kgotla* (Mogotsi 1995, 55). Indeed, a *kgotla* is used by all of the local level institutions. The main functions of the district councils include primary education, collection of local taxes and licensing fees, control of the brewing and sale of traditional beer, sanitary services and water supplies, construction and maintenance of local public roads, and supervision of local markets (Keulder 1998, 115).

Holm (1988, 187) considers the local council system in Botswana to be the "centerpiece" of its democracy. The local councils act as intermediaries between the central government and local communities. Moreover, the local councils have democratized local government—essentially replacing hereditary leaders with elected representatives. Indeed, the councils and other institutions, such as the land boards, have assumed many of the powers formerly held by chiefs and other traditional authorities. In so doing, these local government institutions, created shortly after independence, have "left the chiefs with basically ceremonial duties of representing the tribe and control over traditional courts."

■ House of Chiefs

Nonetheless, a formal role has also been established for chiefs at the national level, in the form of the House of Chiefs. As noted, the House of Chiefs is a fifteen-member body, consisting of eight ex officio members— the chiefs of the eight Tswana subgroups; four elected members chosen from the subchiefs of four specific locales; and three more members elected by the other twelve members of the House (Keulder 1998, 109). The House of Chiefs has no capacity to make laws; indeed it has only an advisory function, which is often ignored by the National Assembly. Initially, according to Christiaan Keulder (1998, 109), even that advisory function was limited because of the lack of participation of House of Chief members "and the fact that only five were literate enough to read and comment on the bills that were forwarded to them." It was because of this that the three more "better qualified members from outside the chieftancy" were added, in the hopes that the House of Chiefs would be able to "perform its duties more effectively and command more confidence." Despite the shortcomings of the House of Chiefs, however, it has contributed to the successful governing of Botswana:

> It facilitated a better understanding of state policies by the ordinary rural population as its debates were heard on national radio and reported in the national press. Issues raised and matters discussed in the house were reflected upon and clarified by the chiefs on their return to their respective kgotlas. Thus they continued to act as a link between rural society and the central legislature, and most importantly, as agents of transparency. (Keulder 1998, 110)

In establishing a formal role for traditional leaders at the national level, the government of Botswana accrued certain benefits. First, the government secured expert advice on traditional institutions and life in the rural areas. Second, an acceptable channel was established through which grievances could be articulated and channeled. Third, by providing a formal means for chiefs to participate in government, the government avoided severing an important link with the rural areas. Fourth, it was expected that the chiefs could be relied upon to assist in the modernization of the rural areas (Keulder 1998, 109).

■ *Party Systems and Elections*

As noted, Botswana has a multiparty political system, but one in which one party, the BDP, has dominated thoroughly. Indeed, the BDP has won every national election since 1965, although the percentage of the popular vote won by the BDP has dropped in recent elections, to as low as 55 percent in 1994, 54 percent in 1999, and 51 percent in 2004 suggesting an increasingly competitive political arena. Up to and including the 1994 election, the BDP was challenged at each election by three parties—the Botswana National Front (BNF), the Botswana People's Party (BPP), and the Botswana Independence Party (BIP). In 1999 the challenge came from two other parties, the Botswana Congress Party (BCP) and the Botswana Alliance Movement (BAM). In mid-2004 the BNF, BAM, and BPP formed an alliance—known as the Election Pact—to oppose the BDP in the late 2004 election. Of the three parties in the pact, only the BNF garnered seats in parliament, winning twelve out of fifty-seven. The BCP won one seat. A number of commentators have argued that in recent years Botswana has actually moved away from being a dominant-party system (Wiseman 1998;

Holm and Darnolf 2000). Such commentators focus, in particular, on the 1994 National Assembly election, in which the BDP received its first serious threat from another political party, in that instance from the BNF. According to John Wiseman (1998), the BNF has been increasingly successful at the local level for even longer, beginning with the 1984 election, in which the BNF gained control over the Gaborone town council. In 1989 and 1994 the BNF won control over several more town councils, including Selebi-Phikwe and its first district (rural) council. In several other town and district councils the BNF became a serious contender for power, even though it did not win the election.

Wiseman (1998) explains the slow decline in support for the BDP as follows. Founded in 1961, the BDP was the party that led the country peacefully to independence. More important, however, was Seretse Khama's leadership of the BDP. As Wiseman observes (and many others concur): "It would be difficult to overstate the importance of Seretse to the development of the BDP, or indeed to the development of Botswana, during the late colonial and early independence period." Wiseman describes Khama as the BDP's "most politically valuable asset." Once Khama was elected president, his personal prestige "virtually guaranteed" the BDP's repeated election victories up until his premature death in office in 1980. Further, according to Wiseman, because of the groundwork laid by Khama, the political succession by his vice president Quett Masire "passed off remarkably smoothly and without acrimony" (Wiseman 1998, 248–249). Under Masire, and his successor, Mogae, however, the BDP has been less ably led and has been increasingly riven by factionalism and disunity.

In addition to its association with Seretse Khama and its status as the party of independence, the BDP "derived very considerable electoral bene fit from having presided over the dramatic growth and development of the [country's] economy" (Wiseman 1998, 249–250). For decades, the BDP steadfastly warned that the election of opposition parties would jeopardize Botswana's economic successes. At the same time, with the knowledge that mineral resources are finite, and some indication that the country's boom years came to an end by the early 1990s, the BDP's ability to benefit from the country's economic successes is waning. In addition, during the early 1990s the BDP's reputation for financial efficiency and rectitude was undermined by successive scandals involving the sale of land and provision of houses in and around Gaborone, and problems at the National Development Bank. These corruption scandals are considered to have contributed to the BDP's poor showing in the 1994 election.

Paradoxically, these very issues may result, in part, from Botswana's growth and development under the BDP. For example, rapid urbanization and economic growth greatly enhanced the value of urban land and demand for housing, thereby creating preconditions in which corruption can occur. Further, the massive road-building program the government has undertaken has also had the effect of "democratizing" travel, thereby eroding advantages the BDP may have enjoyed as the party in power in reaching the rural areas. Moreover, the massive improvements in education and literacy have also meant a better informed and more discriminating electorate able to take advantage of national political reports to be found in an increasingly independent press (Wiseman 1998).

By the same token, while the BNF had been weakened by disunity and leadership problems until the mid-1980s, by the mid-1990s these were decidedly less pronounced. Moreover, the BNF increasingly sought support from among non-Tswana groups in the country. At the same time, the primary support base for the BNF has come from urban areas, in particular the urban working class and unemployed, both of which are growing, as are the urban areas generally. Indeed, Holm and Darnolf (2000, 120) suggest that "urbanization has been gradually bringing about the emergence of a two-party state where the one represents predominantly the cities and the other the rural areas." The BNF also benefits, according to Wiseman (1998), from considerable organizational and other support from students and faculty at the University of Botswana in Gaborone. As Wiseman concludes his discussion of the changing party system in Botswana, he emphasizes the interplay of structure and agency:

> Both human agency (what political elites do, or fail to do) and structure (the socioeconomic environment in which politicians operate) are essential components of an overall explanation of what does, or does not, occur. Structural change creates a range of new opportunities and new difficulties for party leaders to build or sustain support in a changing electorate. The evidence suggests that in Botswana, party system change has lagged behind socioeconomic change. Whilst the latter has been the most dramatic in sub-Saharan Africa the party system has been marked by significant levels of stability and continuity with only a very gradual erosion (which is still incomplete) of the dominant-party system. The initial creation of a dominant position for the BDP by its pre-independence leaders has shown remarkable persistence in spite of the death of the most important of those leaders (Seretse Khama) more than a decade and a half ago. However, in more recent times the BDP elite has been rather less successful in making the sort of adaptations which might have sustained that dominance in the context of socioeconomic change. (1998, 258)

In the aftermath of the 1994 election, according to Lekorwe and colleagues (2001), the BDP sought outside assistance in developing a strategy for the future. Among other things, it was recommended that the party honorably retire some of its older leaders, at the same time as it bring into the party a dynamic new leader who was "untainted" by factional fights. It was in this context that Seretse Khama's eldest son, Ian, was made Festus Mogae's vice president when Mogae assumed the presidency in 1998. Still, it is not entirely clear whether the BDP (barely) won the 1999 election because of Khama's influence and increased stature within the party, or because of a split within the BNF out of which the new Botswana Congress Party was formed. In July 2003, Khama became the new national chairman of the BDP, in a "landslide victory" at a party congress, thereby settling a long-standing factional rivalry within the BDP. Following the 2004 election, Khama was reelected vice-president of the country by the National Assembly.

While the electoral outcomes at the national level have evolved slowly over the years, it has never been alleged that elections in Botswana have been anything but free and fair. According to Wiseman (1998, 245), "with the exception of one 'missing' ballot box in 1984 (the Supreme Court ordered the election to be rerun in the constituency in question) there has never been any serious allegation of electoral malpractice." Interestingly, in an effort to broaden Botswana's democracy and enhance elections in the country, an independent electoral commission was created in 1997. At the same time, the voting age was lowered from twenty-one to eighteen and provision was made for the use of an absentee ballot (Lekorwe et al. 2001, 2).

■ Civil Society

The general consensus around civil society in Botswana seems to be that it has been "historically absent" in the country, only showing some signs of life from the early 1990s onward (Good 1996; Tsie 1996; Holm and Darnolf 2000; Lekorwe et al. 2001). Holm and Darnolf (2000, 129–130) write that a few interest groups did emerge during the colonial period, primarily among "the educated class which found itself marginalized during the policy-making process." These included groups such as the Botswana Teachers Union, the Botswana Civil Servants Association, the Red Cross, and the Young Women's Christian Association. Since independence, according to Holm and Darnolf, the government has in some respects monitored the growth of civil society, mandating that organizations register with the government, but only after meeting certain requirements. Among other things, this means that those groups representing more educated sectors of the population are advantaged, and those from the rural areas are disadvantaged.

Other challenges to civil society organizations in Botswana mirror those of other countries in southern Africa, including lack of sufficient funding, stable staffs, and large memberships. In trying to affect government policy, moreover, organizations often find themselves co-opted (by access to resources, employment opportunities, and so on) by the very ministries they are seeking to influence. In Holm and Darnolf's view (2000, 133), "civil society exists as an extension of the bureaucracy rather than as a set of independent actors confronting politicians and civil servants."

Although civic organizations tend to lack the vibrancy and visibility of their counterparts elsewhere in the region, Holm and Darnolf's assessment appears to be overstated. Perhaps most notable, women's organizations have been at the forefront of civil society activity in Botswana. As Judith van Allen (2001) describes, a significant women's rights movement emerged in Botswana in the early 1990s as a result of an intensive mobilization around a single initiative, namely the challenge to Botswana's citizenship law. Whereas at independence citizenship in Botswana had been determined by birth, this was changed in the early 1980s to birth by descent, and for married women the citizenship of the father only determined the citizenship of a child. Within a few years of the new law's passage a women's rights organization, Emang Basadi, emerged to challenge it. This challenge was ultimately victorious and led to further challenges to discriminatory laws and practices.

In a similar vein, women's organizations were particularly prominent during the 1994 election campaign, a campaign marked by the "appearance of a number of active and articulate civic and community groups" (Good 1996, 56). Among these groups, however, women's organizations have "multiplied faster and scored the highest number of successes." For example, they were reportedly able to convince political parties to add clauses to their party constitutions that were more favorable to women. Although two political parties were led by women, these were admittedly insignificant. Perhaps more telling, concerns raised in the *Women's Manifesto,* issued in 1994 by Emang Basadi, found their way into the programs of the leading political parties. However, as Good (1996, 57) argues, it was not simply the increased activism of women and their groups, but the breadth and depth of the issues raised: "The 'growing militancy of women,' in attaining equal participation and basic human rights, was in fact contributing significantly to the 'changing character' of politics in the country." During the 1990s more than a dozen women's organizations emerged seeking to influence government policy in a number of arenas.

Other types of civil society organizations in Botswana include human rights organizations and indigenous rights organizations, with some overlap between them. Ditshwanelo, the Botswana Center for Human Rights, was formed in 1993 and has focused, among other things, on the government's failure to ratify a number of international conventions—for example, on the rights of children—or failure to adhere to the provisions of those conventions already signed. Another concern of human rights activists inside (and outside) Botswana has been the treatment of the Basarwa, or San, people, an issue mentioned earlier. By the 1990s a number of San "self-help" organizations had emerged in Botswana. For example, a group called the First People of the Kalahari works on the dispossession of land among the San. Their plight has worsened since independence, as wealthy cattle farmers have sought more land for themselves. Much such activity takes place at the local level, with protests lodged at district councils and land boards, with some few San even venturing into elected office at the local level in order to advance their cause (Good 1996, 59–60).

In many parts of southern Africa, trade unions have been particularly powerful actors in civil society—for example, helping to topple the apartheid regime in South Africa and initiate a democratic transition in Zambia. Though initially powerless in Zimbabwe, in recent years unions in that country have emerged to challenge the state as well. In Botswana, by contrast, trade unions have been notoriously weak. Indeed, only in 1977 did the labor movement in Botswana come together to form the Botswana Federation of Trade Unions (Tsie 1996, 606). Balefi Tsie provides a number of reasons for the weakness of organized labor in the country. First, Botswana suffers a low level of industrialization—a vestige of its colonial-era role as a labor reserve for South African mines and a source of beef exports to South Africa. Second, and related, until the 1980s there was only a low level of formal sector wage labor in the economy. Third, what labor movement has existed has always been plagued by poor organization and lack of effective leadership. Fourth, strikes, an important tool of labor organizers, have effectively been prohibited in Botswana; indeed, there has never been a legal strike in the country since independence (Tsie 1996, 607). Botswana's nascent labor movement (urban workers) is considered to form a core of support for the BNF, and as the BNF's fortunes grow, so too may the power of the labor movement.[13]

While civil society in Botswana may be weaker than in other countries in the region, it is not because civil society organizations have not learned from their counterparts elsewhere in southern Africa. Indeed, it is important to note that civil society organizations in Botswana have extensive ties with similar groups in the region. For example, the founders of many of the trade unions in Botswana first learned about labor mobilization as migrant laborers in South Africa and Zimbabwe—and continue to consult with more experienced trade unionists in South Africa today. Similarly, women activists in Botswana have been involved in research and publication projects with other women activists across the region and have exchanged ideas and best practices, including the idea of a women's manifesto, subsequently adopted in Namibia (Holm, Molutsi, and Somolekae 1996, 51).

■ Fundamentals of the Political Economy

Botswana's economic transformation since independence has been quite stunning. At independence it was considered a very poor developing country that would likely remain dependent upon foreign assistance to finance its national budget and upon beef exports to Britain and South Africa for foreign exchange earnings. Yet by the 1980s it had the highest economic growth rate in the world, averaging about 10 percent per year—and this despite six years of drought that negatively affected the country's cattle industry (Hwedie 2001b). While this economic growth rate has slowed in recent years, Botswana's annual economic growth rate still exceeds that of the rest of sub-Saharan Africa (Taylor and Mokhawa 2003, 262). Botswana has significant foreign exchange reserves, has very little external debt, and until recently has never had a budget deficit.

Much of this economic good fortune rests on the discovery of diamonds in the early 1970s, luckily for Botswana, after independence rather than before. By 2003 Botswana was the largest producer of diamonds by value in the world. And since the cost of diamond production in Botswana is low compared to the diamonds' overseas sale value, diamond sales are extremely profitable to the country. Moreover, in 1975 the government successfully negotiated with the De Beers diamond company for a fifty-fifty share ownership in all of the country's diamond mines (Taylor and Mokhawa 2003, 263). Unlike other host governments in Africa that effectively surrender their natural resources to exploitation by multinational corporations, the Botswana government pressed De Beers for a number of conditions on its investment (Samatar 1999, 19–20). The result was that government retains considerable influence over the national diamond-mining company, known as Debswana, in areas such as wage policies and production levels. By 1981 diamonds had replaced beef as the country's leading foreign exchange earner (Taylor and Mokhawa 2003, 263). With the revenue from the diamond mines the government was able to invest in other mineral industries as well, including copper and ash.

At the same time, mining is capital- rather than labor-intensive. Therefore, diamond mining has not greatly increased employment, nor has it expanded the formal sector of the economy. "This has had the knock-on effect," according to Ian Taylor and Gladys Mokhawa (2003, 263), "of maintaining high levels of income inequality and poverty." One of the government's strategies for increasing employment has been to try to expand its manufacturing sector, though this has met with limited success. Some of its initiatives in this realm include the establishment of a regional development project that used special incentives to attract foreign industry, in the copper- and nickel-mining town of Selebi-Phikwe, and the location of a Hyundai assembly plant in Gaborone for the manufacture of Hyundais to southern Africa's transport hub, South Africa. Neither of these efforts was successful in the long run, in the first instance because of the government's failure to adequately assess the quality of the companies seeking to locate in Selebi-Phikwe, and in the second case because of deep hostility on the part of the South African government and trade unions to the competition created by the Hyundai plant in Gaborone (and the government's failure to negotiate directly with the Hyundai corporation, rather than a shaky subsidiary) (Good and Hughes 2002). Indeed, these two failures have been a serious blow to Botswana's attempts to attract quality investment and to diversify more significantly its manufacturing sector.

Moreover, Botswana's diamond industry has, somewhat ironically, become embroiled in the worldwide campaign against conflict diamonds. Also called blood diamonds and dirty diamonds, these are diamonds that are illegally excavated and traded from conflict-ridden places such as Angola, Sierra Leone, Liberia, and the Democratic Republic of Congo and then also used to fund (and so exacerbate) the conflicts in those same places (Taylor and Mokhawa 2003, 264). The anti–conflict diamond campaign has sought to "stem the sale of diamonds that originate from areas under the control of forces opposed to elected and internationally recognized governments, or are in any way connected to those groups." The campaign was ultimately successful in that in 2001 the World Diamond Council agreed to the development, implementation, and oversight of a tracking system for the export and import of diamonds in order to prevent conflict diamonds from entering the global market.

Botswana's role in the campaign has in many ways backfired. Botswana has been very concerned that the campaign not impugn the reputation and product of "clean diamond" countries such as itself and Namibia. Thus, while it has supported international restrictions on conflict diamonds, the Botswana government has worked hard to assert that its own diamonds are clean (Taylor and Mokhawa 2003, 271).[14] But this assertion came under intense scrutiny recently as Botswana found itself in its own controversy over diamonds. In brief, the government has expedited its plan to remove the San people from the Central Kalahari Game Reserve, which was established in 1961 on the ancestral lands of two San groups as a home for them. The reasons given for the removal of the San from the reserve are related to the government's plan to develop the area for tourism—and possibly diamonds (Taylor and Mokhawa 2003, 276). In late 2002, in its effort to relocate the Basarwa, the government went so far as to seal boreholes and destroy property of inhabitants of the reserve. One London-based nongovernmental organization, Survival International, has led the outcry over the Botswana government's moves against the Basarwa (allegedly in search of diamonds). The government response has been, according to Taylor and Mokhawa (2003, 279), "intransigent, illiberal and chauvinistic." Of course Botswana's diamonds are still not conflict diamonds, officially defined, but they have certainly been tarnished by association with the forced removal of the San from the game reserve.

■ Challenges for the Twenty-First Century

Botswana faces many challenges in the twenty-first century, chief among them the second highest HIV/AIDS infection rate of any country in the world—close to 40 percent of the adult population. As a consequence, as one source reported, "the nation spends its weekends at funerals" (Grunwald 2002). Unlike in other parts of Africa, however, the government of Botswana has openly acknowledged the problem and is working vigorously to combat it. A key weapon in the war has been President Mogae, who has provided aggressive leadership, "warning his people in fiery speeches that they are 'threatened with annihilation,' chairing his country's AIDS council and badgering his health officials with questions about condom distribution in prisons and construction timetables for clinics" (Grunwald 2002). In July 2003 President Mogae was quoted as saying that all of Botswana's gains are being reversed by HIV/AIDS ("Fearing Extinction" 2003). In 2000 Botswana embarked upon a five-year "African Comprehensive HIV/AIDS Partnership" involving the Bill and Melinda Gates Foundation and the pharmaceutical company Merck. Each has pledged U.S.$50 million over the five-year period, with Merck also offering an unlimited supply of the antiretroviral drugs that have done so much to prolong the life of HIV-positive people elsewhere in the world. Among other things, this has allowed Botswana to be the first country in Africa to offer free antiretrovirals to anyone who needs them. Another element of the five-year plan is a training program for health care workers and a new research laboratory in Gaborone, both established by Harvard University.

So far those Batswana who have opted for the antiretroviral therapy have shown very high adherence rates—an initial fear about the antiretroviral therapy in the developing world had been that because of impoverished circumstances, people would not be able to adhere to the often difficult drug regimens (and drug-resistant strains might result). At the same time, according to reports, the partnership is still struggling to recruit doctors, nurses, and social workers to build much needed infrastructure, and to "change the deadly culture of denial that still swirls around AIDS in Botswana" (Grunwald 2002). But Botswana's program is not only about treating those who are already infected, but also about preventing further infections. Condoms are widely available and prevention messages are being disseminated over the airwaves, on billboards, in classrooms, and more.

An additional challenge is one faced by many other countries in the region and continent, namely how to deepen democracy. A 2000 survey of Batswana (Lekorwe et al. 2001, iv) indicates that democratic attitudes run deep in the country: "The results reflect long-standing democratic values and the firm entrenchment of democratic institutions. Batswana demonstrate their satisfaction with democracy and the legitimacy of the state by claiming that the government exercises power within legal means and equally represents the interests of all citizens." At the same time, a changing array of opposition political parties has failed to wrest power from the ruling party in Botswana, though they have managed, over time, to lure significant support away from the BDP. But many would argue that until there is an alternation of power at the national level in Botswana, democracy remains elusive.

Like other countries in the region, Botswana is challenged by the need to further diversify its economy, lest it find itself one day without diamonds and once again reliant upon cattle and migrant labor. Indeed, in announcing the country's ninth national development plan in July 2003, President Mogae said the plan would focus on diversifying the economy and ensuring the country's global competitiveness. Among other things he called for increasing the supply of trained people, intensifying research and development, and fostering financial markets ("Botswana Launches" 2003).

In general, the government seems cognizant of the need to plan for 2040, when diamonds are forecast to run out. A strategy, branded Vision 2016, elaborates where Botswana would like to be fifty years after independence. Vision 2016 calls for a continued average growth rate of 8 percent, a trebling of per capita incomes, and the elimination of poverty. This is to be achieved through diversification into manufacturing and services, in particular financial services. To that end the country is investing massively in the education of its young people and has established an international financial services center and a booming stock exchange, and has welcomed a growing number of foreign banks (Johnson 2003). Botswana's historical neglect of industry (in favor of large scale cattle ranching and diamonds) and the concentration of existing industrial assets in non-Batswana hands may make its industrial objectives more difficult in the competitive international environment of the early twenty-first century, however (Samatar 1999, 133). At the same time, given Botswana's developmental characteristics, the state's capacity to realize its "vision" would appear to be among the strongest on the continent.

A final challenge for Botswana reflects its geographic position in southern Africa—it shares long borders with three countries and close proximity to others, some of them deeply troubled. Indeed, the challenges of the 1970s and 1980s, when Botswana faced considerable danger due to its warring neighbors, have in some respects reemerged in the early 2000s. In particular, Botswana has suffered and stands to suffer more from the effects of the worsening situation in Zimbabwe. In April 2003 several members of parliament demanded that the Mogae government take a stronger stance against the Mugabe regime, blaming Mugabe for an influx of illegal Zimbabwean migrants into Botswana. More generally, the MPs expressed concern that "the deteriorating sociopolitical and economic situation in Zimbabwe was having a knock-on impact on their country" ("Botswana Legislators" 2003). For example, veterinarians blamed two outbreaks of foot and mouth disease in the early 2000s on a lack of effective control measures in Zimbabwe and the spread of the disease across the border ("Zim Cattle Spread FMD" 2004). Among other things, reports of foot and mouth disease in Botswana threaten lucrative contacts with the European Union for the country's beef exports. Outside Francistown a new prison was erected in 2002 just to accommodate the massive influx of illegal immigrants, primarily from Zimbabwe. Another concern is a possible downturn in the tourism industry as potential visitors fear the turmoil in the region and avoid Botswana too.

The potential spillover effects from the crisis in Zimbabwe, and the repercussions already experienced, provide a solemn reminder of the interconnectedness of the region. Yet Botswana's history augurs well for its ability to prosper regardless of how quickly—or slowly—Zimbabwe's crisis comes to resolution. After all, Africa's developmental state achieved that status in part because it was able to establish and maintain policy rationality, domestic security, political stability, and economic growth in an often hostile regional environment.

■ Notes

1. The people of Botswana are referred to (in the plural) as Batswana; the language of the Tswana is Setswana.

2. The earliest inhabitants of what is today Botswana, and the only inhabitants until Bantu-speaking groups arrived in the sixteenth century, were the Basarwa, otherwise known as the San or Bushmen.

3. This was the period of the *mfecane,* during which the Zulu kingdom under Shaka Zulu was created. "The resultant process of conquest, warfare, population flight, and social dislocation affected the people of the entire subcontinent from the Fish River in southern Africa to the southern shores of Lake Victoria. These events directly affected the demographic features of the populations of what eventually became the independent states of Botswana, South Africa, and Zimbabwe" (du Toit 1995, 20).

4. Indeed, about 80 percent of the population lives in one eighty-mile-wide strip of eastern Botswana. The population is concentrated along the railroad line that travels through the eastern part of the country (Picard 1985, 4).

5. Neil Parsons (1985, 37) calls this idea one of "the most cherished myths about Botswana's history." According to him, the origins of modern nationalism in Botswana can be traced to the 1920s and two branches of an intellectual nationalist movement, one among "progressive [though still autocratic] chiefs" and another more democratic nationalist tradition.

6. Quett Masire, by contrast, the main organizer behind the BDP, was "a commoner whose family had risen from the bottom of society as entrepreneurial farmers and teachers" (Parsons 1985, 38).

7. According to Wiseman (1998, 248): "Although the marriage was approved

by the Bamangwato at a huge public meeting of the tribe it ran into serious opposition from the British colonial authorities who, under pressure from the South African government (which at the time was constructing the apartheid system of strict racial segregation), stripped Seretse of his hereditary rights to the chieftancy and, for a time, banned him from the territory."

8. The number of seats in the National Assembly has grown considerably since independence—from thirty-one in 1965 to forty in 1994 to fifty-seven in 2004—with the increasing number of constituencies reflecting the country's rapid demographic growth and change (in particular urbanization).

9. In 1997 the constitution was amended to limit the presidency to two five-year terms.

10. "To accomplish its regional goals, the [South African] government beefed up SADF capabilities for fighting interstate wars; increased domestic arms production; intensified its nuclear arms development; and reinforced the police and the military to improve their ability to fight a counterinsurgency war" (Ohlson and Stedman 1994, 63).

11. Molomo (2001) attributes this statement to Jackie Cilliers, executive director of the Johannesburg-based Institute for Defense Policy.

12. Du Toit (1995, 58) quotes President Khama as saying in 1967: "We would never sacrifice efficiency on the altar of localization."

13. The BNF's support from labor stems from the fact that the party's base is in urban areas anyway, where workers tend to be located, and from the fact that the BDP has not been particularly friendly to workers, for example by prohibiting legal strikes.

14. Indeed, as many others have done, the government has gone so far as to assert that "Botswana's diamonds had been fundamental in bringing about social and economic development. The gist of the campaign was to assert that diamonds in Botswana have been used to provide health care, build houses, educate Batswana and, most importantly, create a politically sound environment that, so the argument goes, has contributed to the country's longstanding liberal democracy and relative stability" (Taylor and Mokhawa 2003, 272).

5

Mozambique: Reconstruction and Democratization

On May 8, 2001, President Joachim Chissano of Mozambique announced to a meeting of the Central Committee of the ruling party, Frente de Libertação de Moçambique (Frelimo), that he would not be the party's candidate for the presidential elections due in December 2004. Chissano, who won the presidency in the country's first multiparty elections in 1994 and was reelected in 1999, actually had served as head of state since 1986, when he assumed the presidency upon the death of Samora Machel. Despite his long tenure in office, Chissano's withdrawal might well be regarded as extraordinary, both within Mozambique and the region. Indeed, there was considerable initial doubt among supporters and critics alike that the president would actually abide by his decision (Marshall and Jaggers 2001), and their skepticism was justified. The list of state presidents in the region who have made similar pledges to retire from office, and who subsequently sought ways to preserve their grip on the presidency, is a long one. In addition, Chissano himself had said once before, in 1999, that he would not stand for reelection before ultimately choosing to run (reportedly because no suitable alternative could be found within Frelimo; Mozambique News Agency [MNA] 2001).

Another reason Chissano's decision was unexpected lay in its "legal voluntarism." The Mozambican constitution (1990), which established the institution of direct, popular elections for the office of president, expressly states that "the President of the Republic may only be re-elected on two consecutive occasions" (*Constitution of Mozambique* 1990, art. 118). While this is regarded by some as a flaw of constitutional design, it nonetheless would have permitted Chissano to stand in 2004, since he was elected in 1994, and reelected only once, five years later (MNA 2001). Nevertheless, unlike his regional counterparts Chiluba, Robert Mugabe, Bakili Muluzi, and Nujoma, Chissano appeared genuinely anxious to relinquish the reins of the presidency, notwithstanding the existence of this convenient consti-

Mozambique: Country Data

Land area 799,380 km²
Capital Maputo
Date of independence June 25, 1975
Population 18.1 million, 41% urban
Languages Portuguese (official), and three main African language
  groups: Makua-Lomwe, Tsonga, and Sena-Nyanja
Ethnic groups African, 99.66% (Shangaan, Chokwe, Manyika, Sena,
  Makua, and others); European, 0.06%; Mestico, 0.2%; Asian,
  0.08%
Religions indigenous beliefs, 50%; Christian, 30%; Muslim, 20%
Currency metical (MT); meticais per U.S. dollar: 23,595.00 (July
  2003)

Literacy rate 45.2% (male, 61.2%; female, 30.0%)
Life expectancy 39.2 years (male, 37.4 years; female, 40.9 years)
Infant mortality 125 per 1,000 live births

GDP per capita U.S.$200
GDP per capita (PPP) U.S.$1,140
GDP per capita growth rate 4.3% (1990–2001)

Leaders since independence
  • Samora Moisés Machel, president, 1975–1986
  • Joaquim Alberto Chissano, president, 1986–2004
  • Armando Guebuza, president, 2004–

Major political parties
  Ruling party: Front for the Liberation of Mozambique (Frelimo)
  Other parties: Mozambique National Resistance (Renamo)
  Party for Peace, Development, and Democracy (PDD)

Women in parliament (lower/single house) 30.0% (1999)

Note: Data from 2001 unless otherwise indicated.

tutional loophole. In May 2001 a senior member of the Frelimo Central Committee sought to allay lingering doubts, suggesting that "president Chissano believes that standing for the presidency again would violate the spirit, if not the letter, of the Mozambican constitution. President Chissano believes that, were he to stand again, in reality he would be asking for a fourth term. For he was already president when the 1990 constitution, establishing limits on terms of office, was approved. President Chissano had then been elected in 1994 and 1999, so he now regarded himself as already in his third term" (Fernando Ganhao, quoted in MNA 2001).

Although hardly universally popular, Chissano held considerable power within both the party and the state, and enjoyed substantial benefits of incumbency. Given these resources, a Chissano victory in 2004, while not ensured, was perhaps very likely. Hence, even the official Frelimo explanations for his unexpected recusal appear credible. Indeed, in June 2002, Chissano ensured his retirement when Armando Guebuza, leader of the Frelimo Parliamentary Group, was elected as the party's new secretary-general and its candidate for the 2004 election.

We cite Chissano's decision to step down from the presidency as an important, albeit symbolic step in the inculcation of democratic practices in Mozambique. While certainly not a panacea for Mozambique's myriad problems—including deep poverty, growing corruption, lingering political violence, and overcentralization of power by the regime—Chissano's departure may represent a significant harbinger of democratization in the country and the region as a whole. First, it marked an important reversal of the trend in the region in which presidents attempted to subvert constitutional term limits and nascent democratic institutions by using, in effect, extraconstitutional means to extend their terms in office. While these efforts undermined the rule of law and threatened fragile political institutions elsewhere, Chissano was apparently willing to buck the trend and step down, despite his preeminent role in the Frelimo party hierarchy.

Thus the Mozambican precedent undoubtedly has and will have a regional impact. Indeed, it may have emboldened anti-third-term activists in Zambia and Malawi, where bids by incumbent presidents Frederick Chiluba and Bakili Muluzi were thwarted in 2001 and 2002, respectively. At the same time, however, care should be taken not to overstate the regional demonstration effect of Chissano's decision: after all, Robert Mugabe's power in Zimbabwe has continued since 1980; Malawi's Muluzi continued to explore the third-term possibilities long after Mozambique discarded the idea, and Namibia's Sam Nujoma also considered, though did not pursue, a second constitutional change to allow himself a fourth term. Such a prospect, though unlikely, remains theoretically possible in South Africa. Cases like Mozambique thus represent important incremental steps toward instilling a regional norm of presidential term limits and constitutional governance.

Second, and perhaps more significant, Chissano's departure from the scene briefly introduced, however unwittingly, the prospect for alternation of political parties in Mozambique. Although Frelimo has enjoyed a strong monopoly on elected office, the polity has been quite competitive. The 1999 national election revealed this close divide, as Afonso Dhlakama, the candidate of the principal opposition party, Resistência Nacional Moçambicana (Renamo), came within 5 percent of victory in a disputed presidential election, and Renamo actually won a majority of the votes in six provinces. Moreover, it was widely believed that Frelimo's selection of Armando Guebuza, also a controversial and polarizing figure, as Chissano's successor (Economist Intelligence Unit [EIU] 2002a), would provide a singular opportunity for Renamo and its longtime leader, Dhlakama, to at last capture the presidency. Alternation in power, although not an end in itself, is an important aspect of the consolidation of democracy (Diamond 1999; Carothers 2002). At the same time, however, the prospect of alternation—at least a Dhlakama/Renamo victory—posed its own risks in Mozambique.

In any event, the December 2004 national elections saw Frelimo not only retain control over the reins of government but expand it substantially. Whereas the possibility remains that Frelimo will be magnanimous in victory, such an outcome appears unlikely. In most of the country's three decades of independence, politics has been a zero-sum game, in which Frelimo has been little interested in any semblance of power sharing or even national representation of Renamo's views, and many of the institutional structures discussed below reinforce the ruling party's monopoly. The capacity of Mozambique's democracy to deepen, despite these long-standing political cleavages, and despite its fragile institutions, is a central concern in this chapter.

Mozambique experienced tremendous change in the 1990s, beginning a positive, albeit sometimes halting trajectory toward stability and democracy. The country emerged from fifteen years of civil war to achieve a negotiated peace in 1992. As the one-party state gave way to political pluralism, founding multiparty elections were conducted in 1994, a second set of national elections occurred in 1999, and the third in 2004. A decade of peace and democratic rule, however flawed, suggests strongly that conflict in Mozambique is now situated in the political realm, rather than on the battlefield. Positive developments are also apparent on the economic front. Although still a desperately poor country, Mozambique averaged impressive gross domestic product (GDP) growth of nearly 10 percent annually in the 1990s, and high growth rates have continued in the present decade.

Despite these auspicious signs, however, political and economic problems in Mozambique cannot be underestimated. Substantial tensions persist between former combatants Frelimo and Renamo, as alluded to above. Social problems such as AIDS and income inequality have multiplied.

Corruption among party elites, particularly concerning the privatization of state assets, has become a major issue and has threatened state and government legitimacy.

Four centuries of Portuguese colonialism and, thereafter, state socialism, still complicate modern Mozambique. The legacy of Portuguese colonialism distinguishes Mozambique from the rest of the region, save Angola, and left Mozambique with precious few resources and an illiteracy rate among the highest in Africa. The economic destruction wrought by the rapid and unexpected decolonization in 1974–1975, the civil war that followed, and inappropriate development policies left the economy in shambles by the 1990s (Pitcher 2003). Whereas today Angola has oil and diamonds on which to base its economy, Mozambique's development relies on exports of prawns and cashew nuts; on services, transport, and trade; on energy such as hydropower and, increasingly, natural gas; on commercial fishing; and of course international aid.

The enormity of these political and economic problems therefore presents a difficult legacy to overcome. Thus the Mozambique case raises a number of questions. Most important among these concerns is the durability of the political and economic institutions Mozambique has created in the past decade. Can Mozambique's institutional structures withstand the changes in personnel that occurred in 2004, allowing democracy to become increasingly entrenched? Will Chissano's successor attempt to reignite latent divisions for political gain? Conversely, will Renamo respect Frelimo's now significantly enlarged electoral majority? In fairness, not all these questions are completely answerable with the evidence now available. Yet this chapter's examination of a range of developments in Mozambique helps us to answer them as fully as possible.

■ Historical Origins of the Mozambican State

The Portuguese established one of the first permanent trading posts in southern Africa in the contemporary Mozambican province of Inhambane in 1534. Most of the European activity was initially centered on coastal trade, including trade in slaves. It later expanded to include trading and mining activity in the interior. The Portuguese granted large concessions to foreign companies (principally British) to help finance the colony; however, only one, Sena Sugar Estates, which like the other companies was given near-complete control over African labor and administration, had any measurable success (Alden 2001, 2). Indeed, since most of "these commercial activities were not tremendously successful," Mozambique became a transit and service-based economy almost from the outset (Rupiya 1998, 10).

Most of the peoples initially subjugated by the Portuguese were in the northern "cultural band," comprising significantly the Macua-Lowme, who today make up some 47 percent of the population. In the south, the Tsonga people (23 percent of the contemporary population) were part of the Gaza empire, which put up intense resistance to Portuguese rule through the nineteenth century (Weinstein 2002, 144). It was not until 1914 that the whole of the indigenous population was subjugated by the Portuguese (Alden 2001, 2). Subsequently, thousands of indigenous people were forced into the colonial wage economy. Mozambican labor was made available for the South African mining industry by formal agreement in 1901; a similar agreement was later made with Southern Rhodesia. Of course, these were completely unconcerned with the conditions of labor or the rights of workers, and the bulk of remittances were paid to the Portuguese colonial state rather than to the miners themselves. Thus, "for all intents and purposes, the Mozambican economy was under foreign (non-Portuguese) control" until the 1930s (Alden, 3). In 1932 the Portuguese government sidelined the trading companies and imposed direct rule over Mozambique for the first time.

Substantial Portuguese settlement did not begin until the late nineteenth and early twentieth centuries and only accelerated after World War II. Still, by the 1940s, there were only around 33,000 Portuguese living in Mozambique (Alden 2001, 4), and several thousand Indians who worked in the trades. As with French colonialism in Africa, there was never an expectation in Lisbon or among Portuguese settlers in Africa that control would be ceded to the indigenous population. Moreover, with a settler population numbering 100,000 in 1960, there was also a vested self-interest opposing majority rule among resident whites. Thus Mozambique actually bears considerable resemblance to other settler colonies in southern Africa, namely Namibia, South Africa, and Zimbabwe, where emergent African nationalism encountered settler resistance and precipitated a violent struggle for independence. Indeed, Mozambique's peak European population of around 200,000 by 1973 (Alden 2001, 4) is also quite comparable to the peak white population levels in Zimbabwe and Namibia.

Black nationalism coalesced within Frelimo, which was formed in 1962 under the leadership of Eduardo Mondlane, an anthropologist and onetime United Nations employee. In September 1964, the first shots of revolution were fired in the northern province of Cabo Delgado. Frelimo, which later adopted Marxism-Leninism, was not at the time explicitly Marxist, but it was eventually the recipient of "radical African, Arab, Eastern European and Chinese aid" (Rupiya 1998, 11). Mondlane "from the outset found himself mediating between two opposing perspectives within the organization": one nationalist and concerned with Mozambican liberation, the other committed to scientific socialism (Alden 2001, 4–5). However, Mondlane was assassinated in Dar es Salaam, Tanzania, where the movement had set up its exile headquarters in 1969, prompting escalating conflicts within the party (Rupiya 1998).[1] Following Mondlane's death a three-person leadership council briefly ran the movement. When one of the members, Una Sinango (who was accused of taking part in Mondlane's assassination), was forced out of the movement, Samora Machel, one of the remaining two leaders, moved to the forefront and quickly consolidated his control over the party and its military operations (Weinstein 2002, 146).

The remaining years of Portuguese colonialism bear many similarities to the dying days of settler rule in Zimbabwe. As in Zimbabwe's guerrilla war, Frelimo advances, though probably incapable of toppling the colonial government, nonetheless constituted "a major psychological blow to the Portuguese" (Rupiya 1998, 11). The Portuguese response was extreme, and included such tactics as the use of napalm, scorched earth policies, forced removals of rural poor, and internment camps. Again, as in Zimbabwe, non-combatant civilians were not spared the effects of the colonial regime's attempts to crush the rebel movement. In April 1974, however, the military coup in Portugal that toppled the fascist Salazar regime paved the way for independence in the former colonies. Immediately thereafter, Portugal withdrew its 60,000 troops (Rupiya 1998, 11).

Interestingly, white colonists in Lourenco Marques (now Maputo) briefly considered a unilateral declaration of independence following the Rhodesian example of 1965, but decided against it (Rupiya 1998, 12). The Lusaka Accord of September 1974 officially ended colonial rule and gave power to a provisional government dominated by Frelimo. The People's Republic of Mozambique became independent on June 25, 1975.

Independent Mozambique was extremely ill-suited to the achievement of democracy and development. As noted above, Portuguese colonialism had very shallow roots and very limited investment in human or physical infrastructure. Ninety percent of the population was illiterate, and Frelimo was ill-prepared to govern. Most settlers with needed skills fled the country and many departing colonists destroyed much of the limited economic base (Rupiya 1998, 12). The white population fell to 30,000 by 1977, and international capital flight also occurred as a reaction to the new government's Marxist rhetoric (Alden 2001, 5). In terms of a policy agenda, nationalization of productive assets and the provision of public health were among Frelimo's early concerns. However, economic policies, including "white elephant" industrial projects and Soviet-style collectivization of agriculture, forced resettlements, and the establishment of inefficient state farms, proved disastrous (Alden 2001, 7; Bowen 2000, 10–12). From the beginning, independent Mozambique was a one-party state under the strict control of Frelimo, which formally transformed itself into a Marxist-Leninist "vanguard party" at its 1977 party congress. Links were established to the Soviet Union and Eastern Europe for political and military support (Rupiya 1998).

The death of Mondlane in 1969 contributed to the ascendance of the radical faction within Frelimo (Alden 2001, 5–6). Nonetheless, Frelimo's

Mozambique appears to fit rather uncomfortably with more doctrinaire Afro-Marxist regimes of the period, and in any event the commitment to Marxism proved fairly short-lived. For example, while allegiances were established with the Eastern Bloc, Mozambique also maintained significant economic relationships with the United Kingdom and even South Africa. Moreover, in 1981, the Council for Mutual Economic Cooperation, the institution that managed trade and assistance among the communist countries, rejected Mozambique's appeal for membership, effectively cutting off the country. Thereafter, Mozambique's only economic recourse was the West, and the "capitalist road" was formally, if not rhetorically, embarked upon by 1983 with the adoption of initial liberalization measures under the direction of the international financial institutions (Alden 2001, 8–9). Indeed, in the 1980s, even the U.S. government, under the staunchly anticommunist Reagan administration, regarded Frelimo as only superficially Marxist (see Crocker 1992). Hence in the global support for anticommunist insurgencies funded by the U.S. government under the so-called Reagan Doctrine, the Mozambican rebel movement Renamo was unable to secure U.S. government support at all, although plenty of support flowed from right-wing think tanks in the United States. In this sense, Frelimo's rhetorical commitment to Marxism throughout the 1980s—like Robert Mugabe's avowed "socialism" in neighboring Zimbabwe—was more an effort to maintain "radical" bona fides than a genuine ideological commitment. In any event, the retreat from this weakly expressed Marxism accelerated in the 1980s, so that by Frelimo's July 1989 party congress, Marxism-Leninism had been officially abandoned (Rupiya 1998, 14).

Mozambique's postcolonial stability and economy were also undermined by military conflict. Renamo, known until 1981 as the Mozambique National Resistance (MNR), was established in 1977 by the Rhodesian Central Intelligence Organization. The MNR was designed to serve as a destabilizing force within Mozambique that would sabotage communities, as well as government economic and military installations, in an effort to punish Machel's government and to undermine Zimbabwe's National Liberation Army guerrillas who were using Mozambique as a staging area for attacks on Rhodesian forces (Vines 1996, 15–20). Although the MNR was a Rhodesian creation (supported by apartheid South Africa after Zimbabwe's independence) and engaged in massive human rights abuses, it was able nonetheless to tap into substantial anti-Frelimo sentiment in the central and northern provinces of Mozambique. However, according to Martin Rupiya (1998, 13), the MNR was not a serious threat to the Frelimo government until around 1982, when, with South African support, its fighting strength was dramatically increased. South Africa's interests in destabilizing Mozambique were multiple and complex; its principal objectives were to increase regional dependence on South Africa, and to undermine

Frelimo and its support for African National Congress (ANC) operations in Mozambique.

In 1984, the Frelimo government signed the Nkomati Accords, a nonaggression pact with apartheid South Africa. The parties agreed that Frelimo would shut down ANC bases, and that the South African military would halt its support for Renamo. The South Africans violated the pact, however, and continued to arm and support Renamo, albeit indirectly, thus ensuring the continuation of war in Mozambique (Rupiya 1998, 13). After 1984, Renamo supported its activities through civilians, whom it routinely brutalized and mutilated (Rupiya 1998; Minter 1994). "In seeking to control and instil fear in rural populations, [Renamo] became particularly well-known for mutilating civilians, including children, by cutting off ears, noses, lips and sexual organs. These tactics were part of a standard terrorist strategy intended to advertise the rebels' strength, to weaken symbolically the authority of the government and to undermine the rural production systems on which Mozambique depended" (Rupiya 1998, 13; see also Vines 1996).

By the late 1980s, it had become clear that the war was reaching a stalemate and that the conflict was increasingly "ripe" for negotiation. Unlike Angola, Mozambique lacked the natural resources and fungible commodities like oil and diamonds that would have allowed the combatants to sustain the war. Moreover, the changing global and regional environment—the end of the Cold War, the transition in Namibia, and the initiation of dialogue in South Africa—meant that fewer external actors were interested in sponsoring or prolonging the conflict. Thus, after several years of negotiations at various levels and brittle cease-fires, a lasting general peace agreement (GPA) finally was signed in Rome in October 1992. A UN force (ONUMOZ) of 6,800 troops was assigned to monitor the peace agreement, demobilize nearly 100,000 troops, create a new unified national army, resettle up to 6 million internally displaced persons, and organize elections (Rupiya 1998, 15).

At independence in 1975, Frelimo had formal military units numbering around 10,000 troops in the Popular Forces for the Liberation of Mozambique, which later became known as the Armed Forces of Mozambique (FAM by the Portuguese acronym) (Berman 1996, 43). FAM was not a formidable, disciplined military force and it was unable to completely counter Renamo after about 1980, when the latter gained South African support. Of course, the government's forces were entirely incapable of confronting the South African Defense Force (SADF), which attacked Mozambican-based ANC targets "with impunity" in the 1980s. By 1990, in response to the Renamo threat, the total armed forces of the government numbered 72,000 troops, some 60,000 of whom were in the army. Renamo's guerrilla forces, by contrast, started quite small—in the dozens—but reached several thousand by 1979. Once the South Africans took over as Renamo's sponsors, the number of fighters escalated, apparently to 16,000 by 1984 and 20,000 by the time the GPA was signed in 1992 (Berman 1996, 45–46, 48).

The government received almost all its weaponry from the Soviet Union, but "the relationship was never that close" and the size of the arsenal was limited. Moreover, the Soviets were unwilling to supply the weapons that Frelimo sought, and replacement parts were scarce (Berman 1996, 49–50). Light arms, on the other hand, were provided to the government not only by the Soviets and Eastern Bloc, but also by the United Kingdom and Portugal. Renamo also had a significant number of small arms (but almost no mechanized weapons), which were supplied by the South Africans and purchased with contributions from anticommunist organizations in the West (Berman 1996, 52).

As Carrie Manning (2001, 146) points out, Renamo was "best known to the world for its grotesque campaign of terror against Mozambican civilians," although recent analyses reveal that during the war, government forces also committed atrocities. Nonetheless, the scale of "brutality and savagery" practiced by Renamo guerrillas is widely believed to have been much greater, including the destruction of villages, rape, mutilation, murder, forced conscription, and the use of child soldiers (Berman 1996, 55; Minter 1994; Vines 1996). At war's end, the enormous task of reintegrating these competing factions into a single society, including into a combined military, fell largely to the United Nations. Following the signing of the GPA, the process of implementing demobilization began. However, it was not until December 1993 that troops began to register (Berman 1996, 67).

Forces from each of the armies were required to register at separate assembly points and indicate their willingness to join the new combined army, renamed the Armed Forces for the Defense of Mozambique (FADM), or reenter civilian life (Berman 1996, 60). The expectation was that the new FADM would number 30,000 (mostly army), and that 50 percent of these troops would come from each side (Berman 1996, 69). Astoundingly, however, only 5–6 percent of FAM troops and 10 percent of Renamo soldiers were willing to join the new force. War weariness and fairly generous pensions to former combatants provided strong disincentive to join the FADM. Thus some 78,078 soldiers (57,540 government and 20,538 Renamo) were demobilized by August 1994 (Vines 1996, 155).[2]

The transitional elections were delayed by mistrust between the parties, but were ultimately held on October 27–29, 1994. In the 250-seat National Assembly, Renamo got 112 seats, while Frelimo won an absolute majority of 129; a small coalition party, the Democratic Union, won 9 seats. In the presidential race, Chissano convincingly defeated his rival, Renamo leader Afonso Dhlakama, by a margin of 53.3 percent to 33.73 percent, with some ten other candidates splitting the remainder. The 88 percent turnout among 6.2 million registered voters and peaceful transition to pluralist politics revealed the deep frustration with war shared by Mozambique's population, which numbered 16 million at that time. The peace negotiations in the early 1990s, culminating in the 1994 elections, laid the groundwork for marked economic advances and a decade of relative stability and "normal politics" in Mozambique. However, these processes did not eliminate the cleavages that often reinforced the support for parties in the conflict, nor did they give rise to "consolidated" democracy.

■ Society and Development: Enduring Cleavages

Like many other countries in the region, Mozambique underwent a protracted liberation struggle, from 1962–1974, and like its Lusophone counterpart Angola, it was subsequently ravaged by civil war. Thirty years of violent conflict destroyed much of the fabric of the country and undermined its development potential. Not surprisingly, then, by the 1990s Mozambique was one of the poorest, most economically backward states in the world.

Renamo, for its part, was an externally created insurgency, which often relied on gruesome tactics meant to sow terror and compel obedience (Vines 1996). Thus, in one sense, Renamo was an illegitimate actor. However, it would be wrong to suggest that the movement did not also cultivate its own constituency by tapping into anti-Frelimo sentiments. The basis of these grievances are multiple. As noted above, the economic policies of the Frelimo government alienated the rural peasantry and created deep resentments of the collectivization program (Bowen 2000). Moreover, Frelimo's use of incarceration to "reeducate" political dissidents created a wellspring of ill-will against the party. The Frelimo government's hostility toward the Catholic Church also fostered divisions (Baloi 1996), as did Frelimo's targeting of chieftaincy structures, which the party saw as vestiges of Portuguese colonialism; these were important institutions to Renamo and its predominantly rural supporters (Harrison 1996). Finally, the overwhelmingly southern bias of the Frelimo leadership contributed to ethnolinguistic tensions and turned many residents of Mozambique's central provinces in particular—where the party's support was always tenuous—away from Frelimo (Weinstein 2002).

To some extent, then, several of Mozambique's important social cleavages correspond to divisions in the historical support bases for Frelimo and Renamo—as well as other minor parties. Mozambique is ethnically diverse as well as religiously plural.[3] Catholicism tends to be national and is represented in each of Mozambique's nine provinces, whereas Protestant churches are more concentrated regionally. Catholic clergy have offered criticisms of both parties, but Catholic lay people tend to support Renamo. Other religious identities, as with ethnic identities, tend to correspond to regional bases and are reflected in Renamo and Frelimo voting patterns.

Luis de Brito notes a severe regional split in parties' support bases in the 1994 elections. Frelimo's leaders historically come from the southern provinces (de Brito 1996, 470), and Frelimo's main areas of support are found in those four southern constituencies and in the far north. In the 1994 election, for example, Frelimo won three provinces, plus Maputo city in the south, and two in the northern region, Cabo Delgado and Niassa. The central area of the country was the site of the greatest activity by the Portuguese in their efforts to combat Frelimo, as well as the site where the Rhodesian government first established Renamo. Thus, this is a region both distrusted and disaffected historically by the regime. Likewise, people in Manica, Sofala, and Zambezia provinces in particular felt marginalized by the Frelimo state, not only as a result of their neglect during the war, but also due to long-standing policies of state socialism that effectively punished the peasantry (de Brito 1996, 472).

The Frelimo-Renamo divisions are more regional, social, and historical than ethnic. Yet whereas Mozambique does not have the degree of fractious ethnic-based politics seen elsewhere on the continent, the perception of a southern, urban bias in Frelimo was reinforced in the 2004 campaign. The fact that presidential candidate Guebuza also represents the "old guard" of Frelimo sent a signal as well to the electorate that little has changed in the party's orientation. On the other hand, the leadership hierarchy of Renamo has historically been predominantly Ndau, and "Ndau chauvinism" has been a defining feature of Renamo's existence (Vines 1996, 130)—so much so that the Ndau language became a lingua franca during the war (versus Portuguese in Frelimo) (Vines 1996, 83). Yet this Ndau chauvinism has not prevented Renamo from developing a national profile. Indeed, Frelimo may be more likely to be penalized electorally for its regional bias because it has a record of neglect of the central provinces.

Importantly, since 1994 the zone of conflict between Renamo and Frelimo and their supporters recently appears to be entrenched in the *political* arena. The stakes are increasingly about political power and policy delivery and, not inconsequentially, control over resources. Writing in 1996, Alex Vines observed that "Renamo has entered a new chapter in its history, its artificial origins and brutal reputation increasingly forgiven, though not forgotten, by communities across the country. . . . If Renamo exploits Frelimo's mistakes . . . and succeeds in transforming its election votes into grass-root support it stands a chance of becoming a future government" (1996, 193). This assessment may have proved premature, since Renamo made a series of tactical missteps in the intervening years, which are discussed below in the section on political parties. Nonetheless, the competitive 1999 elections revealed that Renamo and especially Dhlakama were seen by a large segment of the populace as viable alternatives to another decade of Frelimo rule.

Whereas a return to open hostilities appears highly unlikely, some scholars suggest that interparty tensions and escalating violence, evidenced by the deadly November 2000 clashes in Montepuez, Cabo Delgado province, should serve as "a warning" that political violence may "threaten the stability of the whole state" (Orre 2001, 190).[4] Interparty and interregional tensions remain in Mozambique and threaten to again boil over. Moreover, Renamo, and specifically Dhlakama, believe that they have been denied their rightful national political representation by Frelimo, both by fraudulent electoral practices and through malfeasance in various commissions. Frelimo, for its part, has regularly dismissed Renamo's (often illegitimate) concerns and resisted accommodation (Manning 2001, 163). Consequently, the relationship between the parties is increasingly zerosum, even though the electoral system theoretically protects minority party representation and positive-sum outcomes should be feasible. This suggests that the stakes in the December 2004 national election involved more than simply which party was entitled to form the next government. Although widespread interparty violence did not materialize in the run up to the election, it remains to be seen whether events like those in Montepuez in 2000 represent a mere "'bump in the road' to democracy and reconciliation" (Orre 2001, 193), or a harbinger of renewed conflict. Whereas most opposition leaders stopped far short of inciting violence, Renamo's unexpectedly large defeat in 2004 prompted claims of massive electoral fraud and possibly signaled an unwillingness to abide by the results ("Frelimo Wins" 2004). We regard as unlikely a return to violence on a measurable scale. Nonetheless, several fundamental structural conflicts and societal cleavages were not sufficiently addressed in the 1990s.

Finally, the cleavages in Mozambique do transcend the Frelimo-Renamo dichotomy. Indeed, the challenges that minority parties and interests face in accessing the political sphere are formidable. Mozambique's proportional representation electoral system in fact fails to accommodate minority interests because of a 5 percent electoral threshold. Frelimo's centralization of state authority, therefore, does more to inflame than diffuse conflicts.

■ Organization of the State

Mozambique is divided into ten provinces, plus the capital city, Maputo, which has the status of a province. Each province has a capital, which serves as the headquarters of the provincial government. The provinces in turn are subdivided into districts and localities. Despite this multitiered political architecture, Mozambique is a highly centralized polity with administrative power and functions vested in the national government in Maputo (Orre 2001). At the apex of this structure is a president who is head of state. The president appoints a prime minister, who serves as head of government, and he also appoints the ten provincial governors.

■ Executive

Directly elected by separate ballot in 1994, 1999, and 2004, a president with accountability to the voters (via the ballot at least) is still relatively new in Mozambique. When the Portuguese departed in 1975, no elections or national referenda were held: Samora Machel was simply appointed president of Mozambique and Frelimo was designated as the country's only legal party. Following President Machel's death in 1986, the Frelimo Central Committee designated Joaquim Chissano as his successor; only in 1994 did constitutional changes take effect permitting direct presidential election. International observers to the 1994 election certified the results as relatively free and fair, and Renamo and its presidential candidate Afonso Dhlakama accepted the results and agreed to cooperate with the Frelimo government in the new democratic order (Marshall and Jaggers 2001). Chissano, however, resisted calls for a government of national unity, designed on the South African model, and instead appointed an all-Frelimo government.

The Mozambican presidency is invested with substantial powers, and while Chissano is not widely suspected of abusing that authority, skeptics suggested that his pledge to step down was hollow and that he was planning a third term in office (Marshall and Jaggers 2001). Hence, when Chissano's pledge was confirmed commensurate with the ascendance of Armando Guebuza as his successor in 2002, this no doubt strengthened Chissano's legacy as a democratic leader. Ironically, however, it may have weakened his own presidency by making him a lame duck with a full two years remaining in office. The selection of Armando Guebuza, who was not preferred by Chissano, as "president-in-waiting" undermined President Chissano's authority, according to some sources (EIU 2002a, 7). Further, although Chissano was something of a darling of the international community, Guebuza is regarded as a hard-liner by both foreign and local observers. Indeed, though it is too soon to evaluate his approach to governing, as early as 2002, some observers suggested that a Guebuza presidency "has negative implications for the quality of governance and political pluralism in the country. He is closely associated with Frelimo's more authoritarian instincts and has been involved in human rights violations and other abuses in his previous positions in government" (EIU 2002a, 7).

What remains unclear at the time of writing is the status of the *institution* of the presidency in Mozambique. As we have seen most prominently in the cases of Zimbabwe and Zambia, even recognized democratic constitutions in southern Africa have fallen victim to strong executives who disregard such legal encumbrances. Until the 2004 election, at least, Mozambique diverged from the negative precedent set by its neighbors because a closely divided parliament between Frelimo and an alliance of Renamo and several minor parties acted as something of a bulwark against abuse of executive authority, even where other, and presumably more permanent, institutional constraints on executive domination themselves remained immature. The domination of the new legislature by Frelimo may alter this calculus.

Legal Institutions and Constraints on State Power

Judiciary. Mozambique's judicial system has been characterized by outside observers as stricken with "paralysis and incompetence," and much of the responsibility for this state of affairs is believed to rest with President Chissano, although it is not clear whether this results from neglect or a deliberate effort to undermine the judiciary (EIU 2002a, 13, 17). Even Mozambique's own Ministry of Justice described the judicial system as "sick," though it blamed this illness not on political interference, but on "obsolete laws" that lead to "'a frightful absence of ethics, zeal, and dedication' in entities charged with administering justice" (cited in Freedom House 2002). In any event, the massive backlog of judicial cases has "led to near impunity for criminal activity" (EIU 2002a, 13).[5] Freedom House (2002) notes overcrowded jails, excessively long detentions, and "rampant corruption," including frequent bribery of judges. In addition, the legal system is critically understaffed: just 170 judges and approximately 200 defense lawyers serve a population of 19 million. Perhaps more worrying, "many observers consider that the judicial paralysis is not accidental, but is encouraged to facilitate criminal activity and complicity at the highest level" (EIU 2002a, 18).

The 1975 constitution made little pretense of separation of powers and subjugated the courts to the government. After promulgation of the 1990 constitution, however, such political interference was supposed to be eliminated. Yet both interference with and neglect of the judicial branch were commonplace in the 1990s. Indeed, the lack of judicial independence and the excessive burdens on the system were each revealed in the aftermath of the 1999 elections.

According to the constitution (Article 167), the Supreme Court is intended to be the nation's highest court (having both appellate and original jurisdiction). In regard to constitutional matters and supervisory authority over the electoral process, however, a Constitutional Council, similar to South Africa's Constitutional Court, is supposed to have special jurisdiction that supersedes that of the Supreme Court (Article 181). Yet even by 1999 a Constitutional Council had not been formally established. Thus when Renamo alleged fraud in the 1999 election, the Supreme Court had to perform the duties of the nonexistent council. Acting in this expanded capacity, the court ruled in favor of Frelimo, and failed to address a number of issues raised by Renamo concerning the transparency and credibility of the count (Manning 2001, 157). These issues were unlikely to change the result, but the actions of the court failed to engender wider support for the legitimacy of the electoral process, and the courts (Carter Center 2000, 27). At bottom, a culture of judicial autonomy, or even competence, has yet to materialize.

Constitutionalism. The 1990 constitution was accepted by the all-Frelimo parliament in January 1990, and after substantial public debate it was formally signed in November of that year. It was promulgated without any formal inclusion of Renamo and other nascent opposition parties, which then called for the formation of a constituent assembly, but Frelimo rejected the idea (Alden 2001, 20). Renamo members were permitted to contribute to the constitutional debate as individuals, however. Moreover, since some of the provisions of the GPA, signed two years later, were incorporated into the constitution by amendment—notably provisions about the formation of political parties, freedom of association and expression, and details on the electoral process (which were later codified in a separate electoral law)— the final constitution was not objectionable to Renamo (Carrilho 1996, 129). The 1990 constitution superseded the 1975 constitution, which had established a one-party "people's republic," and the post of president was held by the party president of Frelimo (Carrilho 1996, 130).

Among the key provisions of the constitution are separation of powers, presidential term limits, the freedom to create political parties as "the expression of political pluralism . . . and the fundamental instruments for the democratic participation of citizens in the governing of the country" (*Constitution of Mozambique* 1990, pt. 1, chap. 3, art. 31), pluralism of opinion and the freedoms of expression and the press, the right to meet, associate, and demonstrate, and the establishment of legal equality between men and women "in all spheres of political, economic, social and cultural affairs" (Article 67). As a matter of practice, however, many of these impressive liberal dimensions of the 1990 constitution have been erratically applied and sporadically enforced. For example, the judiciary has not escaped executive interference, as discussed above. The violent clashes between the regime and Renamo supporters in Cabo Delgado and elsewhere in late 2000 also called into question the right of habeas corpus and freedom to demonstrate, rights enshrined in the constitution.

Lacking a strong constitutional tradition, Mozambique faces the challenge of living up to its constitution rather than having a poor-quality document. However, two prominent features constrained constitutional manipulation. As with other countries in the region, constitution alteration requires approval by a two-thirds majority in the National Assembly. The rough balance of power between Renamo and Frelimo in the legislature in the 1990s precluded abuse of the constitution by the ruling party.

This balance disappeared in 2004 when Frelimo's victory gave it 160 of 250 seats in the assembly—barely 7 seats short of a two-thirds majority. However, a feature not seen in other countries moves the debate from the partisan parliamentary realm to the population at large and provides a vital institutional safeguard against frivolous or politically driven constitutional changes: "If the proposed amendment implies fundamental changes in the rights of citizens or in the organization of public powers, the proposal, after adoption by the Assembly of the Republic, shall be submitted to public debate and to a referendum" (*Constitution of Mozambique* 1990, art. 199). This important provision would appear to safeguard the integrity of the constitution, insulating it from the type of political meddling witnessed elsewhere in the region.

■ Representation and Participation

▒ *Parliament*

Under the 1975 constitution, the ten provincial assemblies, plus the Maputo City Assembly, elected the National Assembly of the Republic (Carrilho 1996, 132–133). With effect from the first multiparty elections in 1994, however, the populace has a much greater role in political life, directly electing members of the 250-seat unicameral parliament. Still, constituency representation remains weak. As in South Africa, elections to parliament are conducted on a party list system with proportional representation. However, an important distinction is Mozambique's 5 percent threshold, which bars any party receiving less than 5 percent of the national vote from gaining a seat in the assembly. As discussed below in the section on political parties, this leads to considerable exclusion; in 1999, minor parties that collectively received nearly 13 percent of the vote gained no seats in parliament. Independent candidates are also barred from contesting parliamentary seats under the electoral law.[6] The combination of the threshold and the importance of parties privileges Renamo and Frelimo at the expense of smaller parties and their supporters.

The number of seats allotted to each constituency is based not on population, but on the number of registered voters in each constituency (Carrilho 1996, 137). This feature of the electoral law places extremely high importance on the voter registration exercise, yet because Mozambique engages in annual voter registration, this practice may actually result in more equitable and accurate distribution of deputies in the assembly. At the same time, however, it poses the risk that the most populous provinces may be underrepresented simply because of inadequate registration. It is necessary to point out that in recent elections, this apparently has not been the case: the most heavily populated provinces, Zambezia, Nampula, and Sofala—all Renamo strongholds—did receive the highest number of seats. Nevertheless, lingering questions about the neutrality and independence of the National Electoral Commission (CNE) and delimitation bodies must also raise concerns about the possibilities for illicit gerrymandering of parliamentary seats (Carter Center 2000).

Renamo rejected the idea of a majoritarian, single-member constituency system in the course of the Rome peace negotiations in 1992 (Carrilho 1996, 136). In the 1994 election, using the proportional representation system Renamo favored, it won 112 seats to Frelimo's 129. Political science research on electoral models in divided societies suggests that a proportional representation system facilitates positive-sum outcomes: various parties and their constituencies can gain seats in parliament proportional to their share of the vote (Lijphart 1977; Horowitz 1985; Sisk 1995). In the fragile context of postwar Mozambique, the application of a "winner-take-all" model might have risked reigniting the conflict. Renamo's deep discontent over its minority status since 1994 aside, it is a particular irony that, had the 1994 election been held under a majoritarian system, *Renamo* would have emerged with an absolute majority in parliament, 152 seats to just 98 for Frelimo (assuming the same provincial constituencies); in fact, Renamo would have swept the elections in Tete, Manica, Sofala, Zambezia, and Nampula provinces (Carrilho 1996, 139).

In the second legislative elections, held in December 1999, Frelimo again gained a majority, increasing to 133 seats, and Renamo, in partnership with several smaller parties under the banner Renamo-UE (Electoral Union), won 117 seats. Although no other party or coalition gained a seat because they failed to win 5 percent of the vote nationwide, Renamo-UE's significant presence in the assembly gave it a platform. Renamo has been able to influence national legislative debates, though it is incapable of effecting meaningful legislative change as the minority. The Mozambican system is strongly presidentialist, which makes it impossible for parliamentarians, particularly in opposition, to gain a platform to challenge presidential authority. Certainly the Frelimo majority has not impeded executive branch initiatives.

■ *National Elections and Electoral Institutions*

Until the adoption of the new constitution in 1990, National Assembly deputies were elected indirectly by the provincial assemblies. "There was a direct vote only in electing deputies at the grassroots level, namely to the popular assemblies in localities, villages and neighborhoods. In the election of district and provincial assemblies, the votes were cast by delegates at electoral conferences," rather than directly by voters (Carrilho 1996, 132–133). Hence, absent meaningful authority and voting at the popular level, there was scant need for an electoral infrastructure.

The Electoral Law of Mozambique (Law no. 4 of 1993) established the National Electoral Commission. The CNE consists of an unwieldy nineteen members, appointed to five-year terms by the president, although some are proposed by opposition parties. In the 1999 elections, the CNE was viewed as partisan toward Frelimo. This is not surprising; indeed, questions about electoral commission independence, frequently justified, have proved endemic in Africa's transitional democracies. Many CNE procedures were ad hoc, largely because of ambiguities in the 1999 electoral law, and there was a lack of transparency in the critical final stages of vote tabulation (Carter Center 2000, 30). Yet these are precisely the elements an opposition needs to trust the integrity of the process and the legitimacy of the final result: well-defined electoral laws and an independent commission. Indeed, Renamo members of the CNE refused to validate the results in 1999 and filed the complaint with the Supreme Court.

The 1999 elections were the first in the era of "normal politics." Whereas the number of registered voters climbed from 6.2 million in 1994 to 7.1 million in 1999, turnout among registered voters fell from 5.4 million (88 percent) in 1994 to 4.8 million (just over 68 percent) in 1999. Although still an impressive level for the region, the lower turnout in 1999 reflects the lower stakes—peace was no longer on the ballot—and diminished popular expectations. (Local government elections in 1998, discussed below, may have also depressed enthusiasm for the 1999 election. Renamo boycotted in 1998, and turnouts ranged between just 6 and 15 percent.) In any event, the election was close, and unexpectedly so at the presidential level, where Chissano defeated Dhlakama by a margin of 52.3 percent to 47.7 percent.

In January 2000 the Supreme Court found in favor of Frelimo. Although the court acknowledged that about 377,773 potential valid votes had been excluded in the vote-tallying process, it did not provide any further information about their provincial distribution, their probable impact on the election outcome, or the fact that this figure significantly exceeded Chissano's margin of victory (205,593 votes) (Carter Center 2000, 27). As noted earlier, Dhlakama would have had to receive the overwhelming majority of these excluded votes, which was unlikely, to alter the final result (Manning 2001). Yet the lack of transparency damaged the integrity of the electoral system.

Denied recourse through the courts, Dhlakama announced initially that Renamo would refuse to take its seats in parliament, but subsequently reconsidered (Manning 2001, 163–164). Although its parliamentary boycott backfired, Renamo was joined by other political and civic groups, as well as international observers, in calling for revisions to the electoral law and removal of its apparent contradictions. Also demanded was a restructuring of electoral institutions, namely the CNE and the Technical Secretariat for the Administration of Elections, the administrative arm of election management institutions, which operates only during elections. A multiparty Parliamentary Advisory Commission was established to revise both parliamentary procedures regarding elections and the structure of the CNE and to make needed changes to the electoral laws at the local and municipal and national levels. However, this body was beset by partisanship and was unable to reach consensus between its Frelimo and opposition members on the extent of reforms (EIU 2002a, 17). Manning (2001, 164–165) suggests that much of the blame for the failure of various such commissions lies with Renamo, which often seemed to prefer the spoiler role to that of partner.

■ The 2004 Elections

The December 2004 elections for the Assembly of the Republic and the presidency resulted in a decisive victory for Frelimo and for its presidential candidate, Armando Guebuza. In the legislative contest, Frelimo garnered some 62 percent of the vote, whereas Renamo could muster only 29.7 percent; the remainder went to minor parties, all of which failed to reach the 5 percent threshold for representation. As a result, Frelimo was awarded 160 seats, whereas Renamo's parliamentary representation fell to 90 seats from its previous level of 117. Guebuza, for his part, amassed more than double the votes of Afonso Dhlakama: approximately 2 million (63.7 percent) to 998,000 (31.7 percent) ("Frelimo Wins" 2004). Given the closeness of the 1999 election, at the parliamentary and especially the presidential level, the magnitude of the Frelimo victory is striking. Moreover, although overall voter turnout fell precipitously from 5.3 million in 1999 to just 3.5 million in 2004 (approximately 45 percent of registered voters), this redounded chiefly to the detriment of Dhlakama, who "has lost more than 1 million supporters in the past five years" (Mozambique Political Process Bulletin).

Perhaps not surprisingly, the electoral process was marred by allegations from Renamo and the minor opposition parties of massive fraud on the part of Frelimo and the electoral administration. Although such charges had by this time become a familiar Renamo tactic, they were not entirely without merit. Indeed, there was evidence of a number of irregularities, as reported by domestic and international observers. These included flawed voter registration, inflated turnouts in favor of Frelimo, wrongfully invalidated ballots, and police intimidation of opposition supporters in some areas ("Frelimo Wins" 2004). In addition, there were logistical problems associated with poor data collection techniques and "computer chaos" by the Technical Secretariat for Electoral Administration (STAE) office in Maputo, resulting in a delayed vote count (Mozambique Political Process Bulletin). Nevertheless, whereas these and other problems raised justifiable concerns, many of the broader accusations could not be substantiated by independent observers; most concluded therefore that the irregularities were not of such a systematic and national scale that they would measurably alter the outcome.

A number of questions have emerged in the wake of the 2004 contest and the altered political landscape. As we have discussed throughout the chapter, a major concern is what Frelimo and President Guebuza will do with their vastly expanded mandate, and conversely, how Renamo and Dhlakama will adjust now that their opportunities to govern appear foreclosed. For the wider populace, the low turnout—a third lower than in 1999—raises several concerns. Whereas turnout was at least in part affected by the onset of the rainy season in Mozambique, it may also reflect, more worryingly, voter apathy. Frustration with the available political alternatives, and perhaps the political process itself, on the part of its citizenry introduces serious challenges to Mozambique's ongoing democratization.

■ Political Parties: Accommodation or Exclusion?

From two-party to dominant party system? At this point it should be clear that the principal political cleavage in Mozambique is between Frelimo and Renamo and their supporters, although this takes on regional, ethnic, and in some cases religious overtones. Historically, the president of Frelimo was also its presidential candidate. Chissano retained this top leadership post in the party, however, leaving Armando Guebuza to contest the national presidency from the position of Frelimo secretary-general, which he was appointed to in June 2002. In one sense, this is a healthy development, since it allows greater separation of party from government.

At the same time, the division of offices exposes Frelimo to internal divisions based on conflicting loyalties and competition between the two leaders.[7] Indeed, after his retirement from office in 2001, President Frederick Chiluba of Zambia also attempted to retain the party leadership of the Movement for Multiparty Democracy (MMD). What Zambians and MMD partisans discovered, however, was that this arrangement was unsustainable, as it engendered competition with his successor, Levy Mwanawasa (also of the MMD), and led to nagging questions about Chiluba's eligibility for state benefits and his status in the party and in the country. Chiluba was forced to eventually relinquish the leadership of the party when the situation became untenable.

Dhlakama faces no such dilemma in Renamo, where his leadership appears unchallenged, especially after expulsion of other senior members after 2000. As a militia movement founded and promoted by external actors to destabilize independent Mozambique, Renamo had no covering ideology, nor, initially, much grassroots support (Vines 1996; Minter 1994). Not until the mid-1980s did Renamo begin to articulate a position loosely favoring a market economy and political democracy, though more a reaction to Frelimo than a clearly defined ideology (Minter 1994). Frelimo itself was changing in the mid-1980s, becoming increasingly capitalist in orientation and accepting multipartyism. In 1987, Frelimo adopted a structural adjustment program, which entailed a "fundamental rethinking of [its previous] economic model," and in 1989 dropped Marxism-Leninism as the official state ideology (Simpson 1993, 329). A year later the multiparty constitution was adopted. In short, Renamo's principal means of differentiating itself was as being anti-Frelimo. In fact, according to some observers, a dearth of ideology and a limited political platform continue to characterize Renamo, whose raison d'être remains its opposition to that of Frelimo, personalized in Dhlakama himself.[8] The expulsions of some of the top leaders in Renamo, including, prominently, former number-two Raul Domingos in 2000, has further concentrated power in the hands of Dhlakama.

Notwithstanding Renamo's difficulties, a decade of democratic governance left Mozambique looking very much like a two-party state, which the electoral system helps to preserve. Yet the depiction of Mozambican politics solely as a two-party competition between Frelimo and Renamo is misleading. For example, at least ten minor parties allied with Renamo in 1999 in order to secure some parliamentary seats in the UE (EIU 2002a). Moreover, fourteen other parties contested the parliamentary elections in 1994 and twelve did so in 1999. These continue to represent a substantial percentage of the electorate, despite having scant official representation in the assembly.

In 1994, almost 18 percent of the electorate chose parties other than Renamo or Frelimo, yet the 5 percent threshold denied all these voters representation except those who voted for the Democratic Union. The share of votes for minor parties dropped to about 13 percent in the 1999 election, but this still amounted to over half a million people. Despite its increased share of parliamentary seats, Frelimo was stung by its performance, particularly the six provinces in the central part of the country that it lost to Renamo. Hence it quickly began to focus its energies out in the districts and the municipal areas in preparation for the 2004 national elections.

For its part Renamo appears ill-prepared to build on its gains in the 1999 election or take advantage of Frelimo changes at the presidential level. Recent internal tensions, including the dismissal of key lieutenants, as well as unexpectedly poor performance in the November 2003 local government elections, have hurt. At one point, the emergence of a so-called third force (in addition to the two major parties) of united new and existing opposition groups was thought to hold electoral promise, but this now appears unlikely. One such party, the Party for Peace, Development, and Democracy (PDD) (formerly a nongovernmental organization known as the Institute for Peace and Democracy, IPADE), led by former Renamo leader and member of parliament Raul Domingos, contested the December 2003 local and municipal elections and the 2004 national election but fared quite badly. Domingos, who ran as a presidential candidate himself, spoke of a need to "fill up a vacuum between Renamo and Frelimo" ("Mozambique's Former Rebel" 2003); in fact, Renamo's difficulties will likely redound to Frelimo's benefit, rather than to third parties.

Division and exclusion. In July 2000, President Chissano appointed ten provincial governors, all from Frelimo. Dhlakama had insisted that Renamo be awarded the positions in the six central provinces in which it won majorities in 1999. The presumed benefits of proportional representation at the national parliamentary level were thus offset by the lack of provincial autonomy. Combined with Frelimo's domination of the local and municipal spheres, discussed in greater detail below, the party obtained a virtual monopoly on power at all levels of government. Not surprisingly, dialogue between the parties was extremely difficult in an atmosphere of mutual recriminations and Renamo's quite public frustration. After failing to make headway on the governorships, Dhlakama announced in July 2000 that "the Renamo Electoral Union and Dhlakama will no longer cooperate in the maintenance of peace in this country. . . . I will no longer appeal to the people to avoid violence. That is to say, from today, people can start acts of violence as they have wanted to do since January. I am not calling on anyone to be violent, but I will no longer stop my supporters from demonstrating against the despotism of Chissano" ("Renamo Boycotts" 2000).

For its part, Frelimo appeared to send mixed messages to its chief rival. On the one hand, Frelimo policies were hardly conciliatory.

Following both the 1994 and 1999 elections, it governed as if the polity were not deeply divided, which of course it was. Yet, Chissano himself suggested that Frelimo's attempts to negotiate with Renamo in good faith on a range of political and economic initiatives were routinely greeted with suspicion by Dhlakama and quickly rejected.[9] Indeed, Renamo confirmed that it was suspicious of Chissano's motives and resentful of his apparent disrespect for the party.[10] It is unlikely that Chissano's retirement offers enhanced opportunities for rapprochement: Guebuza reportedly holds an even dimmer view of Renamo (EIU 2002a).

■ Local Elections and (De-)Centralization

There are just 33 municipalities in Mozambique, although some 411 additional localities were excluded from the municipal governments system because of capacity constraints (Weinstein 2002, 152). The first elections for control over municipal governments (municipal assemblies and municipal presidents), in 1998, were boycotted by Renamo. This left Frelimo with overwhelming majorities, which it maintained in the 2003 municipal elections despite Renamo's participation. Given its strong electoral support in more than half the provinces (notwithstanding its record in the municipalities),[11] Renamo endorsed greater decentralization while objecting to the ill-defined boundaries between "municipal" and "provincial" authority. Indeed, this ambiguity was the principal justification for its 1998 boycott: since Frelimo controlled the gubernatorial posts already, municipal governments could exercise little autonomy, "simply adding more to Frelimo's plate."[12]

Renamo's indictment of Mozambique's centralized state is a reasonable one. Subnational governance structures are quite weak in Mozambique, and municipal as well as provincial governments are dependent on the national government for resources. Moreover, despite some efforts at decentralization, the effective delivery of services by these local governments to the communities they purportedly serve has been quite limited (Orre 2001). The state president appoints all of the provincial governors, who in turn control appointments to every other administrative level down to the district, and the municipal structures are few in number. Consequently, national elections, particularly presidential, take on added importance; rather than diffusing competition, such a system concentrates it. However, as Jeremy Weinstein (2002, 152) observes, "given the bloodiness of Mozambique's recent history, this system should be cause for grave concern."

■ Civil Society

Mozambican civil society is only now emerging from years of war and statist control. In contrast to much of the rest of the region, civil society appears less mobilized in Mozambique. This is not altogether different from Zimbabwe following its independence in 1980, where it took nearly a decade for civil society to find its voice. The empowerment of labor unions, human rights organizations, and the media was delayed by the need to recover from a protracted war and by state elites initially unaccustomed to pluralism. In Mozambique, civil society organizations (CSOs) remain less prominent than in neighboring states. However, there are a number of non-governmental organizations (NGOs) operating in the fields of human rights, such as the Mozambican Human Rights League, and democracy, such as the Mozambique Association for the Development of Democracy, that criticize government. In addition, organizations operate in the areas of gender, health, and development, for example, as well as under the auspices of Christian or Islamic bodies. Several independent media outlets have also emerged in the past decade.

As the sociopolitical climate liberalized, groups have become less inhibited about critiques of government policy. They criticize a lack of consultation by the government, particularly on development initiatives. Although admonishing Frelimo for trying to claim credit for its various development initiatives smacks of naiveté, some CSO criticisms of Frelimo's exclusive approach are cause for concern. For example, the national development program, Agenda 2025, Mozambique's participation in the African Union, the decision to join the British Commonwealth, and the World Bank–funded PRSP each necessitated wide consultation but received little, according to the government's critics.[13] Yet whereas civil society is adjusting to expanded opportunities and an altered role since the constitutional changes of the 1990s, so too is the state. Its history is one of top-down, hierarchical decisionmaking.

The small independent media has faced challenges as a watchdog. A 1990 press law for the first time allowed privately owned media companies and guaranteed press freedoms (da Silva 1996, 58). In response, a number of privately owned newspapers emerged prior to the 1994 election. In addition, two major government-owned newspapers, the daily *Noticias* and the weekly *Domingo,* were privatized in 1993 under a holding company, Noticias SRL. However, the two major shareholders in Noticias SRL are the Bank of Mozambique and the National Insurance Company, both parastatals. Predictably, these newspapers are still beholden to the state, if indirectly, and have shown obvious bias toward Frelimo, particularly in election periods (Carter Center 2000, 16). State-owned television, which is not widely available throughout the country, and state radio, which is, display similar partiality toward the ruling party while demonizing Renamo.

Among independent outlets, which include several private radio and television stations, the newsletters *Metical* and *Mediafax,* both of which are faxed to subscribers, are among the most successful. However, their readership is limited by their method of distribution and widespread illiteracy in rural areas. *Mediafax* was formed in 1992 by a cooperative called Mediacoop. Its editor, the highly regarded Carlos Cardoso (da Silva 1996, 67), was assassinated in November 2000 while investigating a scandal related to the privatization of the Commercial Bank of Mozambique in which several Frelimo elites were implicated. Cardoso's death had a chilling effect, and "criminal libel laws are another important deterrent to open expression" (Freedom House 2002).

■ Political Economy and Development

After it was rejected by COMECON in 1981, Mozambique increasingly looked to the West for assistance in securing the country's economic future. In 1984 it joined the World Bank and International Monetary Fund (IMF) and in 1985 it received its first International Development Assistance (IDA) loan. For all intents and purposes, Mozambique had by this time moved away from its always tenuous commitment to Marxism-Leninism. Indeed, U.S. economic assistance also increased greatly in the 1980s. In 1987, Mozambique committed itself firmly to the neoliberal path when it adopted an IMF structural adjustment program, which it called the Economic Rehabilitation Program (PRE) (Berman 1996, 57). The PRE legitimized pursuit of individual profit and, in so doing, undermined much of the legitimacy of Frelimo party leaders, who took advantage of market-based opportunities, like privatization, to enrich themselves (Bowen 2000, 198; Pitcher 2003). This opportunism and use of political office for economic gain accelerated in the 1990s (EIU 2002a), and growing popular resentment over Frelimo's consumption and perceived corruption may cost Frelimo the government in 2004. As Merle Bowen (2000, 198) argues, the economic transition begun in the 1980s markedly increased the scope for corruption, which had been "prevalent but petty in the past." The new economic regime has been accompanied by rampant corruption. For example, some U.S.$805 million has been lost in untaxed exports due to corruption among customs officials. One of the most publicized scandals, however, involved the Commercial Bank of Mozambique, from which U.S.$11.5 million disappeared before the institution was privatized in 1996 (Alden 2001, 118). Investigation of this theft, as noted above, led to the murder of journalist Carlos Cardoso.

Frelimo appears to lack the crises of conscience or of identity revealed in the occasional populism of its Marxist-turned-capitalist counterparts in Zimbabwe and South Africa. However, whereas those countries at least had long-standing historical linkages to peasants (Zimbabwe) or workers (South Africa) that could be reinvigorated if politically necessary, Frelimo's "abandonment of Marxism-Leninism [in 1989] only ended its 'official' alliance with peasants and workers. In practice, this alliance had been fraudulent for decades" (Bowen 2000, 200). The election of Guebuza, holder of an expansive business empire and one of the richest men in Mozambique (EIU 2002a), hardly signals that Frelimo will attempt to run on anything but a globalist, neoliberal agenda—regardless of the abject poverty suffered by most of the electorate.

From a global perspective, Mozambique's economy has grown at a phenomenal rate since the early 1990s, and has been labeled in some quarters an "African newly industrializing country" (Nordas and Pretorius 2000). Indeed, the economy grew at over 9 percent per year from 1997 through 2001 in real terms. Although it experienced only 2.1 percent growth in 2000 due to damaging record floods, growth rebounded to 13.9 percent in 2001 (EIU 2002a). The country has also seen some benefits of the enhanced highly indebted poor country initiative, resulting in an external debt reduction from $7.6 billion in 1997 to $787 million in 1998; currently the external debt stands at approximately $683 million (EIU 2002a).

The government published its PRSP in October 2001, the goals of which are "to achieve high rates of sustainable, poverty-reducing growth, consolidate macroeconomic stability, and achieve a quantitative and qualitative increase in the delivery of social service" (EIU 2002a, 8). As in other countries such as Zambia and Malawi, the PRSP program was undertaken as a prerequisite for the advanced highly indebted poor country initiative. A locally owned version, the Action Plan for the Reduction of Absolute Poverty (PARPA), was under way before the PRSP process began, which may be a positive sign that Mozambique's leaders are genuinely concerned about poverty reduction.[14] This version was not signed off in parliament, but was undertaken at the cabinet level and largely technocratic, a move that was criticized sharply by Renamo and several NGOs. This is not unlike in Zambia and Malawi, where recent PRSP strategies were also not widely shared with legislative branches (see Bwalya et al. 2003). Unlike the Zambian and Malawian experiences, however, churches, unions, clubs, and associations were left out of Mozambique's PRSP/PARPA poverty reduction process altogether.

The improved macroeconomic picture and desire of the donors to make Mozambique a "success case" has also aided foreign direct investment (FDI) inflows. Stability and favorable policies led to marked increases in FDI following the war. From 1989 to 1994, FDI averaged an anemic U.S.$21 million per year, but increased to an average of U.S.$153 million from 1995 to 2000 (EIU 2002a, 28). Indeed, in 1997 alone, U.S.$1.8 billion in new foreign investment projects were approved, although U.S.$1.3 billion alone was related to the Mozal aluminum smelter plant. Most FDI, including investment in the smelter project and the development of a major gas pipeline, has come from neighboring South Africa (EIU 2002a).

Mozambique's economic achievements, while remarkable, must be viewed in their historical context. First, whereas recent debt reduction, for example, may be claimed as a victory for the World Bank and the highly indebted poor country program, it is also a just result, considering that much of Mozambique's debt could be considered "odious debt" accumulated in the 1980s in the country's effort to resist destruction by first the Rhodesian armed forces, and later by the SADF and its proxy, Renamo. Indeed, the economic costs of the war from 1977–1992 have been estimated at U.S.$15 billion—including destruction of infrastructure and an estimated 1 million deaths and 5 million displacements (Vines 1996, 1).

Second, Mozambique was at the very bottom of the global economic ladder; thus, even at annual growth rates of 9 to 12 percent, it will still take many years to produce significant structural improvements in the lives of average citizens. As with its neighbors, Mozambique principally exports its primary commodities. Yet Mozambique's particular array of goods scarcely provides the necessary mix for meaningful development. Global demand for such basic commodity exports as prawns (31 percent), cashew nuts (17.4 percent), and cotton (9.5 percent) is limited (EIU 2002a). Moreover, until 2000, the biggest market was Zimbabwe, which has since been devastated by crisis, followed by South Africa. However ironic, Mozambique's economic performance and stability have transformed it into a major aid recipient: such foreign inflows amounted to 36 percent of GDP from 1994 to 1998 (Nordas and Pretorius 2000, 24). In sum, Mozambique's service economy, debt relief, and inflows of international aid are vital, if not necessarily sustainable, components of its near-term economic future. Mozambique still ranks among the world's—and even the region's—poorest countries. The economic boom that has brought such dramatic change and acclaim to Mozambique has been accompanied by deepening inequality. How the state, whose economic functions have been curtailed through liberalization, will address these concerns remains an open question (Pitcher 2003, 264).

■ Challenges for the Twenty-First Century

A dozen years after its historic peace agreement and a decade after its first multiparty elections, Mozambique would appear to be on a path of relative democratic stability and impressive economic growth that few might have predicted. The prelude to the December 2004 presidential elections represented a milestone in Mozambique's modern history. Initially it appeared that the retirement of President Chissano presented a genuine opportunity for *alternance* and for deepening democracy. Indeed, Chissano set an important precedent by announcing in 2001 that he would step aside, allowing Renamo and other opposition groups to prepare for a competitive contest against a nonincumbent.

Clearly the outcome of the 2004 election obviates questions about Renamo's readiness to rule. Yet the situation presents a number of other potential perils. Frelimo's victory sets Mozambique on the path toward one-party dominance. Although this need not, in and of itself, imperil democracy (as the case of Botswana illustrates), Frelimo's style in ten years as the government of a multiparty system has been tailored toward exclusion rather than coalition, and this threatens to worsen under Armando Guebuza's presidency. Guebuza is reportedly even less prepared to compromise with the opposition than his predecessor. This may be of little consequence if the "normal politics" of the past decade is not simply a transient phase. On the other hand, Mozambique remains divided—by rural versus urban residency, by region, by ethnicity, and increasingly by wealth—and the ability of Frelimo alone to speak to the needs of this diverse populace is as much in question today as it was during the war. Hence Frelimo's domination at every level of politics is a potential source of conflict. Renamo, for its part, has matured enormously since its days as a brutal rebel movement with no ideological base and little local legitimacy. Yet time and again under Afonso Dhlakama's leadership, Renamo has dug in its heels where it should have compromised, bluffed where it should have cooperated. It is likely that Renamo will continue to fit quite uneasily, if at all, into the role of "loyal opposition."

Should President Guebuza and the new parliament continue to pursue destabilizing tit-for-tat strategies, a major concern has to be the country's institutions. Key institutions such as the constitutional council, the electoral bodies, and local governments, remain weak, lack autonomy, and appear ill-equipped to manage social conflict effectively. At the same time, institutions of civil society do not yet appear sufficiently widespread and vigorous to offer a meaningful bulwark against the misuse of state power. Although such outcomes may be more difficult under a one-party dominant regime, the strengthening of Mozambique's democratic institutions and the creation of a more equitable and sustainable economy must be top priorities for the new government.

■ Notes

1. Frelimo initially blamed the Portuguese for the assassination, but it is now widely accepted that his murder was part of a leadership struggle within Frelimo (Weinstein 2002, 145–146).

2. As of 1996, the new FADM had less than half its prescribed complement, and represented one of the region's weakest armed forces (Vines 1996). Under UN guidance, the main failing was not the inability to recruit new troops, but rather the failure to confiscate small arms, which are today widely available.

3. The country's thirteen main national languages are Emakhuwa, Xitsonga, Ciyao, Cisena, Cishona, Echuwabo, Cinyanja, Xironga, Shimaconde, Cinyungue, Cicopi, Bitonga, and Kiswahili. There is also significant religious pluralism: African traditional (31.9 percent), Christian (Roman Catholic 24.1 percent and

Protestant 21.5 percent), Muslim (19.7 percent), Hindu (0.04 percent), other (0.6 percent), and unspecified (2.2 percent) (Baloi 1996, 487). There are Muslim majorities in Niassa and Cabo Delgado, and a strong plurality (41.6 percent) in Nampula province.

4. Officially, some forty-four people were killed in initial early November clashes in the north (mainly Cabo Delgado) between police and Renamo supporters, who were demonstrating against Frelimo. Later that month, eighty-four Renamo supporters died in the Montepuez prison cells, reportedly of asphyxiation. A number of reports of political murders followed (Orre 2001, 191–219).

5. For example, the Supreme Court heard 298 cases in 2001; however, the number of cases still pending by year end totaled 1,126. Similar backlogs existed at lower levels of the judiciary as well, according to the EIU (2002a, 17).

6. However, when Renamo expelled five of its MPs from the party, including, in 2000, former leader of the Renamo parliamentary bench and Rome negotiator Raul Domingos, the Frelimo majority argued that the constitution allowed them to keep their seats as independents until 2004. The other four former Renamo members were Almeida Tambara, Chico Francisco, Rachide Tayob, and José Henriques Lopes.

7. Indeed, in the late 1990s it became apparent that splits were emerging between the Frelimo "old guard" and younger members, although the party took some steps to address this divide in its 2002 congress (EIU 2002a).

8. Author interviews with the diplomatic and NGO community, Maputo, June 14–15, 2001.

9. Author interview with Joachim Chissano, June 14, 2001.

10. Author interview with Chico Francisco, Renamo secretary of external affairs, June 14, 2001.

11. Renamo's electoral strength lies in the rural areas, not the urban municipalities (Orre 2001, 85).

12. Author interview with Chico Francisco, June 14, 2001.

13. Author interview with LINK (NGO coalition) leaders, June 16, 2001; author interview with IPADE leadership, Maputo, Mozambique, June 16, 2001.

14. Author interview with Department for International Development (UK) personnel, Mozambique office, Maputo, Mozambique, June 15, 2001.

6

Angola: Peace and the Predatory State

In June 1993 when Margaret Anstee, the UN's special representative, left Angola after overseeing failed elections that were supposed to mark the end of decades of war and herald the start of a new era for Angola, she called the country "the forgotten tragedy" (Pycroft 1994). A decade later, Angola could still be described as a tragedy, but one that had garnered some regional and international attention and that was inching beyond its tragic past. Since April 2002 a cease-fire had been in place between the ruling forces of the Popular Movement for the Liberation of Angola (MPLA) and the rebel forces of the National Union for the Total Independence of Angola (UNITA), and by mid-2004 peace had clearly taken hold. While problems persisted, the demobilization of UNITA troops was complete and, as UNITA made the transition from a rebel movement to a political party, competition was slowly shifting from the battlefield to the arena of party politics. National elections, for the first time in more than a decade, were slated to occur sometime in 2005 or 2006, and a small group of civil society organizations was beginning to assert itself. In the meantime, the MPLA government was under pressure to reach a new economic reform agreement with the International Monetary Fund (IMF) that would in turn facilitate a donors' conference to solicit international assistance for the reconstruction and development of the war-torn country. Increased oil production was contributing to rising economic growth rates for Angola in the early 2000s.

And yet for the majority of Angolans, life remained quite desperate. Large parts of the country's social and economic infrastructure were destroyed or simply collapsed during twenty-seven years of postindependence war. Four million Angolans were internally displaced by the war, 2.6 million since 1998, with most fleeing to urban areas (Tvedten 2002, 12). Among other things, Angolans were fleeing millions of land mines that littered the countryside, making cultivation of the land impossible and imperiling people's lives. As a result of the land mines, Angola ranked first

Angola: Country Data

Land area 1,246,700 km²
Capital Luanda
Date of independence November 11, 1975
Population 13.5 million, 35% urban
Languages Portuguese (official), other African languages
Ethnic groups Ovimbundu, 37%; Kimbundu, 25%; Bakongo, 13%;
    Mestico, 2%; European, 1%; other, 22%
Religions indigenous beliefs, 47%; Roman Catholic, 38%; Protestant,
    15% (1998 estimate)
Currency kwanza (AOA); kwanza per U.S. dollar: 58.17 (July 2003)

Literacy rate 42.0%
Life expectancy 40.2 years (male, 38.8 years; female, 41.6 years)
Infant mortality 154 per 1,000 live births

GDP per capita U.S.$701
GDP per capita (PPP) U.S.$2,040
GDP per capita growth rate −1.1% (1990–2001)

Leaders since independence
• Agostino Neto, president, November 1975–September 1979
• José Eduardo dos Santos, president, September 1979–

Major political parties
    Ruling party: Popular Movement for the Liberation of Angola
        (MPLA)
    Other parties: National Union for the Total Independence of
        Angola (UNITA)
    Liberal Democratic Party (PLD)
    National Front for the Liberation of Angola (FNLA)
    Social Renewal Party (PRS)

Women in parliament (lower/single house) 15.5% (1992)

Note: Data from 2001 unless otherwise indicated.

in the world in number of amputees (Pycroft 1994, 242).[1] As a result of the inability to cultivate the land, half of all Angolans were undernourished and many Angolans relied upon international donors for their food. The public health system in the country had been "reduced to a shambles" (Agadjanian and Prata 2001, 330). Life expectancy at birth in Angola (not yet hit by the AIDS crisis in the same way as other southern African countries) was a mere forty years, and the infant mortality rate was 154 per 1,000 live births, one of the highest in Africa. Even more dramatic, the child mortality rate for children under five was 295 per 1,000 children. There were 5 doctors for every 100,000 people in Angola (a rate among the very lowest in the world) and, not surprisingly, the government spent just 2 percent of gross domestic product (GDP) on health. In the education sector Angola had the distinction of one of the lowest adult literacy rates in sub-Saharan Africa, around 42 percent. Only 37 percent of primary school–age children attended school—again, well below even the sub-Saharan African average (59 percent) (United Nations Development Programme [UNDP] 2003).

These very poor socioeconomic indicators are all the more damning given that Angola is potentially a tremendously wealthy country—endowed with vast oil reserves, gas, diamonds, fertile land on which to grow coffee and other agricultural products, and powerful rivers from which to generate hydroelectricity to sell to neighboring countries. Moreover, Angola has a long coastline and a transport infrastructure that, once rehabilitated, would make it a transportation center for the region. Indeed, Angola's location ties it closely to economies in southern and central Africa and positions it well to become further integrated into and benefit from both. Finally, its capacity to wield military power abroad is also significant. Given these resources, Angola should vie with South Africa for regional superpower status in southern Africa, a role with which Angola's government may already identify (International Crisis Group 2003a, 15).

Not counting Zimbabwe, Angola is the last country in southern Africa to attempt a transition from a very bleak past.[2] Indeed, as Tony Hodges (2004, 199) points out, Angola is actually attempting "a quadruple transition: from war to peace and reconciliation; from humanitarian emergency to rehabilitation, recovery and development; from an authoritarian, one-party system of governance to pluralist democracy; and from a command economy to one based on the laws of the market." As many have observed, each of these transitions would be a tremendous challenge on its own—and Angola faces all four simultaneously. At the same time, Mozambique, with which Angola shares so many common experiences, has made considerable progress over the past decade with these same transitions. Some have suggested that Angola's generous resource endowment, in stark contrast to Mozambique's relative lack of natural resources, goes a long way toward explaining its continued struggle to accomplish these transitions in the 1990s and early 2000s

(Munslow 1999, cited in Hodges 2004, 199). As will be elaborated later in the chapter, the abundance of mineral resources in Angola clearly allowed war to continue as long as it did (long after other wars in the region had ceased)—on the one hand providing a powerful loot-seeking motive for fighting to win or to hold on to power (Collier and Hoeffler 1999, cited in Hodges 2004, 203), and on the other hand providing the means by which both sides could finance their war efforts. In addition, access to resources allowed the government to become and remain fully unaccountable to its people—revenues have been completely mismanaged and outright corruption has become rampant—with the result that a very small elite thrives while the majority of Angolans live in near desperation, bereft of the most basic social services and many of the most basic political rights.

■ Historical Origins of the Angolan State

As in a number of southern African countries, the first inhabitants of what is today Angola were the Khoisan peoples. From the eighth century onward, they were joined by Bantu-speaking peoples from western Africa, during two distinct waves—from the north and from the east—which were part of the great Bantu migrations east and south. The main influx of these peoples into Angola occurred during the fourteenth century, just before the arrival of the Portuguese. By 1500 most of Angola was populated by Bantu-speaking peoples, who first lived in peaceful coexistence with, and later largely absorbed, the original Khoisan population (Tvedten 1997, 10–11). According to Inge Tvedten (1997, 11), "most of the Bantu groups mixed and intermarried with each other and had contact through conquest and trade, but they still maintained distinct ethnic characteristics, including differences in dialect." Over time, villages joined together to form chiefdoms, which were later consolidated to form kingdoms. By the mid–fifteenth century, the Kongo kingdom—the most important of the Angolan kingdoms—stretched over large parts of northern Angola. Other important kingdoms included the Loango kingdom of the Vili in present-day Cabinda, the Mbundu kingdom of Ndongo, the Matamba and Kasanje kingdoms, the Lunda kingdom, and the Kwanyama kingdom, on the border with Namibia. The Ovimbundu people arrived in the southern part of the territory between 1400 and 1600 but never developed a kingdom (Tvedten 1997, 14–16).

The first Europeans to arrive in Angola were the Portuguese, who reached the Angolan coast in 1483, where they encountered the Kongo kingdom. Initially, contacts between the Kongo and the Portuguese were to some extent mutually beneficial. Moreover, according to Tvedten:

> Kongo and Portugal were at this time in many respects on the same economic level. Both were monarchies ruled by kings and a class of nobles in

which relations of kinship and clientage dominated the political system. Social indicators like life expectancy and infant mortality were roughly the same in both societies. Both societies had primarily agrarian economies, and both possessed general purpose money and were heavily involved in trade. (1997, 17–18)

The two groups were very different, however, in that the Portuguese possessed firearms and a superior transport technology that allowed them to move goods, including people, across oceans. Indeed, the Portuguese quickly became involved in a transatlantic slave trade transporting Angolans, first, to sugar plantations in São Tomé and, beginning in 1550, to sugar plantations in Brazil. Relations between the Portuguese and the Kongo quickly soured as Portuguese traders, missionaries, and officials began to interfere in internal Kongolese affairs. Moreover, the slave trade also began to weaken the Kongo kingdom, such that by the end of the sixteenth century "the authority and power of the Kongo kingdom had started to deteriorate" (Tvedten 1997, 18).

Indeed, Angola suffered a heavier loss than any other African country during the four centuries of the transatlantic slave trade. It is estimated that 4 million of the 12 million Africans who survived the Atlantic crossing to be enslaved in the Americas were from Angola—and that another 4 million Angolans died, either in being captured and held in captivity in Angola, or on the journey to the Americas. This represents not only a severe population loss, but also a profound loss in terms of "the development of Angolan society in political, economic, and sociocultural terms" (Tvedten 1997, 18).

In 1576 the Portuguese founded the city of Luanda and the colony of Angola. From that period onward they focused their efforts on conquering the interior of the territory. They met with significant resistance from Angolan kingdoms in the interior, a resistance epitomized by the Queen Nzinga, who dominated the territory from the 1620s to the 1660s. A fierce anticolonial fighter and leader, Queen Nzinga "carried the flag of resistance to the verge of success" in the effort to stave off Portuguese domination (Birmingham 1992, 9). The Portuguese, meanwhile, also had to contend with incursions by other Europeans, including the Dutch, French, and British, who were eager for a share of the lucrative slave trade. After the official abolition of slavery in 1836 (although its practice continued until the 1880s), the Portuguese began to focus on the colonization and exploitation of the Angolan territory. To that end, from the late 1880s onward the Portuguese, bereft of revenues from the slave trade, enacted a brutal policy of forced labor. Moreover, they also implemented a system of local rule that played upon divisions among ethnic groups and weakened traditional political authorities. When all else failed, they engaged in intensive military campaigns to bring the territory under their control. The Portuguese launched their last major military campaign in 1917, stamping out the last vestiges of local resistance; after that "their occupation was complete" (Tvedten 1997, 19–25).

From 1915 onward, Portugal invested considerably in its colony, in order to better exploit it. The Benguela railway, linking mines in the Belgian Congo with the Angolan port city of Lobito, was built, and the Diamond Company of Angola was established and began mining Angolan diamonds in 1917. Coffee production was enhanced and there was rapid development in a number of other industries, including fishing, manufacturing, and later, petroleum. Indeed, from the late 1950s oil production grew rapidly, and during the 1960s foreign oil companies from the United States, in particular, invested heavily in the oil sector. During this period the number of Portuguese settlers increased dramatically as well—from 40,000 in 1940 to 340,000 in 1974 (jumping from 2 to 6 percent of the Angolan population).[3] As in southern Africa's other settler colonies, the intensification of Portuguese settlement in the territory meant an intensification of the expropriation of land in the interior of the colony. Not only were indigenous Angolans expelled from their lands, but they were also forced to cultivate cash crops for export, such as coffee, maize, beans, and wheat, rather than produce food crops for their own consumption (Tvedten 1997, 26–27).

According to Tvedten (1997, 27), the African population in the Angolan colony was subject to a "systematic policy of segregation" in addition to the aforementioned land expropriation and forced labor. This system divided the population into *indígenas* (indigenous peoples) and *assimilados* (assimilated nonwhites) and Europeans. For the vast majority of Africans—considered *indígenas*—the segregation consisted of "an elaborate system of social control (identification cards), economic requirements (payment of a head tax or, alternatively, an obligation to work for the government for six months a year), and lack of political and social rights." Unlike in Botswana, traditional African institutions and leaders played little part in administering the colony; moreover, access to education and health services was extremely limited for the majority of the population. Angolans could be classified as *assimilados,* meanwhile, by meeting certain requirements related to level of educational attainment, proficiency in Portuguese, economic independence, and "abandonment of a traditional way of life." In general, it was *mestíços* in Angola who opted to qualify for *assimilado* status, though the number was always extremely small (Tvedten 1997, 27–28). Thus, whereas Angola had many of the same characteristics as the Anglophone settler societies in Namibia, South Africa, and Zimbabwe, the opportunity for assimilation and potentially citizenship, however negligible, made Angola more like the French colonial model than the British one (Davidson 1994).[4]

The common denominator of colonialism all over Africa, however, was the hardening of ethnic or "tribal" identities, even where only loose, ill-defined groupings existed previously (Vail 1991). Within Angola, over time, ethnic identities among the indigenous population began to solidify and take on a greater salience as well, with three distinctive groupings emerging. The first was the Kongo people, who because of the once power-ful Kongo kingdom had retained a distinctive identity; they also shared considerable ties with Kongo people across the border in Zaire (including a heavy use of the French language). The Mbundu were the second group. They were distinguished by their close interaction with the Portuguese colonists over the years (hence a greater degree of "Westernization" and urbanization) and were associated closely with the urban *mestiço* popula-tion. Finally, the third group was the Ovimbundu, who once dominated the central highlands and were then forcibly removed to coffee plantations in the north, bringing them into potential conflict with both the Kongo and Mbundu (Tvedten 1997, 28–29). By the later years of the colonial period these three groups formed the basis for the three nationalist groups that would challenge Portuguese rule.

Nationalist movements organized somewhat later in Angola than they did in the other southern African colonies. The Portuguese harshly sup-pressed any kind of organized political activity, and the development of an effective leadership was hindered by lack of educational opportunities for most Angolans. Still, not just one but several nationalist movements did emerge. By 1956 the MPLA, led eventually by doctor and poet Agostino Neto, emerged with a support base among the Mbundu people and the *mestiço* population, particularly in the country's larger cities, especially Luanda. In 1962, the National Front for the Liberation of Angola (FNLA), led by Holden Roberto and supported primarily by the Kongo people in the north, was formed, with links across the border in Zaire. Finally, in 1966 UNITA was established by Jonas Savimbi, eventually drawing its main sup-port from the Ovimbundu. The three movements were united in their demand for political independence for Angola but differed in ideological orientation and in terms of the support and resources each ultimately received from foreign backers. In brief, the MPLA, with a Marxist orienta-tion, was the most radical of the three movements and drew international support eventually from Cuba and the Soviet Union. The FNLA was backed by Zaire, with U.S. assistance, from the beginning; paradoxically, the FNLA was also supported by China (Vines 2000, 3). UNITA "never devel-oped any clearly articulated political platform during the 15 years of [prein-dependence] struggle," although it did develop "ethnic Ovimbundu over-tones" (Tvedten 1997, 30–31). Although initially supported by China, by the time of independence UNITA had turned to South Africa for support, and later became a major recipient of U.S. aid. Hodges notes that the three independence movements "proved unable to mount a united front, and at times fought each other." Among other things, this seriously weakened the anticolonial effort in Angola such that by the early 1970s the divided anti-colonial movement in Angola was "little more than an irritant to the Portuguese" (2004, 8).

Among the European colonial powers in Africa, the Portuguese were the least willing to relinquish their colonies. Much less developed than the other European countries by the mid–twentieth century (and a military regime rather than a democracy), Portugal was determined to retain the economic benefits that colonialism provided. As a result, the people of Angola (and Mozambique and Guinea-Bissau) were forced to resort to war to gain their independence. In Angola that war erupted violently in 1961 with uprisings in Luanda and the killing of white settlers in northern Angola (Minter 1994, 18). Over the next thirteen years the three different groups, the MPLA, the FNLA, and UNITA, fought the Portuguese (and at times each other) from exile bases from the north (Congo and Zaire) and east (Zambia) and from inside the country. The Portuguese fought back— indeed they were fighting the same battle in Guinea-Bissau and Mozambique—until the cost of the three colonial wars became too high. In April 1974 the regime that had been in power in Portugal for fifty years was overthrown by lower-level military officers fed up with the African wars, paving the way for independence in the country's African colonies.[5] In January 1975 the three nationalist movements in Angola and Portugal signed the Alvor Accord, providing for a transitional government and elec-tions leading to independence in November 1975 (Minter 1994, 19). But the provisions of the Alvor Accord did not hold, and heavy fighting, aided and abetted by external supporters, quickly broke out among the three movements. Despite the continued fighting, on November 11, 1975, the scheduled independence day, the MPLA declared Angola independent of Portuguese rule and installed itself as the new government. MPLA leader Agostino Neto was named the country's first president and remained so until his death four years later, when he was succeeded by José Eduardo dos Santos, who has held the office since.

■ Society and Development: The Long War and Its Aftermath

Independence, however, did not bring peace to Angola. Rather, a war quickly erupted and continued largely unabated until 2002—despite two substantial attempts at peace in 1992 and 1994. After the MPLA gained power in 1975, the FNLA gradually disappeared as a contender in the fight-ing, and the war became one between the MPLA government and the "rebel" UNITA movement that quickly reorganized in the face of its 1975 defeat. As will be detailed below, two attempts to end the war in the early 1990s—when other regional wars were ending—failed, and with each failed attempt the war became more intractable and more brutal. In the end, it took the assassination of UNITA leader Jonas Savimbi to bring the violence and hostilities to an end. Ultimately, the prolonged conflict took a devastating toll on Angola. By its end in 2002, 1.5 million Angolans had died, 4 million had been displaced from their homes, 300,000 were in exile, and millions were living without access to the most basic public services. In the capital city, Luanda, some 63 percent of the population relied upon the informal sector for their livelihoods (Kibble 2002, 18). A number of factors have been identified as contributing to Angola's devastating postindependence conflict.

Ideological and Ethnic Divisions

As noted above, there were ideological and ethnic differences between the two movements that fed the conflict. In 1976 the MPLA, like its counterpart Frelimo in Mozambique, formally adopted Marxism-Leninism as its official ideology and set out to develop Angola along socialist lines. In 1977 the MPLA declared itself a "vanguard party" and commenced with a program of nationalizing abandoned Portuguese farms and businesses. By the second half of the 1970s the new government was attempting to manage a centrally planned economy (Hodges 2004, 9). But as in Mozambique, the obstacles were formidable. Both countries lacked skilled administrators and technicians who could replace the Portuguese who had fled at independence. Moreover, in each state, according to William Minter (1994, 24), "the post-independence governments took charge of economies in a state of collapse." And the political model that both governments relied upon—again highly centralized—was based upon the Marxist traditions of most of the countries and movements, mainly the Soviet Union and Eastern Europe, that supported them (Minter 1994, 27). Only in the mid-1980s did the MPLA government begin to move away from a centrally planned economy toward one based on market forces (in part due to the poor performance of the economy, but also because of "emergent class interests" stymied by the planned economy [Hodges 2004, 11]). Political liberalization began in 1990 at the MPLA's third party congress.

UNITA, meanwhile, is described by many as not having had a clear ideological position, notwithstanding its eventual South African and U.S. sponsorship. UNITA did have, especially over time, a more pronounced ethnic bias toward the Ovimbundu and other eastern and southern Angolan ethnic groups. Assis Malaquias (2000, 105–107) suggests that the Ovimbundu identification with UNITA was prompted in part by the MPLA government's failure over time to address the needs of most Angolans, particularly those from the southern and eastern regions. According to David Birmingham (2002, 156), Angola's southern elite, "who had not been dealt an equitable hand in the [post-independence] settlements of the late 1970s . . . remained isolated and aggrieved in their south-eastern guerrilla camps on the remote edge of the old Portuguese colonial world." More significant, perhaps, UNITA "relied on loyalty to a charismatic leader—Jonas Savimbi" (who was himself an Ovimbundu) (Minter 1994, 20). In the event, both ideological and ethnic differences were seized upon by a group of external actors with varying motives eager to intervene in the Angolan conflict.

▓ The Cold War: Role of External Actors

A key factor fuelling the war in Angola, and helping to hone the ideological distinctions between the warring parties, was the involvement of several external powers in the conflict, an involvement that began already before independence. Basically, as Steve Kibble (2002, 20) observes, by the 1980s, "Angola was a pawn in Cold War politics." According to Birmingham:

> The role of the Soviet Union in Africa during its last ten years of existence is one factor that needs to be taken into consideration and it may be significant that Angola's second president, José Eduardo dos Santos, was an engineer in the petroleum industry who had been trained in Russia. Another long-distance factor that might be deemed important is the role of the United States which elected a president, Ronald Reagan, who adopted a virulently hawkish agenda during the Cold War confrontations of the 1980s. (2002, 155)

Aside from Zaire, which supported the Bakongo-dominated FNLA from the start, the first external power to become involved in the conflict was the United States, which allocated U.S.$300,000 in January 1975 to provide support to the FNLA (thereby also undermining the Alvor Accord) (Ohlson and Stedman 1994, 81).[6] Shortly thereafter, the MPLA began to receive arms and equipment from Eastern European countries and, by the time of independence, from the Soviet Union. Around the same time the MPLA also enlisted the assistance of some foreign military advisers, including small numbers of Cubans. By mid-1975, South African and Cuban troops were involved in the conflict, on the sides of UNITA and the MPLA, respectively. Also around the same time, the United States embarked upon a U.S.$32 million covert aid program to defeat the MPLA and to counter what was perceived as a Soviet and Cuban communist foothold in southern Africa (Ohlson and Stedman 1994, 81).

If the Angolan war had critical Cold War overtones, it contained a distinctly regional dimension as well. Indeed, regional politics also impinged upon the conflict in Angola, in many ways feeding the proxy war that was taking place between East and West.[7] In the years after independence, two regional liberation movements, the South West Africa People's Organization from Namibia and the African National Congress from South Africa, set up exile bases in Angola, thereby giving apartheid South Africa a pretext for greater military involvement in Angola. The scope of South Africa's involvement expanded considerably after about 1980. In 1981, moreover, the United States introduced the so-called linkage policy, linking Namibian independence to the withdrawal of Cuban troops from Angola and insisting that the MPLA government share power with UNITA. Throughout the rest of the 1980s the fighting and external involvement in Angola increased dramatically. By 1986 the United States was openly providing U.S.$25 million to UNITA.[8] Similarly, South Africa publicly declared that it was also helping UNITA "in every possible way" (Tvedten 1997, 39). By 1985, meanwhile, 40,000 Cuban troops were on Angolan soil and the Soviet Union was supplying large amounts of technical assistance and material aid. A major turning point in the war occurred in 1988, when Angolan government and Cuban troops defeated UNITA and South African forces at Cuito Cuanavale in southern Angola, allowing the government to regain control over large areas of the country previously dominated by UNITA. More important, the battle led to negotiations, beginning in May 1988, to end the thirteen-year war in Angola.

Paradoxically, then, just as external actors helped to prolong and magnify the conflict in Angola, they tried to bring it to an end. According to Minter (1994, 49), by the end of the 1980s, the United States and the Soviet Union "were increasingly in accord on the need for settlements of 'regional conflicts.'" Moreover, antiwar sentiment was mounting in South Africa just as international economic sanctions and domestic political upheaval were wreaking havoc with the South African economy. Pressure for independence in Namibia was rising. As the fighting dragged on, the Soviet Union and Eastern European countries dissolved, Nelson Mandela was released from jail in South Africa, Namibia gained its independence, and the U.S. interest in supporting UNITA waned. By the end of 1990 the MPLA accepted the notion of a new constitution and officially abandoned Marxism-Leninism in favor of democratic socialism (Minter 1994, 52).[9] A nominal multiparty political system emerged in the country by May 1991. Also in May 1991 the Bicesse Accord was signed between the government of Angola and UNITA. The agreement provided for an eighteen-month transition period during which some troops on both sides would be demobilized and eventually joined together to form a national army.[10] During this interim period, "the MPLA was to remain the legitimate and internationally recognized government of Angola, responsible for running the state until new elections could be held" (Vines 2000, 8). At the end of the period, elections for president and the National Assembly were to be held. The agreement was mediated by the United States, the Soviet Union, and Portugal, and the United Nations was charged with overseeing its implementation (Stedman 1997, 36).[11]

Birmingham (2002, 171) writes that the period of eighteen months from May 1991 to September 1992 "was the most spectacular period of optimism and freedom that Angola had ever witnessed." When presidential and National Assembly elections were held in September 1992, 91 percent of the electorate participated, and the vote was deemed largely free and fair by international observers. Yet the results were not respected by the loser in the presidential ballot, UNITA's Jonas Savimbi, who won only 40 percent of the vote, compared to Angolan president and MPLA leader Eduardo dos Santo's 49 percent. Despite the apparent credibility of the electoral outcome, Savimbi immediately cried foul and returned to the bush to carry on UNITA's war against the Angolan government, which he was able to do since UNITA had demobilized very few troops (Stedman 1997, 38). By early 1993 UNITA had gained control of three-quarters of the Angolan countryside. By the end of the year, however, having used oil revenues to acquire additional arms, government forces were able to take back large tracts of territory from UNITA.

In the meantime, the United Nations had also imposed arms and fuel sanctions on UNITA, putting it on the defensive (EIU 2003d, 12). This led to another attempt to end the war in November 1994 with the signing by both parties of the Lusaka Protocol in Zambia. This agreement called for a new cease-fire, demobilization of UNITA troops, UNITA participation in the government, and the establishment of a UN peacekeeping force. But this effort also failed, despite the presence of 7,500 UN peacekeepers and a government of national unity and reconciliation (GURN) established in 1997.[12] When it became clear that UNITA was not disarming as required, its participation in the government was suspended, and in November 1998 President Dos Santos decided to "resume the war in order 'to save the peace,' following the reluctance of UNITA to abide by the Lusaka Protocol" (le Billon 2001, 59; EIU 2003d, 12–13). When this happened, according to Philippe le Billon (2001, 59), "Angola became one of the worst conflict resolution failures of the 1990s." In 2001 the Angolan armed forces began to use "controversial counterinsurgency tactics, clearing civilians from the countryside to refugee camps in the urban centres of the interior in order to deny UNITA access to the support of the civilian population" (EIU 2003d, 13). Eventually, the tide turned against UNITA. Jonas Savimbi was killed at the hands of government forces in February 2002, and Angola's protracted war was finally ended in April that same year.

◾ *The Role of Diamonds and Oil*

Along with Savimbi's role as a "spoiler"[13] in the peace process (Stedman 1997), many have identified access to resources, in particular, oil and diamonds, as a key factor in prolonging the war and preventing a peaceful settlement in Angola in the 1990s (Cilliers 2000; le Billon 2001; Malaquias 2001; Munslow 1999).[14] In brief, the Angolan government was able to rely upon the revenues generated by abundant oil supplies to continue fighting the war against UNITA; moreover, access to the oil revenues meant that the decision to continue the war could be taken by the government alone, without consultation with the people. Similarly, UNITA's access to diamonds allowed, even encouraged, the movement to return to war in 1992 and again in the late 1990s. As le Billon notes, there is a clear relationship between abundant natural resources and armed conflicts:

> Rents generated by narrow and mostly foreign-dominated resource industries allow ruling groups to dispense with economic diversification and popular legitimacy, often resulting in rent-seeking, poor economic growth, and little social mobility outside politics and state patronage. . . . Indeed, quantitative analysis demonstrates that easily taxed or looted primary commodities increase the likelihood of war by providing the motivation, prize, and means of a violent contest for state or territorial control. (2001, 56)

Oil is enormously important to the Angolan economy—providing over 90 percent of official exports and 80 percent of government revenue. Moreover, Angola's oil production is second only to that of Nigeria in sub-Saharan Africa and, with the prospect of still more oil discoveries, "has gained international significance" (le Billon 2001, 61). At the same time, the oil sector very much represents an "enclave economy"—one that has few linkages to other sectors of the economy and that, because it is capital- rather than labor-intensive, provides limited jobs. The oil industry in Angola is geographically isolated from the rest of the country as well— located in the tiny northern Cabinda enclave and offshore. In addition, although oil revenues could have been used over the years to diversify the Angolan economy (for which there is much potential), this has not happened. Finally, in Angola oil revenues were also used to make possible the government's war on UNITA (particularly through the purchase of more than U.S.$5 billion worth of arms in the 1990s), to service debts, and to subsidize the lifestyle of a small elite. "Rather than mitigating the impact of the war and consolidating state governance, the oil revenue has thus reinforced distortions and undermined popular support for the government" (le Billon 2001, 63). Oil revenues have also provided enormous opportunities for corruption, which have been exploited. It has been asserted from many quarters that "the highest levels of government officials allegedly embezzle part of the oil rent" (le Billon 2001, 66), such that a popular slogan in Angola went, "MPLA steals, UNITA kills."

Diamonds have proved a very similar resource for UNITA. As with oil, Angola has an abundant supply of diamonds—indeed, the country is the world's fourth largest producer of diamonds by value (le Billon 2001, 67). They are located primarily in the northeastern part of the country—over "vast and lawless areas" far from government control—and some of them (alluvial deposits) are easily exploited. According to le Billon (2001, 67) diamonds were a revenue source for UNITA since the late 1970s, when UNITA forces simply raided existing companies and freelance diggers. From 1983 UNITA "professionalized its diamond operations, training its staff in diamond sorting and investing in mining equipment." UNITA's diamond exploitation was expanded considerably in the late 1980s and exponentially in the 1990s, as UNITA lost support from the United States and South Africa. According to le Billon (2001, 69), once war resumed in late 1998, UNITA developed new mines in central and southeastern Angola, and even in the southern Democratic Republic of Congo (DRC). From 1992 to 2000, it is estimated that diamonds produced under UNITA's control were worth U.S.\$3–4 billion (le Billon 2001, 69). Le Billon (2001, 71) and others clearly trace UNITA's ability to return to war in 1992 to the movement's access to the diamond revenues. In the early 2000s, however, the international campaign to halt the purchase of conflict diamonds reduced UNITA's diamond revenues, weakening the movement relative to the government. In the event, UNITA's war effort collapsed in the months following Jonas Savimbi's February 2002 assassination.

■ State Failure

A final factor contributing to the protracted struggle in Angola has been identified as state failure, defined by James Busumtwi-Sam (2002, 95) as "a situation where a state's claim to be the authoritative political institution over a population and territory is strongly contested." Moreover, state failure—as manifest in a weak domestic support base for a government—also contributes to leaders seeking outside sources of support, even direct military assistance, as happened in Angola. According to Busumtwi-Sam (2002, 96), state failure in Angola occurred almost immediately after independence. From the start, the authority of the MPLA government was violently contested by UNITA. By the mid-1980s "Angola had *de facto* dual sovereignty with each side controlling large areas of the country." Further, as Kibble (2002, 20) observes, UNITA was aided in its quest to eliminate the MPLA "by the lack of full legitimacy of the MPLA." This lack of legitimacy shaped Angola in the years after independence, according to Kibble: "The MPLA—though it controlled the capital and most of the country on independence day—was never granted the undisputed nationalist legitimacy which it aspired to and claimed."

Consistent with the conditions of state failure, the Angolan state was "no longer able to carry out vital functions associated with governance including forms of domination, the nature of surplus extraction, and the patterns of resource allocation. Most of these functions are now formulated and carried out by powerful agents who are not accountable to the public" (Malaquias 2000, 108). The vacuum created by the absence of the state and its institutions creates opportunities for "warlords," a term popularized by William Reno (1999, 79) to describe situations in which local "strongmen have used commerce to consolidate their political power within a coalition of interest among themselves, businesspeople, and local fighters." Indeed, state failure "serves the interests of 'warlords' in society to the extent that the disorder that ensues creates avenues for maintaining their power and profits" (Busumtwi-Sam 2002, 99). This, of course, describes well UNITA under Jonas Savimbi and the movement's involvement in the highly lucrative illicit diamond trade.

Thus a whole series of factors served to prolong Angola's deadly conflict that erupted with independence. These included early ideological and ethnic differences between the warring parties that were hardened over time; the external intervention of ideologically driven regional and international players who exaggerated the ideological dimension to justify their own actions and who exacerbated the two sides' ethnic bases; access to two highly profitable resources, oil and diamonds, that helped each side to finance the war and carry it out with impunity and without regard for the needs and wishes of the Angolan people; and a state failure bordering on warlordism that left the populace without access to the most basic services and the elite with enormous opportunities for accumulation. Finally, one individual agent in particular, Jonas Savimbi, has been identified by many as refusing to sanction or abide by any efforts to bring the conflict to an end (though in the case of the 1992 election, the United States and United Nations have also been held culpable for failing to prevent Savimbi from spoiling the process); indeed, it took Savimbi's death in early 2002 to finally bring an end to the war and allow peace to take hold.

■ Organization of the State

On April 4, 2002, the Angolan government and UNITA signed a memorandum of understanding, technically an addendum to the Lusaka Protocol, which formalized the cease-fire between the two parties in effect since Savimbi's February 2002 death. As set out in the memorandum, UNITA "recommitted to the peace framework in the 1994 Lusaka Protocol, returned all remaining territory to Angolan government control, quartered all military personnel in predetermined locations, and relinquished all arms. In August 2002, UNITA demobilized all military personnel and in September 2002, together with the government, reconstituted the UN-sponsored Joint Commission to resolve all outstanding political issues under the Lusaka Protocol" (U.S. Department of State 2003a). As of late November 2002 the government and UNITA declared all outstanding issues resolved and the 1994 Lusaka Protocol fully implemented. By the early 2000s Angola was in the early stages of the transitions that other countries in the region had already completed.

▨ *Constitution*

Political liberalization, meanwhile, had actually commenced a decade before, in the early 1990s, when hopes for peace and a resolution of the conflict in Angola were high. At its party congress in December 1990 the MPLA had formally renounced Marxism-Leninism as its guiding doctrine and in mid-1991 a law to revise the country's constitution was enacted. The constitutional revision law "proclaimed a democratic state based on the rule of law and respect for human rights, and introduced a multi-party political system" (Hodges 2004, 55). This new law was accompanied by others that loosened restrictions on associations, political parties, the right of assembly, the right to strike, and the media. A year later, in anticipation of the September 1992 elections, further laws were passed that established a new electoral system, permitted private radio stations, set up a national press council, and made it easier to register political parties. A second constitutional revision law was passed in September 1992 dealing with decentralization and local government. At the same time, the name of the country was changed from the People's Republic of Angola to "the less ideologically charged" Republic of Angola (Hodges 2004, 55). In the end, however, the return to war threatened, though did not fully reverse, the attempted liberalization. As the Economist Intelligence Unit (EIU) (2003d, 14) notes, the 1991 constitutional reform "nominally established Angola as a democratic state based on the rule of law, multiparty politics and guarantees of press freedom, right to assembly and right to strike. In practice, respect for these freedoms is weak and the country remains a heavily centralized state under the political hegemony of the MPLA." At war's end in 2002 the process of constitutional reform began anew, though by mid-2004 a new constitution still had not been approved by parliament. Rather, a new constitution and electoral law had become part of an overall struggle between the ruling MPLA and opposition political parties about the timing of new elections.

▨ *Executive*

In 2004 José Eduardo dos Santos remained president of Angola after nearly a quarter century in office. Dos Santos, who ascended to the presidency upon the death of his predecessor, Agostino Neto, in 1979, was reelected president in the first round of presidential voting in 1992. From 1998, when the position of prime minister was abolished, to 2002, the president of Angola was both chief of state and head of government. In December 2002 the post of prime minister was restored, although power remained highly concentrated in the executive, particularly in the presidency (EIU 2003d, 15). Indeed, Birmingham (2002, 177) argues that after the failed 1992 elections and resumption of war, President Dos Santos decided to concentrate still more power in his own hands: "From being a single-party state with a disaffected opposition thinly scattered in the provinces and abroad, Angola became a presidential state in which power emanated from the palace." From his presidential complex, known as the Futungo, dos Santos made decisions that bypassed "government ministries, party cells and state bureaucracies."

This highly centralized presidential system represents a continuation of past practice in Angola. While the head of state, as president of the ruling party, president of the country, and commander of the armed forces, was a highly centralized role under President Neto, it became even more centralized after dos Santos came to power in 1979 (Hodges 2004, 52–53). In particular, in the face of the external threats outlined above, dos Santos was able to effect changes within the ruling MPLA that greatly enhanced his own position. His powers were further strengthened with the establishment of a defense and security council in 1984, chaired by the president, which quickly became the country's top decisionmaking body (Hodges 2004, 53). Within little time power became "increasingly personalized" around the person of the president and a personality cult developed around dos Santos, though never quite on the scale as the one that emerged around Savimbi (Hodges 2004, 54).

The constitutional changes of 1991–1992, notwithstanding the liberalization that did take place, according to Hodges (2004, 55), "confirmed the concentration of power in the presidency, establishing in effect a presidential system of government." The executive branch is composed of the president, the prime minister, and the Council of Ministers, all of whom are appointed by the president. Governors of the country's eighteen provinces are also appointed by the president and serve at the pleasure of the president. And the president remains the commander in chief of the armed forces. According to the U.S. Department of State (2003a), government in Angola "is based on ordinances, decrees, and decisions issued by the president and his ministers or through legislation produced by the National Assembly and approved by the president."

■ *Judiciary*

According to numerous reports, the judiciary, like other branches of government, is in a state of incomplete transition. As throughout southern Africa, the legal system in Angola is a dual one, based on Portuguese and customary law. On paper, at least, Angola appears to conform to many of the internationally accepted rules and norms of jurisprudence and has authorized the establishment of appropriate legal institutions and structures. In fact, however, the legal system is "weak and fragmented. Courts operate in only 12 of more than 140 municipalities. A Supreme Court serves as the appellate tribunal; a Constitutional Court with powers of judicial review has never been constituted despite statutory authorization" (U.S. Department of State 2003a). Indeed, since the statutory authority for the Constitutional Court is the Angolan constitution, "ironically, the failure to create the Constitutional Court may itself be unconstitutional" (International Bar Association [IBA] 2003, 4). Other institutions, including a judicial protectorate (ombudsman) intended to prevent and combat judicial corruption, have also yet to function, and the penal code, incredibly, dates to 1886, leaving much to judicial discretion (IBA 2003). Furthermore, although Angola is a signatory to several international legal covenants, including the International Covenant on Civil and Political Rights, the Convention on the Rights of the Child, and the International Covenant on Economic, Social, and Cultural Rights, it has failed to report to these bodies as required (IBA 2003).

Not surprisingly, given the veritable absence of a functioning legal-institutional framework, the criminal justice system is in a shambles. The right of habeas corpus is applied inconsistently, if at all, and pretrial detentions lasting two to three years are not uncommon. A major factor that helps to explain the moribund court system and the backlog of cases is that the judiciary is woefully understaffed, poorly remunerated, and insufficiently educated. The justice system also lacks prosecutors and defense attorneys, for similar reasons (IBA 2003). Moreover, historically, the police force has played a paramilitary role in support of the armed forces' war effort, rather than emphasizing its law enforcement functions. Finally, the physical infrastructure of the legal system is also severely degraded: war and neglect destroyed police stations and courts, computers are not available, and communications are limited (Culolo 2001).

These deep-seated problems impact both the commission and the prevention or prosecution of criminal activity at all levels of the Angolan polity. Indeed, Angola's long-contested sovereignty, the centralization of power within the MPLA elite, particularly in the figure of President Dos Santos, the propensity toward warlordism in the countryside, and the country's weak or nonexistent legal institutions have combined to foster an environment in which not only common criminal behavior can become embedded, but also political corruption and organized crime can flourish virtually unchecked. Even the office of Angola's attorney general has noted that corruption is widespread at all levels of the public service and that "Angola is fast moving toward a culture of corruption." Tellingly, however, "there are almost no cases of corruption in the Angolan court rolls," in part because of fear of reprisals (Culolo 2001).

Military

The military in Angola, represented by the Angolan Armed Forces (FAA), is described as "battle-hardened" after decades of internal war.[15] The FAA comprises three forces—an army, navy, and air force. The largest of the three is the army, with 130,000 members. The navy has 3,000 personnel and the air force 7,000. There is a separate presidential guard, which reports directly to the office of the president (U.S. Department of State 2003a). At the time of the April 2002 peace settlement, UNITA had an 85,000-strong army that required demobilization, according to terms of the peace accord (EIU, 2003a). By late October 2002, 5,000 UNITA soldiers had been integrated into the FAA. For other former UNITA combatants, the "Nando Commission for the Social and Productive Reintegration of the Demobilized and Displaced" promised to help reintegrate them into civilian life (Kibble 2002, 25). But, according to the EIU (2003a), the government rushed to conclude the demobilization of UNITA forces without adequate support. "As a result, UNITA personnel are not receiving proper assistance to resume civilian life and may drift into banditry." The issue of properly demobilizing UNITA soldiers is of paramount concern, because the failure to do just that has been identified as one of the key problems in the failed peace efforts in 1992 and 1994 (Kibble 2002, 21).

Since independence the armed forces and police have been the recipients of substantial government resources, making them the "only real manifestation of a 'strong state'" in Angola, according to Hodges (2004, 72). Indeed, Christine Messiant (2001, 293) implicates the upper levels of the police force and the general staff of the armed forces in Angola in widespread corruption that has led to the massive personal enrichment of a small elite who provide the support base for the MPLA government.[16] FAA officers, for example, have exercised significant authority over legal and illicit concessions in the diamond fields, and many have arrayed vast forces of small prospectors in conditions of extreme exploitation (Dietrich 2000, 177–178). Hodges (2004, 74) identifies poor morale, discipline, and leadership as key problems of the FAA. These weaknesses derive, he suggests, from "low pay, arrears in wage payments, the lack of a motivating 'cause' and the preoccupation of much of the officer corps with business activities."

The security forces in Angola, including the police and the armed forces, have been accused of widespread abuses, including extrajudicial killings, disappearances, beatings, torture, and rape (U.S. Department of State 2003b). The worst transgressions among the army reportedly ended with the signing of the April 2002 cease-fire, except in the oil-rich Cabinda province, where the Front for the Liberation of the Enclave of Cabinda–Armed Forces of Cabinda continues to engage in rebel actions against the government of Angola (U.S. Department of State 2003b).

Given its size, experience, arms, and equipment, Angola's military can also be considered a regional superpower. Moreover, it has been involved in wars outside Angola's borders, including the war in the DRC. According to the EIU (2003d, 13), the government of Angola became involved in the war in the DRC (on the side of the DRC government) in an effort to deny UNITA territory from which to operate. By early 2003 the government of Angola claimed that all Angolan troops had been withdrawn from the DRC (EIU 2003d, 21). Of course at the height of the conflict between FAA and UNITA troops, from late 1999 to late 2001, the war also spilled over into neighboring Namibia, whose government, much to the dismay of the populace, granted permission to the FAA to pursue UNITA onto Namibian soil.

■ Representation and Participation

▓ *Legislative Branches*

At the national level, Angola has a unicameral legislature, the 233-member National Assembly.[17] Twelve parties won seats in the National Assembly in 1992, which nonetheless remains dominated by the ruling MPLA. Based on those election results, the MPLA holds 129 seats compared to UNITA's 70, with the rest held by smaller parties. But until a government of national unity and reconciliation was formed in 1997, UNITA deputies did not even take their seats in the National Assembly. In the early 2000s, with Angola's political transition far from complete, most observers were quite cynical about the powers of the country's legislature. Messiant describes the legislative process as follows:

> A regime now disposing of an absolute majority in parliament can thus, even after the formation of the GURN, continue to function as it has in the past, making and unmaking laws according to its own whims or, more prosaically, ignoring the law altogether, whether in the form of disregarding the rights of citizens and of the opposition or by itself functioning largely through channels which are extra-legal and contemptuous of any institutional or juridical procedure. (2001, 291)

Like many others, Messiant describes a country in which predation and corruption—for example, embezzlement of government funds or oil revenues, illegal profit taking, widespread disbursement of patronage—are rampant among a small privileged elite, often referred to as the *nomenklatura*. Messiant (2001, 292) contends that substantial government revenues go wholly unaccounted for: "Parliament faithfully votes each year to approve a budget in which a substantial portion of the monies received by the Angolan state simply does not appear. The official budget is thus a document which bears no relationship to reality, and in any case is not implemented for the most part."

According to Tvedten (2002, 5), there has been very little decentralization of political power to the regional and local level in Angola. Provisional governors are appointed by the president and not elected, and so have little accountability to the populations in their provinces. And while elected local authorities are provided for in the 1991/1992 constitution, they have yet to be established. In addition to national elections in the near future, local elections are also needed.

■ *Elections in Angola: Not Yet a Tradition*

The first democratic, multiparty elections in Angola, for National Assembly and president, were held on September 29–30, 1992. As noted, the results of the election, which showed Jonas Savimbi trailing President Dos Santos by a slight margin, were deemed fraudulent by Savimbi (though not by any of the international election observers), and resulted in UNITA returning to war. A runoff election was supposed to be held between the two presidential candidates, as neither Savimbi nor dos Santos received more than 50 percent of the vote.[18] That second round of voting never took place, however, as Savimbi refused to participate, and was officially canceled in February 1999.

By mid-2004, new elections, a key ingredient in Angola's incomplete political transition, had not yet been scheduled. The MPLA government refused to set a date until seventeen preconditions were met. These included the adoption of a new constitution and new electoral law and improvements in basic infrastructure that would allow the holding of elections in all parts of the country. Only then, the government contended, could voters be registered and an electoral commission installed. The government estimated that all of the preconditions could not be met before early 2006. Hodges (2004, 65) concedes that organizing credible elections in Angola will require "a huge and complex voter registration exercise, since much of the adult population does not possess identity cards or other forms of identification, because of the war, population displacements and the breakdown of civil registration systems." Still, a group of civil society organizations and political parties, calling itself the "Campaign for a Democratic Angola," demanded in early 2004 that elections be held in 2005. The group charged that the MPLA government had imposed a "permanent coup d'état" on the country and, having ruled since independence, was running the national economy as a monopoly and forestalling "a course of action [elections] which might be able to bring the country to constitutional and socioeconomic normality" ("New Opposition Grouping" 2004).

■ *Political Parties*

Despite the Campaign for a Democratic Angola, party politics in Angola remains largely dominated by the MPLA and UNITA. In the ill-fated 1992 elections, several small, independent political parties won seats in the National Assembly, but their influence has been limited—felt mostly with regard to work carried out in conjunction with civil society organizations— for example, in promoting peace or opposition to corruption. None of the smaller parties, including a revived FNLA, has seriously challenged the position of either of the two major parties, described by Hodges (2004, 66) as the "two traditional 'army-parties.'" Moreover, according to Tvedten (2002, 5), representatives of the smaller parties in the National Assembly are dependent on the ruling MPLA for everything—from pencils to salaries.

And yet neither the MPLA nor UNITA seems to hold much widespread appeal. The MPLA, "once Marxist-Leninist, now espouses an ill-defined democratic socialism but in reality serves the interests of the governing elite. It is also suffering from something of an identity crisis, as its oil-rich elite becomes more distant from most Angolans" (EIU 2003d, 15). By contrast, "UNITA portrays itself as representing the 'real Africans' of the interior against domination by what it sees as the urban and mixed-race bias of the MPLA elite in the coastal areas" (EIU 2003d, 15). To a significant degree, Malaquias confirms this growing detachment of the MPLA from its ideological and ethnic moorings. Indeed, the party retains only tenuous links to the ethnic Mbundu elite on whom it was built, and instead is dominated by "a political and economic elite—composed predominantly of *mulattos* and descendants from indentured laborers from [the former Portuguese colony of] São Tomé—[who] used their superior education, political skills, and economic power to take control of the party from the Mbundu elite" (2000, 109).

At the same time, however, UNITA's core support remains largely confined to the Ovimbundu people of the central highlands, but even this ethnogeographic base is also misleading. Under Savimbi, UNITA was controlled by his Bieno subgroup, though the Bailundo and Uambo subgroups are more numerically dominant "and traditionally [were] more powerful politically, militarily and economically." In fact, "the civil war in Angola [hid] potentially violent intra-group divisions" (Malaquias 2000, 105–106). Moreover, there were clear political divisions within UNITA as well. After the return to war in 1992, UNITA split into a number of factions, including "Savimbi's armed rebels, overseas representatives generally loyal to the organization, parliamentarians and others in Luanda holding ambiguous relations with Mr. Savimbi and the MPLA, and a rival, MPLA-supported faction of UNITA defectors, UNITA Renovada" (EIU 2003d, 15).

Since the April 2002 peace agreement these groups have reunited, thus transcending past divisions. In June 2003 the consolidated UNITA elected a new leader, Isaias Samakuva. Samakuva is considered "a more moderate and urbane figure who is well regarded and it is expected that he can provide more constructive opposition for the country" (EIU 2003d, 15). It is generally held that under new leadership, UNITA will garner more widespread political support. According to many observers, however, the MPLA—with its access to state resources and other advantages—will do everything it can to prevent that outcome. By mid-2004 many opposition party leaders had come together to protest the government's refusal to set a date for new elections, suspending their participation in a constitutional commission until a definite timetable for holding elections could be approved ("Political Maneuvers" 2004).

▣ Civil Society

After decades of war, civil society in Angola is considered by many to be fragile at best. As Fernando Pachecho (2002, 54) observes, "with a politically bipolarized society and with people's preoccupations essentially focusing on survival mechanisms, little time, energy and attention are left for associative life and collective action." Still, as part of the reforms of the early 1990s, previous restrictions on nongovernmental organizations (NGOs) were lifted, with the result that, according to Hodges (2004, 88), "a more vibrant, active civil society came into being for the first time since the post-independence crackdown on independent organizations." At the same time, the growth and development of these organizations was hampered in the late 1990s by the "return to war, the politico-military division of the country and actions taken by the government to prevent these organizations, in particular the unions and the press, from posing a threat to its hold on power."

And yet there is a nascent but growing civil society in Angola today. Pachecho (2002, 55) cites a range of groups: churches and religious organizations, which in the context of Angola's unstable past "constitute important points of stability" and devote themselves to issues of peace, national reconciliation, humanitarian and social assistance, protection of human rights, and so on; a variety of issue-based NGOs dedicated to such diverse causes as education, health, development, women's emancipation, external debt forgiveness, and redemption of cultural values; professional associations and trade unions, which represent member interests and seek to influence public policy (though with Angola's weak and disorganized formal sector, the labor movement has not been particularly strong); cultural groups, which contribute to the civic education of the population; the privately owned mass media, which promote spaces for public debate and political pluralism; and peasant organizations, which have helped over the years to meet the needs of the population (unmet by the state) and contributed to the population's autonomy.

While these organizations exist and are growing, according to Pachecho (2002, 57) they may well be perceived by government "as adversaries or enemies of the state. This is to a certain extent due to the reciprocal difficulties in finding mechanisms of co-existence and negotiation and, ultimately, to the lack of democratic culture in the country in general." In seeing these groups in an adversarial light, the Angolan government risks missing out on a main benefit of a vibrant civil society. As Pachecho writes: "The Angolan state has not yet clearly understood that by facilitating the action of civil society it would legitimise itself."

Messiant (2001, 294) takes a cynical view of government relations with civil society in Angola. She describes an Angola, before the April 2002 cease-fire, in which the government strategically moved to co-opt certain sectors of civil society in an effort to neutralize any political opponents or independent critics. According to her, the government did this through the use of state subsidies for certain NGOs. Sometimes such government support was combined with repression and intimidation, and proved very "effective in taming or at least marginalizing potential opponents."

Another aspect of the government's attempt to "take over" civil society, according to Messiant (2001, 287), was the creation in 1996 of the Eduardo dos Santos Foundation (FESA). Ostensibly, FESA is modeled on foundations in liberal democracies around the world "dedicated to the pursuit of social, cultural and scientific progress." Some observers suggest, however, that FESA is a fount of patronage, using its tremendous wealth and patronage resources (principally from oil revenues) to centralize power within the presidential palace and to marginalize even the ruling MPLA (Messiant 2001, 287; Malaquias 2000, 111). Birmingham (2002, 178) refers to the creation of the FESA as "one of the small institutionalized steps on the road to totalitarian presidentialism in Angola."

The media are typically considered to be an integral part of civil society. In Angola, though freedom of the press is now enshrined in the constitution, it is rarely respected (EIU 2003d, 26). Moreover, journalists are routinely harassed, and self-censorship among them is routine—though some are becoming more outspoken (Tvedten 2002, 6). Overall, however, the state-owned media, including *Jornal de Angola,* the Angop news agency, Rádio Nacional de Angola, and the national television network, Televisão Popular de Angola, still dominate. As elsewhere in southern Africa, media outlets that are state-owned and state-controlled lack both the autonomy and the incentive to criticize their patrons in the regime. There are a number of independent print weeklies, but these are very expensive and so their readership is largely confined to an urban elite. There is one independent radio station run by the Catholic Church.

■ Fundamentals of the Political Economy

In 2001 the estimated per capita GDP at purchasing power parity in Angola was U.S.$2,040 (UNDP 2003). The bulk of national revenue comes from the petroleum sector, which represents some 61 percent of GDP and over 90 percent of exports. Diamonds are also a significant natural and financial resource, but their significance is dwarfed by oil, which supplies Angola's government with considerably greater and more consistent revenues (Reno 2000, 219). Much of Angola's oil production, conducted by multinational oil companies and overseen by the national oil company, Sonangol, finds its way to U.S. markets—particularly as the United States tries to diversify away from its dependence on oil from the Middle East (EIU 2003d). And yet Angola's per capita GDP and oil wealth greatly disguise the true nature of the political economy in Angola today. Indeed, as noted earlier, on nearly every socioeconomic indicator Angola ranks at the very bottom among nations. Four decades of war have taken a devastating toll in Angola, and since the onset of peace the extent of the damage has been even more evident. Moreover, the nearly intractable conflict helped to spawn an astonishing level of predation and corruption in Angola, centered around the two resources that funded the war, diamonds and oil. That corruption, in turn, has exacerbated the already glaring discrepancies between rich and poor in Angola and has facilitated a centralization of power in Angola that threatens the country's recovery and future development.

It is not surprising, therefore, that "there is also much overt criticism that the Angolan government is not doing more to use its own vast oil wealth responsibly and for the benefit of its own people" (EIU 2003d, 30). The United Kingdom–based organization Global Witness (2002a) has documented how "the progressive impoverishment of a country during almost four decades of war and civil conflict has gone hand-in-hand with rising oil revenues." In brief, at the same time that Angola's socioeconomic indicators have fallen dramatically, the country's oil revenues have risen markedly. And those revenues have largely "been diverted straight into parallel budgets of the shadow state." In one year alone (2001), for example, up to U.S.$1.4 billion in oil revenues was unaccounted for. And this at the same time that international aid agencies were scrambling to find funds to feed about a million internally displaced Angolans. Moreover, as noted earlier, during this same period government officials were enriching themselves through their involvement in "a highly over-priced military procurement process" (Global Witness 2002a). In other words, as the Global Witness investigation documented, "it is clear that the political and economic disorder brought about by the civil war has been deliberately exploited to enrich the ruling elite. Meanwhile, the failure of the Angolan state to provide for its citizens has been blamed on the conflict."

Angola's undisclosed and unaccounted-for national revenues have been the main reason for a series of economic policy failures (EIU 2003d, 29). At independence, in keeping with its Marxist-Leninist doctrine, the MPLA government sought to establish a centrally planned economy. From the late 1980s onward, the government announced a series of economic reform programs, though most were abandoned after failing to achieve their objectives. Then in 1990, as part of the larger liberalization effort, the government moved to adopt market-based reforms. After failing to carry out the conditions of some IMF-sponsored economic reform packages, however, the government announced in mid-2002 that it wanted no more of them. This stance had significant repercussions with potential donors who were wary of giving aid to Angola unless the conditions existed to make that aid effective. Indeed, many potential donors have been engaged in an "aid boycott" of Angola until the government is able to demonstrate effective governance, improved accountability, and an end to corruption ("Aid Boycott Eases" 2004). In early 2004 the government of Angola moved closer to reaching an agreement with the International Monetary Fund that would open up the way for IMF loans to Angola and for increased donor assistance to the country ("Recent Moves Welcomed by IMF" 2004).

Alongside the egregious disparities in income and wealth in Angola are regional imbalances. Most of the development in the country since independence has been concentrated in the coastal areas and large cities and towns under government control, particularly Luanda. Some agricultural activity has been possible in southwestern Angola, which has been less affected by the war, though agriculture represents only 6 percent of GDP, a fraction of its contribution in 1990. Importantly, just four provinces— Cabinda and Zaire (oil) and Lunda Norte and Lunda Sul (diamonds)— account for 98 percent of export revenues (EIU 2003d, 31). Nonetheless, inhabitants of the four regions have benefited little from those revenues.

■ Challenges for the Twenty-First Century

In the early 2000s Angola was just embarking on the transitions that other countries in southern Africa had already completed, in some cases many years earlier. For the first time since the independence movements emerged in the early 1960s, the country was at peace. New political parties had been formed and UNITA was in the process of remaking itself from a rebel movement into a political party vying for public office. The constitution was in the process of being revised again and national-level elections were promised—though far from scheduled. The government was negotiating with the International Monetary Fund to restructure the economy. Although IMF-sponsored adjustment programs are not without their detractors and have proved problematic elsewhere, the return of such actors as the IMF would signify a fundamental change in Angola's relationship with the global political economy. Moreover, it would provide the country with renewed access to international finance, and perhaps a measure of economic oversight long absent in Angola. Indeed, considerable international attention was focused upon the predation and corruption endemic to the MPLA regime and the need for greater scrutiny and accountability.

To be sure, Angola faces enormous development challenges, greater than any in southern Africa. In addition to devastating social conditions, shallow political institutions, and economic malaise compounded by endemic corruption condoned by a host of domestic and international actors, Angola must also contend with healing a populace that has known little else but war, repression, and fear for decades. At the same time, Hodges contends (2004, 206), the end of forty years of war should mean new opportunities for progress—removing justification for further mismanagement of resources and restrictions on democratic freedoms, raising expectations of better times ahead, easing the culture of fear, and changing the political landscape "by ending the bipolarism in Angolan politics that has barred the emergence of a credible civilian opposition with an agenda for progressive change." If Angola's many resources could be put to constructive rather than destructive purposes the country would be better placed to confront its significant challenges. Among other things, this will require a complete transformation of the way politics and business have been conducted over the past decades. Indeed, with its wealth of natural resources, its potential transport infrastructure, and its significant domestic and regional markets, Angola stands to become a country to be reckoned with in southern Africa and the continent as a whole—if the economic, political, and social challenges can be surmounted. After forty years of deadly conflict and unspeakable privation, the people of Angola may yet have a chance to experience what should have been the fruits of independence.

■ Notes

1. According to David Birmingham (2002, 159), it has been estimated that 9 million mines were laid in Angola in order to deny farmers or their families access

to land. "Such a number of mines made Angola's killing fields comparable to those of Cambodia."

2. Lesotho and Swaziland, not discussed in this book, represent two other outliers.

3. During the early colonial period very few Portuguese women had migrated to the colony, resulting in a significant *mestíço* population in the country (as Portuguese men "mixed" with indigenous women)—1.1 percent of the population by 1974. By then there were 31 *mestíços* for every 100 white Portuguese (Tvedten 1997, 26).

4. According to Tvedten, personal e-mail communication, July 24, 2004: "A very important aspect of Portuguese colonialism (which partly explains why relations between Africans and whites are so different in the five former Portuguese colonies) is the presence of a large number of poor white Portuguese, who fought with Africans for jobs as maids, taxi drivers, bush traders, etc."

5. According to Hodges (2004, 8), "it was the success of liberation movements in Mozambique and Guinea-Bissau, not Angola, that eventually brought the downfall of the Salazarist regime of Marcello Caetano, thereby paving the way for the independence of all five Portuguese African colonies."

6. As Tvedten (1997, 37) notes: "The question of 'who came first' has been the subject of much debate"; this question is not pursued in full in this chapter.

7. In contrast, the postindependence conflict in Mozambique had only a limited East-West dimension. In fact, the unwillingness of the United States and the Soviet Union to insert themselves (or their official proxies) into the Mozambican conflict on a substantial scale may be one factor in its more rapid cessation.

8. In 1976, covert assistance to UNITA was prohibited by the Clark Amendment. However, the Clark Amendment was repealed by the U.S. Congress in 1985, allowing the resumption of covert support to UNITA, totaling approximately U.S.$250 million between 1986 and 1991 (Vines 2000, 7).

9. According to the Economist Intelligence Unit (2003d, 12), Marxist-Leninist ideology in Angola gradually softened after José Eduardo dos Santos came to power in 1979, following Agostino Neto's death in office.

10. A combined force, to be called the Angolan Armed Forces (FAA) was to number 50,000 troops. At the time of the Bicesse Accord, the government army numbered 120,000, whereas UNITA's army was 65,000. Both were expected to contribute equally to the new FAA (Vines 2000, 9).

11. According to Birmingham (2002, 170): "The peace, orchestrated by Portugal with help from the superpowers, was to be monitored by the United Nations, which sent Margaret Anstee to supervise Angola's first ever democratic election. Down in the Luanda slums the 1991 accord was gratefully known as Margaret's peace."

12. Birmingham (2002, 176) describes the GURN as a "political initiative designed to prevent a renewed outbreak of war. . . . As part of the search for a policy which would defuse the anger of the opposition and minimize the danger of a return to war the president created a 'government of national unity.'" The principle of a GURN was included in the Lusaka Accords (Vines 2000).

13. Many pages have been devoted to trying to figure out who was responsible for this failed attempt at a peaceful transition in 1992. Stephen John Stedman (1997, 5) suggests that the greatest risk to peace making endeavors is "spoilers"—"leaders and parties who believe that peace emerging from negotiations threatens their power, worldview, and interests, and use violence to undermine attempts to achieve it." What determines whether spoilers will succeed or fail, according to Stedman, is the role of international actors "as custodians of peace" (1997, 6). In the Angolan

case in 1992, the consensus is that the United Nations and the United States, in particular, failed to prevent Savimbi from spoiling the outcome of the peace process. See also Anstee 1996 for a firsthand account of the process.

14. See especially Hodges 2004, chaps. 6–7.

15. EIU 2003d, 20. The government's armed forces were known as FAPLA prior to the Bicesse Accords. "By 1994, the army had been retrained and renamed under the banner of the FAA," which was originally intended to be the name given to the *combined* UNITA-MPLA armies, as stipulated in Bicesse (Vines 2000, 9).

16. According to Birmingham (2002, 184): "In the national army of the 1990s, officers dominated the now privatized trade in diamonds and invested their wealth in the Luanda housing market, earning large fortunes as landlords to the foreign employees of oil companies, diplomatic missions and international aid agencies."

17. In fact, only 230 members were elected to the National Assembly in 1992. Three seats for Angolans living abroad were not filled (U.S. Department of State 2003a).

18. The law required a runoff election if the top vote-getter received less than 50 percent of the vote; dos Santos had 49.6 percent and Savimbi 40 percent.

7

Zimbabwe:
State and Society in Crisis

Zimbabwe, which achieved independence only in 1980, was not long ago regarded by observers as one of the most stable, prosperous, and indeed promising countries in Africa. Its postcolonial industrial and commercial agricultural development provided a solid base that augured positively for Zimbabwe's future economic performance (Stoneman and Cliffe 1989). The country was hailed as a model of postcolonial racial reconciliation for its apparent accommodation of blacks and white former settlers. Moreover, from a political standpoint, although never entirely democratic, Zimbabwe was nonetheless a *constitutional* polity, with an independent judiciary and largely protected civil liberties.

Two decades after independence, this promising portrait of Zimbabwe has been shattered. Indeed, the first years of the twenty-first century witnessed Zimbabwe sliding into a deepening political, economic, and social crisis. The level of economic and sociopolitical decline is staggering, much of it beginning only in 1997. Zimbabwe's economic infrastructure has been severely degraded in all sectors, and the losses there may prove irreversible. A June 2003 report (Mkalipi et al. 2003), drawing on Zimbabwe's own government statistics, painted a grim picture. Gross domestic product (GDP) plummeted 30 percent in the preceding three years. The once heralded manufacturing sector, already battered by economic liberalization in the 1990s, declined by 17.2 percent in 2002. Similarly, the mining sector fell by 7.1 percent. Moreover, inflation reached 208 percent in January 2003 and continued to rise thereafter. Social statistics were equally disturbing. The collapse of the health care sector means that the AIDS epidemic, which has ravaged Zimbabwe, continues with little prospect of abatement. A politically induced food shortage, combined with drought, meant that in March 2003, 7.2 million Zimbabweans—or 60 percent of the population— needed food aid. Finally, a decline in real wages of 28 percent between 1982 and 1997 (that is, before the current phase of the crisis) contributed to

Zimbabwe: Country Data

Land area 390,580 km²
Capital Harare
Date of independence April 18, 1980
Population 12.8 million, 36% urban
Languages English (official), Shona, and Ndebele
Ethnic groups Shona, 82%; Ndebele, 14%; other, 2%; Coloured and
    Asian, 1%; European, less than 1%
Religions syncretic (part-Christian, part-indigenous beliefs), 50%;
    Christian, 25%; indigenous beliefs, 24%; Muslim and other, 1%
Currency Zimbabwe dollar (Z$); Zimbabwean dollars per U.S. dol-
    lar: 852.58 (July 2003)

Literacy rate 89.3% (male, 93.3%; female, 85.5%)
Life expectancy 35.4 years (male, 35.5 years; female, 35.4 years)
Infant mortality 76 per 1,000 live births

GDP per capita U.S.$706
GDP per capita (PPP) U.S.$2,280
GDP per capita growth rate –0.2% (1990–2001)

Leaders since independence
  • Robert Mugabe, prime minister, 1980–1987
  • Robert Mugabe, president, 1987–

Major political parties
    Ruling party: Zimbabwe African National Union–Patriotic Front
    (ZANU-PF)
    Other parties: Movement for Democratic Change (MDC)

Women in parliament (lower/single house) 10.0% (2000)

Note: Data from 2001 unless otherwise indicated.

an environment in which, as of 2000, over 75 percent of households lived in poverty, and this number has since grown.

The political situation is a mirror image of the socioeconomic one. Zimbabwe once had many democratic features. Although President Robert Mugabe revealed occasional authoritarian tendencies in the past, the country had generally strong institutions that helped to constrain most autocratic impulses of the president and the ruling party.[1] Today, the rule of law has all but collapsed. The once famously independent judiciary is stocked with pliant judges who answer to the ruling party. Police no longer uphold the law, and sometimes participate in breaking it. Ruling party militias roam the country as formal and informal security forces and, acting as agents of the regime, frequently terrorize opposition supporters. As a result of the country's disregard for the rule of law, human rights violations, including torture, the forcible seizure of white-owned property (principally commercial farms), and abrogation of international agreements, Zimbabwe has become an international pariah, at least outside of Africa. It was suspended from the Commonwealth in 2002, has since been hit by economic ("smart") sanctions by the European Union, Japan, and the United States, among others, and financial flows from Western countries, except urgent humanitarian assistance, have slowed to a trickle (Economist Intelligence Unit [EIU] 2003l). Within Africa, and the southern African region in particular, Zimbabwe's status is somewhat more ambiguous, though the crisis certainly holds profound implications for its neighbors and the continent.

Among the most striking features of Zimbabwe's decay is the rapidity with which it occurred. Admittedly, in 1997, the year generally regarded as the turning point in the country's recent collapse, Zimbabwe's prospects were somewhat tentative. The country was recovering from two debilitating droughts earlier in the decade, and although agricultural growth had returned impressively, the effects on the wider economy were still apparent. Moreover, an economic liberalization program (the economic structural adjustment program [ESAP]), which was enacted in 1991, had concluded and a successor program was under consideration. ESAP had contributed to considerable socioeconomic hardship for many Zimbabweans, and some scholars argue that there is a direct causal link between its impact and the economic decline that followed later (Bond and Manyanya 2002; Carmody and Taylor 2003). Nonetheless, there were still some indicators in early 1997 that a social partnership could emerge that might ameliorate some of the effects of a renewed ESAP (Zimbabwe Congress of Trade Unions [ZCTU] 1996).

Linked to this, but perhaps of greater importance, was the fact that civil society had begun to play an increasingly active role in the political life of the country. Independent media outlets were expanding, and criticism of government was generally tolerated; labor unions and human rights organizations were gaining unprecedented influence; and cracks were beginning to appear in the de facto one-party state that had dominated since independence, providing some evidence of a maturing political culture (Sithole 2000). Conceivably, had these influences been utilized by the regime rather than marginalized and attacked, a more democratic future, rooted in strong social institutions, might have emerged.

The fact that the country was in shambles just half a dozen years later begs a number of questions, two of which preoccupy us in this chapter. First, is it possible to identify the factors that explain Zimbabwe's collapse? Second, given the country's myriad problems, what are its prospects for democracy and economic recovery? Although these questions defy easy answers, an examination of the various interactions between social and political actors and the context in which they operate in Zimbabwe can shed light on this inquiry.

There is disagreement among scholars and other observers about the root causes of Zimbabwe's "plunge" (Bond and Manyanya 2002). Among those who adhere to economic explanations, some blame it on structure, history, and uncorrected racial and socioeconomic imbalances that date from the independence agreement in 1979, or soon thereafter (Bond 1998; Bond and Manyanya 2002). Others, although still looking to structural factors, fix a more recent date, and cite the international financial institutions, the World Bank and International Monetary Fund (IMF), as the principal culprits (Carmody 2001; Stoneman 1998). These authors suggest that the painful choices and harsh conditionalities of Zimbabwe's 1991–1995 ESAP undermined the socioeconomic fabric of Zimbabwe and destroyed the economic foundation on which its prior development and stability once rested. Conversely, economic liberals suggest that the government's *abandonment* of the neoliberal program in 1997 accounts for the collapse (World Bank 1995; Brett and Winter 2003). Advocates of the neopatrimonial paradigm, with its emphasis on the role of the "big man" in Africa, emphasize that weak state structures and institutions allow, indeed promote, the emergence of patrimonial leaders like President Robert Mugabe (Bratton and van de Walle 1997). Still others engage in what might be labeled a psychosocial analysis of history; these interpretations cite greed, power lust, corruption, and incompetence among the factors, but their common thread is a demonization of Mugabe and his political cronies (Rotberg 2000; Meredith 2003; Blair 2002). Such personalist approaches, however, tend to be the least analytically rigorous because they discount the significant role of institutions, however weak, as well as interactions and the international context (Herbst 1990, 245–249).

In reality, the crisis in Zimbabwe requires an understanding of this complex mosaic of interlocking factors. Thus history, structure, and agency are essential components to consider. The framework employed in this book therefore allows examination of institutions and actors as well as material resources, and the interactions between these factors. With this in mind, we can begin not only to make sense of the situation in Zimbabwe, but also to determine the degree to which it is exceptional—or representative—in the region. Zimbabwe remains an important case study in the southern African region, and on the continent as a whole. A little more than a decade ago, Zimbabwe was seen as a bright light in the region; today its importance reflects negative concerns—that is, the threats that Zimbabwe's seemingly inexorable collapse and intractable political crisis may pose for such issues as regional stability, new pan-African initiatives, and Mugabe's counterparts in southern Africa.[2] These concerns, as well as the future of Zimbabwe itself, are very much at stake.

■ Historical Origins of the Zimbabwean State: Context, Key Actors, and Issues

The area now known as Zimbabwe was established as territory of the British South Africa Company (BSAC) in 1890, under charter from the British crown. Together with the territory to its north (modern-day Zambia), the area became known as Rhodesia around 1895, after Cecil Rhodes, the British-born magnate who headed the BSAC. At the time, Zimbabwe was inhabited by two principal ethnic groups, the Ndebele, who had arrived in the region only three generations earlier from South Africa, and the numerically dominant Shona, who were heirs to a once vibrant trading empire that thrived between the eleventh and fifteenth centuries. In 1888, Rhodes's representatives signed the Rudd Concession with the Ndebele king, Lobengula, a treaty that granted them certain "legal" rights to explore mining opportunities in the region. Later, beginning in 1889–1890, Rhodes's men used several deceptions, including Lobengula's alleged subjugation of the Shona peoples to the north, as a pretext for violating the treaty and seizing control over all of Lobengula's kingdom, including the parts inhabited by both the Shona and Ndebele groups.

In 1896–1897, the Africans—both Shona and Ndebele—rebelled against their new colonial masters in what became known as the first *chimurenga* ("rebellion" in Shona). When the revolt was put down, with significant African loss of life, BSAC rule was secured. Thereafter, the white population of the territory steadily increased, although when the anticipated mining concessions proved to be far more limited than initially thought, most white settlers came as farmers. After evicting the indigenous Shona, they established large farming tracts mainly in the central plateau and eastern highland regions of the country; in the southern Matabeleland region previously dominated by the Ndebele, mostly ranching activities were initiated.

The second phase of Zimbabwe's modern history can be dated from 1923, the last year of "company rule." Government of the territory, which by then had become known as Southern Rhodesia, was turned over to the settlers, whose population and self-interest had increased markedly in the three prior decades. This was a pivotal period in Southern Rhodesia. Not only were the settlers granted substantial self-government, but they also opted to remain semiautonomous (with some links to the colonial office), rather than accept an offer to amalgamate with South Africa. The decision to remain autonomous was based in part on Rhodesians' desire to avoid being swallowed up by their larger neighbor and its ascendant Afrikaner population. Hence, as Pierre du Toit (1995) notes, this was a important stage in the shaping of a distinctly Rhodesian nationalism, which was to set the stage for events that unfolded over four decades later.

From 1923 through 1964, Southern Rhodesia experienced tremendous growth and the emergence of an efficient settler state apparatus that ensured the comfortable lifestyle of white residents. The federation with Northern Rhodesia and Nyasaland (Malawi) from 1953 to 1963 further fueled Southern Rhodesia's development, as Malawian labor and Northern Rhodesia's substantial copper wealth flowed almost unidirectionally toward Southern Rhodesia's far greater industrial base. Politically, although the federation's central government powers included defense, trade, industry, and finance, the members retained power over local government, African education, health, agriculture, and land policy. This left the authorities in each of the colonies a considerable degree of autonomy in determining "native policy," and Southern Rhodesia, with the highest number of settlers, had the most repressive native policy (Wills 1964; Sithole 1988). Indeed, in Southern Rhodesia, blacks were stripped of most of their land; forced into the wage economy but denied the right to strike; restricted in their livelihood, place of residence, and movement; and required to carry passes (du Toit 1995).

African nationalism in Southern Rhodesia gathered speed during the federal period, influenced both by the nature of settler rule and by the independence movements that had emerged elsewhere on the continent, including in federation partners Malawi and Zambia. Unlike those states, which gained their independence in 1963 and 1964, respectively, Southern Rhodesia's large settler population was highly resistant to the prospect of a transition to independence that would result in majority rule. In fact, in the face of mounting black nationalism throughout Africa, Southern Rhodesian politics had begun to shift sharply to the right in the late 1950s (Houser 1976, 5). A nascent African liberation movement, the Southern Rhodesia African National Congress, headed by Joshua Nkomo, was banned in 1959, and new repressive legislation was enacted.[3] Yet neither banning nor imprisonment could prevent the emergence of formal resistance movements in the African community. Nkomo subsequently played a leading role in the formation of the Zimbabwe African People's Union (ZAPU) in 1960, which was banned in 1962 but survived underground. A breakaway group, including Robert Mugabe, formed the Zimbabwe African National Union (ZANU) in 1963. ZANU was banned later that year but also continued underground.

As was the case elsewhere in the region where African nationalist movements encountered substantial settler populations, there was resistance to change, and eventually violence. Settlers' self-interest—defined by their social, political, and financial stake in the territory, both real and perceived—made compromise difficult.[4] The prospect of independence in Northern Rhodesia and Nyasaland provoked an even greater conservative backlash among Southern Rhodesia's settler population, and resulted in a victory for the staunchly conservative Dominion Party (later the Rhodesia Front [RF]) in the 1962 legislative elections in the territory (Houser 1976).

In 1965, under pressure from London, but opposed to making any concessions to its African population, Southern Rhodesia issued a unilateral declaration of independence (UDI) from Great Britain. Backed by the white population, RF premier Ian Smith vowed never to surrender to majority rule.[5] Zimbabwe's third historical phase thus dates from the UDI and continued for the next fourteen years. Despite the conditions under which the UDI was declared, including the imposition of UN sanctions in 1967, the Rhodesian economy flourished. After a small drop in national revenues immediately following the UDI, the economy underwent tremendous growth: real GDP increased nearly 40 percent between 1965 and 1970, and a further 35 percent by 1975 (Stoneman and Davies 1981, 97). In fact, in the face of sanctions, the Smith regime pursued an aggressive policy of import substitution industrialization that greatly enhanced the country's industrial base. Rhodesia also achieved self-sufficiency in a number of agricultural crops, including wheat, sugar, and maize, but despite international sanctions, trade relations continued with apartheid South Africa and, less openly, even with the United States and Great Britain. Still, the economy experienced sharp declines after 1975.

The African nationalist movements that emerged in the 1950s solidified during the 1960s and started to press for full independence. What began as scattered and disorganized attacks as early as 1966 led to full-scale war in 1972, when the Zimbabwe National Liberation Army (ZANLA) and the Zimbabwe People's Revolutionary Army (ZIPRA), sponsored by ZANU and ZAPU, respectively, commenced a primarily guerrilla war against the Rhodesian army (Stedman 1991, 37–39). The combination of gains by the African liberation movements and the prospect of a continued military stalemate and the exhaustion of the "easy" phase of import substitution that had helped to fuel the Rhodesian economy finally led the Smith regime to the negotiating table, although full negotiations with ZANU and ZAPU did not begin until September 1979 (Stedman 1991). After a brief interregnum in 1978–1979 in which the country was known as "Zimbabwe-Rhodesia" (a transparent attempt by Smith and the RF to maintain power by installing an African prime minister, Bishop Abel Muzorewa, which never gained popular legitimacy), the principal combatants reached a negotiated settlement in 1979 (Davidow 1984).

With the British acting as brokers, the negotiations took place at Lancaster House in London and included plans for a new constitution and the transition period, and arrangements for the cease-fire (Stedman 1991, 177). Of these issues, the constitution was the most critical element, and its final version was extremely favorable to settler interests. Among its most noteworthy provisions were the establishment of a parliamentary constitutional model; the reservation of 20 seats for whites, elected on a separate roll, in the new 100-seat legislature; the protection of white property rights and land security, with the sale of land on a "willing buyer–willing seller" basis only; guaranteed pensions for white civil servants and military personnel; and a bill of rights (Stedman 1991, 177–183).[6] The final agreement, signed at Lancaster House on December 17, 1979, endorsed the constitution, formally ended hostilities between the warring parties, put in place a plan for the demobilization of armed forces on both sides, and set forth a timetable for a transition to majority rule beginning with national elections in February 1980.

The events of the fourth phase of Zimbabwe's history, from independence in 1980 to 1997, and the fifth, which marks the precipitous decline beginning in 1997 and continuing to the present, are addressed in greater detail in the remainder of the chapter. Nonetheless, a few key themes are worth highlighting here. ZANU, which claimed a "Marxist-Leninist" orientation, handily won the first independence elections and formed the first independence government. Despite its avowed socialist orientation, however, the new government pursued policies of relative economic and social moderation. Although the 1980–1997 period was marked by the emerging dominance of ZANU-PF[7] and the decline of white political power, the period was also characterized by continued white economic hegemony in the key commercial agriculture, manufacturing, and mining sectors. Scott Taylor (1999b) argues that a symbiotic relationship, of sorts, emerged between ZANU-PF and the white agroindustrial elite on whom ZANU-PF, and the country as a whole, were financially dependent. Hence, "Marxism-Leninism" figured more as a rhetorical device, although the development of an autonomous *black* middle class was discouraged by the state (with important later implications). The economy endured two major recessions in the 1980s, and given pressure from industrialists and the international financial institutions, Zimbabwe adopted a structural adjustment program in 1990 that ultimately had severe consequences.

After 1997, the country's overall economic situation did not improve and the Mugabe government began to adopt an increasingly populist platform as it attempted to insulate itself from growing societal unrest and—after 1999—a serious political opposition. Mugabe also embroiled the country in the war in the Democratic Republic of Congo (DRC) beginning in August 1998, which provided patronage opportunities for military and political elites, but drained the national treasury of an estimated U.S.$1 million *per day* for over three years (Nest 2001; United Nations Security Council [UNSC] 2002). At the same time, Zimbabwe's ever-worsening economic situation was matched by growing repression, aimed at political opponents and others. ZANU-PF's erstwhile white allies were among the principal targets of President Mugabe, who sought to blame white Zimbabweans, particularly commercial farmers, for pervasive landlessness among blacks and, by extension, the country's larger economic problems. As we demonstrate below, this was largely a search for scapegoats by Mugabe.[8] Nonetheless, by 2002 over 80 percent of Zimbabwe's 4,500 white-owned commercial farms had been forcibly seized by the government. The chaotic, corrupt, and violent "solution" to Zimbabwe's historical landownership disparities has precipitated economic collapse and contributed to the prevailing environment of lawlessness.

In response to growing international and domestic pressure, President Mugabe has dug in his heels. The cooperation and patronage flows that once sustained the relationship between whites and ZANU-PF have fractured. Further, although some politically connected elites continue to access rents in the DRC, the regime's domestic sources of patronage are severely constrained due to the hemorrhaging of the local economy. In other words, the state lacks the resources to placate dissent through side payments to societal clients, and instead must increasingly rely on coercion and repression. With both formal and informal resources drying up and society in chaos, the endgame may be approaching for ZANU-PF, at least under Mugabe's direction. Many of these issues are elucidated below; however, four particular events from this most recent period should be highlighted. First was the crash of the economy in November 1997, heralded by the 75 percent loss in the Zimbabwe dollar's value—in one day—and the events that precipitated the currency's dramatic fall. The second event was the February 2000 constitutional referendum, in which the government's effort to change the constitution to increase presidential power and permit seizures of white farms was defeated by civil society. Third was the June 2000 parliamentary election, which saw genuine interparty competition for the first time between ZANU-PF and a formidable new opposition party, the Movement for Democratic Change (MDC). Last was the March 2002

Chronology of the Crisis in Zimbabwe

March 1996 Presidential elections won by Mugabe. Uncontested after Muzorewa and Sithole withdraw.

March 1997 War Victims Compensation Fund scandal breaks. Looting of ZW$4.5 billion in pensions discovered (siphoned off by ministers and party hacks).

June/July 1997 Mugabe agrees (without cabinet approval) to compensate "war veterans" lump sums of ZW$50,000 each, and stipends of $2,000 per month.

November 1997 When Mugabe's plans emerge, donors balk, the economy slides: Zimdollar falls 75 percent against major currencies in one day.

November 1997 There are 1,503 farms (4.8 million hectares) listed for compulsory acquisition by the state.

January 1998 Strikes led by labor groups effective.

September 1998 International Donors Conference on Land: produced agreement to resettle just 118 farms over a two-year period (with international support).

February 1999 All designated farms dropped by courts due to government inaction.

September 1999 Opposition party, Movement for Democratic Change, launched.

February 2000 ZANU-PF referendum on constitution defeated.

February 2000 Land invasions begin.

June 2000 MDC wins 57 seats of 120 contested.

September 2001 Abuja Agreement: Mugabe agrees to end land seizures.

February 2002 Land Acquisition Act (1992) amended to allow any minister to order farms vacated. Legislation becomes effective May 2002.

February 2002 Over 100 people, mostly MDC supporters, reported killed in election-related violence since 2000.

March 2002 Presidential election: Mugabe defeats MDC candidate Morgan Tsvangirai with approximately 56 percent of vote. Result widely condemned as illegitimate.

March 2002 In wake of election results, more international sanctions applied; Zimbabwe suspended from Commonwealth.

June 24, 2002 Twenty-nine hundred white farmers given forty-five days to vacate properties.

August 8–10, 2002 Eviction orders take effect; defiant farmers are arrested.

August 12, 2002 In a series of speeches, Mugabe appears conciliatory toward whites, but reverses course quickly.

September 2002 United States and donor countries continue to press South Africa, Nigeria, and other African states to place more diplomatic and economic pressure on Zimbabwe or risk aid reductions.

2003 Zimbabwe's decline continues. An estimated 600 white farmers remain on land, with only 300 actively farming. "Acquired" farms fallow. Emergency food aid continues; ZANU-PF accused of providing it only to partisan supporters.

presidential election, in which the seventy-eight-year-old Mugabe won a controversial and violent election against the MDC candidate, Morgan Tsvangirai. This ushered in the latest wave of violence and repression as the regime, now without popular legitimacy, continued to cling to power.

■ Society and Development: The Politics of Racial and Ethnic Pluralism in a Postsettler Society

▨ *Race Relations*

From the time Europeans began settling in Zimbabwe, race has formed the principal cleavage in that society. White economic privilege was absolute in the colonial period. Africans were deprived of land, freedom of movement, and rights as they were forced into subservient positions in the Rhodesian economy. Ironically, the economic advantages that accrued to whites disproportionately before the liberation war continued through the 1990s (S. Taylor 2002).

The violence of the liberation struggle in Zimbabwe was considerable, a struggle that was very clearly defined in racial terms between white settlers and black nationalists.[9] When it became clear by the mid-1970s that the Rhodesian army would not defeat the liberation armies militarily and that some form of political settlement would be necessary, many white Rhodesians fled, including to apartheid South Africa. In the year 1978, for example, over 13,000 whites emigrated (Stedman 1991, 162). Even more left the country in the aftermath of independence. However, some 130,000 whites remained in 1980, although they represented only about 2 percent of the population.

Notwithstanding the violence of the liberation struggle, the nature of the settlement at Lancaster, and the surprise—even fear— among whites and the international community over Mugabe's victory in the February 1980 elections, reconciliation of racial animosities quickly became the order of the day. The white population had fallen considerably from its peak of 270,000 in 1961 (Herbst 1990, 223), but remained significant. Whites still controlled virtually all industrial and commercial resources, the large-scale commercial farming sector, and most private managerial and senior bureaucratic positions (S. Taylor 2002). Indeed, in many ways the new government's policy of national reconciliation was a pragmatic one, forged out of concern for the country's economy:

> On 4 April 1980, Robert Mugabe addressed the nation as its new prime minister: "We will ensure that there is a place for everyone in this country. We want to ensure a sense of security for both the winners and the losers. There will be no sweeping nationalization; the pensions and jobs of civil

servants are guaranteed; farmers will keep their land. Let us forgive and forget. Let us join hands in a new amity." (quoted in Nhema 2002, 101)

The speech was greeted with relief by most white residents and ushered in a period of rather astounding "reconciliation" in which even those who had been skeptical of the settlement *and* Mugabe's election victory were put at considerable ease. Indeed, despite their self-proclaimed "Marxist" sympathies, ZANU and Mugabe quickly revealed through their policies that they would adhere to the provisions of Lancaster and safeguard white property rights.

This reconciliation was apparently so entrenched that Jeffrey Herbst (1990, 221) could argue less than a decade after independence that "the fact that 100,000 Whites live peacefully in Zimbabwe means that reconciliation can be called Zimbabwe's greatest success." Today we know that Herbst's account proved premature and overly optimistic: what passed for reconciliation was merely preservation of the preindependence status quo. For their part, whites used Mugabe's apparent nod to reconciliation as a basis for continued wealth accumulation and maintenance of their landholdings, and relative tardiness about "affirmative action" in corporate and industrial ranks (Strachan 1986, 1989; S. Taylor 2002). Herbst claims this was part of an "implicit bargain" between the state and white residents: specifically, established farmers and businesspeople could stay, unmolested; however, their children would be discouraged from staying. Herbst thus saw blacks gaining control over economic resources through a process of attrition and demographic change (Herbst 1990, 221, 223).

By definition, this bargain was implicit and "never discussed publicly" (Herbst 1990, 221); however, the existence of an "implicit" bargain like this presupposed that the Mugabe government was itself committed to black advancement. Subsequent research has called this assumption into question by suggesting that Mugabe and ZANU were content with continued white economic dominance because it could forestall the emergence of a black middle class that might present a challenge to ZANU's political hegemony (Raftopoulos 2001; Taylor 1999b). Moreover, what Herbst (and later du Toit [1995]) failed to recognize is that the implicit bargain, to the extent it truly existed, could be superseded or extended because of the mutually beneficial linkages between black political elites in ZANU and white economic elites. Therefore, although this relationship between "strange bedfellows" may not have continued indefinitely, its final collapse in 2000 is not adequately explained through the implicit bargain thesis.

In any event, one observation receives broad consensus: although the relationship between the races was substantially characterized by Mugabe's "new amity" for most of the independence era, many whites were able simply to continue a colonial lifestyle following independence (Herbst 1989;

1990; Raftopoulos 2001; Bond 1998). In fact, some whites remained unreconstructed and unapologetic racists (Weiss 1994; Godwin and Hancock 1993).[10] Many felt scant need to alter their behavior by integrating socially or politically, or through economic sacrifice, however limited (Bond and Manyanya 2002); indeed, this was an inherently rational strategy, since whites felt very little pressure from the new regime to adjust their behavior (S. Taylor 2002). Yet this also left them vulnerable to later attack by the state. Indeed, one can see how many whites would have been blindsided by Mugabe's resort to seemingly unbridled racism beginning in the 1996 presidential election. After all, amity *had* prevailed, the government had supported white economic interests consistently, even at the expense of black ones, and had only halfheartedly embraced "indigenization" (S. Taylor 2002).

Nonetheless, although race became a political smokescreen intended to distract the populace from the government's own failed policies on land, indigenization, economic redistribution, and general improvement of the black condition, it did gain some political traction for the ruling party in some quarters (Taylor 1999b). Moreover, some argue that following the assault on white farmers, mostly between 2000 and 2002, race has ceased to be a major cleavage in Zimbabwe: many whites have abandoned commercial activities or fled the country altogether (Cooke, Morrison, and Prendergast 2003). Regardless of whether Zimbabwe's racial divisions have been "resolved" in this manner—that is, the coerced emigration of the vast majority of whites ipso facto obviates the racial conflict—the victimization of white Zimbabweans by their former collaborators in the government makes clear that Mugabe can no longer use whites as scapegoats for the country's mounting problems.

▇ *Ethnic Relations*

The departure of large numbers of whites refocuses attention on the other major societal cleavage in Zimbabwe: ethnicity. The majority Shona, who compose approximately 82 percent of the population, have been the dominant black actors since independence. The remainder of the population is divided among the Ndebele (16 percent) and several other smaller groups. However, the Shona are also quite diverse, consisting of six subgroups who show recent signs of intraethnic competition as political and economic resources have become scarce (Maroleng 2003). Just prior to colonialism, the Shona, who arrived in modern-day Zimbabwe between the eleventh and fifteenth centuries, had been a subject people to the Ndebele, who settled in the area only in the 1830s, fleeing their own subjugation under the Zulu during the *mfecane* (the period during which the Zulu kingdom under Shaka Zulu was created). A century and a half later, interethnic friction contributed to the eventual division between the two liberation movements, ZAPU under Joshua Nkomo and ZANU under Ndabaningi Sithole (and later Robert Mugabe), where the former became identified with Ndebele and the latter with Shona.[11]

The level of contestation for resources in Zimbabwe between ethnic groups is itself a subject of debate (du Toit 1995). Importantly, the Shona and Ndebele have seen periods of conflict and cooperation. The ZAPU and ZANU parties together formed a loose "patriotic front" in 1976 as a basis for joint negotiations with the settler state. In 1980, Mugabe invited the predominantly Ndebele ZAPU to join his first cabinet. His rival Nkomo took the post of home affairs minister. Mugabe also appointed Canaan Banana, an Ndebele, to the then largely ceremonial position of president in the first independent government. Alfred Nhema (2002, 101) argues that this was part of an emergent "tradition" of ethnic balancing, which was earlier evidenced in the Muzorewa Zimbabwe-Rhodesia period.[12]

On the other hand, interethnic relations have also endured great tension in the postsettler period. For example, when arms caches were discovered on ZAPU-owned property in February 1982, ZANU suspected a ZAPU plot to reconstitute its armed forces and to seize power. Nkomo and several other ZAPU ministers were sacked, and Nkomo subsequently fled to London in March 1983, where he remained until August 1983 (Nhema 2002, 114). When former ZIPRA soldiers did rebel in Matabeleland and the Midlands province beginning in 1982, the government responded by sending the army's Fifth Brigade to put down the disturbances. Between 1982 and 1985, 1,500 people, mostly Ndebele, were killed, according to the official estimate (du Toit 1995, 132); however, some recent estimates place the death toll as high as 7,000, including many innocent civilians. Debate about the period has resurfaced in recent years, as civil society organizations began to reexamine the roots of President Mugabe's authoritarianism. The leader of the Fifth Brigade, Air Marshall Perrence Shiri, is today one of the most senior members of the Zimbabwean military, and some critics have called for Mugabe to be investigated for war crimes because of the actions of the army under his direction.

In part due to ongoing Ndebele resentment, some of the strongest zones of support for the new opposition party, the MDC, are found in the two Matabeleland provinces, where Ndebele populations are numerous, in particular in the city of Bulawayo. Moreover, although it is quite inaccurate to label the MDC an Ndebele party, several senior positions in MDC are occupied by Ndebeles. Nonetheless, it is too simplistic to view intra-African relations in Zimbabwe through an exclusively ethnic lens. Ndebeles have served as prominent members of the government and cabinet, even during periods of great national tension. Indeed, Mugabe has demonstrated great skill at co-opting Ndebele nationalism and potential rivalry. For example, after several years of negotiations, the 1987 Unity Accord brought ZAPU and Nkomo back into government through a formal merger—absorption, really—into ZANU-PF. Nkomo remained in Mugabe's government as a vice president until his death in 1999. Moreover, a few Ndebeles occupy senior positions in government, including John Nkomo, the current minister for special affairs in the president's office, and Jonathan Moyo, the minister of information.[13]

■ Organization of the State

■ *Executive*

At independence, Zimbabwe was bequeathed a Westminster parliamentary model, courtesy of the Lancaster House agreement. Between 1980 and 1987, Mugabe was prime minister and the presidency was a ceremonial office. However, when the Lancaster provisions barring changes to the political system expired in 1987, Zimbabwe adopted an executive presidency, which provided for two vice presidents appointed by the president. Mugabe, who sought to adopt a presidential model even prior to independence, assumed the office, and the post of prime minister was eliminated (Nhema 2002). Like most other contemporary African states, Zimbabwe has a strong executive with significant powers and resources at his disposal. Moreover, as head of the party in a system of single-party dominance, the president commands loyalty in the parliament as well as the party structures. By and large, the parliament has served as a rubber stamp for executive authority. Notably, even with substantial MDC representation after 2000, parliament is incapable of providing the balance of power required to prevent the presidential model from sliding into dictatorship.

The executive is supported by a cabinet that as of 2003 consisted of twenty line ministries responsible for specific portfolios, and five ministers of state. In addition, there are twelve deputy ministers, and the eight provincial governors are intended to carry out executive functions at the regional level. A hallmark of Mugabe's approach to governance has been the repeated reshuffling of cabinet members: ministers have been reassigned, demoted, or sacked altogether with increasing frequency. Again, this relates to threats and perceived threats to the president's authority: loyalty is rewarded, whereas those who are seen as "counterrevolutionaries," or as potential rivals to the president, are marginalized (EIU 2003l).

In the ZANU-PF case, the party central committee and politburo are also supporting bodies involved in policymaking. Although their purview lies in party affairs, historically party and state were interchangeable in Zimbabwe. As a result, these entities serve to enhance and concentrate presidential power. "The Politburo is chaired by President Mugabe, and consists of Secretaries of the ten departments, their deputies, and 4 Committee members. It has 24 members who hold regular meetings once a month. This is a decision-making organ between the meetings of the Central Committee. The second organ is the Central Committee which has 150 members who meet once in three months. This is a decision-making body between [party] congresses" (http://www.zanupfpub.co.zw).

Thus the ZANU-PF party structure is also an important part of the government's executive functions and provides a mechanism to reward and punish individuals within the senior ranks of the party. The ZANU-PF Central Committee, for example, was enlarged from only 26 members in the early 1980s to 90 members by 1990, and to 280 members by 2000. The ZANU-PF Politburo is appointed by the president and key members of the central committee and deals with all regular party matters (Stoneman and Cliffe 1989, 79).

■ Constitutionalism: From Lancaster House to the 2000 Referendum

Constitutional principal has been subverted to executive authority in Zimbabwe, and the ruling party now ignores constitutional restrictions with impunity. Yet the 1979 Lancaster agreement provided a comprehensive constitutional blueprint for the independent state. Its more notable provisions have been enumerated above, including reserved parliamentary seats for whites, an independent judiciary, a bill of rights, a stipulation that land transfers could only be made on a "willing buyer–willing seller" basis rather than forcibly acquired, and a council of chiefs.[14] It was, in short, an inherently conservative document, intended to restrict the agenda of the new government and provide certain guarantees for white residents. Although the Lancaster agreement stipulated that the constitution could only be changed with a 100 percent majority in the parliament, the constitution could be altered after ten years by a two-thirds majority. Many of the provisions agreed to at Lancaster had earlier expiry dates. The white seats, for example, were guaranteed only until 1987. It was believed that the ten-year expiration of the Lancaster constitution would give time for the new Zimbabwean state to become institutionalized and for constitutional protections to become entrenched.

In September 1987 the first of these changes took place. The twenty reserved white seats were abolished, and the eighty African members elected twenty new members to the lower house (eleven of whom were white) (Nhema 2002, 117). The ten white reserved seats in the upper house were abolished. In October 1987 the Westminster model was abandoned in favor of an executive presidency. Finally, by December the two-chamber parliament was abandoned in favor of a unicameral system, with a single, 150-member chamber, effective from the 1990 general election (Nhema 2002, 117).

Nonetheless, the 1979 constitution, with these and other amendments, has remained the basic legal framework in Zimbabwe. Thus by 1998 the National Constitutional Assembly (NCA), a movement that had emerged in mid-1997, was lobbying for a new constitution. The NCA was a coalition of some ninety-six civil society organizations, including academics and legal experts, labor unions, churches, and human rights groups who argued that, at its core, the constitution of Zimbabwe still contained many colonial-era provisions and that numerous amendments had had the effect of reducing individual rights (EIU 2003l, 7). The NCA successfully pressured the state to establish a constitutional commission in April 1999. To the dismay of the NCA, however, at least 300 members of the government's 400-member commission were also members of ZANU-PF. The NCA refused to accept the legitimacy of the process (Raftopoulos 2001, 15), and continued its own unofficial constitutional-drafting exercise in parallel.

On the one hand, the very emergence of the NCA was a striking example of the maturation of civil society in Zimbabwe, because a diverse range of interests and institutions came together around one goal. On the other hand, the NCA's exclusion was a reflection of the unwillingness of the ZANU regime to make the constitution a truly popular, *modern* document, appropriately reflective of people's concerns in the contemporary Zimbabwean state.

Confident of its ability to control the outcome, the government put the constitutional commission's version of the constitution to a national referendum. In Zimbabwe's first-ever plebiscite, held on February 12–13, 1997, 54.7 percent of the population voted to reject the government proposals. The NCA had rallied its supporters and others in the wider populace to vote no to the narrowly tailored, partisan document, which would have increased presidential powers and undermined property rights by abolishing the last vestiges of legal protections against state seizure of (largely white-owned) commercial farms. This marked the first electoral defeat President Mugabe had faced in twenty years of power, and later events revealed that he was unwilling to tolerate additional losses.

If it is possible retroactively to fix the start of Zimbabwe's collapse in November 1997, as suggested above, it is equally clear that the country took a sharp and irrevocable downward turn after the release of the referendum results in mid-February 2000. Prior to this date, most stakeholders and government opponents held firm to the belief that the economic and increasingly political crisis gripping the country could be addressed through popular means—including not only marches and periodic demonstrations, but also mediation and consultation. Moreover, civic confidence that change might be possible via the ballot box was significantly boosted via the referendum process itself; indeed, President Mugabe appeared initially magnanimous in defeat when he announced the results (Raftopoulos 2001).

Very shortly after the referendum, however, the national environment became quite different. The defeat of the referendum ushered in a level of violence not seen in Zimbabwe in almost two decades, rising lawlessness, state disinterest in restoration of order, and government manipulation of race and the land issue for political ends. Since late February 2000, then, Zimbabwe has been characterized by an intolerance of dissent and gross human rights violations—including state-sanctioned torture, illegal imprisonment, the use of food aid as a weapon, and nearly 200 politically motivated deaths. Paradoxically, what began as a worthy effort to enshrine constitutionalism was so warped by the state that it succeeded in destroying its foundation.

▪ Other Branches of the State

The judiciary and judicial-presidential relations. In a system of genuine balance of power, the judiciary should have been capable of mitigating Zimbabwe's slide toward authoritarianism. Zimbabwe long had an autonomous judiciary, as enshrined in the Lancaster agreement. Sections 11–26 of the 1979 Zimbabwean constitution include a "Declaration of Rights" that guaranteed freedom of expression, association, and assembly. Hence, government actions and decrees were regularly taken to the High Court, where it was not uncommon for the government to lose decisions, which it generally accepted, albeit grudgingly.[15]

However, starting with its defeat on the constitutional referendum in 2000, the executive branch pursued a strategy of intimidation and harassment, often simply ignoring judgments from the bench. More alarming, prominent jurists, including former Supreme Court chief justice Anthony Gubbay, were forced to retire under threat. In 2001, Gubbay was replaced by the more government-friendly Godfrey Chidyausiku. As noted above, presidential and executive authority has been increasingly dismissive of unfavorable judicial decisions, roughly since 2000–2001. Whereas Mugabe was long chastened by judicial review of presidential directives, his administration no longer seems concerned about legal opinion. An artifice of checks and balances exists, but even this pretense is seldom maintained in an atmosphere increasingly characterized by lawlessness. ZANU-PF has become a law unto itself; in some cases, the response to unfavorable decisions from the bench has been to change the law. In other cases, however, the courts have simply been ignored.

The latest period has seen not only the erosion of constitutional protections, but also an array of repressive legislation intended to consolidate the power of the ruling party and clamp down on dissent. Although passed with intent to influence the March 2002 presidential election, these laws have had sweeping ramifications well beyond that event. The notorious Public Order and Security Act of 2002, for example, which contravenes Section 11 of the constitution, prescribed penalties of up to twenty years' imprisonment for any threat to organize civil disobedience. The Citizenship Act of 2002 outlawed dual citizenship and was designed to prevent whites and the descendants of farm workers born in neighboring countries from voting for the MDC in the 2002 presidential election. The Access to Information and Protection of Privacy Act of 2002 restricted access for foreign reporters and imposed tight controls on local media. It also created a state-appointed commission to license journalists, with penalties of up to two years in prison for violating the regulations ("Zim Parliament" 2002).

The newly pliant judiciary has largely concurred with the application of these laws, though there have been interesting exceptions. David Blair (2002, 76) traces the breakdown of the rule of law to a single event: on March 17, 2000, as the land invasions were escalating and 630 farms were then occupied, the farmers' main representative body, the Commercial Farmers Union (CFU) sought and obtained a court order from High Court justice Paddington Garwe (who has ties to ZANU-PF himself) naming key agents of the regime as respondents.[16] The order, which was agreed to by the parties, stipulated that the farm occupations were illegal, and that farms must be vacated. Garwe gave the police seventy-two hours to execute the order. However, encouraged by the president himself, at the end of the period the number of occupations had ballooned to 742, indicating the powerlessness of legal institutions in contemporary Zimbabwe. The turning point identified by Blair is compelling, and it has been followed by numerous other assaults on judicial independence. Indeed, several other recent examples stand out as stark illustrations of the breakdown of the rule of law and the subversion of the judiciary to the political whims of ZANU-PF.[17]

The military. Since independence the Zimbabwean military has not played a visible role in the country's politics, with the exception of the killing of noncombatants by the Fifth Brigade in the early 1980s. Outside of that notorious unit, in general, the military—which was established by merging ZANLA and ZIPRA forces and initially some members (especially senior officers) of the Rhodesian forces as well—was regarded as professional and apolitical. As in other southern African nations, military interventions have been uncommon, and coups unheard of. The post-1997 period, however, witnessed the emergence of a newly politicized and enriched military establishment, which poses a looming threat to continued civilian rule in Zimbabwe. The military began to emerge as a political force following Zimbabwe's 1998 intervention in the war in the DRC. Zimbabwe sent as many as 15,000 troops to the Congo, severely stretching the country's deployment capacity (EIU 2003l).

Though the DRC intervention became a national economic disaster for Zimbabwe as a whole, military and political elites have enriched themselves in the DRC through mining and timber concessions, supply and transport contracts, and so on. Party- and military-owned and affiliated companies, such as Zimbabwe Defense Industries and Operation Sovereign Legitimacy (Osleg), managed to secure lucrative and controversial contracts in the DRC, as well as joint ventures with the Congolese government (see Nest 2001; UNSC 2002; Global Witness 2002b). Thus the generals have become intricately linked within the ZANU-PF patronage web. The rank and file, however, have not fared as well; the troops remaining following the substantial pullout in October 2002 reportedly were there to protect Zimbabwean investments—far from the original mission, which was allegedly to protect the Congo's sovereignty (EIU 2003l).

Nonetheless, the senior officers now have a vested interest in preserving the status quo of ZANU-PF rule, which is an inherently political position; indeed, any threat to ZANU-PF power poses a corresponding threat to the military elite. The risk lies not only in the prospect of lost patronage, but also in the potential of facing prosecution by a reformist, civilian government headed by the MDC or another opposition party. As a result, the military inserted itself into domestic political affairs (or was asked to do so). For example, "in an unprecedented display of strength and hubris prior to the 2003 presidential election, the military declared that it will be the final arbiter of who governs Zimbabwe" (Carmody and Taylor 2003, 13). Commander in chief of the armed forces, Lieutenant-General Vitalis Zvinavashe, stated, in effect, that a Tsvangirai victory would not be tolerated and any presidential aspirant would be subjected to a liberation war "litmus test":

> We wish to make it very clear to all Zimbabwean citizens that the security organisations will pursue Zimbabwean values, traditions and beliefs for which thousands of lives were lost. . . . We will therefore, not accept, let alone support or salute, anyone with a different agenda that threatens the very existence of our sovereignty, our country and our people. (quoted in Carmody and Taylor 2003, 13)[18]

■ Representation and Participation

▦ *Legislative Branch*

As the ZANU-PF executive branch has concentrated authority and drawn on the military to solidify its power and insulate itself from challenges, the power of the legislature has remained marginal. Since 1989, when the upper house of parliament (the Senate) was discarded, the unicameral parliament has been composed of 150 members, 120 of whom are elected on the basis of a common voters' roll by a first-past-the-post, simple majority in single-member constituencies. The remaining thirty members are appointed by the president and include the eight provincial governors, ten traditional chiefs (elected first by an electoral college of chiefs), and twelve others (Commonwealth Observer Group 2000, 9). The president's capacity to appoint members—an anachronism also found in neighboring Zambia—not only impedes the independence of the legislative chamber, but also vests extraordinary power in the president and potentially dilutes the will of the electorate by rendering opposition representation in the chamber less competitive.[19] Until 2000, when the MDC captured fifty-seven seats, the competitiveness of the chamber was unimportant; it was dominated by ZANU-PF, which served as a rubber stamp for President Mugabe's decisions. However, the unchecked rise of executive authority described above, coupled with a slim electoral margin of the ZANU-PF majority[20]—and the thirty *appointed* members of parliament—means that a once compliant parliament has been marginalized even further from the political process.

▓ *Party System and Elections*

Zimbabwe has been a nominally multiparty state since independence in 1980. Although the country flirted with de jure single-party rule in the late 1980s, the ZANU-PF government, which had long pushed for such a change, abandoned the effort in 1990. In any event, a single-party option proved unnecessary: by the late 1980s, ZANU-PF attained a virtual lock on elective office, cemented in the 1990 elections (Sylvester 1995). Not until the emergence of the Movement for Democratic Change in September 1999, and the parliamentary elections that followed in June 2000, was the dominant-party regime seriously challenged at the ballot box.

The country's two principal liberation movements, ZAPU, led by Joshua Nkomo, and ZANU, led by Mugabe, were the leading contenders in the first independence elections, held in February 1980 under the conditions agreed to at Lancaster House in December 1979. ZANU captured fifty-seven of the eighty African seats, defeating ZAPU, which garnered twenty seats. Bishop Abel Muzorewa's United African National Council (UANC) picked up three seats. The Rhodesia Front, under Ian Smith, captured all twenty of the seats on the white voters' roll (Nhema 2002).

The elections in 1985, 1990, 1995, and 1996 each saw the steady consolidation of ZANU hegemony. In 1985, ZANU gained sixty-four seats in the hundred-seat lower house; Muzorewa's UANC lost all its seats; ZANU-Sithole (later ZANU-Ndonga) gained one seat; and the RF (renamed the Conservative Alliance [CA] in 1983) gained fifteen of the twenty white seats. A liberal RF breakaway group, the Independent Zimbabwe Group, could muster only five seats. Mugabe was publicly critical of whites for their continued support of Ian Smith's party, the CA. Nhema (2002, 116) argues that such behavior led Mugabe to believe that "by voting yet again for Smith, whites had spurned his government's hand of reconciliation. As he put it, 'the vote [for the CA] proved that [whites] had not repented in any way'" (Nhema 2002, 116, n. 79, quoting *The Herald,* July 1, 1985).

The elections in 1990 were significant because they confirmed the consolidation of ZANU-PF political power after the 1987 Unity Accord. Former ZANU-PF secretary-general Edgar Tekere and his Zimbabwe Unity Movement party were defeated at the polls, and the opposition only managed to garner three seats. At the same time, however, this outcome also masked a latent discontent with ZANU-PF rule that was to escalate exponentially in the 1990s. Tekere's party actually received more than 19 percent of the vote nationally. Moreover, turnout of just under 60 percent reveals that substantial numbers did not bother to vote, suggesting a reservoir of anti–ZANU-PF sentiment in the country (Sylvester 1995, 411). In any event, the ruling party was able to draw on the substantial resources of incumbency that it exploits in every election. These include privileged, often exclusive, access to the state-owned media; the ability to dispense food in poor rural areas, typically in the form of maize or seed; and sole access to an electoral fund (amounting to Z$30 million annually in the elections of the 1990s), which was not subject to public audit (Zimbabwe Human Rights Association [ZimRights] 1996). In addition, the plurality electoral system in single-member constituencies, which favors incumbents and underrepresents supporters of other parties, also worked in ZANU-PF's favor. In the 1995 and 1996 elections, these factors as well as the deteriorating macropolitical and economic situation combined to produce apathy rather than voter mobilization. Although opposition parties gained 18 percent of the national vote in the parliamentary contest, turnout fell to 57 percent (Sylvester 1995, 411). In the 1996 presidential election, Zimbabwean nongovernmental organizations (NGOs) claimed that the government engaged in rampant vote buying and distribution of maize, seed, and fertilizer to shore up rural support (ZimRights 1996, 9). The turnout for the 1996 elections was an anemic 31 percent of registered voters, which ZimRights (1996, 11–12) and other domestic observers interpreted as a vote of no confidence in ZANU-PF.[21]

Despite ZANU-PF's substantial margins of victory, one important trend that emerged from the 1995–1996 elections was the loss of ZANU-PF support in the urban areas, where poverty, unemployment, and labor activism all were on the increase. This created legitimacy problems for ZANU-PF, and exposed its growing vulnerabilities. Internal decay within the ruling party, declining living standards in the 1990s, and the emergence of a credible alternative to ZANU-PF were to set the stage for major changes in the years that followed, culminating in the MDC's performance in the 2000 and 2002 elections, when it swept the urban vote. Notwithstanding the MDC's inability to secure a majority of the 120 seats it contested, the June 2000 election nevertheless was a watershed event in modern Zimbabwe (see Alexander 2000; Kriger 2000; International Crisis Group [ICG] 2000; Sithole 2001). Although fifteen political parties contested the June 24–25, 2000, parliamentary elections, ZANU-PF and the ascendant MDC were the principal contenders.[22] ZANU-PF captured sixty-two seats to the MDC's fifty-seven, but the results from over thirty constituencies were immediately challenged by the opposition as fraudulent. Nonetheless, with the widespread irregularities, the harassment of MDC supporters, including the deaths of nearly thirty people (mostly MDC partisans) in election-related violence prior to the poll, and the benefits of incumbency, the MDC's achievement was noteworthy (Kriger 2000).

The presidential election was held on March 9–10, 2002. It took place in an electoral context of rising repression and attacks on MDC supporters (this time over 100 people lost their lives). Moreover, the draconian legislation introduced prior to the election helped to tilt an already unlevel playing field further in ZANU-PF's favor. Despite these advantages, MDC candidate Tsvangirai garnered, officially, over 42 percent of the vote. On March 13, 2002, Mugabe was declared the winner, defeating Tsvangirai by an official margin of 1.6 million to 1.2 million votes. These results were immediately challenged by the MDC, its supporters, and much of the international community.[23] Fraud was certainly a factor in the government's victory; by some estimates, it accounted for more than the 400,000-vote margin of Tsvangirai's defeat.[24] Indeed, these findings were consistent with the results of opinion polls conducted in the months prior to the election, which showed a substantial lead for Tsvangirai.[25]

▓ Civil Society and Social Groups

The MDC's origins clearly lie in a civil society that became energized in the late 1990s. Indeed, opposing voices to ZANU-PF were neither as organized nor as capable in the first decade of independence (Sylvester 1995). Of course, organized interest groups existed in the 1980s, and before. However, they were able to strike an increasingly resonant chord with the wider society as the 1990s wore on, due to a confluence of factors. Prominent among these was the worsening economic situation for average Zimbabweans: real wages were declining, industrial closures were becoming commonplace, and the ability of the state to provide a social safety net was rapidly eroding. The economic structural adjustment program, which was intended to address many of these concerns, suffered from both flaws in design and implementation, and the program therefore contributed to deepening hardship (Carmody and Taylor 2003).

The trade unions, human rights organizations, and later the emergent MDC were able to capitalize on this discontent (ZCTU 1996; Bond and Manyanya 2002). Civil society's awakening, therefore, was both consequence and cause of ZANU-PF's declining hegemony. Civic organizations arose to challenge ZANU-PF's neglect of social, economic, and political concerns, and as more groups were emboldened, the regime no longer appeared impenetrable. In the Zimbabwe case, however, civic expression came at an enormous medium-term cost: the greater the voice of civic actors, the more repressive the regime response—a desperate measure consistent with dying authoritarianism.

The MDC emerged partly out of the labor movement and partly out of the NCA, but it came to attract myriad other interests as well, including NGOs, human rights organizations, churches, and legal groups. The well-known linkage between civic organizations and the MDC is an important factor in explaining why groups from human rights NGOs, church and religious groups, to women's organizations have been targeted, intimidated, and frequently arrested by state authorities. Below we examine the role of several of these key "traditional" elements of civil society: labor, human rights organizations, and the media. It is important to note that Zimbabwe has a rich history of economic interest groups that play a critical mediating role in the economic arena as well. These actors have been the subject of numerous studies (e.g., Herbst 1990; Skalnes 1995; Taylor 2004), and have served as key societal partners, and sometime critics, of both the Rhodesian and Zimbabwean governments over the years. Since the role of these groups is drastically curtailed, if not eliminated, as a result of the economic crisis, we instead concentrate on civil society actors who are more actively engaged in criticism or support of ZANU-PF's political agenda. Thus this section does examine those organizations that have been co-opted by the state. Among these, groups such as the liberation war veterans association admittedly stretch our very conception of civil society, since they are increasingly funded, organized, and utilized by the state for expressly political purposes.

Labor. Unlike in some other African countries, including South Africa and Zambia, trade unions in Zimbabwe lacked strength historically. At independence, Zimbabwean labor was "weak, divided and had played no significant role in the discussions over the transition to majority rule at Lancaster House in 1979" (Raftopoulos 2001, 4). In the 1980s, labor was restrained as part of a state corporatist framework (Shaw 1989). Indeed, as Brian Raftopoulos (2001, 4) argues, the main labor umbrella, the Zimbabwe Congress of Trade Unions (ZCTU), was effectively a wing of ZANU-PF in the 1980s; Robert Mugabe's brother, Albert, even served as ZCTU secretary general until his death. Moreover, the nominally socialist government of ZANU-PF instituted repressive antilabor legislation such as restrictions on shop floor organization and dealt harshly with strikes in the early 1980s, even prohibiting the right to strike.[26] These measures were welcomed by employers, and the mostly white business community benefited. Beginning in 1987, however, new leadership emerged within the ZCTU, including Morgan Tsvangirai as secretary-general. With the familial link to ZANU broken, the ZCTU began to distance itself from the ruling party and actually represent worker interests. Despite the historical weakness of labor in Zimbabwe, the state was wary of its potential power, even in the early 1990s.[27] Thus, as relations between the state and the union federation became more antagonistic, the state began to harass and arrest labor leaders, including Tsvangirai, who were later acquitted by the still autonomous High Court (Raftopoulos 2001, 8).

The early 1990s were a difficult time for the union movement in Zimbabwe, as they were in other countries of the region such as South Africa and Zambia, which adopted inherently antilabor structural adjustment programs. Patrick Bond and Masimba Manyanya (2002, 86) have disapprovingly stated that the ZCTU and "Tsvangirai sought an accommodation with neoliberalism." Arguably, this was the only way labor could avoid being marginalized, since economic policy decisions were being made chiefly between international donors and the state, and thus the parameters of economic policy "choice" were already set. In this vein, the ZCTU articulated a position in its 1996 "Beyond ESAP" report (ZCTU 1996) that largely accepted the hegemony of the neoliberal agenda.

Nonetheless, the second half of the 1990s saw the reemergence of strikes and stay-aways called by the ZCTU. The ESAP deepened, if not caused, declines in real wages and sharp escalation in unemployment in all sectors except commercial agriculture (Carmody and Taylor 2003). Protests mounted, and the ZCTU gained a prominent role. First, it supported a strike by a previously unaffiliated union, the Public Sector Workers Union, over pay increases in early 1996. Later, the ZCTU called the first of its own strikes in December 1997 (Raftopoulos 2001, 10–12; Bond and Manyanya 2002, 88). The ZCTU's December 1997 action marked a critical turning point for the organization. Called in response to a Mugabe-proposed tax that would severely undercut the already precarious position of workers, the threat of the strike induced the government to capitulate on the issue. However, the status of the unions as a genuine political force was ensured when the ZCTU went ahead with the successful strike anyway (Raftopoulos 2001, 13; Bond and Manyanya 2002, 88).

The events of this period in 1997, including but not limited to the role of the ZCTU, set off a chain of events that permanently altered the political and economic landscape in Zimbabwe. By early 1998 the ascendant ZCTU was playing a central role in the launch of the NCA, which was chaired by Tsvangirai. The "spectre of the Chiluba route to power," to quote Raftopoulos (2001, 8), was certainly apparent by September 1999, when much of the ZCTU leadership assumed prominent positions in the newly formed MDC. Tsvangirai became leader of the MDC, which gained the staunch support of not only labor unions, but also business groups and the urban middle class.

Human rights organizations. The mid-1990s marked a period when, it could be argued, ZANU-PF and Mugabe were at their weakest. The economy over which they presided was under pressure from the combined effects of structural imbalances, two severe droughts, and the ESAP. The elections of 1995 and 1996, although swept by ZANU-PF, showed the party's vulnerabilities. Finally, the regime's then latent authoritarianism permitted political and legal space in which to criticize the government.

In addition to the labor efforts noted above, a number of critical organizations arose in this period. Among these was the Zimbabwe Human Rights Association (ZimRights), which was actually established in 1992 but rose to prominence mid-decade as an outspoken government critic. By 1998 it claimed 15,000 members. In attempting to fulfill its organizational objectives, ZimRights clashed with ZANU-PF over many functions, including civic action, democracy and good governance, HIV/AIDS, victim support, voter education and election monitoring, as well as more "conventional" human rights concerns—lobbying the government to adopt international human rights norms (ZimRights 2002). One of the organization's most valued functions since the June 2000 parliamentary elections has been to serve as an information conduit to international human rights organizations.

Finally, the Crisis in Zimbabwe Coalition was established in 2001, between the elections, as land invasions and political violence escalated, and it appeared that ZANU-PF would attempt to rig the presidential elections. The coalition actually contains nine other entities, including the NCA, the ZCTU, and the Media Institute; altogether, the nine subgroups represent some 500 NGOs. Among the coalition's chief objectives are the promotion of "freedom and democratic values through encouraging dialogue, tolerance and the shaping of ideas by Zimbabweans from all walks of life" (Crisis in Zimbabwe Coalition 2003).

The media. As in most of Africa, the biggest player in Zimbabwe's media is the state, which has profound implications for the dissemination of ideas, the representation of alternative viewpoints, and the competitiveness of opposition parties and groups. The government-owned *Herald* newspaper, and the *Sunday Mail,* are among only three English-language dailies and have the widest circulation in the country. The government press, and the principal television broadcast company, ZBC, take an unapologetically ZANU-PF line. Similar progovernment views are espoused on state-run radio. Indeed, there are great risks for not doing so: the head of the state-owned press company, Zimpapers, was dismissed in the 1990s for not toeing the government line sufficiently.

On the other hand, the independent media (especially print) have fought tirelessly to publish dissenting viewpoints. Several weekly newspapers, such as the *Financial Gazette,* the *Zimbabwe Independent,* and the *Sunday Standard,* have criticized the government, at great risk to journalists, editors, and sellers of the papers. The only independent daily newspaper, the *Daily News,* was established in April 1999 and immediately took an antigovernment position and attracted a wide readership. However, the *Daily News,* which developed a pro-MDC bias, paid a heavy price. Its press was bombed twice; both times army personnel were suspected, based on the devices used. Reporters and staff of the *Daily News,* like those from all the independent papers, have been harassed and imprisoned. Even before the promulgation of the new media law, the Access to Privacy and Protection of Information Act (AIPPA), journalists risked imprisonment, fines, or worse.[28]

As noted above, the passage of AIPPA in January 2002 made it a criminal offense to publish certain kinds of stories, imposed licensing requirements on reporters—a privilege granted, and subject to revocation, by the state—and established registration procedures for news agencies. Given the hostile climate for journalists, it is a testament to the dedication of both local and foreign correspondents in Zimbabwe that they continued to publish stories in the wake of this legislation. However, the state continues to go to great lengths to control the dissemination and use of information. Reporter Andrew Meldrum, a longtime Zimbabwe resident but American citizen, was deported in 2003 for publishing unfavorable stories, while in September 2003 the government shut down the offices of the *Daily News* and confiscated its equipment, alleging company registry violations. The now pliant courts declined to overturn the draconian media law.

Progovernment groups: war veterans and the new militias. The institutions and actors discussed above tended to coalesce around opposition to the regime and its policies. The Zimbabwe National Liberation War Veterans Association (the "war vets"), conversely, emerged as a significant player on the national stage beginning in July and August 1997, but provided an important plank in ZANU-PF's otherwise dwindling popular constituency. Under Chenjerai Hunzvi, a Polish-trained doctor (who actually spent the liberation war in Eastern Europe), the war vets became a formidable organization. The black guerrillas of the liberation war had indeed been wronged. At the end of the war in 1979, they were demobilized and returned, sometimes quite uncomfortably, to civilian life. Their Rhodesian army counterparts were given substantial pensions, which were guaranteed by the Lancaster agreement. Senior war veterans in the ruling party penetrated the highest ranks in the army, police, and state bureaucracy (Kriger 2003). However, for years after independence, many of the "rank and file" among the former guerrillas suffered from unemployment, landlessness, and homelessness, although collectively their contribution to independence was of course widely recognized (Bond and Manyanya 2002). "When it was discovered in 1997 that the War Victims Compensation Fund had been looted, to the tune of Z$450mm by senior officials in ZANU-PF, war veterans organized mass demonstrations," including against the president himself (Carmody and Taylor 2003, 10) at the Heroes Day celebration in August 1997.

Reportedly "shaken" by this threat from one of ZANU-PF's most vital constituencies, Mugabe unilaterally agreed on pension payments to the vets—all tax free. He also promised free education for dependents, free health care, free land, and interest-free loans of up to Z$20,000 (Nhema 2002, 143–144). Shortly after this massive giveaway, estimated at a total cost of some Z$4.5 billion, was announced, the Zimbabwe economy collapsed; the Zimbabwean dollar fell 75 percent against the U.S. dollar in one day (Nhema 2002, 144). Hunzvi, whose own war veteran credentials were dubious, and who was believed to have been involved in a scheme to secure thousands of dollars for bogus compensation claims to war "injured," nonetheless was a skilled and charismatic leader who was able to put the war veterans on the center stage of national politics. However, revealing that the agreed payout was as much about contemporary politics and patronage as about compensation for the liberation war effort, "about 50,000 people were given the cash, even though fewer than 30,000 war veterans had been demobilized when the war ended in 1979" (Blair 2002, 39).

The liberation war vets were perhaps the only group with the standing to threaten President Mugabe, and he dared not respond with the repressive tactics he had so successfully used against his other societal foes. Indeed, the entirety of his revolutionary bona fides rested on accommodation of the fighters in the liberation struggle, with whom he identified politically, as well as the peasant farming community, on whose behalf the war was supposedly fought. Thus the promise of land reform, attained through the seizure of white-owned commercial farms, could shore up some much needed support for ZANU-PF among these essential constituencies. Raftopoulos (2001) argues that Mugabe rapidly capitulated to the war vets because he feared an alliance between labor and war vets that could undermine his government. Indeed, according to Raftopoulos (2001, 12), a potential alliance between the war vets and the ZCTU was discussed in

1996, but never came to fruition. Instead of an oppositional role, however, the war vets—many of whom were far too young to have fought in the actual independence war—became the shock troops of the farm invasions that began in February 2000 and continued unabated thereafter (ICG 2002). As such, they have been key players, and occasional pawns of the state, in the devastation of Zimbabwe's commercial farming-based economy.

■ Fundamentals of the Political Economy

At independence, Zimbabwe had a solid industrial infrastructure, an experienced commercial agriculture sector, and an internationally competitive mining industry. The combination of increased state spending after 1980, the impact of two recessions and regional droughts, the burden of repaying Rhodesian-era war debts, as well as the need to import vital industrial infrastructure led to the adoption of the structural adjustment program, ESAP, in 1990. The program, which was implemented in 1991, was supposed to provide a foundation for growth. Instead, it helped precipitate a series of economic changes that had a devastating impact on the Zimbabwean economy (Gunning and Oostendorp 2002; Jenkins and Knight 2002). Determining who bears responsibility for the failure of ESAP depends on whom one asks, although a strong case has been made that its flaws were principally of design rather than implementation (Bond and Manyanya 2002).

However, even if ESAP and the economic hardship it spawned pertain to structural factors, this is not to suggest that *agency* is not also important in the analysis. ESAP precipitated a series of events. How those events unfolded and were reshaped, however—including the rise of the opposition; the collapse of the relationship between ZANU-PF and the white economic community; the emergence of destructive populist economic policies, including land invasions and seizures; the massive authoritarian reaction of the regime to popular discontent; and finally, complete economic collapse—was the result of interactions and of *actors'* decisions, which were shaped by context. Particularly since the turn of the century, ZANU-PF's stewardship of the economy has been an unmitigated disaster (EIU 2003h).

Thus the 1990s witnessed a series of policy missteps that ultimately allowed the political space for opposition to emerge. The state struck back by targeting the politically weakest group in Zimbabwe—its former benefactors, the white farming community. By seizing the populist mantle of land reform, Mugabe thought he could cling to power. This strategy has called for the displacement of urban discontent and opposition support to the rural areas where ZANU-PF is strong traditionally (Carmody and Taylor 2003).

Government-sanctioned farm invasions began in February 2000 and escalated through 2002. As a consequence of targeting whites, a deliberate pattern of patronage flows, or "resource networks," between the ZANU-PF state and the white community have been permanently ruptured. To be fair, the land distribution under the status quo ante was grossly imbalanced in favor of a tiny white farming community, a dilemma that has been the subject of many comprehensive analyses (Bowyer-Bower and Stoneman 2000; Moyo 1995, 2000). Yet at the same time, the large-scale commercial sector *produced,* contributing half a million formal sector jobs, more than 20 percent of GDP, and it contributed, if indirectly, to the ZANU-PF patronage base (Taylor 1999a). ZANU-PF attacked whites because it needed a *political* scapegoat, not because the maneuver made sense economically. Indeed, the predictable global condemnation and agroeconomic collapse that ensued are evidence that Mugabe's land seizures and demonization of whites was an economic cul-de-sac (Cooke, Morrison, and Prendergast 2003). Although some 11 million of roughly 13 million hectares of white-owned farms have been seized, much of the land has gone to political cronies of the regime, or poor black farmers who have not been given the means to farm effectively or productively; the state, of course, itself destitute, lacks the ability to provide these resources. Agricultural production fell by an estimated 22 percent in 2002, following hefty declines the previous two years (EIU 2003h, 6).

The seizure of white farms and the corresponding declines in agricultural output did not begin until after the 2000 referendum, although some 1,471 farms were listed for acquisition already in 1997. The ability to resist takeover for two and a half years is a reflection of the institutional capacity of the farming interest associations to resist the move, international carrots and sticks to prevent abrogation of property rights norms, and the fact that the white farmer presence (and performance) remained important to the state for some time (Taylor 2003). Even as late as 2001, it appeared as if Mugabe's so-called fast-track land reform program might be reversed. Indeed, at the special Commonwealth meeting in September 1997, the government even consented to halt the invasions, restore the rule of law, and initiate an orderly, internationally supported land reform process ("Edited Text" 2001). However, Mugabe subsequently reneged on all commitments. The genie of land reform became impossible to put back in the bottle after February 2000; it was the only tool, however blunt, ZANU-PF could use to try to demonstrate its populist and "revolutionary" credentials against an ascendant MDC.

■ The Informalization of the Zimbabwean Economy

Economic policymaking has become a question of "crisis management" rather than planning for the future (EIU 2003l). As noted earlier in the chapter, by 2003 all formal sectors were in decline, with the exception of platinum mining. The country's GDP continues to plummet (approximately 13 percent per year in 2002 and 2003), despite the fact that there is little left to shrink after declines in prior years. With inflation continuing to spiral out of control, running at an annual rate of over 350 percent, the currency has collapsed; the government has responded by instituting new price controls (EIU 2003l, 2003h). To make matters worse, the widely respected finance minister, Simba Makoni, who was appointed in July 2001 in an apparent effort to shore up international confidence that the economic regime could be turned around, resigned in 2002. Makoni was replaced by the far more pliant Herbert Murewa, who failed to distinguish himself in previous ministerial appointments, including as head of industry and commerce. Murewa was himself replaced less than two years later.

The collapse in the formal economic sectors, namely commercial agriculture and manufacturing, and of state-owned enterprises and their employment bases, led to increasing informalization of the economy. For most Zimbabweans, survival has become increasingly difficult and shortages of even the most basic commodities are commonplace. International food aid, imported in 2002–2003 to prevent an estimated 6.2 million people from starving, was employed as a political weapon in the hands of the government, which denied food relief to MDC supporters (EIU 2003l). Fuel is frequently inaccessible and imported goods are out of reach because of chronic foreign currency shortages. Barter, parallel market currency transactions, and elaborate schemes to find policy loopholes have become the norm. Not surprisingly, millions of Zimbabweans have sought refuge abroad, principally in South Africa, for both economic and political reasons.

Zimbabwe was once among the world's top three producers of tobacco. Today, formal trade has evaporated, as Zimbabwe lacks the production for export and the foreign currency for imports. At the same time, obligations to regional partners have also increased and caused tremendous unease. Mozambique and especially South Africa are owed enormous sums (Cooke, Morrison, and Prendergast 2003). Moreover, Libya's Muammar Qaddafi stepped in to become the new international benefactor and a major supplier of Zimbabwe's fuel. However, 2003 saw even the Libyans becoming increasingly uncomfortable due to Zimbabwe's nonpayment, and the country has been forced to mortgage state-owned assets to the Libyan and Malaysian governments in return for services.

In the prevailing survivalist environment, it is difficult for those who oppose the regime to exert much pressure on it. Yet the regime could not maintain its control without substantial basis of support from those who benefit from its policies. In fact, the ZANU-PF government may find itself endangered ultimately not by the MDC and a reinvigorated civil society (which anyway is being suppressed), but by dissatisfied clients in its own midst. For now, the regime has secured the support of military elites like General Zvinavashe, retired general Solomon Mujuru, and Air Marshall Shiri by awarding them lucrative contracts in the DRC and political influence (Nest 2001; UNSC 2002). Within ZANU-PF erstwhile challengers to Mugabe have been sidelined by frequent cabinet reshuffles, which have claimed possible Mugabe successors like former ministers Edison Zvogbo and Makoni. For those who remain, access to power and resources remains a considerable elixir: an incentive to maintain the status quo. Moreover, many senior military and party officials may harbor some fear of who comes next within ZANU (or worse, an MDC ascendance to power), leading party officials to cling to Mugabe as the "devil they know" (see Maroleng 2003).

In sum, the regime has momentarily placated the leadership (but perhaps not the rank and file) of its potentially most dangerous constituents, the "war vets," by empowering them through lawless militias and land occupations, and the military through the DRC. It has co-opted business interests not related to the military as well, awarding them business opportunities, shares of state companies, and various illegitimate contracts throughout the 1990s (S. Taylor 2002).

Nonetheless, the essential element in the maintenance of clientelism is resources; in short, patronage *costs.* Although some, such as military elites and senior political figures like Speaker of Parliament Emmerson Mnangagwa, maintain access to patronage resources through their extensive linkages to Congo mineral wealth, other illicit networks face severe difficulty in light of Zimbabwe's economic implosion (Global Witness 2002b). Unlike oil- and diamond-rich states like Angola, there is no unlimited source of wealth upon which to draw in Zimbabwe. Thus the present status quo is unsustainable over the long term. When the state has mortgaged all its assets to Libya and others, and has become prohibitively indebted to its neighbors, and the principal remaining sources of foreign exchange have been exhausted with little hope of rebound, the regime must face collapse—or be forced to reach political compromise with the MDC (EIU 2003h). If not, the very forces that are currently sustaining ZANU-PF—the military businessmen, party elites, and cronies of the regime (including, ironically, as the UNSC [2002] points out, some whites)—will revolt against Mugabe or his designated successor.

■ Challenges for the Twenty-First Century

The economic challenges highlighted in this chapter provide a clear indication that the current phase of the crisis in Zimbabwe will face an inevitable endpoint. The question concerns how this will come about and what will follow. Frighteningly, it is not difficult to imagine a scenario that is worse than the status quo. Among the options: a coup d'état by the increasingly politicized military, a popular uprising, a civil war, a descent into warlordism.

However, there are more positive alternative futures that also warrant consideration. For example, there remains a prospect, if slight, for interparty dialogue and some sort of a collaborative—or more remotely, power-sharing—arrangement between ZANU-PF and the MDC. Another possibility assumes an MDC victory in a rerun presidential election (EIU 2003h). Given President Mugabe's intransigence and autocratic methods, both of these more optimistic outcomes would seem to rely on the removal or retirement of the president from office. Were Mugabe to retire, however, the constitution requires a new election if the president chooses to step down before the end of his term, and there is no guarantee that a ZANU-PF successor, if victorious, would be any less hostile to the embattled opposition.

Nonetheless, beginning in January 2003, rumors surfaced that President Mugabe might be considering retirement, a subject long regarded as taboo in ZANU-PF. A dialogue was reportedly initiated between agents of Mnangagwa and General Zvinavashe and Morgan Tsvangirai. Tsvangirai, already standing trial in 2003 on an alleged treason plot, made the information public, whereafter it was immediately disavowed by the government. Ultimately, it was not clear that Mugabe himself had ever sanctioned the discussions (Mkalipi et al. 2003; Cooke, Morrison, and Prendergast 2003). In any event, by 2004 Mugabe appeared firmly ensconced in office, and unwilling to relinquish his office any time before the end of his term in 2008.

The security of Mugabe's position may explain why the first of two treason counts—which carried the death penalty—against Morgan Tsvangirai was dismissed in October 2004. Rather than herald restored judicial independence or newfound magnanimity on the part of President Mugabe, however, Tsvangirai's victory bore the hallmarks of a momentary appeasement, *by the regime,* of the international and regional communities in advance of Zimbabwe's March 2005 parliamentary elections; Zimbabwe's neighbors will no doubt look upon the decision favorably. In any event, the largely spurious charges against Tsvangirai had their intended effect: to further undermine MDC and its leaders and to crush the once formidable threat to Mugabe's rule.

Although it is unwise to locate all Zimbabwe's problems in the person of Mugabe as some authors do, or to overstress the "personal rule," there is no denying that Mugabe has become a major obstacle to reaching an accord. The death of Jonas Savimbi in Angola in March 2002 and the election of Levy Mwanawasa in Zambia in December 2001 remind us how important individual leaders can be in shaping—or misshaping—the histories of their countries. In other words, agency is a critical factor. Thus the prospect of a Mugabe withdrawal from the scene is important from the standpoint of moving the process forward (Cooke, Morrison, and Prendergast 2003; ICG 2003c). However, as we have argued, one must not lose sight of structural factors as well: Zimbabwe is constrained by region, and by its position in the international and regional political economy.

Many of the ruinous policies of the Mugabe government—for example, laws that repress civil and political liberties—can be repealed fairly quickly. A settlement will bring immediate relief from the international community, and efforts to repair Zimbabwe's industrial and commercial infrastructure could probably begin almost immediately, although their completion would take many years. Yet the country faces long-term problems as well, regardless of who holds the presidency, and which party the president represents. Although Mugabe has claimed victory on the land problem, the issue is far from resolved. Will white farmers, many of whom have fled to Mozambique, Zambia, and elsewhere, be allowed to return to reclaim their legally acquired title deeds to their lands? Will they *want* to come back? What then happens to genuine land reform, not to mention the thousands of black Zimbabweans already resettled? Other structural problems are no less daunting. Over 25 percent of the adult population is infected with HIV, yet the social and medical system was ill-equipped to deal with this population even before the current crisis. In addition, unemployment stands at over 70 percent and an equal percentage of Zimbabweans live below the poverty line.

A successful post-Mugabe transition in Zimbabwe will require reengagement with the West and the region, as well as considerable healing of deep domestic fissures. The once enviable promise of Zimbabwe has now eroded almost completely—astoundingly, in a little more than half a decade. Surely it will take far longer to restore Zimbabwe's position as an economic and political leader in the region.

■ Notes

1. One respected scholar even suggested that presidential and ruling party authoritarianism was "eroding" as recently as 1999 (Sithole 2000).
2. South African president Thabo Mbeki is widely regarded as a key figure in brokering a compromise in Zimbabwe, but he has resisted any aggressive role, much to the consternation of Western nations (Cooke, Morrison, and Prendergast 2003). The major pan-African initiative is the New Partnership for African Development, which was launched in 2002.
3. Including the Preventive Detention Act, the Unlawful Organizations Act, the Emergency Powers Act, the Native Affairs Amendment Act, and the Law and Order Maintenance Act. Never rescinded, the latter continues to be employed to repress dissent.
4. Rhodesia had the status of a "self-governing colony" since 1923, and thus

had long enjoyed considerable autonomy from the colonial office in London. This was something of an anomaly in the era of British imperialism, since the British in fact had little control or influence over the Southern Rhodesian polity (Stedman 1991, 36).

5. The UDI was declared in November 1965, following a referendum with 58,000 whites in favor and just under 7,000 opposed (Houser 1976).

6. According to Stephen John Stedman (1991, 182–183), it was the pledges from the British and U.S. administrations to support the cost of land reform and pensions payments that enabled ZANU to agree to the draft constitution. The Lancaster agreement preserved the landownership status quo, in which some 7,000 white farmers owned nearly a third of the country's agricultural land (Moyo 1995).

7. In 1987, former rivals ZANU and ZAPU merged to form ZANU-PF, thus resuscitating the old "patriotic front" title. Although the name came into use earlier, we use "ZANU-PF" in this text to refer to the merged entity.

8. It was also extremely hypocritical, since ZANU-PF had long tolerated marked disparities in landownership (Taylor 1999a). ZANU-PF also blamed the British for not fulfilling their commitment to finance land reform (Bond and Manyanya 2002).

9. The war cost between 30,000 and 40,000 lives, most of them black (Stedman 1991, vii).

10. Ian Smith remained in Zimbabwe unmolested following independence, and although also proclaiming the reconciliation mantra, he continued to spout racist, paternalistic invective, mostly directed at his black successors (see, for example, Smith 2002).

11. ZAPU, which predated ZANU, was until the early 1970s a multiethnic organization. It was led by Nkomo, himself Ndebele. A series of Shona defections, based more on ideology than ethnic tensions, led the parties to be increasingly perceived as "Ndebele" or "Shona"; eventually reality came to reflect these perceptions (Sithole 1988).

12. Muzorewa, a Shona, appointed an Ndebele, Josiah Gumede, as ceremonial president in 1978.

13. Nkomo is viewed in some circles as a possible successor to Mugabe, although this would appear highly unlikely, not least because of his Ndebele identity.

14. The colonial-era chieftaincy structure was maintained despite the conflicts between chiefs and guerrillas during the war; many chiefs were seen as collaborationists with the Rhodesian state (see Nhema 2002, 99).

15. For example, the government lost cases pertaining to its illegal acquisition of private land in the early 1990s (Taylor 1999a). It was also rebuffed by the courts in its efforts to use security laws to bar competition from a private mobile phone network (Taylor 1999b). In these and other cases, the government consented to the court's findings.

16. The CFU action named prominent ZANU-PF officials who were spearheading occupations of white-owned farms in order to intimidate their owners. Specifically, War Veterans Association leader Chenjerai Hunzvi, Minister of Youth and Sport Border Gezi, and Police Commissioner Augustine Chihuri were named as respondents.

17. In July 2002, for example, the top legal officer in the country, Minister of Justice Patrick Chinamasa, was found guilty of contempt of court. Chinamasa not only ignored the summons to appear, but also publicly scoffed at it. In February 2003 the government ordered police to arrest sitting High Court judge Benjamin Paradza, at the courts, on trumped-up charges. The actual intention was to intimi-

date Paradza, who had issued several rulings unfavorable to the government, and any others who would follow his precedent (Meldrum 2003).

18. Zimbabwe Alert 2002.

19. Namibia's president also appoints six members of parliament who are, unlike in Zambia and Zimbabwe, nonvoting.

20. Itself achieved in the controversial June 2000 election, marred by substantial irregularities.

21. However, the opposition was fragmented and poorly organized. The two other presidential candidates, Ndabaningi Sithole (ZANU-Ndonga) and Abel Muzorewa (United Parties) withdrew in the days before the election, although their names remained on the ballot.

22. Other parties were the reconstituted ZAPU, Muzorewa's United Parties, the Liberty Party, Margaret Dongo's Zimbabwe Union of Democrats, and ZANU-Ndonga. The latter four formed a "voting pact" prior to the elections (Commonwealth Observer Group 2000).

23. "U.S. Says Zim Election Fundamentally Flawed" 2002; Cowell 2002.

24. Ignatius 2002; sources cited in the article claim that, absent fraud, Mugabe would have lost by 466,000 votes.

25. R. W. Johnson (2000, 52) envisioned "a Tsvangirai landslide." An August–September 2001 poll of 3,013 people, conducted by Target Research for Zimbabwe's independent *Financial Gazette,* revealed a narrower gap. It found that 52.9 percent of Zimbabweans supported Morgan Tsvangirai, while 47.1 percent favored Mugabe (*Financial Gazette,* November 8, 2001).

26. As Raftopoulos (2001, 5) notes, the state arrested hundreds of striking workers in the 1980–1982 period, and thereafter passed a new labor relations act in 1985 that severely restricted the right to strike. Of course, labor activism was further curtailed by the clientelistic relationship between the ruling party and main labor body, the ZCTU.

27. Interestingly, Raftopoulos (2001, 8) argues that since organized labor, and particularly Zambia's ZCTU, played such an instrumental role in ending one-party rule in that country, ZANU-PF was clearly haunted in this period by "the spectre of the Chiluba route to political power," and thus sought to repress union activity even further.

28. Two reporters from the weekly *The Standard* were imprisoned and tortured in January 1999 after publishing a story, based on anonymous sources, suggesting that a military coup was being plotted. Earlier, in 1995, journalists and editors from the independent *Financial Gazette* newspaper were jailed for raising questions about President Mugabe's relationship to his secretary, whom he subsequently married. Among the independent newspapers, however, the *Daily News* has probably been the chief victim of a sustained government campaign (Sandra Nyarira, political editor, *Daily News,* personal comment to the author, November 2002).

8

Namibia: Limits to Liberation

At independence in 1990 Namibia was viewed throughout Africa and the world as a potential exception on a continent wracked by ethnic violence, economic crisis, political decay, and social malaise. Despite a twenty-five-year war in the northern part of the country, Namibia boasted an enviable economic infrastructure and considerable resources—minerals, fish, and livestock—to match. Following a largely consensual process between previously antagonistic parties, Namibia had adopted a new constitution hailed as one of the most liberal and democratic in the world. And despite decades of South African–imposed apartheid rule, Namibia possessed a fairly educated and healthy society—notwithstanding major differences among groups—enhanced by tens of thousands of returning Namibian exiles, many of whom were highly educated and highly skilled. At independence in March 1990, President Sam Nujoma and his South West Africa People's Organization (SWAPO), back after decades of exile, appeared ready to reconcile with their onetime adversaries and to commence with the business of governing their new country. Though some remained skeptical, the former adversaries—mostly white Namibians and a few others—seemed willing to give the new leader and government a chance. "Africa's last colony" was poised to set a new example for Africa. And with Namibian independence a product of the end of the Cold War, Namibia seemed to embody the hopes and aspirations of a continent for a new post–Cold War global order that would be more friendly to Africa.

In the intervening years, much of that promise has been realized. In more than fifteen years of independence, Namibia's exemplary constitution has been largely respected. Since the first universal franchise elections for a constituent assembly in November 1989, largely free and fair elections have been held routinely, with all but the first assembly election held under Namibian auspices. The rule of law has been maintained and the rights of the Namibian populace have for the most part been upheld. Government

Namibia: Country Data

Land area 824,269 km^2
Capital Windhoek
Date of independence March 21, 1990
Population 1.8 million, 31% urban
Languages English (official), Afrikaans, African languages
Ethnic groups Ovambo, Herero, Nama-Damara, Kavango, Lozi, San,
  Coloured, European
Religions Christian, 80–90%; indigenous beliefs, 10–20%
Currency Namibian dollar (N$); Namibian dollars per U.S. dollar:
  7.44 (July 2003)

Literacy rate 82.7% (male, 83.4%; female, 81.9%)
Life expectancy 47.7 years (male, 45.5 years; female, 49.2 years)
Infant mortality 55 per 1,000 live births

GDP per capita U.S.$1,730
GDP per capita (PPP) U.S.$7,120
GDP per capita growth rate 2.2% (1990–2001)

Leaders since independence
• Sam Nujoma, president, March 1990–March 2005
• Hifikepunye Pohamba, president, March 2005–

Major political parties
  Ruling party: South West Africa People's Organization (SWAPO)
  Other parties: Congress of Democrats (COD)
  Democratic Turnhalle Alliance (DTA)
  United Democratic Front (UDF)

Women in parliament (lower/single house) 25% (2005)

Note: Data from 2001 unless otherwise indicated.

commitments to health and education are manifest in a substantially expanded health infrastructure and improved school enrollment and literacy rates since independence. Women have made great strides in the electoral arena—reaching nearly 30 percent of members of parliament (MPs) in the National Assembly, among the highest in Africa and the world, and more than 40 percent of local councillors, far above the world average. A fairly active civil society, including women's groups, churches, and human rights associations, has asserted itself since independence and attempted to hold government accountable to the people. An independent media, operating alongside a government-owned one, has remained very vocal and very vigilant in the years since 1990. Economically, Namibia appears to have held its own as well. With a per capita income of U.S.$1,960 in 2001 (U.S.$6,700 at purchasing power parity), Namibia is considered a lower-middle-income country by the World Bank (2003b, 235). The traditional primary sectors have continued to dominate Namibia's economy—with the country's fishing stocks considerably replenished after independence. And with major improvements made to the port at Walvis Bay and the completion of the Trans-Kalahari Highway, the opportunity exists for Namibia to become the much vaunted "gateway to the Southern African Development Community"—and its 200 million people. In the intervening years, Namibia's tourism industry—targeted at the high-end tourist—has seen steady growth as well.

At the same time, there are indications that Namibia may be following bad examples, rather than setting a new one. Though there have been regular elections at the local, regional, and national levels in Namibia since independence, there has been no alternation of power at the national level. While Namibia is still technically a multiparty democracy, with seven political parties represented in the National Assembly, the ruling SWAPO party holds a better than two-thirds majority in both houses of parliament and has done so since 1994. When a new political party emerged in 1999, largely from the ranks of disaffected SWAPO members, the ruling party engaged in a deliberate smear campaign against it, and worked to ensure that the new party did not attain "official opposition" status in parliament, though it had clearly earned it. Moreover, in a move reminiscent of one-party states around Africa, SWAPO managed to have the constitution amended in 1998 to allow President Nujoma to stand for a third term of office in 1999. In another repetition of past practice among single-party states, SWAPO remains wedded to the model of political party and sectional affiliates. In a clear bid to forestall the emergence of a rival political movement with a readily mobilized base—à la the Movement for Multiparty Democracy in Zambia—the ruling party has held a tight rein over affiliates such as the country's largest trade union federation, the National Union of Namibian Workers (NUNW). The SWAPO government also managed to embroil

Namibia in two foreign wars around century's end—in neighboring Angola and the Democratic Republic of Congo (DRC)—and did so without consulting with the people's elected representatives first. In the view of many observers, Namibia's involvement in the DRC stems at least in part from President Nujoma's close association with Zimbabwe's autocratic relic Robert Mugabe. The other trends reflect a pattern in a number of countries in the region—where a liberation movement steeped in authoritarian patterns of rule and undemocratic practices is now the ruling political party.

Unfortunately, Namibia is also one of the countries in southern Africa hardest hit by the AIDS crisis, with significant consequences throughout the economy and society. Additionally, like many countries in the region, semiarid Namibia faces recurrent drought and the threat of water shortage remains a potential impediment to growth and development. The land question is another sensitive issue in Namibia, with overall land distribution skewed to the advantage of a white minority.

Like Botswana, Namibia is a very large country, very sparsely populated by only 2 million people. With such a small population, Namibia will never be the economic powerhouse that neighboring South Africa is. Moreover, given its small market, Namibia will never attract a level of foreign investment comparable to South Africa or even Angola. But if it is able to resolve its land question peaceably, carefully cultivate existing natural resources, attract high-end visitors to its stunning landscapes and varied wildlife, become a trade and transport hub for the region, and create more jobs through export processing zones, Namibia may set a positive example for what a lower-middle-income country can accomplish. Similarly, if Namibia is able to weather the transition to a new president in 2005, embrace more sincerely a multiparty political system in which opposition political parties are welcome, and witness the emergence of a more diversified and dynamic civil society, then it may again provide a model for what a postsettler society in Africa can achieve. This chapter explores the factors that will help to influence Namibia's future—whether as a progressive regional leader or as a continental hangover from a previous era.

■ **Historical Origins of the Namibian State: Context, Key Actors, and Issues**

Namibia has experienced a historical trajectory unlike any other in the region, though there are some important similarities with the other former settler colonies of South Africa and Zimbabwe. Namibia was the only colony in southern Africa to be colonized by the Germans, albeit only until World War I.[1] When the Germans arrived during the late 1880s in what is today Namibia, the territory was already occupied by several groups. In the northern part of the country (indeed extending into what is today Angola), the Ovambo people (the largest ethnic group in Namibia) practiced mixed farming, allowing for a "greater concentration of population and for the evolution of more cohesive and centralized social and political structures." Indeed, precolonial Ovamboland was dominated by a series of independent kingdoms (Emmett 1999, 42–43). Farther east along the Kunene River, the Kavango people, an Ovambo group who developed independently of the main group in Ovamboland, lived less densely in a region of higher rainfall and therefore greater agricultural potential and fewer land pressures. Farther east still, in the contemporary Caprivi region, lived the Masubia and Mafue groups, both of which are related to communities in Zambia (Emmett 1999, 43). The rest of Namibia, because of lack of rainfall, was, and remains, suitable only for livestock raising—large livestock in the central plateau and small livestock in the southern region of the country. When the Germans arrived, the Herero people, "widely recognized as outstanding and dedicated cattle farmers," dominated the "prime hardveld areas of the central and northern plateau" (Emmett 1999, 43). As pastoralists, the Herero experienced a wide dispersal of population and decentralized political authority. The Hereros had to contend with incursions from the Nama people from the south, who tended smaller stock in smaller herds and relied more heavily "on strategies more commonly associated with hunter-gatherers"—for example, raiding. There was a relative lack of social cohesion and centralized authority among Nama groups (Emmett 1999, 45). Two other hunter-gatherer groups, the San and Damara, lived in much smaller numbers in central and southern Namibia and in some subjugation to the Nama and Herero.

Much of Namibia then was characterized by a harsh, semiarid climate suitable only for raising small or large livestock, depending on the region of the country. At the same time, Namibia did posses a wealth of minerals of keen interest to early explorers and traders and, eventually, to European colonizers. These included diamonds in the southern part of the country, copper, zinc, some gold, and several other minerals in the center and north of the country, and eventually, even uranium was discovered. Ultimately, Namibia's long Atlantic Ocean coastline would provide ample stocks of fish, though in the early colonial period the main interest was in collecting guano from offshore islands. Moreover, the cattle herds maintained by the Herero were greatly coveted by early visitors to the territory.

After initially being managed by German trading companies, South West Africa, as it was then called, became a settler colony of the Germans (Emmett 1999, 53). Tensions over land between German settlers and especially the Herero but also the Nama, led to the outbreak of wars in 1904 that lasted until 1907. The wars were conducted with such brutality on the part of the Germans that by the time of their end in 1907 "an estimated 80 percent of the Hereros, 50 percent of the Namas and 30 percent of the

Damaras perished" (Emmett 1999, 59). Moreover, at war's end "the land and livestock of all black groups which had participated in the rebellions were confiscated." As in South Africa and Zimbabwe, regulations were put into place that required Africans to carry passes and "service books" that detailed any labor contracts they had entered into. Among other things, these regulations laid the groundwork for forced labor in the colony (Emmett 1999, 59).

German colonial rule in South West Africa ended less than a decade later when British forces defeated German forces in the territory during World War I. The 1919 Treaty of Versailles allowed the Allied powers to take over all of Germany's colonies, and South West Africa was entrusted as a "C Mandate" to the Union of South Africa by the League of Nations in December 1920. Between the two world wars, "native reserves" were established and "native commissioners" were appointed throughout the territory, including in the far northern Ovambo area, which had not fallen under direct German administrative rule before World War I. Also during this interwar period, South African authorities actively encouraged settlers from South Africa to take up farming in South West Africa. Finally, legislation introduced during these same years helped to regulate an emerging migrant labor system that would provide indigenous labor to the mines, commercial farms, and growing towns in the young colony.

With the creation of the United Nations in 1945 and the dissolution of the League of Nations in 1946, South West Africa's political status changed again as it became a trust territory of the UN, despite protestations from the South African government, which favored direct incorporation of the territory into South Africa. The UN General Assembly rejected direct incorporation in December 1946, however, and from then on South Africa sought to make South West Africa a de facto, but not de jure, fifth province of South Africa. A few years later the same legislation that began to formalize apartheid and the policy of separate development in South Africa was extended to the fifth province. This included, for example, the policy of transforming previous "native reserves" into "ethnic homelands," although none of Namibia's ethnic homelands was ever granted even nominal independence, as in South Africa.

South Africa's de facto incorporation of Namibia into its territory was not accepted by much of the population or the international community. From the 1940s and 1950s leaders such as Chief Hosea Kutako of the Herero Chiefs Council, Chief David Witbooi of the Nama, and others began petitioning the United Nations for an end to South African rule in the territory. By the end of the 1950s, moreover, an incipient nationalist movement had emerged, first among Namibian contract migrant workers in Cape Town (the Ovamboland People's Congress in 1957), and then among migrant workers in Windhoek (the Ovamboland People's Organization

[OPO] in 1959). At the same time, ordinary Namibians continued to resist colonial rule and its oppressive regulations. When colonial authorities sought to forcibly remove residents from Windhoek's black township in 1959 and relocate them, the ensuing protest resulted in the shooting deaths of eleven and wounding of forty-four others. In the aftermath of the shootings, much of the nationalist leadership was imprisoned, banned, or restricted by the South African colonial authorities, with the result that many opted for exile. The activities of the OPO ground to a halt and, outside of the country in New York City in April 1960, OPO leader Sam Nujoma was elected president of the recently renamed nationalist movement, the South West Africa People's Organization.

In 1962 SWAPO leaders made the decision to take up arms against the South Africans and began training future combatants in Egypt. Armed struggle began when SWAPO's military base in Ongulumbashe in northern Namibia was discovered by the South Africans in 1966. More than 200 activists, most of the remaining internal SWAPO leaders, were arrested or fled into exile. In those early days SWAPO's exile base was in faraway Tanzania, though with independence in Zambia, and later Angola, the liberation movement shifted its exile camps closer to home. Tensions and unrest increased considerably inside Namibia, meanwhile, following two developments in the early 1970s: a massive general strike by contract migrant workers in 1971–1972 and the related imposition of emergency regulations in Ovamboland (to which most of the migrant workers returned during the strike), and South African efforts to grant self-government to the ethnic homelands, particularly Ovamboland. Protest rallies sponsored by the SWAPO Youth League and school boycotts by high school students were met with detentions and trials, as well as the meting out of brutal punishments by tribal courts in the north. These factors, together with the proximity of new SWAPO exile camps in Zambia and Angola, led to an exodus of thousands of young Namibians from the territory from 1974 onward.

By then northern Namibia had become a war zone. Cross-border incursions by SWAPO combatants were more frequent as exile bases were established in Angola, and from late 1975 South African Defense Force (SADF) troops were airlifted into the north. Civilians were ordered to withdraw from border areas of Ovamboland and emergency regulations first imposed in Ovamboland in 1972 were extended to Kavango and the Caprivi in 1976. Martial law was declared throughout the north. In 1977 the SADF began recruiting Namibian volunteers for ethnic military units to fight the externally based nationalist movement and attempt to restore order in the north.

It was against this backdrop that the South Africans initiated the first of two attempts at an internal settlement of the Namibian situation in the form of an interim government established in 1980. This government lasted only three years before it collapsed amid charges of corruption and incompetence, and was followed in 1985 by the second attempt, a transitional government of national unity, which lasted until 1989, when an internationally sanctioned and monitored transition to independence began. Indeed, by the 1980s international diplomatic efforts to rid Namibia of South African colonial rule, centered at the United Nations, began to bear fruit. These were further aided by the collapse of the Soviet Union and end of the Cold War in the late 1980s and were linked to a strong regional and international commitment to ending the war in Angola and achieving Namibian independence. The Brazzaville Accord, signed in December 1988, laid the groundwork for a year-long UN-supervised transition to independence that began in April 1989 under the auspices of Security Council Resolution 435. During that transition, SWAPO combatants—the People's Liberation Army of Namibia (PLAN)—as well as an indigenous force that had been created by the South Africans—the South West Africa Territorial Force (SWATF)—were demobilized by a UN Transitional Assistance Group and SADF troops were sent home to South Africa. Tens of thousands of Namibian exiles from around the world, but mostly neighboring Angola, along with the former PLAN combatants, were repatriated to Namibia. In November 1989 UN-supervised elections were held for a constituent assembly to draw up a new constitution. On March 21, 1990, political independence was finally granted to Namibia.

Scholars have interpreted Namibia's transition to independence in different ways, with different implications for Namibia's future.[2] Michael Bratton and Nicolas van de Walle (1997), for example, view Namibia's transition to independence as one of many attempted democratic transitions across Africa in the late 1980s and early 1990s. They suggest that the prospects for a successful transition to democracy were likely somewhat better in Namibia than elsewhere in Africa because Namibia was one of a few African countries in which an "elite pact" provided the foundation for the democratic transition.[3] It happened this way in Namibia, they contend, because Namibia was one of two remaining settler oligarchies in Africa at the time of its transition.[4] And while transitions from settler oligarchies were often violent and protracted, as in the Namibian case, they typically ended through negotiation (Bratton and van de Walle 1997, 178): "The contenders for power struck a series of political, military, and economic agreements that divided power (at least for an interim period) and protected minority interests." Moreover, settler oligarchies were also aided by the fact of having had some heritage of institutionalized political competition, albeit sharply restricted by race in the southern African context. Still, Bratton and van de Walle (1997, 179) argue that in such a situation, political liberalization becomes the somewhat easier task of expanding the franchise to allow greater political participation, rather than one of trying to institutionalize previously unknown principles of political pluralism.[5]

To a large extent Namibia conforms to Bratton and van de Walle's description of a settler oligarchy. In Namibia, as in South Africa, "the dominant group used the instruments of law to deny political rights to ethnic majorities, usually through a restrictive franchise and emergency regulations backed by hierarchically organized coercion" (1997, 81). From the beginning of colonial rule, black Namibians lost not only political but also economic and social rights through a series of laws and regulations governing nearly every facet of their lives. By the end of colonial rule, emergency regulations had been in effect in the northern Namibia war zone for decades. For the most part, in Namibia "settlers reproduced functioning democracies within their own microcosmic enclaves, with features like elections, leadership turnover, loyal opposition, independent courts, and some press freedom, all reserved exclusively for whites" (Bratton and van de Walle 1997, 81). For much of the twentieth century white Namibians had some form of elected representation, although their representatives often acted only in an advisory capacity or had jurisdiction over very limited areas. Namibia deviates from this characterization in that whites had no control over their executive; rather, he was appointed in South Africa.

Joshua Forrest describes Namibia's transition only slightly differently. In his view, the 1988 Brazzaville Accord may be considered "'a transitional pact' to which the nation's leading politicians lent their approval in the context of emerging from an authoritarian political system toward a democratic framework of government." Though the accord was signed by a number of countries external to the conflict in Namibia, it was made possible by a series of meetings outside Namibia during the 1980s between SWAPO and representatives of white political and economic interests inside the territory. Such a pact, according to Forrest (1998, 42), establishes "basic guidelines within which the country's political leaders can determine the exact nature of the constitution and decide on the democratic institutions to be established." Gerhard Erasmus (2000), moreover, focuses very heavily on Namibia's constitution, referring to the transition to independence as a "transition through constitutionalism"—a transition in which the constitution played a central role in the founding of an independent Namibia. Like Forrest, Erasmus (2000, 77) emphasizes the way in which the transition was "structured and guided by a prior agreement," which included a commitment to a "strong" constitution. "Thereafter, this constitution had to continue to fulfill other important functions. It had to constrain the inherent tensions in the Namibian body politic, and guide the young state along a path of constitutionalism and the rule of law. In this manner, it was hoped, stability and progress could be achieved and another 'African disaster' prevented."

Interestingly, these authors suggest reasons to think that the perils of Africa's first wave of independence might be avoided in Namibia. Another group of authors (Bauer 1998; Dobell 1998; Leys and Saul 1995; Melber 2003), by contrast, worry that liberation without democracy could well be

Namibia's fate, with the nature of the liberation struggle and the impact that this had on the liberation movement accounting for such an outcome. Indeed, Colin Leys and John Saul (1995, 5) suggest that "the possibility exists that the very process of struggling for liberation, especially by resort to force of arms, almost inevitably generates political practices that prefigure undemocratic outcomes." This view contrasts markedly with a once popular view that suggested that "the logic of protracted struggle . . . made the politics of armed liberation movements more democratic and radical than those of other nationalist movements and more likely to lead to genuinely socialist [progressive] outcomes in the post liberation phase." With hindsight, that view has evolved considerably. As Henning Melber (2003, 5) observes: "There is a growing insight that the armed liberation struggles were in no way a suitable breeding ground for establishing democratic systems of government after gaining independence. The forms of resistance against totalitarian regimes were themselves organized on strictly hierarchical and authoritarian lines, otherwise they could hardly have had any prospect of success." In the case of SWAPO, there is ample evidence that while in exile in Zambia and in Angola in the 1970s and 1980s, hundreds if not thousands of SWAPO members were detained, starved, tortured, imprisoned in underground dungeons, and even killed—by the movement itself. Democratic voices within the movement were clearly silenced (Leys and Saul 1995, 4). To make matters worse, since independence, SWAPO has steadfastly refused to account for or confront its policies and practices while in exile (Saul and Leys 2003). What does this legacy of authoritarianism in the liberation movement turned ruling party portend for Namibia's future? Moreover, the extent to which SWAPO was even a "liberation movement" with the goal of transforming Namibia in some meaningful way after independence, rather than simply a nationalist movement seeking political independence, has also been called into question (Bauer 1998; Dobell 1998). These issues have great significance for Namibia's political future and are revisited later in this chapter.

■ Organization of the State

▨ *Executive*

As defined in Article 1 of its constitution, Namibia is a sovereign, secular, democratic, and unitary state. Government comprises the typical three branches (executive, legislative, and judicial), with a popularly elected president who is both head of state and head of the executive, and an appointed prime minister. Executive power in Namibia vests in the president and the cabinet. The national legislature is a bicameral parliament consisting of a national assembly with seventy-two elected members and six nonvoting members appointed by the president, and a national council with twenty-six members elected from among thirteen regional councils. The constitution provides for the separation of powers and hence an independent judiciary. Judicial power in Namibia is exercised by a supreme court, a high court, and a number of lower courts.

According to Namibia's original constitution, the president was limited to two consecutive terms in office, with presidential and National Assembly terms running concurrently. Before the 1999 elections, however, the constitution was amended to allow President Nujoma to run for a third term of office. The decision to amend the constitution to allow this change in presidential terms was taken by SWAPO at its May 1997 party congress. The party argued that President Nujoma was not popularly elected by the Namibian people in 1989 (he was elected by the Constituent Assembly in February 1990), so voters should be allowed a second opportunity—in 1999—to vote for him (*The Namibian,* September 1, 1999). Proponents of the change pledged that it would be applicable only to the 1999 elections and that future presidents would serve only two terms. With a two-thirds majority for SWAPO in both houses of parliament, there was never any doubt that the amendment to the constitution would be approved, as happened in late 1998. In the December 1999 presidential elections, President Nujoma easily won a third term of office, polling 76.7 percent of the vote.[6] During his third term of office, President Nujoma sent mixed signals about his intention to stand for a fourth term. Then, in a May 2004 extraordinary congress, SWAPO selected the party's vice president, Hifikepunye Pohamba, minister of lands, resettlement, and rehabilitation, to be the party's presidential candidate in 2004 (*The Namibian,* May 31, 2004). Pohamba, Nujoma's age mate and comrade from the liberation struggle, was clearly Nujoma's personal choice to succeed him; indeed, Nujoma went so far as to dismiss from office two potential contenders for SWAPO presidential candidate: Prime Minister Hage Geingob in August 2002 and Foreign Minister Hidipo Hamutenya in May 2004.[7] Pohamba easily won the 2004 presidential race with 76.4 percent of the vote.

One implication of the third term for President Nujoma has been an increasing concentration of power within the office of the president. Indeed, in the view of some observers a "rising presidentialism" has existed for some time within the executive branch of government. This has been evident, for example, from President Nujoma's insistence on making political appointments himself (particularly ministers and deputy ministers) and his past practices of keeping political rivals at bay with periodic cabinet reshuffles, of choosing the first several of seventy-two candidates on SWAPO's party list for the National Assembly elections, and of retaining much of the preindependence SWAPO leadership in key cabinet posts.

Citing some of these practices, Christiaan Keulder raises concerns about the growing influence of the executive branch over the legislative branch in the years since independence. The situation is exacerbated, in Keulder's view (1999a, 6–7), by the existence of a "tight single party cabinet" (all members appointed from one party only) and by the fact that all cabinet members are appointed by the president. Moreover, because all of the ministers and deputy ministers are MPs in the National Assembly, they outnumber ordinary SWAPO MPs by a ratio of two to one. The result of this, according to Keulder (1999a, 7), is that "as far as the ruling party is concerned, the National Assembly is little more than the Executive in disguise." This of course has immediate negative implications for the autonomy of the National Assembly.

■ Constitutionalism

Namibia's constitution was drawn up by the seventy-two-member Constituent Assembly elected during the special UN-supervised election held in November 1989. By many accounts, the drafting of the constitution was a remarkably consensual process.[8] Indeed, Forrest (1998, 43) marvels at the way in which SWAPO, "with its history of guerilla nationalism," and the main opposition group at the time, the Democratic Turnhalle Alliance (DTA), "with its history of collaboration," were able to work together to forge a national constitution. In Forrest's view, this represented "an impressive example of successful bargaining by opposing political elites in a transitional democratic context." This was possible, according to Forrest (1998, 43–44), because SWAPO and the opposition parties perceived it to be in their own respective best interests to participate in the bargaining process "and forge a workable democratic framework." Forrest concedes that the commitment to democracy on the part of SWAPO and DTA elites may have been instrumental, "but even instrumental commitment may make possible the consolidation of democratic rule so long as both ruling and opposition politicians act as democrats and treat their opponents as democrats."

At the same time, it is important to note that much of what was ultimately included in the Namibian constitution was determined far in advance of the meetings of the Constituent Assembly in late 1989 and early 1990. In fact, a set of constitutional principles had been adopted in 1982 as part of the UN effort to bring about an international settlement of the conflict in Namibia. According to Erasmus (2000, 81), these principles go a long way toward explaining Namibia's remarkable constitution: "One of the most obvious explanations for the basic features of the Namibian Constitution and its liberal-democratic values lies in the framework that the Constitutional Principles comprised, and from which no deviation was permitted." Thus one might assert, as Erasmus does, "that Namibians actually did not enjoy a completely free hand in writing their own constitution." At the same time, Erasmus notes that while "the blueprint for the Constitutional Principles had originally been drafted by the Western Contact Group consisting of Canada, France, Germany, Great Britain and the USA," Namibian parties, including SWAPO, had accepted the principles as providing the basic framework for gaining independence.

When it was adopted in 1990, Namibia's constitution was hailed as one of the most liberal and democratic in the world. Indeed, some observers consider it to be the linchpin of Namibia's multiparty democracy. The Namibian constitution contains entrenched clauses guaranteeing fundamental human rights and freedoms, including freedoms of association and expression (including a free press) and peaceable assembly. The constitution also includes the proscription of arbitrary arrest, detention without trial, and the death penalty, and enshrines the right of individual property ownership and the payment of just compensation for any expropriation of property. The constitution also provides for the establishment of two offices meant to protect democracy and promote accountability in Namibia, namely the offices of the ombudsman and the auditor general. Both offices were established in 1990 and have operated actively, albeit with limited resources, ever since.

As noted, Namibia's constitution has been largely respected since independence—the single, but significant, change was to allow a third term for President Nujoma—and the rule of law has largely prevailed during that same period. There were some concerns in the early 2000s about the government's respect for the human rights of its citizens, primarily in northern conflict areas. At the same time, there have been no reports of political prisoners being held, academic freedom being restricted, or journalists being subjected to harassment or violence by the police.

■ Judiciary

As noted above, judicial power in Namibia is vested in a supreme court, a high court, and lower courts presided over by magistrates. By 2002 there were thirty magistrate courts established in Namibia. The Supreme Court serves as a court of appeals and constitutional review court. In recent years, the greatest impediment to the administration of justice in Namibia has been long delays in hearing cases within the court system, a problem afflicting other judiciaries in the region. According to the U.S. Department of State (2003d), during 2002 "the lack of qualified magistrates, other court officials, and private attorneys resulted in a serious backlog of criminal cases, which often translated into delays of up to one year or more between arrest and trial, contravening constitutional provisions for the right to a speedy trial." Moreover, many of those awaiting trial were reportedly "treated as convicted criminals," contravening the constitutional right to a fair trial with a presumption of innocence until proven guilty.

As in most of southern Africa, there is another set of courts in Namibia—so-called traditional courts. Namibia's constitution allows customary law in effect at the time of independence to remain in effect as long as that customary law does not conflict with the constitution or any other statutory law.[9] According to M. O. Hinz (1998, 10), this "constitutional recognition of both customary law, and through it, traditional government, has freed customary law and traditional government from its marginalization as an inferior way of living." Indeed it is likely that most of Namibia's rural residents first encounter the nation's legal system through customary law and the traditional courts. These traditional courts deal primarily with minor criminal offenses such as petty theft and "infractions of local customs among members of the same ethnic group" (U.S. Department of State 2003d). One problem, however, has been that within the traditional courts there tends to be "an uneven application" of protections provided by the constitution (U.S. Department of State 2003d).[10]

▪ Military

As in the rest of southern Africa, the military has played a minimal role in politics and society in Namibia to date. This despite the fact that the main military force, the Namibian Defense Force (NDF), was formed at independence by bringing together former combatants from both sides of the independence war: from SWAPO's People's Liberation Army of Namibia and the South African–sponsored South West Africa Territorial Force. NDF troops numbered about 9,000 in 2003. Another 6,000 troops belonged to the Special Field Force (SFF), the paramilitary police unit recruited primarily from among former PLAN combatants in the mid-1990s. The SFF, along with the rest of the Namibian police, are supervised by the Ministry of Home Affairs, and the NDF is supervised by the Ministry of Defense. The two forces share responsibility for Namibia's internal security. The National Central Intelligence Service covers national security–related intelligence inside and outside the country (Economist Intelligence Unit [EIU] 2003f, 16; U.S. Department of State 2003d).

Namibia's military was active outside its borders for about four years, from 1998 to 2002, participating in wars in two neighboring states. Namibia's involvement in the regional war in the DRC and the civil war in Angola caused considerable consternation among the populace and some opposition politicians. According to several reports, President Nujoma ordered the initial deployment of Namibian troops in the DRC (in support of embattled DRC president Laurent Kabila) in August 1998 without first consulting his cabinet or parliament (Melber 2003, 15). Opposition party

MPs strongly condemned this "surreptitious" deployment of Namibian troops outside of the country's national borders (*The Namibian*, October 19, 1998). Moreover, this was one of the issues cited by Ben Ulenga when he resigned as Namibian high commissioner to the United Kingdom in August 1998; months later he would go on to form the most significant opposition party to emerge in the country since independence.

Criticism of Namibia's involvement in the war mounted as, by the end of 1998, the government became increasingly reluctant to reveal any information about it. Indeed, in early 1999 it was reported that the minister of defense, backed by the prime minister, had instructed his staff in late 1998 to refuse further information to the media about Namibia's participation in the war.[11] President Nujoma and SWAPO MPs justified Namibian involvement in the DRC war on the grounds of international solidarity and the need to secure Namibian peace, stability, and democracy. At the same time, many observers stress the importance of close political ties between SWAPO and the ruling parties in Angola and Zimbabwe "forged during the years of the armed liberation struggle" and suggest that those ties led Namibia to join the two countries in the war in the DRC (EIU 2003f, 15). By 2002 all NDF soldiers were withdrawn from the country.

In December 1999 Namibia became involved in the internal war in Angola when the government gave permission to the Angolan Armed Forces to launch attacks from northern Namibia into southern Angola against troops of the National Union for the Total Independence of Angola (UNITA). This decision by the Namibian government prompted retaliatory action by UNITA against Namibia, which in turn provoked NDF involvement in the conflict. By early May 2000 the NDF had set up military bases inside Angola in an attempt to prevent UNITA rebels from carrying out retaliatory attacks on Namibian soil (*Daily Mail and Guardian*, December 23, 1999; *The Namibian*, May 2, 2000). However, the expansion of the Angolan war into Namibia had swift and significant consequences, including the killing of several civilians. Coupled with the general fear caused by the fighting, losses to the tourism industry mounted as anxious potential visitors canceled trips to Namibia (*Daily Mail and Guardian*, January 7, 2000; *The Namibian*, February 15, 2000). The extension of Angola's civil war into Namibia also resulted in widespread charges of human rights abuses by NDF and SFF members in the Kavango and Caprivi regions, where the fighting was concentrated. Those abuses decreased significantly once cross-border fighting from Angola came to an end following the Angolan cease-fire in April 2002 (U.S. Department of State 2003d).

Finally, during this same period, Namibia's military and security forces became involved in an internal conflict. On August 2, 1999, separatist rebels, calling themselves the Caprivi Liberation Army and demanding independence for the Caprivi region, launched armed attacks on the police station, army base, and Namibian Broadcasting Corporation office at Katima Mulilo, Caprivi's largest town. The Namibian government responded by declaring a state of emergency in the region and detaining hundreds of suspected rebel collaborators (*Daily Mail and Guardian,* August 6, 1999; *The Namibian,* August 2, 1999, August 3, 1999, August 6, 1999). The rebellion was led by onetime DTA leader and Caprivi native Mishake Muyongo, who subsequently fled to Botswana and then Denmark. Unrest in the region and the security forces' harsh response to the alleged secession attempt prompted thousands of ordinary Caprivians to flee to Botswana as well. By 2002 tension in the region had largely subsided, though NDF and SFF members continued to kill alleged secessionists, and several others accused of high treason for their alleged involvement in the plot died in police custody (U.S. Department of State 2003d).[12]

■ Representation and Participation

▨ *Legislative Branches*

As noted above, Namibia's bicameral parliament consists of a national assembly (lower house) with seventy-two elected members of parliament and six nonvoting members appointed by the president, and a national council (upper house or house of review) with twenty-six members elected from thirteen regional councils. Members of the National Assembly are elected every five years under a closed list, proportional representation electoral system. Members of the National Council serve six-year terms, with two members from each regional council being elected to the National Council. Shortly after independence, the country was divided into thirteen geographic regions (as opposed to the ethnically based designations of the previous regime), each with a governor and council. For purposes of elections, each region is further divided into constituencies, with the number depending on the region's population. At the local level, municipalities, towns, and villages—in some cases newly proclaimed after independence—are governed by municipal, town, and village councils, respectively (Toetemeyer 2000, 118–123).

As Table 8.1 indicates, SWAPO easily dominates legislative bodies at all three levels in Namibia, from local to national, with its support ranging from roughly 60 percent at the local level to more than 75 percent at the national level from 1989 to 1999. In part, the choice of electoral system may be influencing electoral outcomes in SWAPO's favor. According to Keulder (1999b, 5), at the regional level at least, SWAPO is overrepresented in that the party's share of seats exceeds its share of votes. This can be attributed to the use of the first-past-the-post electoral system for regional elections, which requires a simple majority for the winner to take all. In

Table 8.1 Election Results in Namibia by Party, 1989–1999 (percentages)

	Nov. 1989 Constituent Assembly	Dec. 1992 Local Authorities	Dec. 1992 Regional Councils	Dec. 1994 National Assembly	Feb. 1998 Local Authorities	Dec. 1998 Regional Councils	Dec. 1999 National Assembly
Voter turnout	98.05	82.33	81.07	76.05	33.75	40.01	62.00
SWAPO	56.90	58.02	68.76	73.89	60.35	67.92	76.30
DTA	28.34	33.26	27.68	20.78	23.91	23.91	9.40
COD	—	—	—	—	—	—	9.90
UDF	5.50	5.88	2.49	2.72	6.66	4.45	2.90
FCN	1.55	—	—	0.24	—	0.17	0.10
DCN NPF/ACN	5.09	0.06	0.20	0.83	0.53	—	0.30
SWANU (NNF)	0.79	1.49	0.72	0.53	0.23	—	0.30
MAG	—	—	—	0.82	—	—	0.70
Residents' associations	—	—	—	—	8.22	—	—

Sources: 1989–1998: Keulder 1999b, 61; 1999: The Namibian, December 7, 1999, and December 9, 1999.
Note: Percentages do not sum to 100 due to spoiled ballots and trace percentages to smaller parties.

addition, the prevalence of uncontested SWAPO constituencies (as many as twenty-nine of ninety-five constituencies in the 1998 regional election) has enhanced SWAPO's representation at the regional level.

Though SWAPO may be overrepresented at the regional level, Forrest (1998, 300–301) argues that regional councils and the National Council, regardless of party composition, are making an important contribution to the consolidation of democracy in Namibia. He describes Namibia's national councillors, elected from among the country's regional councillors, as performing an important grassroots transmission role—serving as a "state-society connecting agency" on behalf of Namibia's predominantly rural areas. Against all odds and the expectations of the Ministry of Local and Regional Government and Housing, regional councillors, regional governors, and national councillors have managed to assert important roles for themselves and their institutions, tackling issues of significance to their largely rural, arguably neglected, constituents. This is all the more interesting given that the ruling party, SWAPO, was initially strongly opposed to the notion of a second chamber of parliament, most likely because members would be elected (indirectly) on the basis of constituencies rather than party lists. SWAPO only agreed to the National Council on the condition that it would only review, and not veto, legislation passed by the National Assembly.

Electoral systems have other important implications for the National Assembly and the independence of the legislative branch. Indeed, the use of a closed list, proportional representation system in the National Assembly elections means that MPs are not elected directly by constituents; rather they are elected because their name is placed high enough on a party list to win a seat. What this also means is that MPs hold office at the pleasure of their party and are not accountable to anyone beyond the party. As Keulder (1999a, 9) notes, "members of the lower house are not turning to well-defined constituencies when seeking office, but rather to those that control the composition of the list. This undermines legislators' autonomy and restrains their potential to rebel against policy decisions taken in the executive." As in the Mozambican and South African proportional representation systems, the absence of genuine linkages to constituencies is a cause for concern.

A more benevolent result of Namibia's use of the closed list, proportional representation system for the National Assembly elections (combined with voluntary quotas on the part of political parties) has been a very high percentage of women in the National Assembly—up to 29.2 percent in 2004 (falling to 25 percent in 2005). Along with Mozambique and South Africa (both about 30 percent), Namibia now has one of the highest percentages of women in a national legislature in Africa and in the world. The representation of women is even greater at the local level in Namibia, where gender quotas are mandated by law. More than 40 percent of local councillors and many mayors and deputy mayors in Namibia are women.

An additional, "lower" level of representation exists in Namibia, in the form of traditional leaders and traditional authorities. This level can be extremely important, however, in countries that are predominantly rural, like Namibia, in that in many rural communities traditional leaders may "continue to control most of the important rural survival strategies: allocation of land, natural resources, communal labour practices and in some instances law and order" (Keulder 2000, 150). In Namibia, the Traditional Authorities Act of 1995 recognizes two types of traditional leadership: chieftanships and headmanships (but not kingships) and makes provision for remunerating both. In 1996 it was estimated that around 150,000 families, or 855,000 people (about half of Namibia's population), were living in communal areas under the jurisdiction of a traditional leader of some sort (Keulder 2000, 161). At the same time, however, the establishment of regional councils effectively transferred to the regional councils all of the administrative powers previously allocated to traditional authorities (Keulder 2000, 161). In general, traditional authorities have no role in local authorities, regional councils, or local land boards, except for an advisory role. The 1995 act also makes provision for a council of traditional leaders that would have an advisory role to the president; otherwise its sole jurisdiction would be over the traditional authorities at the local level.

◼ *Party Systems and Elections*

Beginning with the Constituent Assembly elections in 1989, elections have been held on a regular basis in Namibia—every five years for the National Assembly and presidency, every six years at the local and regional level. Since 1989 all elections have been held under Namibian auspices and all have generally been deemed free and fair, although serious concerns were raised about the quality of the 1999 National Assembly and presidential election campaigns. With the exception of the 1998 local and regional elections, voter turnout in Namibia has generally been fairly high, ranging from 98 percent in 1989 to 62 percent in 1999. By contrast, the voter turnout rate was only 33.75 percent in the February 1998 local elections and 40 percent in the December 1998 regional elections. In both cases, according to post-election analyses, these low turnouts resulted from three broad factors: negative feelings toward political actors, special circumstances relating to the electoral process, and apathy or lethargy (Keulder 1999b, 18–19).

In the 1989 Constituent Assembly elections, ten parties fielded candidates and seven were represented in the first National Assembly. In the 2004 National Assembly elections, seven parties won seats, up from five in the 1999 elections. With the exception of the 1998 local and regional elections, the ruling party, SWAPO, has steadily increased its share of the vote in each election, such that by 1999 (and again in 2004) it received 76 percent of the vote. At the presidential level Nujoma won reelection overwhelmingly in 1994 and 1999, and his hand-picked successor, Pohamba, won an easy victory as well in 2004. These trends have caused many observers to consider Namibia a state of single-party dominance.

Indeed, institutionalizing strong multiparty political systems is one of the challenges facing many African countries today as they seek to transition from decades of authoritarian single-party rule to more democratic rule, and Namibia is no exception. The freedom to form and join political parties clearly exists in Namibia, and since independence dozens of political parties have come and gone, or reorganized themselves into coalitions or alliances with other parties. At the same time, none has managed to challenge effectively the ruling party or to encroach significantly upon its base of support. A number of reasons have been put forward to explain this, including SWAPO's role as the leading nationalist organization in the struggle for independence and other parties' continued association with preindependence "interim" governments (a liability for the DTA, in particular), SWAPO's access to generous resources of the state, SWAPO's strong and unwavering support among the majority Ovambo ethnic group, SWAPO leader Sam Nujoma's continued appeal as "founding father" of the nation, a lack of significant ideological differences among nearly all political parties, and a lack of financial resources for the smaller opposition parties (Bauer 1999, 439–441).

Prior to the 1999 National Assembly and presidential elections there had been speculation that SWAPO's dominance might be seriously challenged by a new party, one that emerged from among the ranks of disaffected SWAPO members in the late 1990s (Kalenga 1999; Lodge 2000). That party, the Congress of Democrats (COD), was formally launched in March 1999. The party has been led, since its inception, by former SWAPO member of parliament Ben Ulenga, deputy minister and high commissioner to the UK. COD members, including Ulenga, explained their defection from SWAPO by "the failure of Swapo to transform itself from a secretive and exiled armed nationalist movement to a mass-based governing party." They complained that SWAPO allowed very little space for constructive dialogue within the party, and accused President Sam Nujoma of copying "the tactics of his old ally and good friend, President Robert Mugabe of Zimbabwe" (Kalenga 1999, 26–27).

The new party quickly gained the attention of the SWAPO leadership; President Nujoma accused Ulenga and others of engaging in "rebellious activities" against the ruling party (*The Namibian,* April 6, 1999, March 31, 1999). The attacks continued during the campaign for the 1999 national elections. For example, SWAPO issued a pamphlet that described the COD leadership as "political malcontents, who have been driven to their defection from the party by personal ambitions and infantile opportunism" (*The Namibian*, September 2, 1999). In northern Namibia, the home affairs minister called the COD a group of "traitors and spies" who wanted to bring back "a white government like that of the Boers during the liberation struggle," echoing Robert Mugabe's verbal assaults on the opposition Movement for Democratic Change in Zimbabwe (Kalenga 1999, 25; Lodge 2000, 28).

The COD did not do as well as anticipated by many in the 1999 election, garnering only 9.9 percent of the vote in the National Assembly elections (translating to seven seats), compared to SWAPO's 76.3 percent. Moreover, the COD clearly lured votes away from the DTA, the hitherto strongest opposition party, rather than from the ruling party (Lodge 2000, 26). SWAPO's anti-COD campaign, historical dominance, and structural advantages as ruling party surely contributed to the final result as well. Following the election, the ruling party was successful in denying the COD its rightful place as the official opposition in the National Assembly. SWAPO played a role in the hasty formation of a coalition between the DTA and the United Democratic Front (UDF); with their combined nine seats the DTA-UDF coalition was regarded as the official opposition.[13] Nonetheless, the COD is considered to have better long-term prospects than the DTA, which remains tarnished by its association with preindependence governments. In the 2004 election, the COD won more votes than in the 1999 election, but lost two seats in parliament; the DTA fared worse, losing votes and three seats in parliament.[14]

One consequence of the move toward a political system of single-party dominance has been a steady blurring of the distinction between party and state, a characteristic of one-party states throughout Africa. Party membership, for example, is essential for appointment to senior positions in government and parastatal organizations. Indeed being a "loyal Namibian," according to the party, is essential for obtaining any government job. Cabinet reshuffles have been justified on the basis of "party discipline," and SWAPO party leaders rarely, if ever, articulate policy positions distinct from those of government (Bauer 1999, 433). The Economist Intelligence Unit (EIU) (2003f, 13) suggests that this blurring of the line between party and government "has hampered the rooting out of corruption, which has become prevalent at both senior and junior levels."

■ Civil Society and Other Groups

While a "dense network" of voluntary associations may not yet fully exist in Namibia, civil society and its organizations have grown considerably in the years since independence. According to one recent survey there are currently about 220 nongovernmental organizations (NGOs) in Namibia: 160 NGOs and 60 community-based organizations (though many of these are very small, even inactive). The major areas of NGO intervention in Namibia are agriculture, rural development, education, and training. Organizations of civil society in Namibia work both with government, to address critical development needs, and on their own, identifying their own agendas for social, political, and economic action. NGOs in several sectors work in tandem with their relevant ministries; others collaborate with the National Planning Commission on development policy and programs or participate in the legislative process by attending committee hearings or meeting with legislators and their staffs. Several NGOs focus on independent organizing, constituency mobilization, and provision of information, all essential elements in expanding civil society's role and strengthening its voice. These include some of the larger, more prominent NGOs in Namibia, such as the Legal Assistance Center, the Labor Resource and Research Institute, the Namibian Society for Human Rights, Sister Namibia, the Namibian Economic Policy Research Unit, the Institute for Public Policy Research, and the new local chapter of Transparency International. The Namibia NGO Forum, formed in 1991, acts as an umbrella body to many of Namibia's NGOs.

■ Trade Unions, Churches, and Student Groups

Independent organizing is a relatively new phenomenon in Namibia. Before independence, both the South African–sponsored interim government and the externally based liberation movement worked hard to ensure that little in the way of independent organizing occurred outside their respective spheres of influence. During the 1970s and 1980s, a national trade union federation and affiliated unions, a church federation, and national student organization were all formed inside Namibia and have continued to exist, in different guises, up to the present. The emergence of trade unions from among the ranks of SWAPO supporters in the mid-1980s was only sanctioned by the exiled liberation movement when it became clear in the final days of the struggle that they had value as a mobilizing force (Bauer 1998). Indeed, upon independence SWAPO moved quickly to ensure that the recently formed federation—the National Union of Namibian Workers—affiliated itself formally with the party. In the early years of independence there were attempts on the part of some union members to move the unions away from the ruling party, but they were never successful. Such efforts were always met with great consternation, even threats, from SWAPO (Bauer 1999). The NUNW was one of the few organizations to state its "unequivocal" support for a third term for President Nujoma and for Namibian intervention in the DRC (*The Namibian,* October 1, 1998). As noted earlier, the ruling party, cognizant of the recent role of labor movements in opposition politics in Zambia and Zimbabwe, has been very vigilant with respect to the nation's trade unions. A clear part of the government's co-optation effort has been the steady flow of trade union leaders into government, including as SWAPO members of parliament and deputy ministers.

The churches followed a slightly different trajectory with respect to the party. The Council of Churches of Namibia (CCN), representing about 80 percent of the Namibian population by the early 1980s, has a long-standing association with SWAPO; indeed, by the 1980s it was referred to by some as the party's "internal religious wing" (Steenkamp 1995, 99). The church had played an active part in early protests against South African rule in Namibia. In the urban areas, CCN offices tried to address the health, education, and economic development needs of the neglected majority population. After independence, however, the federation was rebuked by the ruling party for its demands that SWAPO address "the detainee issue"—those SWAPO members still missing from exile. The party even attempted to prevent the CCN from holding a national conference to address unresolved issues concerning the detainees. Ultimately, the conference was held in March 1998, though SWAPO pointedly sent no delegates (*The Namibian,* March 9, 1998). Moreover, during the Angola and DRC wars, the CCN called for dialogue rather than war as a means for ending armed conflicts in the region (*The Namibian,* February 10, 2000). Thus, unlike the trade unions, the churches and their national federation have maintained some independence vis-à-vis the ruling party.

Organized youth have also wrestled with the ruling party since independence. First formed in 1984, the Namibian National Student Organization (NANSO) also considered itself part and parcel of the liberation movement inside the country in its early days (Maseko 1995, 120). Shortly after independence, however, in 1991, NANSO voted to disaffiliate from SWAPO, given concerns that affiliation prevented the organization from recruiting non-SWAPO students and youth, concern about preventing outside control of NANSO processes and structures, and a general desire to preserve the inner organizational democracy and autonomy of the student organization (Maseko 1995, 127–128). Leaders of the disaffiliation effort were labeled "foreign agents" by the SWAPO leadership and shortly thereafter a splinter student organization was formed with the assistance of the ruling party. Thereafter the original NANSO lost significant numbers of members and began to experience administrative, financial, and organizational difficulties (Bauer 1999, 437–438).

This obvious reluctance on the part of the ruling party to sanction, never mind encourage, independent organization (and voices) outside of party structures is of great significance to the prospects for the consolidation of democracy in Namibia. As Leys and Saul (1995, 4) noted in the early years after independence: "While a formally democratic system has indeed emerged in Namibia, it seems fair to say that little popular empowerment has been realized." As Melber notes more recently (2003, 15), criticism is not taken lightly by the ruling party: "Loyalty to Namibia is equated with loyalty to Swapo's policy and in particular the party's president. Dissenting views are marginalized."

▒ *Media*

An integral part of an active civil society is a free and independent media. Indeed, a significant level of media freedom has existed in Namibia since independence. Namibia has an impressive array of government, private, and community media sources. The national radio station broadcasts throughout the country in every Namibian language. In recent years, there has been a proliferation of independent radio stations, including a community radio station in Katutura, the black township outside Windhoek. The national television network, the Namibian Broadcasting Corporation, is government owned, as are a number of newspapers and magazines, but operates with some measure of independence. Three independent dailies and a host of smaller, private newspapers and magazines vie with one another for readers from among the national populace. The privately owned and operated media in Namibia are fiercely independent, and editors and columnists freely voice their criticisms of government and other institutions.

The Media Institute of Southern Africa (MISA), whose secretariat is based in Windhoek, monitors press freedom in the region. One issue of recent concern to MISA was the Namibian government's decision in late 2000 to withdraw advertising from the privately owned newspaper *The Namibian,* and then to withdraw government purchases of the newspaper for all government offices (MISA 2000, 68). This was because of allegedly critical and unpatriotic reporting by *The Namibian.* Yet in the view of MISA's regional director, Luckson Chipare, press freedom is much greater in Namibia than in some other MISA member countries. Among southern African countries, Namibia was in the middle range in terms of action alerts issued by MISA during 2000. According to Chipare, a key concern for Namibia must be maintaining editorial independence throughout the media and achieving the three-tier system of public, commercial, and community media that MISA advocates throughout the region.[15]

■ Society and Development: Enduring Cleavages

▒ *Politics of Race in Namibia*

Namibia is a multiracial and multiethnic society. Most of the population is black, divided among several ethnic groups; just under 10 percent is mixed race or "Coloured" and just under 5 percent of the population is white. About two-thirds of the white population are Afrikaans-speakers, with the rest being German-speakers descended from German colonists and English speakers of South African origins. After decades of colonial and apartheid rule, most white Namibians are far better off than their black counterparts—although the discrepancies are probably not as great as in South Africa. Indeed, the United Nations Development Programme (UNDP) (2000, 20) reports that 55 percent of aggregate income in Namibia accrues to 10 percent of the population. A small minority of Namibians live like their middle-class counterparts in the industrialized world (or better) while the majority of Namibians live like their counterparts in the rest of sub-Saharan Africa. For this reason, it is very misleading to speak about a per capita income in Namibia and to rank the country on that basis. According to the UNDP, "in terms of its income and asset distribution, the Namibian economy is so extreme that the 'average' Namibian, in social and economic terms, is a rarity."

The persistence of disparities is reminiscent of the other postsettler societies in southern Africa and reflects, in part, the fact that each eschewed a policy of redistribution after independence. Namibia, like South Africa and Zimbabwe, turned to a policy of national reconciliation in an effort to move beyond the decades of apartheid rule and race-based oppression. Immediately upon his return to Namibia, Sam Nujoma stated his support for a policy of national reconciliation: "The first thing we have to do is pursue a policy of national reconciliation and open a new page of history, founded on respect for human life, human rights and equality, and build a new life for the whole society. Everybody has suffered; this war has affected everyone. Even whites" (*The Namibian,* September 19, 1989). Nujoma's views were echoed repeatedly by other members of the new government after independence.

National reconciliation had a distinct economic component. The new government was keen not to antagonize the largely white private sector, whether local or foreign, which controlled commercial agriculture, the retail sector, and the mining industry. One of the National Assembly's very first acts was to pass a bill that provided generous conditions for foreign investment and various guarantees on the security of those investments. In the intervening years, however, it appears that the positions of President Nujoma and the ruling party have hardened. White commercial farms have not been invaded, businesses have not been nationalized or even looted, white Namibians have not been given any indication that they are welcome but their children are not.[16] At the same time, verbal attacks on whites, in particular foreign whites (who in some cases are the owners of businesses or land in Namibia), have been growing. "Whites" are most typically criticized for attempting to intervene in internal Namibian affairs. For example, white Namibians and foreigners were accused of instigating the protests (for environmental and cultural preservation reasons) against building the Epupa dam in northern Namibia (*The Namibian,* May 29, 1997). President Nujoma rails against homosexuality in Namibia, considering it a white or foreign import. At the World Summit on Sustainable Development in

Johannesburg in September 2002, Nujoma publicly castigated foreign (European) donors, suggesting that Namibia did not need foreign aid.

Interestingly, there has been a clear trend away from including whites in senior positions in government. Whereas the SWAPO government that took power at independence in 1990 was a careful blend of party leaders from exile, party leaders from inside the country, and white Namibians, "this mix has gradually altered in subsequent cabinet reshuffles so that there are no longer any white ministers, although there are still several white deputy ministers and permanent secretaries" (EIU 2003f, 7). In some cases prominent whites in government have left of their own accord, while others have been asked to leave.

As indicated in President Nujoma's first words on the subject, national reconciliation in Namibia has always been about moving on, about burying the past rather than confronting it. Unlike South Africa, Namibia never established a truth and reconciliation commission that would have investigated past practices and atrocities of the South African administrations in Namibia and, perhaps more importantly, of the liberation movement. As Erasmus (2000, 78) charitably observes: Namibia "adopted a different policy of national reconciliation [from South Africa] by deliberately moving away from the unpleasant memories of the past and instead focusing on what was postulated as the building of a unified nation." This was not for lack of calls for such a commission in Namibia, but those calls went totally unheeded. To this day, the relatives of those young SWAPO members who never returned home from SWAPO exile camps in Angola call for the movement to be held accountable.[17]

Ethnic Conflict and the Politics of Pluralism

In a decade and a half of independence Namibia seems to have avoided significant ethnic conflict. Official government documents downplay ethnicity by presenting population and other statistics almost exclusively by region, rather than race or ethnicity, and only occasionally by "language group," the primary marker for ethnicity in southern Africa. The largest single ethnic group in the country comprises the Ovambo-speaking people, who constitute just over half of the population and live primarily in the four northern regions of Ohangwena, Omusati, Oshana, and Oshikoto, and in some urban areas such as Windhoek and Oranjemund.[18] The Nama and Damara people together make up about another 12 percent of the population. Herero- and Kavango-speakers each make up about another 10 percent of the population. Namibians of mixed-race origin compose less than 10 percent of the population and whites under 5 percent. Other groups include Lozi-speakers, who live in the Caprivi, and the San, the most marginalized and deprived group in Namibia, who no longer have a territorial base (EIU

2003f, 17–18). The Ovambo are further divided into eight subgroups, of which the Kwanyama are the largest and most significant.

There are clear reasons for the government of Namibia to avoid ethnic labels. Throughout colonial Africa perceived ethnicity was used by colonial authorities to divide, in order to more easily subjugate, colonial peoples.[19] This was even more true in apartheid South Africa and Namibia, where significant settler populations sought to deprive indigenous populations of even the most basic rights and did so on the basis of racial and ethnic classifications. Creating ethnic homelands, for example, was all about depriving black Namibians and black South Africans of Namibian and South African citizenship, respectively. In response, of course, the nationalist movement led the struggle for independence with the battle cry "One Namibia! One Nation!" and, like many other nationalist movements, sought to incorporate members of all ethnic groups into the movement, in particular into visible leadership positions.

At the same time, ethnic prejudice does appear to have reared its ugly head within SWAPO in exile. For example, it is charged by many that those most heavily persecuted by the movement in exile were predominantly Nama-Damara or Herero-speaking Namibians, or that they were "Ombuitis"—Ovambo-speakers from the central and southern urban areas rather than the rural north. More often than not these might also have been the more educated and politically progressive SWAPO cadres (Bauer 1998, 165; Saul and Leys 2003, 54–55). Those accused of perpetrating the crimes in exile include Kwanyama-speakers from the north. According to the EIU (2003f, 16) there is a Kwanyama bias within Namibia's military today: "Kwanyama ex-PLAN commanders hold most senior NDF posts, and state security appointments have a similar ethnic bias." But the EIU notes that there have been few reports of intertribal tensions within the army.

Many people suggest that, as in other multiethnic societies, enduring ethnic allegiances in Namibia may prove a stumbling block to the consolidation of democracy. For example, SWAPO's long-standing and steadfast base of support has been from the Ovambo-speaking people. Since they compose more than half the population, should Ovambos continue to vote along ethnic lines for the ruling party, then no other party will ever defeat them. Similarly, if other political parties are organized largely along ethnic lines, then no other parties will ever garner more than about 10–12 percent of the vote. For the most part, political parties in Namibia do have an ethnic base, although there is significant crossover and some melding of ethnic allegiances into one political party.

Finally, there have been claims of an ethnic bias on the part of the SWAPO-led government. For example, during 2002 "some citizens complained that the Swapo-led government provided more development assistance to the numerically dominant Ovambo ethnic group of the far north than to other groups or regions of the country" (U.S. Department of State 2003d). Forrest (1998, 323) argues that one of the reasons that significant ethnic tensions have not emerged in Namibia is that regional governments—by "contributing to the moderation of village-level tensions and providing an outlet for grievances against central government ministries"—have helped to defuse the potential emergence of regional or ethnic challenges.

To date, the main exception to this appears to have been in the Caprivi, where long-standing ethnic concerns were seen by many to be at the heart of the alleged secession plot uncovered by the government in late 1998. Indeed, the movement was felt to have valid reasons (with certain ethnic overtones) for its disgruntlement with the Namibian government, including far fewer development projects in the Caprivi than in the more favored four northern regions, high levels of unemployment in the region, and the appointment of government and other officials from outside the region.

■ Fundamentals of the Political Economy

Since independence, the government's economic goals have focused on achieving a sustainable economic growth rate, achieving a real increase in per capita incomes, diversifying the economy, expanding employment opportunities, and improving education and health services. In recent years, there has been a heightened focus on reducing income inequalities and enabling black economic empowerment. During 1995 to 2000 real gross domestic product (GDP) grew at about 3–5 percent per year, sometimes short of the targeted 5 percent. In 2002 the real GDP growth rate was still short, at about 3 percent. In 2000 unemployment in Namibia was estimated at about 20 percent, not counting those no longer looking for work. About 30 percent of Namibians are estimated to be employed in agriculture, primarily subsistence agriculture in the communal areas. The government hopes to increase employment opportunities by promoting small and medium-sized enterprises and by tripling manufacturing employment to 20 percent of all formal sector jobs (EIU 2003f, 27). Whereas manufacturing in the past was primarily confined to the processing of fish and meat products, in recent years several large Asian-owned textile factories have opened in Namibia as part of a larger government strategy to attract foreign investment to the country. Indeed, legislation in 1995 provided for the establishment of export processing zones in the country and by 2000 two dozen companies with such status were operating in the country. Textile companies, meanwhile, are seeking to take advantage of Namibia's eligibility under the Africa Growth and Opportunity Act to export textiles and clothing duty-free to the United States. Otherwise, mining, commercial agriculture, and fishing remain the mainstays of the Namibian economy.

Significant effort has also been invested in building the tourism industry in Namibia.

As in the other postsettler southern African societies the land issue remains a contentious one in Namibia. Like income, land is very inequitably distributed in Namibia; about 4,000 white commercial farmers own about 6,400 holdings on 30.5 million hectares, or about 37 percent of Namibia's land area. Much of this is arid land devoted to livestock ranching (EIU 2003f, 8). Much of the rest of Namibia's land, generally better watered, supports about 150,000 subsistence farm families in the over-crowded northern communal areas. So far, the redistribution of commercial farmland in Namibia has proceeded on a willing buyer–willing seller basis, as provided in the 1999 commercial land reform bill. The policy is also in keeping with Namibia's constitutional right to private property and reflects government's realization of "the importance of maintaining efficient commercial livestock ranching" (EIU 2003f, 7). The redistribution of land has been hampered, however, by the high prices of commercial farms and a lack of government funds to purchase them. In April 2003, however, a new land tax was imposed that is expected to raise significant funds that will then be used to purchase land for redistribution and resettlement. And in June 2003 new legislation provided government the right to acquire land for resettlement "in the public interest." Land still has to be purchased, but not at the market prices mandated by the willing buyer–willing seller policy (EIU 2003j).

It has been suggested that the demands for land redistribution have not been as great in Namibia as in South Africa or Zimbabwe, because the majority of Namibians, the Ovambo-speaking people from the north, were not actually dispossessed of their land during the colonial period. Rather it was the Herero and Nama-Damaras from central and southern Namibia whose land and livestock were taken; moreover, these groups do not form the core of the ruling party's support base in the way that the Ovambo do. By the same token, there is also a crying need for land reform in the northern communal areas. There, the fencing of communal lands by the rich and politically powerful, as well as the historical neglect of the northern communal areas (in terms of agricultural extension services, access to credit and other inputs, environmental degradation, etc.), have limited access to land and income among subsistence households.

■ Challenges for the Twenty-First Century

And so we return to our original question: whether Namibia will set a new example of Africa's promise in the twenty-first century or whether it will follow the example of so many neighbors to the north toward disintegration and decay. The structural constraints are numerous and it seems that there is only so much that individual or even collective agents can do. Economically, the challenges abound. A generous resource endowment and healthy infrastructure are mitigated somewhat by a harsh climate marked by water shortages and recurring drought. Unemployment and lower-than-anticipated economic growth rates threaten continued improvements in living standards that are expected by the population and that are necessary to narrow the disparities across racial and ethnic groups. Foreign investment, one source of jobs, remains the double-edged sword it has always been—damaging the environment and people's health, eroding hard-won labor standards, and yet providing some source of livelihood for many.

Socially, Namibia faces a dire challenge in the form of a burgeoning AIDS crisis that threatens to impact every facet of life in devastating ways. On this front at least, Namibia is leading the way, with its decision in 2003 to begin producing generic versions of antiretroviral drugs and to make available to pregnant women other drugs that help to reduce mother-to-child transmission of the virus. And while Namibia has made enormous strides in terms of primary health care and education provision since independence, both still need to reach large segments of the population. Moreover, a very rapid rural to urban migration—as many as 600 people arrive in the capital city every month—puts a remarkable strain on local government resources and services, contributes to rising crime rates, and provides a ready reserve of disaffected people to threaten Namibia's hard-won political stability.

Finally, politically, the country faces the same challenges of many African and developing countries that have attempted recent democratic transitions: how to create a tolerant democratic political culture after decades of authoritarian colonial rule and decades of undemocratic practices within a liberation movement in exile; how to institutionalize a viable multiparty political system in which opposition political parties (with social bases that are other than ethnic) can thrive and not be labeled disloyal for daring to utter a criticism; how to carry out peaceful presidential successions on a continent where leaders have usually been removed only by force. Though President Sam Nujoma elected not to stand for an unconstitutional fourth term of office, he essentially handpicked his successor—his "most loyal lieutenant," Hifikepunye Pohamba. Though Pohamba was "selected" by delegates at a SWAPO extraordinary congress in May 2004, his selection was clearly engineered by President Nujoma. Moreover, President Nujoma remains leader of the party until at least 2007, thus suggesting he might be "president by proxy" (Sherbourne 2004). In the end, Namibia's first presidential succession was marked by far less than complete transparency and by the retention of power by the first, older generation of once-exiled liberation leaders.

■ Notes

1. For more on the history of Namibia, see Katjavivi 1990; Hayes et al. 1998; Dobell 1998; Ngavirue 1997; and Emmett 1999.

2. For more on the transition, see Cliffe et al. 1993 and Weiland and Braham 1994.

3. Bratton and van de Walle 1997, 178. An elite pact is one in which "moderate factions in the government and opposition seek common ground through negotiations." In such a situation "incumbent and opposition leaders meet behind the scenes to provide mutual assurances that each would respect the vital interests of the other in a future democratic dispensation."

4. According to Bratton and van de Walle (1997, 81), settler oligarchies "resembled the bureaucratic-authoritarian regimes constructed by Europeans in those parts of the colonial world where white settlers gained *de facto* control of the state." They "approximate exclusionary democracies." Political competition was high but participation low—with settlers reproducing functioning democracies for themselves, while fully excluding the indigenous majority.

5. "Where cultural and organizational contexts are unsupportive, the introduction of political contestation can lead to division, polarization, and instability. If this logic is correct, then the prospects for gradual, negotiated political opening are generally better in bureaucratic-authoritarian regimes, provided they display some heritage of political competition, than in neopatrimonial regimes" (Bratton and van de Walle 1997, 179).

6. In the 1994 presidential race, Sam Nujoma was reelected with 74.5 percent of the vote; rival candidate Mishake Muyongo of the Democratic Turnhalle Alliance (DTA) polled 23.1 percent of the vote. In the 1999 presidential race, Nujoma was again reelected, with 76.7 percent of the vote; Ben Ulenga of the Congress of Democrats garnered 10.6 percent of the vote, the DTA's Katuutire Kaura polled 9.7 percent of the vote, and the United Democratic Front's Justus Garoeb received 3.0 percent of the vote. *The Namibian,* December 7, 1999. In 2004 SWAPO's Hifikepunye Pohamba won 76.4 percent of the vote to Ben Ulenga's 7.3 percent and Katuutire Kaura's 5.1 percent of the vote. *The Namibian,* November 22, 2004.

7. In a cabinet reshuffle in August 2002, Geingob, who had served as prime minister since independence, was offered the post of minister of regional and local government and housing. Rather than accept this obvious demotion, Geingob resigned from office. Speculation about the reasons for Geingob's demotion centered around his campaign in early August 2002 to become the SWAPO party vice president. Instead, President Nujoma's favored candidate, Pohamba, became the party's vice president. In early April 2004 a SWAPO Central Committee meeting selected Hamutenya, Pohamba, and longtime higher education minister Nahas Angula as contenders for SWAPO presidential candidate. Just days before the congress to select the candidate, Hamutenya was abruptly dismissed from office by President Nujoma.

8. Erasmus (2000, 81) calls it "a remarkable process of compromise and reconciliation."

9. According to F. M. d'Engelbronner-Kolff (1998, 62–63), "describing the essence of customary law is a controversial and complicated matter. The entire discourse about customary law, as well as the distinction between custom and law, relates to the autonomy, or for legal purposes, the sovereignty, of social groups outside the central government." Many seem to reconcile this contradiction by seeing

customary law in terms of "society's semi-autonomy—the fact that it can generate rules and customs and symbols internally, but that it is also vulnerable to rules and decisions and other forces emanating from the larger world it is surrounded by." Importantly, customary law must also be understood as dynamic, "rather than being a static body of rules and principles."

10. For example, the U.S. Department of State (2003d) claims, citing a January 2003 case, that "some traditional leaders reportedly continue to detain and imprison persons accused of minor offenses without recourse to police or judicial review."

11. *The Namibian,* January 4, 1999, January 5, 1999; *Daily Mail and Guardian,* January 6, 1999.

12. Saul and Leys (2003, 338) note that interrogators from SWAPO's detention centers in Lubango, Angola, during the 1980s have been "reincarnated as members of the Security Service or the President's Special Field Force."

13. *The Namibian,* April 13, 2000. Certain privileges are accorded the official opposition, such as the leader being able to respond first in major debates introduced by the ruling party, and at times being able to speak for an unlimited period in the National Assembly. The leader of the official opposition also receives a higher salary than ordinary members of parliament.

14. In the 2005–2010 National Assembly SWAPO retains 55 of 72 seats, and the opposition parties retain 17 seats divided as follows: COD 5, DTA 4, UDF and NUDO 3 each, and MAG and the Republican Party 1 each. *The Namibian,* November 22, 2004.

15. Author interview, Windhoek, March 1, 2002.

16. See Chapter 7 for a discussion of this issue in Zimbabwe.

17. See Saul and Leys 2003 for an account of "forgotten history" as politics in contemporary Namibia. As they observe (2003, 337): "Swapo's domestic critics have continued to make clear that, in their view, it is not differing philosophies and strategies of reconciliation but rather Swapo's desire to cover its own tracks that does indeed provide the most convincing explanation of the path the movement has chosen."

18. Most, though not all, of "historically disadvantaged Namibians"—those people particularly discriminated against under South African rule—live in these four regions plus the Kavango and Caprivi regions.

19. As Leroy Vail (1991, 7) reminds us "ethnicity is not a cultural residue but a consciously crafted ideological creation." In southern Africa three variables were at play from the late nineteenth century onward: the need for a group of cultural brokers for the nationalist project, the practice of "indirect rule," and a reach toward "traditional values" in a period of rapid social change. European missionaries played a tremendous role in "creating" African ethnic identities.

9

South Africa: Contending with the Contradictions

In its first-ever, all-race election in 1994, South Africa achieved what only a short time before had seemed unthinkable: a peaceful transition of power from a white minority regime to a democratic, popularly elected black majority government. As a result of that election, the principal and long-standing liberation movement, the African National Congress (ANC), emerged as the leader of a new Government of National Unity (GNU). More astoundingly, the ANC was joined in the GNU by its erstwhile enemy, the National Party (NP), and its main black rival, the Zulu-based Inkatha Freedom Party (IFP). Accordingly, the election outcome and the new government were hailed around the world as a miracle; the election's importance is not to be underestimated. Indeed, in contrast to South Africa's very recent past, "it is difficult not to be enthusiastic about its accomplishments and its future" (Mattes 2002, 22). Just a few years earlier, South Africa had been ruled by a racist white minority government under the brutally oppressive system of apartheid. It also faced a low-level guerrilla war and economic stagnation, and was considered a pariah by the international community. The 1994 election allowed South Africa to reenter the community of nations and immediately claim a leadership position on the African continent.

Several of South Africa's attributes proved auspicious in its renewed promise and newfound legitimacy: the country's economic base, its leadership, and the nature of its negotiated transition to democracy. First, although the last years of apartheid and National Party rule had badly damaged the economy, South Africa could nonetheless claim a level of gross domestic product (GDP) and industrial development, as well as an economic infrastructure and degree of sectoral diversity that is unsurpassed in Africa. Thus the country was poised to play a leading role on the continent economically as well as politically. Second, the new South Africa was substantially personified by the ANC's Nelson Mandela, who became the first

South Africa: Country Data

Land area 1,221,038 km²
Capital Pretoria
Date of independence May 31, 1961, declared a republic
Population 43.2 million, 58% urban
Languages Official languages: Afrikaans, English, IsiNdebele,
    Sepedi, Sesotho, Swazi, Xitsonga, Setswana, Tshivenda,
    IsiXhosa, and IsiZulu
Ethnic groups African, 75.2%; European, 13.6%; Coloured, 8.6%;
    Asian, 2.6%
Religions Christian, 68%; Muslim, 2%; Hindu, 1.5%; indigenous
    beliefs, 28.5%
Currency rand (R); rand per U.S. dollar: 7.43 (July 2003)

Literacy rate 85.6% (male, 86.3%; female, 85.0%)
Life expectancy 50.9 years (male, 47.7 years; female, 54.4 years)
Infant mortality 56 per 1,000 live births

GDP per capita U.S.$2,620
GDP per capita (PPP) U.S.$11,290
GDP per capita growth rate 0.2% (1990–2001)

Leaders since 1994
    • Nelson Rolihlahla Mandela, president, May 1994–June 1999
    • Thabo Mvuyelwa Mbeki, president, June 1999–

Major political parties
    Ruling party: African National Congress (ANC)
    Other parties: Inkatha Freedom Party (IFP)
    Democratic Alliance
    New National Party (NNP)

Women in parliament (lower/single house) 32.8% (2004)

Note: Data from 2001 unless otherwise indicated.

president of the democratic state. Mandela's lack of bitterness, despite twenty-seven years of imprisonment by the apartheid state, and his quest for reconciliation between the races brought him and his country world-wide acclaim and respect. More important, his leadership was essential in guiding South Africa through a very fragile period in its history. Third, the process of negotiation between former combatants, in which Mandela was instrumental, helped to establish the rules of the game for the democratic transition and set a positive and peaceful course for the future.

These accomplishments, however, mask a great number of problems. Notwithstanding the promise of majority rule, and indeed the promises of the ANC government itself, South Africa has failed to live up to many expectations both domestically and internationally. On the economic front, the growth anticipated in 1994 simply has not materialized. South Africa requires more than 6 percent annual GDP growth in order to achieve per capita increases in wealth and well-being; due to a variety of domestic and international forces, however, democratic South Africa averaged less than 3 percent in its first decade. The country continues to be one of the most unequal in the world, measured by income disparities that still largely fall along racial lines. In the rural communities, a land reform program that dwarfs Zimbabwe's is behind schedule and below expectations. While a small number of blacks in the urban areas have joined the ranks of the new middle class, poverty remains entrenched and has deepened in many areas, with unemployment in the black community reportedly running as high as 40 percent.

Not surprisingly, given the social demands on the state and its economic constraints, crime has skyrocketed, and South Africa today has the dubious distinction of having one of the highest and most violent crime rates on earth. Similarly, although the state has made gains in rural and urban health care provision, the AIDS crisis threatens to devastate South Africa's fragile health and social infrastructure. With an astounding 4.7 *million* HIV cases in the country, South Africa has the highest number of infected persons anywhere in the world.

The widely hailed reconciliation process that was embodied by President Mandela, Archbishop Desmond Tutu, and others, and orchestrated by the Truth and Reconciliation Commission (TRC) from 1996 to 1998, has revealed numerous shortcomings. Mandela, of course, retired from the presidency in 1999. More significant, although efforts at reconciliation have been far deeper than in Zimbabwe in 1980, rising black alienation and white resentment suggest renewed social conflict is possible. Coupled with a belief that the TRC failed to punish—or even identify—all the perpetrators of apartheid-era crimes, this has led to bitterness and disillusionment in a substantial segment of the black community and among some members of the white population as well.

Finally, political challenges also threaten to undermine South Africa's meticulously negotiated transition. Thus, "if one looks at South Africa's new democracy in a comparative perspective, one's enthusiasm is greatly tempered, if not altogether removed" (Mattes 2002, 22). South Africa under the ANC has once again become a dominant-party system, albeit in the context of democratic institutions, including an impressive and inclusive constitutional structure and regular multiparty elections (Lodge 1999). The concentration of power, however, holds implications for governance, for these institutions, and for the country's nascent democratic culture, which may be showing premature signs of decay (Mattes 2002).

Numerous theoretical and analytical approaches attempt to explain South Africa's performance in the first decade of independence. Critics on the left decry what they see as the ANC's abandonment of its social-democratic roots and its commitment to nationalization and economic redistribution in favor of a neoliberal, market-based development model (Saul 1999; Bond 2000). They argue that the ANC's unfettered embrace of market capitalism, which became apparent in the mid-1990s, has amounted to a betrayal of labor, and black interests more broadly, and has contributed to lasting social instability. Those on the right, to be sure, are generally less critical of the ANC's economic program, with its emphasis on property rights, supply-side policies, and an overall framework that promotes growth *before* redistribution. Nonetheless, the ANC has not escaped criticism from those on the right, who criticize what are regarded as political choices, such as the enactment of affirmative action and labor legislation that they believe threatens corporate interests (Adam 1997). In addition, Thabo Mbeki, who succeeded Mandela as South African president, occasionally resorts to populist rhetoric that hints at a penchant for redistribution, and thus causes some concern among capitalists, although this has yet to be taken seriously by those closest to the government (Bond 2000; I. Taylor 2002).

Many of the virtues attributed to South Africa, as well as the challenges it faces a decade after its transition to democracy, are reminiscent of Zimbabwe in the same period (Herbst 1989; Stoneman 1988). Indeed, the countries have similar historical, economic, and political endowments. Although overstating those commonalities is unhelpful, some parallels warrant closer consideration. These include the nature and depth of reconciliation; the disparities in income, land, and resources between the black and white communities; the choice of economic development strategy; and the pitfalls of one-party dominance. Examination of these issues can shed light on the critical questions facing contemporary South Africa: What are the prospects for economic growth and social stability? How strong—or conversely, how fragile—is South Africa's democracy?

■ Historical Origins of the South African State

Formal European contact with South Africa dates to 1652, when the Dutch East India Company established a way-station in the western Cape region for its Indian Ocean trade. Initially no settlement was intended, but the territory gradually attracted Dutch and French Huguenot farmers, and by 1672 a colony had been established (Omer-Cooper 1994). The area was not uninhabited, however, and white settlement led to the decimation of the local population, known as the Khoi. Many of these indigenous peoples died, and miscegenation between white men and Khoi women was also common.[1] Dutch hegemony eventually gave way to the superior military and commercial capacity of the British, who established control in the Cape colony between 1795 and 1803. In 1828 the British annexed the other South African territory of Natal, to the east. The arrival of the British in South Africa gave rise to centuries of tension between English-speakers and the descendants of the original Dutch-French settlers, who became known as Afrikaners.

Cultural and economic clashes between the European populations— over, among other things, the *modestly* more liberal British policies toward indigenous peoples—led a significant portion of the Afrikaner population to push farther into South Africa's hinterland, and in 1836 many of them migrated from the principal areas of European settlement in the British-controlled Cape and Natal colonies. This "Great Trek," as it came to be known, led to the establishment of the Transvaal Republic and the Orange Free State. One of the great foundation myths of the Afrikaner people was that the vast territories of the country that they settled were empty and uninhabited; in fact they were home to several hundred thousand Khoisan and several million Bantu-speaking peoples, including Xhosa on the eastern frontier and Sotho-speakers and Zulu subgroups to the north and northeast.[2] These early nineteenth-century migrations set the stage for more than a century of racial conflict (Omer-Cooper 1994).

By the late 1870s, most of the African populations had been conquered or subdued, and white South Africa was essentially divided into two British colonies, Cape and Natal, and two Afrikaner-led republics, Transvaal and the Orange Free State, on which the British and English-speaking economic interests long had designs. The discovery of significant deposits of diamonds in the late 1860s, and gold in 1886 in the Transvaal, greatly exacerbated existing tensions between the British and Afrikaner populations. These came to a head with the outbreak of the Anglo-Boer War of 1899–1903. In the course of the war, the Boers (literally, "farmers" in Afrikaans) were brutally defeated by the British forces, suffered an estimated 25,000 deaths of women and children in British concentration camps, and ultimately lost the Transvaal and Orange Free State to British control. Although the prosecution of the war contributed to an enduring enmity between the two groups, the formation of the Union of South Africa in 1910—which joined the Cape colony, Natal, Transvaal, and Orange Free State into a single, self-governing political entity—actually placed Afrikaners on equal legal and political footing with the British for the first time.

The nineteenth century was a period in which South Africa's black populations, including kingdoms, chiefdoms, and less hierarchical communities, lost their autonomy to white control and faced escalating oppression by both British and Afrikaner populations. By the time of the union in 1910, the foundations for the violent, destructive policies that were to become apartheid had all been laid. As indicated in Table 9.1, a series of increasingly restrictive pieces of legislation began the process of forcing blacks into the labor economy, particularly after the discovery of gold in the 1880s spurred the development of a substantial mining industry. These laws served to deprive blacks of their limited franchise (which in any event existed previously only in Cape province), the right to organize, the choice of where to live, as well as land and capital ownership.

The Union of South Africa enjoyed autonomous status vis-à-vis London as a self-governing entity, and the period between 1910 and 1948 witnessed the alternation in power of political parties that represented a mix of Afrikaner and British influences, though pro-British, English-speaking politicians predominated. Nonetheless, the racial policies of the Anglophile governments were hardly progressive, and mirrored those of other British settler colonies such as Rhodesia (Zimbabwe). For example, during this period, laws were passed that regulated sexual relations between blacks and whites, mandated a pass system for black males, deprived blacks of most jobs in an effort to eliminate economic competition for "poor whites," and eliminated the vestiges of black franchise in the Cape. In 1948 the Afrikaner-dominated National Party won the elections, and for the first time a non-British-influenced party gained control over the South African state. The National Party had campaigned on a platform of racial separation known as apartheid, and immediately began to institute its policy, which called for total social and territorial separation of the races. Having consolidated control of the South African state by the 1958 elections, the National Party's hegemony lasted for over four decades. In the process, the nationalists created a system of gross inequality and unchecked brutality, whose legacy continues to affect South African state and society.

■ **Apartheid and Its Legacy:
Enduring Cleavages in Politics and Society**

The four-decade history of apartheid has been extraordinarily well chronicled: activists and scholars, the victims of apartheid as well as its archi-

**Table 9.1 Key Pieces of Preapartheid and Early Apartheid-Era
Legislation**

	Year Enacted	Function
Preapartheid Laws		
Glen Grey Act	1894	Restricted black landholdings (principally in the Cape)
Mines and Works Act	1911	Barred Africans from skilled positions
Native Lands Act	1913	Limited African landowner-ship to 7 percent of land (all in "native reserves")
Natives Trust and Land Act	1936	Limited African landowner-ship to 13 percent of land
Natives (Urban Areas) Consolidation Act	1945	Mandated carrying of passes in urban areas
Apartheid-Era Laws		
Prohibition of Mixed Marriages Act	1949	Outlawed interracial marriages
Population Registration Act	1950	Classified South Africans by "race"
Group Areas Act	1950	Outlawed interracial communities and created racially defined residential areas
Suppression of Communism Act	1950	Granted state broad police powers to prevent "communist" activity
Bantu Education Act	1953	Consigned Africans to menial education
Reservation of Separate Amenities Act	1953	Outlawed integration of public facilities
Native Labor (Settlement and Disputes) Act	1953	Made African strikes illegal

tects, all provide thorough documentation (Luthuli 1962; Carter 1980; Mandela 1995; O'Meara 1996; de Klerk 1999). In short, it is well known that the apartheid-era policies were brutally repressive. In broad strokes, apartheid entailed an economic program intended to advance the interests of Afrikaners, undergirded by hypernationalism, maintained by a system of repression, and rationalized by strict Calvinist religious convictions and a belief that the Afrikaners were "God's chosen people" (Dubow 1995, 258–260). Although scholars differ as to the degree to which any of these factors deserves greater consideration, it is clear that they are not mutually exclusive (O'Meara 1983; Giliomee 1983; Dubow 1995, 259–260). The Afrikaner-dominated state after 1948 therefore sought to serve class, ethnic, and religious interests, and did so by enacting a draconian and ever more intricate web of laws, some of which are highlighted in Table 9.1.

An essential pillar of apartheid was the notion of racial "purity." This required an elaborate racial classification scheme codified in the 1950 Population Registration Act. Without any scientific basis, racial categories were prescribed: white, black, Asian (predominantly those from the Indian subcontinent), and "Coloured" or mixed race (the very existence of whom might have undermined any notion of race purity). Somewhat ironically, these categories persist today.[3]

Nonwhite groups emerged to resist oppression. Initially, their objectives were quite modest and their methods conservative, but opposition grew more radicalized after 1948. The African National Congress was the largest as well as the oldest such organization. Formed in 1912 by educated African elites who sought inclusion *within* the existing political framework at the time, the ANC eventually attracted a mass following and became one of the most racially inclusive black nationalist organizations. A critical step in the ANC's transformation to a more radical organization seeking to fundamentally change the status quo was the establishment of the ANC Youth League in 1944. Originally committed to nonviolence, the ANC formally adopted a policy of armed struggle in 1961 when it became clear that its methods of peaceful resistance and civil disobedience were being met with the slaughter of its people. Many of the ANC's leaders, including Nelson Mandela and Walter Sisulu, were caught, charged with treason, and sentenced to life in prison at the Rivonia Trial in 1964. From there they were sent to Robben Island, where they remained for nearly three decades.

The resistance to apartheid continued, however, and both the struggle and efforts to contain it became decidedly more lethal in the 1970s and 1980s. Domestically, mass actions protesting apartheid policies were met with state violence, as well as the imposition of states of emergency curtailing the already limited rights of blacks. Beginning in the late 1960s, the state developed a massive security apparatus designed to crush dissent in the form of black "subversive" activity. However, this had mixed results and may have contributed to the mass mobilization throughout the country over the years, in which one antiapartheid movement after another surfaced to replace or supplement its predecessor. Over time, the black urban townships, to which South African blacks had been forcibly relocated, became ungovernable.

With the ANC and other African nationalist movements banned, and their leaders exiled or in prison, a number of multiracial movements emerged. The United Democratic Front, for example, which was formed in 1983 by an alliance of some 565 civic, political, and religious organizations, mobilized townships in such activities as rent, consumer, and school boycotts (du Toit 1995). Later in the 1980s, trade unions became more directly involved in antiapartheid activities; in 1989 the Congress of South African Trade Unions (COSATU), the black trade union umbrella body, joined with the United Democratic Movement to form the Mass Democratic Movement, which then initiated a nationwide campaign of civil disobedience designed to weaken the apartheid state.

Internationally, occasional armed incursions from outside the country from the military wings of the ANC and the Pan-Africanist Congress (PAC), regional instability, and global sanctions against South Africa also contributed to the state's "manpower shortages, declining resources, and a weakening resolve" (du Toit 1995, 194). Hence the exponential increase in the human and material cost of state repression, economic crisis, international condemnation, and domestic stalemate contributed to the negotiated end of apartheid (du Toit 1995; Sisk 1995). The negotiated settlement, of course, culminated in the historic ANC victory and ascension of Mandela to the national presidency in 1994.

Given its successful transition to democracy and majority rule—though many had predicted a bloodbath[4]—South Africa is fondly referred to as the "Rainbow Nation" today. However, this label obscures the fact that the colors of this rainbow are in many respects as separate and distinct as ever. Many if not most of South Africa's contemporary problems are rooted in its racist history; thus it is impossible to discount its past experiences and the structural, social, and historical inheritance of the contemporary regime. However, whereas many of the choices made and policies enacted by the ANC government since 1994 were constrained by the domestic and international environment, such structural constraints fail to explain the whole of contemporary South African politics. Indeed, individuals and institutions have "endogenized the exogenous" by shaping external norms to fit the local context.

■ The Politics of Transition and Negotiation

Faced with both domestic and international pressures, the South African state was "substantially weakened" by the late 1980s and early 1990s (du Toit 2001, 20). As Pierre du Toit (2001, 21) notes, many activities were beyond the reach of state control: corruption, dirty tricks, and clandestine murder among them. Thus the prospect of a negotiated settlement brought great risk (the potential loss of hegemony) as well as opportunity (the prospect of stemming economic losses and maintaining political control) for the government, as it did for the ANC. Nonetheless, both parties anticipated that they might use their positions and the perceived weakness of the other party to gain from negotiation.

In fact, the negotiations began as early as 1985, when secret meetings commenced between the imprisoned Nelson Mandela and NP justice minister Kobie Coetsee at the behest of then-president P. W. Botha. These meetings, which were later branded "talks about talks" to reflect their preliminary and exploratory nature, actually lasted several years and coincided with the rapidly deteriorating economic and political environment in South Africa at the time. Mandela and Botha finally met in July 1989, although the two men were unable to arrive at a mutually acceptable program (Mandela 1995). Mandela insisted on a number of state actions, including the unbanning of the ANC and other organizations, the unconditional release of political prisoners, and a plan for majority rule. Botha also sought more concessions than Mandela was willing to grant, such as the renunciation of the armed struggle (Mandela 1995; Sisk 1995).

When Botha suffered a stroke in 1989, the elevation of Frederik W. de Klerk to the South African presidency in September 1989 proved to be a watershed event. De Klerk, previously education minister, and a devoted member of the National Party, was an unlikely candidate for change, yet he proved instrumental in paving the way for the transition to majority rule. With only limited consultation with his party, de Klerk removed the nearly three-decade-old bans on the Pan-Africanist Congress, the ANC, and the South African Communist Party (SACP) on February 2, 1990. He released Mandela unconditionally on February 11, 1990, after twenty-seven years of imprisonment, having earlier released most of Mandela's compatriots (du Toit 2001, 58).

What followed was more than three years of negotiations between, principally, the ANC and the NP, although other parties joined in these discussions (du Toit 2001, 61). The negotiations between the ANC and NP were punctuated by repeated clashes and suspensions and occasionally public accusations that one or the other party was acting in bad faith. Moreover, this very fragile period was overshadowed by a worsening security environment, growing community violence, and accusations, later substantiated, that the state was instigating conflicts in the black community, especially between the ANC and the Inkatha Freedom Party, the Zulu nationalist organization based in the KwaZulu "homeland."

Various explanations have been advanced for why the parties initiated—and more importantly, continued with—negotiations, despite the considerable hurdles. Hermann Giliomee (1997, 126) argues that demographic pressures (namely the growing black population relative to whites), economic stagnation, and swelling black resistance undermined the prior stability of the apartheid state beginning in the 1980s, thereby forcing the regime to capitulate in the early 1990s. Thus, as things began to unravel,

NP elites such as President de Klerk and Minister of Constitutional Development and of Communication Roelf Meyer (who served as the National Party's chief negotiator in the constitutional negotiations) became less interested in the ethnic entrepreneurship that had underpinned apartheid's logic, and more interested in negotiating a position for themselves; indeed, de Klerk and Meyer, among others, retained government positions after the transition (Giliomee 1997, 130).

Taking a less personalist approach, du Toit (2001, 63) contends that "both the NP and the ANC saw themselves as the ascendant power in the negotiating process. . . . Neither considered the other to be an equal." In other words, in the initial period, both parties thought they could *win:* the ANC because of its numerical superiority, and the NP because of its control over the state apparatus and later its perception that it could counter ANC support by appealing to the predominantly Afrikaans-speaking Coloured community and building tacit alliances with the IFP. Conversely, Timothy Sisk (1995, 15, 27) argues that power symmetries actually existed between the parties, and that de Klerk in particular recognized that neither side could impose its solution on the other; he was simply more pragmatic than his predecessors.

In any event, while perceived power symmetries may explain the willingness of both the ANC and the NP to enter into negotiations, the balance of power eventually shifted quite clearly to the ANC. The National Party sought, for example, a guaranteed white veto in the legislature (similar to that assured in Zimbabwe's 1979 negotiations), and a leading role in writing the final constitution. However, when the "Record of Understanding" that would guide the transition process was signed by the ANC and NP on September 26, 1992, it was on terms overwhelmingly favorable to the ANC: it rejected the white veto and stipulated that the final constitution was to be written by an elected assembly (du Toit, 65). Having failed to gain concessions from its numerically superior rival that might preserve elements of white power, the NP's electoral defeat was already ensured by 1993, when the election date was set for April 27, 1994. Clearly, de Klerk and his negotiators did not intend to lose power for the Afrikaner population. Indeed, as Giliomee (1997, 188, 139–140) suggests, they simply lost control of the process in the face of superior ANC tactics.[5]

The importance of Mandela and de Klerk as individual agents cannot be underestimated. Although negotiations with the ANC were initiated under de Klerk's predecessor, it is unlikely that P. W. Botha could have carried them through. Both by demeanor and by professional background in the government's security and defense arms, Botha was scarcely a conciliator. Moreover, in the view of some analysts, the conflict was insufficiently "ripe" for resolution until the early 1990s, when domestic and international circumstances necessitated movement (Zartman 1989, cited in Sisk 1995).

Mandela, for his part, was indispensable in the negotiation and transition. He compromised where necessary, such as by agreeing to "suspend" the ANC's armed struggle; however, he refused to renounce violence until the NP's commitment to the process was clear. Mandela was also implacable when it came to other dimensions of the negotiations, such as setting the dates for the election and the writing of the constitution. Other individuals were also instrumental in achieving a peaceful outcome. Indeed, the finer details of the negotiation were hammered out not by Mandela and de Klerk, but by their subordinates. The ANC's Cyril Ramaphosa and the NP's Roelf Meyer held some forty meetings between June and September 1992 when wider interparty negotiations had stalled (du Toit 2001, 64). Thus, at multiple levels, leadership was essential to keeping the project on track. The ANC won the April 1994 elections overwhelmingly with 62.65 percent of the vote, against 20.31 percent and 10.54 percent for the NP and IFP, its nearest rivals, respectively. With that, South Africa witnessed a remarkable transfer of power to majority rule.

The first postapartheid government, as stipulated in the 1993 interim constitution, was to be a government of national unity. The GNU was an essential, if largely *symbolic,* aspect of the negotiated settlement. The ANC formed the majority, and seven of the twenty-seven cabinet posts were awarded to the NP (in addition, F. W. de Klerk was appointed second deputy president), and three to the IFP, proportionally on the basis of each party's electoral performance. The GNU offered to both the population and the international community a picture of peaceful transfer of power, of power sharing and cooperation, and of reconciliation between former adversaries. In other words, it was a vision of the country, and its future, that all members of the new the government were desperate to present to the wider populace, particularly following the violence that had accompanied the 1990–1994 transition period.[6]

However, the three-party GNU endured for only two of its anticipated five years; in June 1996 the National Party withdrew from the government over disagreements with the ANC. Following the passage of the "final" constitution by the Constituent Assembly, and dissatisfied with the ANC refusal to extend the GNU beyond the 1999 elections, the National Party determined that its prospects were better as a formal opposition party than as a member of the GNU. As discussed below, the NP never regained its strength or its share of the vote subsequently. Nonetheless, its withdrawal from the GNU helped to usher in a period of more conventional opposition politics in South Africa and a period in which observers began to look more critically at the nature of the "miracle" and the country's prospects for reconciliation, for growth and economic revitalization, and for good governance in South Africa's fragile but much heralded democracy.

■ Organization of the Postapartheid State

▨ *Constitutionalism*

Postapartheid South Africa has had two constitutions. The first was the 1993 interim constitution, which established the framework for the transition and the initial years of the new state and came into effect following the elections on April 27, 1994. In 1996, a new, "final" constitution was ratified (effective February 1997), entrenching many of the provisions of the interim version, although it made some important changes. The 1993 document, and its 1996 successor, had a number of international influences, and were modeled on the Canadian, German, and Indian constitutions, as well as the International Covenant on Civil and Political Rights and the European Convention for Human Rights (Dugard 1998, 25). Enshrining many of the protections long-denied to black South Africans, the interim constitution guaranteed equality before the law, freedom from torture and degrading punishment, freedom of speech, assembly, and association, the right to a speedy and fair trial, as well as electoral rights, such as universal adult franchise and the right to political choice (Jeffery 1998, 32). The new constitution also contained provisions for freedom of speech and a constitutional court, the latter intended to provide a "clean slate" for judicial oversight of constitutional matters, given the tainted status of the apartheid-era judiciary (Dugard 1998, 27).

Given its scope, the 1996 South African constitution is celebrated in many circles as one of the most comprehensive and inclusive constitutions in the world. Its preamble clearly establishes the constitution as means to promote both healing and democracy in South Africa. Its preamble states: "We, the people of South Africa, Recognise the injustices of our past, Honour those who suffered for justice and freedom in our land; Respect those who have worked to build and develop our country; and Believe that South Africa belongs to all who live in it, united in our diversity." "Widely seen as a 'state of the art' document," according to Robert Mattes (2002, 24), "it contains a wide array of classic political and socioeconomic rights, institutional innovations . . . and an activist Constitutional Court." Nonetheless, the constitution has also attracted some criticism, including, surprisingly, from many liberals.

For example, committed liberals decry the *qualified* freedom of speech provisions in the constitution (Dugard 1998, 27), although given the abuses by state and society during apartheid it is difficult to condemn South African constitutionalists for banning hate speech and speech advocating violence. Also controversial were aspects of the Bill of Rights, which establishes not only "vertical rights"—that is, protections for the individual from the state—but also "horizontal rights" that extend to relations between individuals (Dugard 1998, 26). This sets up a potential "clash between [individuals'] competing rights, for example, between the right to free speech and [another's] right to dignity" (Jeffery 1998, 34). In the same vein, the Bill of Rights attracts criticism because it is *too* inclusive—containing provisions about the right to housing and health care, for example, which many regard as governmental rather than constitutional functions (Jeffery 1998, 38). In South Africa, however, it may have proved impossible to exclude such elements from the constitution. Mattes (2002, 24), conversely, criticizes the constitution for what it leaves out, "particularly with regard to the interaction among party politics, voter representation, and legislative-executive relations."[7]

South Africa's 1994 and 1996 constitutions each affirmed the country's status as a federal state and acknowledged the role of the nine provinces (expanded from the original four provinces as part of the transition) in this structure. Among the most controversial aspects of the negotiated settlement was the issue of "minority rights" in the new South Africa. Many whites were, and remain, concerned about their place in the new South African society. The desire for an independent Afrikaner *volkstaat* (homeland), for example, continues to define the white far right and is part of the platform of the Freedom Front Party and more radical separatist groups, such as the Afrikaner Resistance Movement. Many blacks too, notably the supporters of the IFP in KwaZulu-Natal, sought some degree of autonomy from ANC dominance. Indeed, the dissatisfaction with the range of powers granted the provinces under the interim constitution led the IFP and others initially to refuse to participate in the 1994 election. Paradoxically, though the interim constitution did not grant territorial autonomy, it did help to alleviate some of these concerns, in part by suggesting that federalism would be a component of a future South African polity.[8]

In fact, however, federalism was weakened in the 1996 document, which centralized many government functions and institutions and strengthened the position of the national parliament vis-à-vis provincial legislatures (*Constitution of South Africa* 1996, chap. 6, sec. 146).[9] The federal senate was replaced as the upper house by the National Council of Provinces (NCOP), which was intended to have greater contact with the provinces. Critics saw these steps as evidence of continued consolidation not only of central government power, but of ANC power specifically (Jeffery 1998, 39–41; Mattes 2002). And in many respects these constitutional changes mirrored centralization of ANC power. Nevertheless, the 1996 constitution was presumed to be relatively insulated from political interference, since constitutional changes required a two-thirds majority, which the ANC did not have.[10]

Concerns about ANC dominance and minority rights were heightened further when the Constitutional Court approved an amendment (signed into law in 2003) that lifted the constitutional prohibitions on party mergers and "floor-crossing" by members of parliament (MPs) between elections. This immediately resulted in a two-thirds parliamentary majority for the ANC, allowing it to change the constitution unilaterally. Ironically, as James Myburgh (2003, 36) notes, this "greatly diminishes the status of the Constitutional Court," the institution charged with protecting democracy in South Africa. "If the court strikes down legislation, the ANC now has the choice of altering the law to make it comply, or changing the constitution." The ANC cemented its super majority by taking 279 seats (69.7 percent) in the 2004 national elections.

Judicial Branch

The 1993 constitution established the principle of constitutional supremacy in South Africa; this was reaffirmed in the "final" constitution. In this sense, the constitution is the supreme law, and "all government bodies, including parliament, were subjected to it, and any action, including parliamentary legislation, inconsistent with the constitution was invalid" (Malherbe 1998, 86). Thus the Constitutional Court became the highest court in South Africa for adjudication of constitutional matters. The Constitutional Court consists of a president, deputy president, and nine other judges, each of whom serves a single twelve-year term (Malherbe 1998, 92). Below the Constitutional Court are the Supreme Court of Appeal, the High Courts, and the Magistrate Courts. "High Courts have jurisdiction in all constitutional matters," except those exclusively reserved to the Constitutional Court (Malherbe 1998, 91). The Supreme Court of Appeal hears, at its discretion, appeal cases, including constitutional cases. It consists of a chief justice, a deputy chief justice, and seventeen judges of appeal. In 2003, all of these judges were male, and sixteen of the nineteen were white; of the remainder, one was Indian and two were African.

As a creation of the new South Africa, the Constitutional Court is multiracial. More important, its members are guided by the principal functions of the 1996 constitution, which include the desire to "heal the divisions of the past and establish a society based on democratic values, social justice and fundamental human rights; Lay the foundations for a democratic and open society in which government is based on the will of the people and every citizen is equally protected by law; Improve the quality of life of all citizens and free the potential of each person" (*Constitution of South Africa* 1996, preamble). In contrast, the lower courts, in which white judges outnumber nonwhites by a two-to-one margin, remain dominated by apartheid-era appointees, who may or may not subscribe to these values. Judicial tenure and civil service protections meant that many members of the judiciary were in fact staunch supporters of apartheid laws. It is a further irony, then, that changes in the South African judicial and political system granted judges far more autonomy and independence than they had enjoyed under the previous system. Absent a jury system model, South African law rests squarely with judges. In situations where judges may lack objectivity, this may foster a crisis of jurisprudence and loss of faith in the system.[11]

■ Executive Branch

The presidency. Most of the countries in southern Africa adopted direct elections for their presidents shortly after independence as a means of centralizing executive power. South Africa's president, by contrast, is elected by the National Assembly immediately after its seating. The South African president is required to be an elected member of the National Assembly; he or she must vacate his or her seat upon being elected president, which is then filled from the party list (Venter 1998, 60). Although this does not ensure legislative oversight, at the very least it preserves some of the linkages between the executive and the legislature found in the parliamentary model. In spite of these institutional constraints, however, the executive is unquestionably the dominant actor in the South African system, and "few mechanisms exist with which the legislature may check executive action" (Mattes 2002, 24). Executive power has become more concentrated, in practice if not in law, under President Thabo Mbeki, who was first elected to succeed Mandela in 1999.[12]

At first glance, this is somewhat surprising, since some constraints exist on the institutional powers of the presidency. For example, the South African president does not have veto power, but can refer bills back to parliament or to the Constitutional Court. The president chairs meetings of the cabinet, but this body, which attempts to reach decisions by consensus, is ultimately accountable to parliament (Venter 1998). However, whereas cabinet members—and the larger parliament through the vote-of-no-confidence maneuver—are theoretically able to impose constraints on presidential authority, the new South Africa is a place of strong parties and party loyalties. More precisely, it is a dominant-party system, much like the apartheid-era system, but with the ANC replacing the NP at its apex. Thus, President Mbeki is far more accountable, if at all, to the national ANC leadership than to the legislature, which his party dominates (Mattes 2002, 25). In practice, however, the party's strength and rigid hierarchy redound to Mbeki's benefit, as president of the ANC: both party leaders and rank and file are unlikely to risk a challenge to the authority or legislative initiatives of the president, since to do so is to risk expulsion from the party and parliament.

The president is constitutionally limited to two five-year terms. Yet this has not quashed the oft-repeated concern of the ANC's rivals that if the party achieves a two-thirds majority in parliament (as it did in 2004; the 1999 election left it one seat short, although it has since achieved this supermajority), the ANC could simply change the constitution to allow Mbeki more time in office, as the ruling party did (for one election only) in Namibia. To be sure, President Mbeki has occasionally displayed an intolerance of dissent, and paranoia about threats both real and imagined (Mattes 2002; Hadland and Rantao 1998). Still, the charge that he will seek a constitutional amendment to extend his term, however worrying to the opposition, is unsubstantiated thus far.

The cabinet. Cabinet ministers are appointed by and serve at the discretion of the president. In the current cabinet, the defense, foreign affairs, finance, law and order, and home affairs portfolios have senior status (Venter 1998, 65); although this is an informal hierarchy, it gives an indication of the priorities of the government. The president may also appoint up to two ministers who are not members of parliament, and the size of cabinet is not constitutionally prescribed, although it has numbered twenty-seven or twenty-eight members since 1994—a fairly large grouping even by regional standards. The original GNU cabinet had twenty-seven members (excluding deputy ministers, who are not members of the cabinet), including seven and three positions apportioned to the NP and IFP, respectively. Although the GNU effectively collapsed with the National Party's withdrawal in June 1996, the IFP continued its governing partnership with the ANC. Mbeki's 1999–2004 cabinet included three members of the IFP who held the arts and culture, corrections, and home affairs portfolios, the latter held by IFP party leader Mangosuthu Buthelezi. The cabinet reshuffle following the April 2004 election saw the dismissal of Buthelezi and the refusal of two IFP members of parliament to assume deputy ministerial posts, while the New National Party (NNP) and the left-wing Azanian People's Organization party were awarded two ministerial appointments.

President Mbeki, as did President Mandela, has also used cabinet appointments to reflect the gender, racial, and ethnic diversity of the country. Mandela's twenty-eight-member post-GNU cabinet (1996–1999) included eighteen Africans (fourteen men and four women), four Indians, three Coloureds, and two whites (Venter 1998, 64). Although Mbeki initially appeared somewhat less inclined to mimic the inclusiveness of his predecessor, he too has sought ethnic, racial, and gender balance in his cabinet appointments, which included four Indians and three whites. In 2004, five women were placed at the helm of ministries. The president may also appoint a deputy president from the sitting MPs (Venter 1998, 63). In the first postapartheid government, Mandela selected as deputy presidents

Mbeki, who had been part of the ANC's leadership in exile during apartheid, and the former state president F. W. de Klerk. The appointment of de Klerk was part of the arrangement for the GNU, in which the NP's second-place finish entitled it to the position. A high-profile member of the government, de Klerk lacked any real authority, although other NP members of the GNU headed line ministries, including finance.[13] In Mandela's administration, Mbeki effectively ran most of the day-to-day activities of the government as deputy president, while Mandela tended to more symbolic functions. Since the constitutional changes in 1996 and de Klerk's subsequent withdrawal of the National Party from the GNU, only one deputy president remains. Thus, when Mbeki became president himself in 1999, he appointed Jacob Zuma as his deputy. The powers and functions of the deputy president are as limited or expansive as those assigned him by the president. Indeed, the constitution simply states that "the Deputy President must assist the President in the execution of the functions of government" (*Constitution of South Africa* 1996, chap. 5, secs. 91–92).

■ Military

Trends and transformation. South Africa's apartheid-era military, the South Africa Defense Force (SADF), was notorious for its role in destabilizing the region as part of then–prime minister (and later president) P. W. Botha's "Total Strategy." Begun in 1977, the Total Strategy linked domestic security and intelligence efforts with a program of regional destabilization designed to root out the ANC and other antigovernment groups operating externally, increase the economic dependence of regional neighbors on South Africa, and ultimately maintain South Africa as a preserve of apartheid and capitalism. As part of this strategy, the SADF intervened militarily in Angola on behalf of that country's UNITA allies, conducted bombing campaigns in Mozambique and elsewhere, and engaged in clandestine activities throughout the region (Minter 1994). Operating with other intelligence and security arms of the state, the military was also involved in gross human rights violations, including torture and biological warfare experimentation (TRC 1999). In short, notwithstanding Botha's insistence that South Africa in the 1970s and 1980s faced a "total communist onslaught," the actions of the SADF could only be seen as "defensive" by this perverse logic.

The transition to majority rule necessitated fundamental changes in the way South Africa's military conducted its affairs. Symbolically, the armed forces were renamed the South African *National* Defense Force to reflect the domestic and defensive nature of the new military, rather than it being a source of regional destabilization.[14] Moreover, the armed forces faced the formidable task of integration. Since the SADF had literally been on the "front lines" of apartheid, and numerous senior civilian and military leaders of the armed forces were later implicated in apartheid-era crimes, this remains an exceedingly complex task. The integration imperative also impacted the liberation movements, whose soldiers and paramilitaries were expected to be combined into the new national force. In addition to the SADF, the liberation movements had armed forces, as did several of the former "black homelands" (although they lacked sovereignty). The process of integrating these former rivals swelled the size of the armed forces well beyond the target of a combined force of 70,000 by May 1997. Indeed, by the late 1990s there were 100,000 military personnel, including 18,300 former members of Umkhonto we Sizwe (Spear of the Nation; the ANC's armed wing), 5,700 former members of the Azanian People's Liberation Army (the PAC's armed wing), and 11,500 former members of the homeland armies (du Toit 2001, 119). The military hierarchy is now mixed, although as of 2005 most of the senior office ranks remained white-dominated.[15]

The military as economic actor. South Africa's apartheid-era military-industrial complex was extensive. It was not only a major purchaser of weaponry, but a major arms manufacturer as well. The state-owned weapons manufacturer, Armscor, was established in 1968. According to Human Rights Watch (2000): "By 1994 South Africa had established itself as the tenth largest arms producer in the world, with approximately 800 arms and arms component manufacturers employing a workforce of 50,000 (down from 160,000 in the 1980s)." Weapons were produced for both domestic and international purposes. Consistent with the National Party's regional strategy, Armscor "was virtually given a free hand in pursuing lucrative markets that often turned out to be located where gross human rights abuses were taking place." However, an arms export scandal exposed in 1994 led to the appointment of an independent commission and subsequently the adoption of major reforms to and restrictions on the arms export regime. The new policies included a strong human rights plank.

As in nearly all developing countries, military spending is controversial; states that are unable to provide basic needs nonetheless spend heavily on militaries. Moreover, these forces are seldom used in defense of national sovereignty, but instead perform domestic police functions, often repressively (Ball 1988). Like the state it replaced, postapartheid South Africa faces no perceptible external military threats. Hence the role of the military in the posttransition environment demanded a reevaluation of its budget allocation. The 1995–1996 Strategic Defense Review suggested that military expenditure would remain more or less constant in the 1990s, at 9.7 billion rand per year. Yet the budget has continued to increase, despite improved security conditions and declines in the offensive *and* defensive capacity of the South African military.[16]

For the government's part, Defense Minister Mosiuoa Patrick Lekota insisted that spending is within reasonable limits, noting that his department is still only allocated 1.62 percent of the GDP and 6.74 percent of government expenditure. In 1999 a scandal broke when the government announced a 29.9 billion rand arms purchase, an extraordinary sum that was immediately greeted with allegations of corruption and conflicts of interest (Mattes 2002).[17] In short, the military is receiving more, but providing less, a troubling scenario in light of the country's myriad underfunded social and economic problems.

■ Representation and Participation

▨ Legislative Branch

South Africa has a bicameral parliament consisting of a 400-member lower house, the National Assembly, whose members are elected directly every five years, and a 90-member upper house, the National Council of Provinces, whose members are elected from the nine provinces. The NCOP, which "is subordinate to the National Assembly because it has less formal power" (Calland 1999, 22), is intended to represent provincial interests. However, as noted above, the NCOP is only a partial substitute for the broad federal powers anticipated during the transition and in drafting the 1993 constitution. Thus the purpose of the NCOP is to provide "a national forum for public consideration of issues affecting the provinces" (Taljaard and Venter 1998, 36). When the National Assembly passes a bill, it goes to the NCOP, which can then pass the bill, pass it subject to amendments, or reject it; in the latter cases, it goes back to the National Assembly for reconsideration (Taljaard and Venter 1998, 44). However, the National Assembly is clearly the superior legislative body in this framework.[18] Further, the NCOP is actually several steps removed from its provincial constituents: NCOP members are not popularly elected; rather they are nominated by the elected members of the provincial assemblies and represented proportionally, on the basis of their party's share of provincial legislative seats.

While lacking single-member constituencies, even these "local-regional" bodies have little local orientation (Lodge 1999). Indeed, for both houses, the legislative-constituency link is quite weak, a structural constraint of the party list proportional representation electoral system, which privileges party loyalty. Combined with the lack of single member constituencies, voters have very limited actual influence over their designated legislators (Mattes 2002, 24).

In South Africa, the proportional representation system is used without minimum electoral thresholds (for example, requiring a party to receive 5 percent of the vote before obtaining any seats in parliament); thus the number of parties represented in the National Assembly increased from seven in 1994 to thirteen in 1999, although the number dropped slightly, to ten, in 2004. The number of seats held by most parties declined, however, while the ANC increased its numerical advantage. Following the historic 1994 elections (shown in Table 9.2), the ANC held a 62.65 percent majority (or 252 seats) in the National Assembly. In the 1999 election it reached 66.36 percent (266 seats), or just 1 seat short of a two-thirds majority. In 2004 the ANC's 289 seats reflected nearly 70 percent of the vote. Not surprisingly, the ANC's electoral dominance has come at the cost of the diversity of opinion and debate in parliament, which have decreased.

As noted above, parliament is supposed to have oversight over the executive as in the traditional parliamentary model. In practice, South

Table 9.2 South African National Election, 1994

Party	Number of Valid Votes	Percentage	Number of Seats
African Christian Democratic Party	88,104	0.45	2
African Democratic Movement	9,886	0.05	0
African Moderates Congress Party	27,690	0.14	0
African Muslim Party	34,466	0.18	0
African National Congress	12,237,655	62.65	252
Democratic Party	338,426	1.73	7
Dikwankwetla Party of South Africa	19,451	0.10	0
Freedom Front	424,555	2.17	9
Federal Party	17,663	0.09	0
Inkatha Freedom Party	2,058,294	10.54	43
Keep It Straight and Simple	5,916	0.03	0
Luso-SA Party	3,293	0.02	0
Minority Front	13,433	0.07	0
National Party	3,983,690	20.39	82
Pan Africanist Congress	243,478	1.25	5
Soccer Party	10,575	0.05	0
Women's Rights Peace Party	6,434	0.03	0
Workers List Party	4,169	0.02	0
Ximoko Progressive Party	6,320	0.03	0
Total	19,533,498	100.00[a]	400

Source: Independent Electoral Commission, South Africa, http://www.elections.org.za.
Notes: a. Total does not equal 100 due to rounding.
Registered voters: 22,709,152
Total ballots (nonvalid included): 19,726,610
Voter turnout: 86.87%

Africa's executive is the dominant institution, contributing to a trend of executive concentration of power. Indeed, this is so severe that, as Mattes (2002, 27) notes, "Parliament may continue to play an active role in developing and amending legislation in areas of no great interest to the executive, but when there is a difference of opinion on matters that are important to the executive, it will always prevail."

In sum, two clear trends are observed. First, the promise of devolution of power to local and regional governments has not been realized. On the contrary, South Africa has seen a growing centralization of authority in the national governing structures. Second, South Africa has acquired all the trappings of the dominant-party state observed elsewhere on the continent and in the region. Although the power of subnational governmental bodies is circumscribed, the ANC nonetheless has consolidated its power at every level of government in South Africa: local, regional, and national.

■ Party System and Elections

The momentous 1994 election notwithstanding, South Africa is not considered a consolidated democracy (Friedman 1999; Mattes 2002). Moreover, South Africa's historic election was itself beset by substantial irregularities (Lodge 1999). While many of the electoral problems have since been addressed,[19] it is now regarded as a truism that elections alone are insufficient to achieve democracy (Carothers 2002). Alternation in power is also an important aspect of democratization, but this prospect appears increasingly unlikely in South Africa in the face of ANC dominance. The risks of a one-party state, even a nominally democratic one, are not insubstantial, and include lack of representation, or more serious, repression of dissent. South Africa's proportional representation system, of course, was designed to alleviate the former problem, and the increased number of parties in parliament is encouraging in this regard. But an emerging popular disconnect from political life, in part related to the ANC, is a matter of great concern (*Afrobarometer* 2003b).

Yet it is unreasonable to fault the ANC alone. In the 1999 election, for example (see Table 9.3), the opposition parties were incapable of mounting a credible campaign against the popular ruling party; their principal rallying cry was the claimed need to block the ANC from gaining the constitution-changing two-thirds majority in the National Assembly, rather than substantive policy alternatives. The once formidable Afrikaner-oriented National Party (subsequently renamed the New National Party) was in shambles, and in 2000 it joined an electoral partnership with the historically liberal, white, and predominantly English-speaking Democratic Party, now known as the Democratic Alliance. This union proved short-lived, however. Indeed, the NNP reemerged a year

Table 9.3 South African National Election, 1999

Party	Number of Valid Votes	Percentage	Number of Seats
Pan Africanist Congress of Azania	113,125	0.71	3
Government by the People Green Party	9,193	0.06	0
Socialist Party of Azania	9,062	0.06	0
United Christian Democratic Party	125,280	0.78	3
United Democratic Movement	546,790	3.42	14
Vryheidsfront/Freedom Front	127,217	0.80	3
Abolition of Income Tax and Usury Party	10,611	0.07	0
African Christian Democratic Party	228,975	1.43	6
African National Congress	10,601,330	66.35	266
Afrikaner Eenheids Beweging	46,292	0.29	1
Azanian People's Organization	27,257	0.17	1
Democratic Party	1,527,337	9.56	38
Federal Alliance	86,704	0.54	2
Inkatha Freedom Party	1,371,477	8.58	34
Minority Front	48,277	0.30	1
New National Party[a]	1,098,215	6.87	28
Total	15,977,142	100.00[b]	400

Source: Independent Electoral Commission, South Africa, http://www.elections.org.za.
Notes: a. Formerly the National Party.
b. Total does not equal 100 due to rounding.
Registered voters: 18,172,751
Total ballots (nonvalid included): 16,228,462
Voter turnout: 89.30%

later when the alliance collapsed, only to enter subsequently into a curious electoral alliance with its old archenemy, the ANC, in late 2001. The National Party's near-constant attempts to reinvent itself merely cemented the perception that it had lost both its ideological and racial compass—the twin sources of its former appeal—in the wake of apartheid's collapse. The National Party was awarded just seven parliamentary seats following the 2004 election. With its dwindling electoral influence confined to the Western Cape province, the party determined in mid-2004 that it would soon shut down entirely.

Nonetheless, there appears to be ideological and policy space in which to challenge ANC hegemony; yet none of the established larger parties has sought to occupy it. Indeed, the ANC's unmistakable rightward shift on economic issues—perceptible since 1990, but dramatic after the 1996 adoption of the misleadingly titled "Growth, Employment, and

Redistribution" program (GEAR)—has co-opted much of the neoliberal economic agenda of the Democratic Alliance and the NNP. (Other parties represent even narrower racial, ethnic, or religious agendas.) The ANC's neoliberal economic stance would appear to make it vulnerable to a challenge by a left-wing party; however, the ANC has been able to effectively block any leftist-populist insurgency. The party maintains a "tripartite" electoral alliance with the trade union umbrella body COSATU and the South African Communist Party—the relationship with both is a vestige of their unity in the antiapartheid struggle—which has endured for over a decade, notwithstanding the fact that ANC economic policies appear increasingly antithetical to leftist interests. Although friction increased noticeably during 2002, particularly with the labor unions, the ANC's dexterity at "talking left, but acting right" (Bond 2000; I. Taylor 2002) has enabled it thus far to successfully co-opt and confuse would-be opposition supporters on either side of the ideological spectrum.

The ANC has proved adept at consolidating its hold on power. As discussed above, party switching ("floor-crossing") was prohibited by the original constitution: any MP who opted to change parties automatically lost his or her parliamentary seat. Although such a restriction increased party strength at the expense of individual autonomy, it ensured that proportional representation was maintained for the life of the assembly, until the next election. The 2003 constitutional amendment permits floor-crossing during prescribed periods in the legislative session. When it was allowed in March 2003, the ANC delegation to the National Assembly immediately gained 9 new members, resulting in a supermajority of 275 seats. The change decimated some opposition parties, such as the United Democratic Movement, whose delegation went from fourteen to four, and poses the same risk for other small parties. Although, theoretically, floor-crossing allows MPs autonomy and political cover to respond to "public opinions running counter to the party line" (Mattes 2002, 24), in reality it has few if any benefits for the electorate in a dominant-party system; in the southern African context, it usually reflects individual opportunism more so than ideological conversion. Moreover, it simply increases ANC party strength (Myburgh 2003). Indeed, this amendment was enacted despite South African voters' *opposition* to party switching by a margin of three to one (Economist Intelligence Unit [EIU] 2003c, 17).

Indeed, there is an alarming indication of growing disaffection with party politics, and perhaps democracy, as practiced in South Africa. As many as 40 percent of individuals surveyed before the 2004 election indicated that they might not vote *at all* in that election (*Afrobarometer* 2003b; Mattes 2002). Surveys conducted in 2002 indicated an overall drop in support for all political parties, including the ANC (votes for the ANC declined to 42 percent from 56 percent two years earlier) (*Afrobarometer* 2003b). Actual voter turnouts foreshadowed this growing problem of political apathy: turnout has steadily declined "from between 86 and 92 percent of all eligible voters in 1994 to 68 percent in 1999. In 2000, turnout in local government elections stood at 48 percent of registered voters and 37 percent of all eligible voters" (*Afrobarometer* 2003b, 2–3). Turnout in 2004 (76.7 percent of registered voters) was better than predicted; however, this represented a drop in turnout of 11.2 percent and 110,000 fewer voters (Independent Electoral Commission 2003). These trends, coupled with the decline of party competition, may be cause for concern about the direction of South Africa's democracy (see Table 9.4).

Table 9.4 South African National Election, 2004

Party	Number of Valid Votes	Percentage	Number of Seats
African Christian Democratic Party	250,272	1.60	6
African National Congress	10,880,915	69.69	279
Azanian People's Organization	39,116	0.25	2
Christian Democratic Party	17,619	0.11	0
Democratic Alliance[a]	1,931,201	12.37	50
Employment Movement of South Africa	10,446	0.07	0
Independent Democrats	269,765	1.73	7
Inkatha Freedom Party	1,088,664	6.97	28
Keep It Straight and Simple	6,514	0.04	0
Minority Front	55,267	0.35	2
Nasionale Aksie	15,804	0.10	0
New Labor Party	13,318	0.09	0
New National Party[b]	257,824	1.65	7
Organization Party	7,531	0.05	0
Pan Africanist Congress	113,512	0.73	3
Peace and Justice Congress	15,187	0.10	0
Socialist Party of Azania	14,853	0.10	0
United Christian Democratic Party	117,792	0.75	3
United Democratic Movement	355,717	2.28	9
United Front	11,889	0.08	0
Vryheidsfront Plus	139,465	0.89	4
Total	15,612,671	100.00	400

Source: Independent Electoral Commission, South Africa, http://www.elections.org.za.
Notes: a. Formerly the Democratic Party.
b. Formerly the National Party.
Registered voters: 20,674,513
Total ballots (nonvalid included): 15,863,558
Voter turnout: 76.73%

■ *The Truth and Reconciliation Commission*

In many ways, the TRC was both postapartheid South Africa's most remarkable achievement and its greatest disappointment. When the TRC was established by the Promotion of National Unity and Reconciliation Act (1995) and began its hearings in 1996, it was widely hailed as a model for postconflict reconciliation. In contrast to regional precedent, as in Zimbabwe, where no formal reconciliation was ever conducted, and in contrast to trials, such as those at Nuremberg following World War II, the TRC was a unique institution (Minow 1998). It consisted of three related activities. The Human Rights Violations Committee was charged with taking written statements and hearing oral testimonies in an attempt to establish a record of apartheid-era crimes and determine a narrative truth about perpetrators and victims of crimes. The Amnesty Committee determined whether or not applicants would be granted amnesty in return for their testimony—"truth telling"—to the TRC about their involvement in an act that was deemed to be *political;* nonpolitical criminal activity was ineligible and a matter for the legal system. The applicant was not required to show contrition, and the victims or their families were not required to grant forgiveness, although clearly this was desired by some of the principals on the TRC (Tutu 1999). Finally, the Reparations and Rehabilitation Committee was charged with ascertaining who should be compensated as victims of apartheid-era violence, and determining appropriate restitution.

The most prominent of the TRC's three committees was the Human Rights Violations Committee, which was chaired by the retired Anglican archbishop and Nobel Peace Prize winner Desmond Tutu. Tutu saw the work of the commission as an essential component of the postapartheid healing process and argued that South Africa could not move forward unless its citizens came to grips with its past through full disclosure of the horrors of apartheid. Supporters of the process believed that, in contrast to punitive trials, the TRC would encourage national healing through forgiveness; unlike in postwar Germany, for example, in South Africa both victims and perpetrators would have to live among one another in the postconflict environment. Punishment, TRC advocates argued, would lead to a cycle of hostilities that might irreparably tear the fabric of the new nation (Minow 1998).

The TRC, which held hearings from 1996 to 1998, is now recognized as a sincere if deeply flawed process (Minow 1998; Krog 1999; Wilson 2001; Graybill 2002). Among other problems, its scope may have been too limited. For example, the commission limited its inquiry to the period from March 1960 (the date of the Sharpeville Massacre, arguably the onset of apartheid-era violence) to April 1994 (the date of the transition). Second, the TRC investigated only 9,980 deaths. Yet between September 1984 and

May 1994 alone there were some 20,500 deaths directly related to apartheid policies and the transition process, indicating that the TRC barely scratched the surface (du Toit 2001, 33). From the start, as du Toit (2001, 32) notes, the number of potential cases meant that the TRC faced "an unattainable task." Another problem was that the TRC received 21,298 submissions or testimonies, but held only 700 public hearings. As a result, many individual victims for whom public truth *telling* might have proved cathartic indeed were merely able to present their stories to a lone TRC representative (Wilson 2001).

In addition, the TRC failed to secure the testimony of, or in many cases even identify, the principal architects of apartheid. While policemen and agents of the security and intelligence services were an occasional presence, very few of apartheid's leaders were ever called to account. Former president P. W. Botha defied the TRC's demand to appear. His successor, F. W. de Klerk, simply denied any knowledge of or responsibility for political killings carried out under his presidency—even though his denials directly contradicted testimony of subordinates. Moreover, the prosecutorial mechanism largely failed to convict, and in many cases to even try, alleged perpetrators like Wouter Basson, former defense minister Magnus Malan, Botha, and others who refused to cooperate with the TRC. On the other side, Nelson Mandela's former wife and chair of the ANC Women's League, Winnie Mandela, downplayed her culpability in political murders of ANC rivals in the late 1980s and early 1990s. In short, "truth" was not always attainable, even in the absence of punishment.

In terms of the prospects for healing generated by the TRC, these too must be questioned. Most white South Africans failed to buy into the process, whether or not they were directly involved in the perpetration of apartheid (Tutu 1999; Wilson 2001). Similarly, the reparations committee, tasked with arguably one of the most important functions of the TRC, proved inadequate. It was not until 2003 that onetime payments of 30,000 rand each were determined, allocated to some 22,000 victims and their families. The delay and the amount of the restitution were a source of considerable bitterness (EIU 2003c).

Thus it appears that, at best, the TRC was a vehicle for initiating a national dialogue, and in that sense had additive value. Du Toit (2001, 35) argues that the TRC made "a modest contribution to the factual knowledge on the subject of political violence." However, it is not clear what impact it had on popular attitudes. In a recent survey (Institute for Justice and Reconciliation 2003), for example, 73.6 percent of black respondents saw whites as having profited *and continuing to profit* from apartheid, whereas just 22.4 percent of whites felt the same way. Indeed, 90 percent of white respondents thought that South Africans should just move on with their lives. In the context of southern Africa, "forgive and forget" is a better method for *deferring* rather than preventing conflict. Conversely, *durable* institutional solutions can help create channels for mediation, communication, and future resolution of conflicts. If South Africa is any more "healed" for having gone through the TRC process, the degree of healing may ultimately prove shallow. This realization, along with South Africa's festering problems with crime, inequality, AIDS, and so forth, threaten to undermine the democratic experiment. To some degree, South Africa's civil society organizations help to preserve the democratic tendencies and compensate for the state's shortcomings.

■ Civil Society and Social Groups

South Africa has a plethora of civic organizations and a vibrant civil society. It has sophisticated media in multiple languages, activist nongovernmental organizations (NGOs), and a historically powerful labor movement. Many of these organizations can trace their development as centers of power outside the state to the apartheid era. Despite the draconian nature of the apartheid state, including its restrictions on movement, labor, association, and so forth, many groups honed their skills in that social context. Indeed, the constraints of apartheid, in which society was tightly circumscribed, and the state was only a tool of repression, compelled the creation of alternative means of interest articulation within communities.

Editors and journalists of black and liberal white media faced harassment and bannings during the apartheid years, and many publications were closed by the state. Similarly, political organizations were banned and forced to operate underground. Trade unions, key players in anticolonial movements around the continent, were legalized much later in South Africa than elsewhere in Africa. Initially resistant, the apartheid state gradually acquiesced to many of the demands of organized labor as the significance of an increasingly skilled black labor force to the white South African economy could no longer be ignored. Business associations also became key players in the apartheid era, and a number of them arguably have as great an influence today (Nattrass 1999). In addition, religious organizations provided both the greatest supporters and the staunchest opponents of apartheid. The various churches in the South African Council of Churches (SACC), for example, played an instrumental role in attacking apartheid both domestically and internationally in the 1980s, whereas the Dutch Reformed Church supplied apartheid's theological foundations. Similarly, cultural groups such as Inkatha (which later established the political party IFP) helped solidify Zulu nationalism and opposition to apartheid, though Inkatha supporters eventually came into conflict with ANC supporters between the dismantling of apartheid in 1992 and the 1994 elections, with deadly results. Long-standing groups like the Afrikaner Broederbond helped cement Afrikaner nationalism and were part of a class project to elevate the status and socioeconomic position of Afrikaners (Dubow 1995; du Toit 1995).

Other civil society organizations began to emerge in the late 1980s and early 1990s, many of which helped to unravel apartheid. Policy advocacy organizations especially thrived in this period. Amid great uncertainty, many of these groups attempted to promote a particular type of democratic and political reform and lobbied both domestically and internationally for change. Among these were organizations that continue to this day, including the Institute for a Democratic Alternative in South Africa, the South African Institute of Race Relations, and the Center for Policy Studies, which generally support a liberal democratic model and liberal to progressive economic policies.

In the wake of the successful transition, the number of NGOs expanded further and many altered their mandates. Among the more recently established civic organizations are those actively engaged in the fight against HIV/AIDS. Such organizations have persevered despite a long-standing resistance in South African political and social circles to discussing the disease and providing access to antiretroviral drugs (see Chapter 10). In an environment in which the government, including the health minister and the president, has been uncooperative, and the wider society has been long in denial, these groups have overcome tremendous obstacles. In 2003, for example, the Treatment Action Campaign (TAC) enlisted the support of the South African Medical Association and religious organizations and scored a major victory that compelled the government to make antiretrovirals available to HIV-positive pregnant women and others at risk from the virus (EIU 2003c, 17).

South African civil society's mobilization clearly reached its zenith late in the struggle against apartheid and in the transition period. The culture of civic activity and organization flourished, at least initially, in the new liberal postapartheid environment, but that activity is more erratic and diverse today as the transition to democracy, which served as a catalyst for mobilization, has passed. This is not to say, however, that the policies of the new South African state do not engender protest, as well as support, among societal actors. Yet whereas civil society organizations such as the unions, AIDS activists, and religious groups have each found ample grounds to challenge the state, particularly on policies perceived as hostile to the poor and labor, their activity has lacked the coordination seen in the past.

Thus, while South Africa is undeniably "procedurally" democratic under the ANC government (Bratton and van de Walle 1997), it lacks many of the *substantive* aspects of democracy, which are concerned with delivery—access to resources, improved quality of life, and the like (Mattes 2002; Friedman 1999). Although these shortcomings might be expected to form an area of coordinated, intense, and sustained debate, this has not materialized. This has led critics on the left to call for a remobilization of churches, NGOs, and even the unions to oppose the ANC's continued embrace of neoliberal economic policies and an agenda seen as "anti-poor" (Saul 1999, 39).

Media. South Africa has among the most vibrant print and broadcast media on the continent. The newspapers have a long tradition. Television broadcasts were introduced only in 1976, but today the country has four free channels and five subscription stations, making it one of Africa's most diverse markets. The English-language press was one of the few media voices against apartheid, though this was limited to one or two newspapers. Most, in fact, supported the National Party fairly consistently. The Afrikaans-language press, of course, was unabashedly pro-NP (Williams 1998, 192). Today the Afrikaans- and English-language presses both are more outspoken in their criticism of the ANC state than they were of apartheid governments. On the one hand, this stems from the democratization process itself, and the fact that press freedoms are enshrined in the constitution. On the other hand, the ANC resents press criticism, and some analysts argue that English-language editors in particular have responded to ANC pressures by being less outspoken (Williams 1998, 195). Nonetheless, the sheer diversity of print outlets today provides far more opportunities for a vigorous fourth estate in South Africa.

The broadcast media have also diversified, though the publicly owned South African Broadcasting Corporation (SABC) remains the dominant actor. The SABC is a state-owned enterprise, but the Broadcasting Act of 1999 seeks to fully commercialize its operation. This is in marked contrast to the state-dominated broadcast networks in other countries in the region. Indeed, South African media critics have precisely the opposite fear from further media commercialization: that it will only deepen the corporation's reliance on advertising revenues. Such private sector "dependence means that programming continues to be marked in many ways by racism, sexism and classism, as advertisers skew programming mainly towards white middle-class men" (Duncan 2000).

Conversely, the alleged biases in programming may be counteracted by a state bias in the SABC's news coverage. During the 1999 campaign, for example, SABC radio and television broadcasts were accused of bias toward the ANC. Indeed, as Tom Lodge (1999, 204) argues, the SABC gained considerable praise as evenhanded and impartial in the 1994 election. However, in the 1999 election, "a series of contentious staff changes at the SABC in early 1999 . . . effectively placed journalists with strong ANC affiliations in charge of the news," a maneuver that eroded the SABC's credibility.

Religious communities. According to 1990 census data, 78 percent of South Africa's population is Christian. There is also a substantial Muslim minority that numbers over 850,000. As of 1996, there were 30,000 Christian churches in South Africa, representing some 130 denominations (Tingle 1998). As noted earlier, the churches have played an ambiguous role in South African history. The Dutch Reformed Church (DRK) in fact provided a religious justification for apartheid, seeking to explain the subjugation of blacks under apartheid in biblical terms. In fact, the first prime minister elected under apartheid in 1948, Daniel Malan, was a DRK minister (Dubow 1995). However, when the DRK declared racism to be a sin in 1986, its declaration helped create a basis for the reform and eventual demise of apartheid among the deeply religious Afrikaner population (Tingle 1998, 200).

In contrast to the DRK, many of the other Protestant churches were important actors in the antiapartheid struggle as members of the South African Council of Churches and the Institute for Contextual Theology. The SACC, which was a prominent platform for antiapartheid theologians such as Archbishop Tutu and Reverend Allan Boesak, was seen as aligned with the ANC by the late 1980s (Tingle 1998, 204).

In the contemporary period, certain ties of "solidarity" persist between the ANC and the church umbrella body. These linkages were strained when the ANC firmly embraced a neoliberal economic model in 1996 (GEAR), which the churches believed hostile to the poor, ostensibly the ANC's (and the churches') primary constituency. Despite South Africa's poverty rates, however, the SACC has not resumed the "oppositional" role it assumed in the 1980s. Other denominations, such as the evangelical churches (which have gained an enormous foothold in the wider region), began to affiliate with the SACC only in the late 1990s. Yet they tend to be concerned with the perceived decline of social mores under ANC rule, following the legalization of abortion, pornography, and gambling, for example (Tingle 1998, 219).

Trade unions. Although it got a comparatively late start, the trade union movement was instrumental in bringing about an end to apartheid. Through such umbrella bodies as the Congress of South African Trade Unions, the black unions organized strikes, mobilized community boycotts, and engaged in mass protests at a time when the core leadership of the various liberation movements were either in jail or in exile. In recognition of that role, and the close alliance between the 1.7 million–member COSATU and the ANC, the two left-leaning bodies joined together with the ANC's long-time ally the South African Communist Party to form a governing partnership in the postapartheid government. Despite these ties, labor (like the SACP) is, at best, a junior partner in the alliance and has complained that the ANC simply dictates policies rather than engaging in consultation. The adoption of the GEAR program in 1996, with its inherent hostility to labor interests, was the most egregious example of what COSATU considered ambush tactics by the ANC (Mattes 2002, 26). As discussed in the following section, the ANC refused to negotiate any aspect of the GEAR program, despite labor objections (Bond 2000). However, the SACP and COSATU MPs sit in parliament as ANC members, which severely curtails their ability to challenge the party (Mattes 2002, 26).

In the meantime, South Africa's economy is facing a labor crisis that has been exacerbated by deindustrialization in key sectors. Unemployment was already extremely high in 1994—31.5 percent by some measures (du Toit 2001). Expectations that overall economic conditions, especially jobs, would improve as envisioned in the initial ANC development strategy, the Reconstruction and Development Program (RDP), were a key part of COSATU concessions to and compromise with its ANC partners in the early 1990s. Yet, the moderately more labor-friendly RDP was replaced by GEAR in 1996, and more recently jobless levels have increased to 40 percent among blacks, who make up the bulk of union membership. Some 500,000 formal sector jobs were lost between 1994 and 1997, putting a major strain on South Africa's "miracle." Black South Africans are disproportionately affected by retrenchments, followed by the Coloured community.

Nevertheless, despite growing disagreement within the tripartite alliance,[20] it is unlikely to be undone by the ANC. Indeed, the ANC has every incentive to attempt to placate its leftist partners. Notwithstanding recent tensions, the ANC has more control over the political direction of the union federation only while ANC remains in a close, formal relationship with the labor body. The experience of Zambia and Zimbabwe's dominant-party states, which saw the rapid rise of formidable, electorally successful labor-based parties, is not lost on ANC elites (Bond and Manyanya 2002). Hence the ANC will continue to "talk left" even as it "acts right." As the following section shows, however, the ANC appears to have abandoned all but its rhetorical claim to the left; hence it is unclear how long it can continue to co-opt, and thereby contain, labor interests.

■ Fundamentals of the Political Economy

Labor friction and deindustrialization have not prevented South Africa from boasting the strongest, most diversified economy on the African continent. Yet it is also one of the most unequal societies, in terms of not only distribution of wealth, but also industry and landownership. Although the economy has grown at an average of approximately 3 percent per year since 1995, analysts have acknowledged that 6–7 percent annual growth is required to combat unemployment and inequality (Mattes 2002, 23).

In search of the right policy mix, but clearly driven by structural constraints of globalization as well, the ANC moved from a socialist perspective calling for nationalization and redistribution, to one promising "growth with equity" to staunch neoliberalism, all within the span of six years. In exile, and until 1992, the ANC advocated a program of democratic socialism, including the redistribution of wealth through nationalization. However, the ANC's letter of intent to the International Monetary Fund (IMF) in 1993 agreeing to pay apartheid's U.S.$20 billion external commercial bank debt cemented the ANC as a firm adherent of "globalization" (Saul 1999, 19). The RDP was briefly tried, but the global and South African capitalist influences on the ANC soon prompted the state to abandon even this modestly statist economic program (I. Taylor 2002).

The Growth, Equity, and Redistribution program, adopted in 1996, is fundamentally a neoliberal structural adjustment program, although it was "homegrown" and not "imposed" on South Africa by the international financial institutions (IFIs) (I. Taylor 2002). Yet where similar structural adjustment programs have earned criticism elsewhere on the continent (Mkandawire and Soludo 1999), the initiation of the program caused some puzzlement in its application to South Africa. Not only did GEAR call for austerity at a time when society was demanding a *greater* state role in the economy, but it was not mandated by the IFIs, nor was it, critics charge, even necessary, as economic alternatives had yet to be fully explored (Bond 2000; Taylor and Nel 2002).

The manner in which GEAR was adopted by the ANC was also a source of considerable controversy. With its market orientation, calls for corporate tax reductions, low government spending, and privatization, GEAR won the full endorsement of business and the international financial institutions. However, it was presented to parliament and to the ANC's governing "partners" the SACP and COSATU as a fait accompli and deemed "nonnegotiable." Objections to the method of GEAR's announcement and adoption were summarized by leftist scholar John Saul (1999, 22), who noted, "It is this kind of coolly self-satisfied, self-righteous, and profoundly ideological thrust on the part of the new ANC elite . . . that is the single most depressing attribute of South Africa's transition."

Although GEAR's critics cannot claim complete vindication, GEAR has had a mixed record. Whereas government spending, inflation, and interest rates are well within parameters (EIU 2003c), GEAR has failed to meet a number of its targets. Employment, as noted above, is off sharply, yet GEAR predicted that the economy would *add* 400,000 new jobs by 2000. Moreover, other key indicators, such as investment and GDP growth, are substantially below targets (Bond 2000, 78; EIU 2003c). In adopting GEAR, South Africa did everything right in terms of neoliberal economic formulations. According to many economic indicators, however, the program has not produced the expected results. Some problems, such as the 60-plus percent declines in the value of the rand in 2001 and the drop in foreign direct investment, were substantially outside the control of South Africa's economic team, but the adverse effects of globalization on the domestic economy have not led to a reevaluation of the policies (I. Taylor 2002). Interestingly, despite the ANC's many concessions on the economic model, some segments of the big business community—now a vital constituency for the once left-leaning ANC—have grown restive with the performance of the South African economy, as evidenced by the transfers overseas of significant portions of the capital base of several larger conglomerates, most prominently Anglo-American (Bond 2000; I. Taylor 2002, 164–167). And on the other side of the spectrum, as noted, the ANC's important political alliance with COSATU and the SACP is under threat. More critically, for the South African populace as a whole, GEAR lacks any real provisions for social development, human resource development, public sector transformation, crime prevention, or infrastructure development, even on the modest level prescribed by the now defunct RDP (Bond 2000, 83).

■ The ANC and the Business Community

The adoption of GEAR and the ANC's noteworthy realignment are in large part a reflection of the influence of South Africa's large conglomerates. These same firms, which represent South Africa's leading mining, industrial, and financial services companies and have roots in the last century, were deeply involved in apartheid. They were supporters of the state and helped provide the economic infrastructure that enabled the apartheid state to endure and indeed thrive, both domestically and internationally (Nattrass 1999). Paradoxically, however, it was many of these same firms that began to chip away at apartheid in the 1980s and may have accelerated its demise. Eventually, apartheid became an extra tax on business. The Physical Planning and Utilization of Resources Act of 1967, for example, blocked industries from expanding their black labor force without state approval. By 1978 there were over 4,000 laws and 6,000 regulations affecting business (du Toit 1995, 160). In short, apartheid produced uncompetitive labor laws, international sanctions, and a worsening domestic economy that led South African business to support its dismantling by the mid-1980s.

Among the leading firms in South Africa today are Anglo-American Corporation, Liberty Life, South African Breweries, Old Mutual, Rembrandt, and Sanlam. Although their principal businesses are in mining, manufacturing, and financial services, these companies are multisectoral conglomerates (they also have substantial "concentration," or vertical integration, as well) that formed the backbone of the South African economy for generations. While three—Anglo, Liberty, and South African Breweries—have become truly global corporations and moved their head-quarters to London (not uncontroversially, as noted above) and delisted from the principal bourse, the Johannesburg Stock Exchange, they remain important actors in the local economy as employers and taxpayers. The leading corporations collectively associate in the South Africa Foundation, a business association that provides one of several avenues for business to influence government policy. Both individually and collectively, the large South African firms have been successful in this regard (Nattrass 1997).

Although the business impact on government is noteworthy given the ANC's history, it is also not surprising, given the national dependence on this handful of firms. Predictably, the business community was cool to the ANC's first major socioeconomic program, the RDP, which called for higher levels of state spending than business regarded as prudent. Business actors (and especially the IMF) saw the RDP as an extra tax on business and a disincentive for further investment, and pushed the ANC hard for an approach that adhered more closely to neoliberal principles. The South Africa Foundation even proposed a program, which it branded "Growth for All." Although this was attacked by government, largely for political reasons, the business community was quite receptive to the government's GEAR program.[21]

■ Race and the Economy: Whither Redistribution?

Since large residual white populations remained in southern Africa after independence, a considerable degree of accommodation has been required to reduce conflict between the owners of the resources and the new majority "owners" of the state. South Africa's 4.5 million whites continue to dominate industry, commercial agriculture, the financial sector, mining, and the vast majority of agricultural lands and resources. However, after more than three centuries, most white South Africans have no ties to an ancestral homeland. Thus a cynical replay of the "Zimbabwe model"—white emigration or de facto state expulsion—is unlikely in South Africa, at least without the violence all parties to the 1994 transition sought to avoid.

Hence the adoption of GEAR and the abandonment of the RDP in 1996 were a concern to many both within and outside South Africa. Rather than rely solely on an unpredictable market mechanism, the RDP explicitly sought to shift some of the responsibility for redress onto the beneficiaries of apartheid, as well as address specific social needs. In fairness, both before and since GEAR's enactment, the state has made improvements in some areas among the urban and rural poor. Since 1994, infant mortality has declined and some black household incomes have increased. By December 1997 the ANC government had constructed 250,000 new houses, provided electricity to 1.4 million homes, built or upgraded 560 health clinics, and completed 1,020 new water projects that provided access to clean water for 8.9 million people (du Toit 2001, 123–124). These improvements are cited in survey data as the most recognizable achievements of the ANC government (*Afrobarometer* 2003a). Yet, glaring inequities continue to exist, not only in regard to basic needs, but also in employment, ownership, and opportunities for advancement.

Some assert that a new black middle class has emerged, which offsets some of the concerns about the macroeconomic framework. This is misleading, however. First, because it overestimates the size and stability of this new black middle class (S. Taylor 2002).[22] Second, it fails to give sufficient attention to the magnitude of South Africa's poverty: 76 percent of South African households are below the poverty line (EIU 2003c, 22) and the *state* is the only institution uniquely suited to address it. The state has taken some proactive steps to stimulate black advancement. It has legislated changes to the Labor Relations Act and implemented the Employment Equity Act (1998), which requires white-run firms to meet specific black employment targets or face fines (S. Taylor 2002), and it recently published its "Black Economic Empowerment" strategy (EIU 2003c). However, most of these policies suffer from erratic enforcement and affect more urbanized, relatively more educated blacks—still a comparatively small portion of the population. Meanwhile, the mass of poor, uneducated, or undereducated black South Africans face few solutions and declining household incomes. They therefore find themselves increasingly desperate, and as some surveys indicate, disillusioned with ANC and democracy (Mattes 2002) and perhaps turning to crime (du Toit 2001). In short, economic deprivation in the black community remains the Achilles' heel of the postapartheid state: it makes plain the absence of substantive democracy and imperils the genuine gains of the 1994 "miracle."

There are some recent signs of backlash against the ANC's embrace of big business and a substantially neoliberal agenda. In addition to several strikes and threatened strikes, in 2004 many of the ANC's labor allies, including COSATU, condemned the black economic empowerment process as enriching only a "few politically connected figures," such as ANC stalwarts Cyril Ramaphosa and Saki Macozoma (Reed 2004). Aware of this growing resentment among much of its labor and urban constituents in particular, the ANC began to, rhetorically at least, move away form its strict embrace of neoliberalism (SouthScan 2004, 1). It remains to be seen, however, whether this will result in any measurable policy change on the part of the ruling party.

■ Challenges for the Twenty-First Century

The economy and poverty remain, in our view, the principal obstacles to future stability in South Africa. As noted, growth is insufficient to meet population needs, and the controversial GEAR policies have to a considerable extent removed the state from the direct provision of economic resources to the poor in terms of redistribution, and have instead placed this critical role in the purview of "the market." It remains to be seen how well this substitutes for direct state interventions. The failure to address poverty, crime, the AIDS crisis, and public discontent over access to basic human needs reveals that South Africa's highly vaunted democracy is fragile in "substantive" terms (Friedman 1999).

If the economy is South Africa's Achilles' heel, however, there are many other areas of concern in the body politic. By substantial majorities, South Africans of all races profess an interest in forgetting about the past, although whites are more likely to want to "just move on" than blacks. While this is in one sense an encouraging phenomenon, the now many intensive studies of the TRC and its aftermath may suggest otherwise. Indeed, many recent analyses suggest that the wounds of apartheid are not yet healed and that, in many ways, the TRC, despite its enormous efforts and considerable goodwill, proved to be little more than a palliative in the end (Wilson 2001; Graybill 2002). Evidence from within the region itself tells us that it is far more difficult to simply "forgive and forget," as Zimbabwe's Robert Mugabe pledged in 1980. Such instructions, whether well meaning or cynical, are particularly challenging to follow if the bulk of the populace lacks the material basis to move forward, let alone the psychological one (Minow 1998; Chua 2003). Ominously, it is not impossible to foresee an "antimarket backlash" against the ANC's embrace of economic liberalism in general, and whites in particular, if the economy and general living standards do not improve markedly (Chua 2003). The Zimbabwe example, however cynical and hypocritical Mugabe's manipulations of race have been, is simply too proximate to ignore. "Reconciliation" is inherently fragile where the inequalities of the past persist and are so visible.

Procedural democracy, too, stands at a crossroads. The regularization of elections and the institutionalization of the Independent Electoral Commission appear to have been substantially achieved. Indeed, the establishment of procedures and improvements in the conduct of elections and respect for their results indicate that "South Africa has traveled quite far along the road to democratic consolidation" (Lodge 1999, 210). Conversely, the concentration of power in the ANC and the party's increasing centralization of authority are matters of concern, as is the corresponding erosion of federalism. The ANC now dominates virtually every level of government in South Africa. The absence of a credible opposition party, or parties, is also problematic "when a governing party sees less and less need to respond to public opinion because it is assured of re-election" (*Afrobarometer* 2003b). The constitutional changes enacted in 2003 to allow aisle-crossing without a compulsory by-election served to further limit contestation almost immediately. The lack of perceived progress on numerous economic and social issues, crime and AIDS prominent among them, coupled with ANC's unbridled dominance, may have grave implications for participation. This is not yet endemic in South Africa, but the lack of genuine parliamentary constituencies means that people are increasingly disconnected from the institutions of government (Mattes 2002). The primacy of the constitution and the role of the Constitutional Court (institutions that a short time ago seemed set to ensure the preservation of constitutionalism in South Africa) have been threatened by the emergence of an ANC supermajority that can change the constitution unilaterally.

Many factors augur positively for South Africa, and the achievements of both its government and society in the decade since the end of minority rule cannot be diminished. Nonetheless, the country faces challenges to democracy of *both* procedural nature and substantive nature. Moreover, as a state of single-party dominance for the foreseeable future, South Africa must internalize the positive lessons of the Botswana model, while avoiding the pitfalls of the Zimbabwe model of single-party dominance.

■ Notes

1. This was generally prior to the arrival of large numbers of European women, after which mixed public unions declined (Omer-Cooper 1994). Nonetheless, it does raise some questions about the "purity" of white Afrikaner culture, which was to become a key part of the Afrikaner foundation myth and of apartheid (Dubow 1995).

2. Many African peoples had been displaced just prior to and during the Great Trek as a result of a series of conflicts, known as the *mfecane,* that resulted in the consolidation of the Zulu kingdom. Not only did the *mfecane* disrupt existing African political structures, but it also made weaker peoples more likely to seek alliances with whites against their African enemies (Omer-Cooper 1994, 68; Hamilton 1998).

3. Although in official discourse "black" has come to encompass all nonwhites, much of the contemporary research, including polling data, continues to utilize the traditional classifications. While we acknowledge their arbitrariness, we nonetheless employ the narrower, more common understanding of "black" in this chapter.

4. As late as 1989, more than 40 percent of Afrikaners said that they would *physically* resist an ANC-led government (Giliomee 1997, 114).

5. Several other parties from both the right and left walked out of the negotiations, most prominently the IFP, which only agreed to participate in the elections several weeks before they were held.

6. A total of 13,546 deaths, or more than 3,000 per year, resulted from political violence in the four-year period 1990–1993 (du Toit 2001, 41).

7. Although these are typically components of electoral rather than constitutional law, it is worth noting that these are issues of major contention, especially since the 1999 election.

8. The interim constitution also established twelve official languages, which was, at the very least, state acknowledgment of cultural pluralism.

9. Compare to Chapter 90, Section 126 of the 1993 constitution, in which legislative competence of provincial assemblies was considerably less circumscribed. The 1993 constitution (Chapter 11A) also contained provisions for the consideration of a Volkstaat, a proposition that was rejected by 1996.

10. The party was fifteen seats short following the 1994 election, but just one seat short after the 1999 election.

11. One prominent example was the widely criticized April 2002 verdict by an apartheid-era High Court judge, Willie Hartzenberg, exonerating biological weapons expert Wouter Basson. Basson was found not guilty, notwithstanding substantial evidence implicating him in the deaths of hundreds of black South Africans during apartheid. Judge Hartzenberg repeatedly frustrated the state's attempts to introduce evidence, dismissed a number of charges, and refused to recuse himself despite apparent conflicts of interest. Blacks, and the government, were justifiably outraged. An interesting early account of the case was written by William Finnegan (2001).

12. Mbeki appointed a cabinet that has great personal loyalty to him, takes a more direct role in policymaking, and enjoys a supermajority in parliament.

13. Indeed, the retention of National Party finance minister Derek Keys helped bolster the credibility of the new government's economic program in the international marketplace, which had feared redistributive policies from the ANC (I. Taylor 2002).

14. However, this domestic defensive emphasis does not rule out engagement in regional or global peacekeeping operations, and the military is committed as well to the creation of a potential African rapid response force.

15. There have been, however, a number of defections at all levels. Many white members of the former SADF retired from the service shortly before and after 1994 rather than serve the new black government led by the ANC. Some of these enlisted in private army operations, most prominently Executive Outcomes, a company that has engaged in controversial mercenary operations in Angola, Sierra Leone, and elsewhere. South Africa adopted a constitutional provision prohibiting "South African citizens from participating in armed conflict either nationally or internationally" (Human Rights Watch 2000). In May 1998 this provision was given enforcement teeth when "the government passed the Foreign Military Assistance Act, a law unique in the world, that limits and controls the activities of mercenaries," including those in private military companies like Executive Outcomes. Established in 1989, Executive Outcomes closed business in South Africa in 1999.

16. Author interview, Institute for Security Studies, Pretoria, June 13, 2001.

17. A parliamentary report found no evidence of "improper or unlawful conduct" by government in the arms procurement (Parliament of South Africa 2001).

18. On bills not affecting the provinces, the National Assembly passes legislation over an NCOP veto with a simple majority. However, even on ordinary bills affecting the provinces, "the National Assembly can ignore the NCOP's wishes if it can muster a two-thirds majority in favor of the measure" (Calland 1999, 23).

19. Elections are overseen by the Independent Electoral Commission, which was restructured and professionalized after 1994. Although considerably more independent than, say, its counterparts in Zambia and Zimbabwe, the commission also relies on the state for financial support. This has led to protracted budget disputes with the Ministry of Home Affairs (Lodge 1999).

20. There was a public exchange of insults between cabinet members, including the president and union leaders, in August 2001, leading to the calling of massive strikes (Mattes 2002, 26).

21. "Growth for All," which detailed a strict neoliberal economic program, was actually distributed several months before GEAR. The fact that the policy prescriptions were nearly identical, however, led observers to conclude that the South Africa Foundation document's release merely showed poor sensitivity toward the political necessity that the *government* show ownership over macroeconomic policy, rather than appear to be a lackey of big business (author interviews, Johannesburg, July 1999).

22. There is also a prominent group of new black millionaires, among them Cyril Ramaphosa, Nthato Motlana, and Don Ncube. However, as Patrick Bond (2000, 42) points out, this "class" of black "filthy rich" numbers fewer than 300 individuals.

10

The AIDS Crisis
in Southern Africa

The HIV/AIDS crisis has taken a devastating toll on sub-Saharan Africa. As of 2003 the disease had affected Africa more gravely than any other region in the world. Although comprising only 10 percent of the world's population, sub-Saharan Africa accounts for 70 percent of the people living with AIDS. Indeed, at the end of 2003, up to 28.2 million people were living with HIV/AIDS in sub-Saharan Africa, almost 3 million of whom were children under age fifteen. During 2003 an estimated 3.4 million adults and children in sub-Saharan Africa were newly infected with HIV, and an estimated 2.4 million lost their lives to the disease. AIDS has become the leading cause of death in Africa (UNAIDS/WHO 2003, 5). Given the current trends, it will be years before the pattern of devastation is halted. Perhaps more alarmingly, the social, economic, and political damage inflicted on the continent, directly or indirectly as a result of AIDS, may take generations to reverse.

And the HIV/AIDS crisis is most severe in southern Africa; with less than 2 percent of the world's population, the region is home to about 30 percent of people living with AIDS worldwide (UNAIDS/WHO 2003, 8). Six countries in the region—Botswana, Namibia, South Africa, Swaziland, Zambia, and Zimbabwe—form "the global epicenter of the epidemic" (Hwedie 2001a, 55). In four of these countries in 2001, "national adult HIV prevalence had risen higher than thought possible, exceeding 30 percent: Botswana (38.8 percent), Lesotho (31 percent), Swaziland (33.4 percent), and Zimbabwe (33.7 percent)" (UNAIDS/WHO 2002, 17).[1] (See Table 10.1.) South Africa, meanwhile, had the highest absolute number of adults infected with HIV in any country in the world—5.3 million at the end of 2002 (UNAIDS/WHO 2003, 9).[2] Until recently, it had been hoped that the HIV infection rate in southern Africa had reached what epidemiologists call its "natural limit," beyond which it would not grow. But this appears not to be the case. Indeed, as UNAIDS (2002b) notes in its *Report*

Table 10.1 HIV/AIDS Estimates for Southern Africa, Sub-Saharan Africa, and the World, 2001

	People Living with AIDS			Deaths, Adults and Children	Orphans, Cumulative Number
	Adult Rate (%)	Adults (ages 15–49)	Children (ages 0–14)		
Angola	5.5	320,000	37,000	24,000	100,000
Botswana	38.8	300,000	28,000	26,000	69,000
Lesotho	31.0	330,000	27,000	25,000	73,000
Malawi	15.0	780,000	65,000	80,000	470,000
Mozambique	13.0	1,000,000	80,000	60,000	420,000
Namibia	22.5	200,000	30,000	13,000	47,000
South Africa	20.1	4,700,000	250,000	360,000	660,000
Swaziland	33.4	150,000	14,000	12,000	35,000
Zambia	21.5	1,000,000	150,000	120,000	570,000
Zimbabwe	33.7	2,000,000	240,000	200,000	780,000
Sub-Saharan Africa	9.0	26,000,000	2,600,000	2,200,000	11,000,000
World	1.2	37,100,000	3,000,000	3,000,000	14,000,000

Source: UNAIDS 2002b, 189.

on the Global HIV/AIDS Epidemic 2002: "If a natural HIV prevalence limit does exist in these countries, it is considerably higher than previously thought."[3]

The scale of the HIV/AIDS epidemic in southern Africa makes it the most threatening issue confronting the region, with implications for nearly every facet of economic and sociopolitical life. This chapter considers those implications in detail. Our intention is to move beyond the statistics that have become so familiar in the international discourse on AIDS that we risk becoming inured to them. What do the numbers *mean* for southern Africa's development? The southern African experience reveals that AIDS is far more than a health crisis; it transcends economic, political, and social boundaries and issues. Of course, the science remains essential. Any hope for a resolution of this crisis, however, requires interventions perhaps best described as sociopolitical, from the level of the state down to the household.

■ A Staggering Impact on the Region

The HIV/AIDS crisis in southern Africa is having an impact on nearly every facet of life in the region. First and foremost, it portends to have a staggering demographic impact, wiping out half a century of development gains in the region. In addition, the crisis is having an impact on sectors as diverse as agriculture, defense, education, health, and industry, with implications for food security and national security, among others. Finally, the crisis also poses a grave threat to national economies, and has ramifications for national politics as well. Indeed, the effects of HIV/AIDS on socioeconomic conditions suggest a bleak future for southern African economies and polities. For example, AIDS has contributed to sharp declines in household income and purchasing power, thereby reducing the demand that can fuel growth in local economies. The growing inability of many children to attend school means greater social problems and a loss of competitiveness in a global economy increasingly dependent on knowledge. Cash and food crops that are not grown due to the disease means revenues that are not earned on exports, or revenues that must be spent on imports. Overall, economic growth rates are expected to be profoundly impacted by HIV/AIDS. While economists generally agree that African countries need annual growth rates of 7 percent in order to reduce poverty in their countries, estimates now suggest that countries with high HIV prevalence rates will experience significant drops in per capita gross domestic product (GDP) growth rates.[4] And this says nothing of the impact on the informal sectors of economies, where much economic activity in southern Africa takes place.

The HIV/AIDS crisis threatens to take a political toll as well. Nearly all of the countries in southern Africa have experienced a significant political transition in the past decade or so—from white minority to black majority rule, from decades of single-party authoritarian rule to multiparty rule, from internal war to, it is hoped, peace and reconstruction. As such, these are all fragile polities that could easily be destabilized. For example, it has been suggested that the AIDS-induced poverty described above "will further increase the risk of ethnic violence as individuals and groups blame others and scapegoat minorities for their increasing economic deprivation" (U.S. Institute of Peace [USIP] 2001, 7). Indeed, the AIDS crisis could prove the ultimate test for governments in the region. An AIDS-ravaged electorate could become increasingly disenchanted by a failure of governments to respond to its needs, in particular regarding treatment and care. And the economic toll—growing inequalities in countries where economic and racial inequalities are already glaring, an inability to compete internationally because of falling labor productivity and skills losses, failure to generate foreign investment, famine and food insecurity—may all be blamed on fragile governments. Moreover, the way in which political leaders and governments in the region respond to the HIV/AIDS crisis will continue to reveal a great deal about their priorities. Shula Marks (2002, 13), in her article on HIV in southern Africa, quotes A. M. Brandt (1998, 148): "The way a society responds to problems of disease reveals its deepest cultural, social and moral values." The net effect of an "AIDS-depleted society," according to the U.S. Institute of Peace (USIP) (2001, 7), "is a hollowing out of the state and social networks that are already under pressure from poverty and sundry other concomitant variables." The end result could be more authoritarianism and even state failure in heavily affected southern African societies.

Life Expectancy and Infant Mortality

The demographic impact of the HIV/AIDS epidemic is already revealed by a series of socioeconomic indicators such as life expectancy and infant and child mortality. For example, "life expectancy at birth in southern Africa, which rose from 44 years in the early 1950s to 59 in the early 1990s, is set to drop to just 45 years between 2005 and 2010 because of AIDS" (United Nations Development Programme [UNDP] 2000, 10). Indeed, according to the *Human Development Report 2002,* life expectancy at birth in 2000 was already as low as forty years for Botswana and Malawi, forty-one for Zambia, forty-three for Zimbabwe, and forty-four for Namibia and Swaziland (UNDP 2002, 151–152). (See Table 10.2.) For Botswana, this drop represents a level "not seen in the country since before 1950" (UNAIDS 2002d). Moreover, Osei Hwedie (2001a, 56) cites one study that suggests that within a decade, life expectancy in Botswana would drop further to thirty-one years for men and thirty for women. Similarly, for Zambia, Nana Poku and Fantu Cheru (2001, 42) report that life expectancy there will fall to thirty years by the end of the decade.

The decline in life expectancy over the past decade is due not only to the deaths of adults, but also to the deaths of children. The HIV/AIDS epidemic is also projected to contribute to substantially higher rates of infant and especially child mortality (under five years of age). According to the *Report on the Global HIV/AIDS Epidemic 2002:* "In the worst affected countries [in Africa], HIV/AIDS has had a major impact on child survival.

Table 10.2 Projected Demographic Indicators for 2010 in Southern Africa With and Without AIDS

	Projected Child Mortality per 1,000 Live Births		Projected Life Expectancy	
	With AIDS	Without	With AIDS	Without
Botswana	120	38	38	66
Malawi	203	136	35	57
Namibia	119	38	39	70
South Africa	100	49	48	68
Zambia	161	97	38	60
Zimbabwe	116	32	39	70

Source: U.S. National Intelligence Council, January 2000.

In seven countries in Sub-Saharan Africa, under-five mortality has increased by 20–40 percent due to HIV/AIDS" (UNAIDS 2002d).[5]

AIDS Orphans

The crisis is impacting children in another way, namely that they are being orphaned as their mothers and fathers die of the disease. Officially defined as children who have lost their mothers or both parents to AIDS, AIDS orphans number just over 12 million in Africa out of a global total of just over 13 million. A study released in Namibia in 2003 found that half of all orphans in that country had lost their parents or guardians to AIDS-related illnesses ("Education Sector" 2003). In South Africa in 2002 an estimated 330,000 children had been orphaned by AIDS, with that number expected to grow to 1.72 million by 2010 (Delius and Walker 2002, 10). For southern Africa as a whole, it was estimated in 1999 that AIDS orphans composed nearly 10 percent of the total population (Delius and Walker 2002, 43).

Typically, grandparents and other extended family members, often with very limited resources, are called upon to care for these AIDS orphans. In Zambia, for example, three of every four households has taken in at least one AIDS orphan (UNAIDS 2002c). In many cases, however, the burdens have simply become too great for surviving relatives. Therefore, many AIDS-affected children, including large numbers of girls, find themselves on the streets, where some resort to prostitution in order to survive, thereby putting themselves at very high risk of HIV transmission (Human Rights Watch 2002). Another grave concern is that increasing numbers of AIDS orphans could contribute to a growing child soldier population, which has so far largely eluded southern Africa. In rural areas, the premature death of parents disrupts the transfer of skills and knowledge from one generation to another, putting future generations at risk. "Children growing up as orphans have fewer opportunities to learn how to use and sustain land and to prepare nutritious food for family members" (UNAIDS/WHO 2002, 28). Similarly, AIDS orphans have significantly fewer opportunities to attend school than their non-AIDS counterparts.

The Household

For most southern Africans, the impact of HIV/AIDS is felt first at the level of the household. Gabriel Rugalema (2000, 538) investigates the impact of HIV/AIDS on rural households in southern Africa, concluding that the epidemic is having "significant adverse effects on household composition, labour, and income," which are then having "knock-on effects on the ability to produce food, schooling of children, cropping patterns, livestock production, labour allocation, access to productive assets and consumption of goods and services essential for household maintenance and reproduction." More concretely, Rugalema has observed that the death of key adult household members often results in a dissolution of the household, forcing remaining household members to leave and join other households. One study in Zambia found that 65 percent of households in which the mother died of HIV/AIDS had dissolved (UNAIDS 2002d). Another study in Zimbabwe found that a similar percentage of households that lost "a key adult female" during 2000 had "disintegrated and dispersed" (UNAIDS/ WHO 2002, 28).

Household responses to illness of a key member due to HIV/AIDS include disposing of household assets; curtailing the number and quality of meals, resulting in poor nutrition or even malnutrition; withdrawing children (mostly girls) from school, thereby contributing to increasing illiteracy levels and a diminishing ability to participate in the global economy; and a general household insecurity and vulnerability, undermining the capacity of households and communities to cope and recover, in the long term. According to Rugalema (2000, 542–543), the fact that "AIDS kills strong people and leaves behind the weak . . . renders households more vulnerable to future shocks than, say famine" or other disasters do.

A number of factors, including loss of income, increased care-related expenses, the reduced ability of caregivers to work outside the home, and mounting medical and funeral expenses, come together to push AIDS-affected households more deeply into poverty. In Zambia, research has shown that "in two-thirds of families where the father died, monthly disposable income fell by more than 80 percent." In Botswana, per capita income for the poorest quarter of households is expected to fall 13 percent between 2000 and 2015, while every wage earner in this group will take on four more dependents as a result of HIV/AIDS. Typically, the burden of coping with the impact of HIV/AIDS on households falls on women "as the demands for their income-earning labour, household work, child-care and care of the sick multiply. As men fall ill, women often step into their roles outside the homes; in parts of Zimbabwe, women are moving into the traditionally male-dominated carpentry industry, for example" (UNAIDS 2002d). And yet, despite this, when men fall ill with HIV/AIDS, more money will be spent on their health care than on women's care when they fall ill.

■ Education

The impact of the HIV/AIDS crisis on education in southern Africa has already devastated the ranks of students and teachers alike. School enrollments are dropping because children are being removed from school to care for ill parents or family members, HIV-affected households can no longer afford school fees and other school-related expenses, children themselves are becoming infected and are therefore not able to complete their schooling, and the number of children is falling due to AIDS-related infertility and falling birth rates (UNAIDS 2002d). In parts of South Africa's KwaZulu-Natal province, for example, enrollments in the first year of primary school were 20 percent lower in 2001 than in 1998. In part this was due to AIDS-imposed economic hardship, but enrollments also dropped because children themselves were dying of the disease (UNAIDS 2002d). In Namibia, it is anticipated that between 2003 and 2010 the number of new entrants to school will drop by 14 percent ("Education Sector" 2003). In Zambia too, the number of school-age children (under age fifteen) by 2010 will be only 5.4 million, rather than the 6.8 million it might have been were it not for HIV/AIDS (Poku and Cheru 2001, 42).

Teachers are another casualty of the HIV/AIDS epidemic, with significant consequences for classroom size and overall quality of education.[6] This is an even greater hardship for rural schools that often rely on only one or two teachers. In Namibia, a study released in 2003 predicted that about 3,360 teachers, or about 20 percent of the country's total teaching staff, would be lost to AIDS-related illnesses by 2010. Without HIV/AIDS the number of teachers lost in the same period would have been only 860 ("Education Sector" 2003). In Zambia, it is estimated that more than 30 percent of teachers are already infected with the virus. The number of teacher deaths in 1998 in Zambia was the equivalent of two-thirds of the annual output of newly trained teachers at all teacher training institutions combined (Poku and Cheru 2001, 42). Indeed, large numbers of skilled teachers will be difficult to replace. "Swaziland has estimated that it will train 13,000 teachers over the next 17 years just to keep services at their 1997 levels—7,000 more than it would have to train if there were no AIDS deaths" (UNAIDS 2002d).

Education is a cornerstone of a society's development. In southern Africa, improvements to the educational system constituted one of the most important achievements of political independence. However, education at all levels, already damaged by economic liberalization, faces further decimation by AIDS. Moreover, in many southern African countries there is a very real concern that resources may be diverted from the education sector to other sectors, such as health and welfare, where the HIV/AIDS-induced needs are more immediate.[7] Severe budget constraints, only partly due to AIDS, force hard choices on governments.

Health

Clearly, health sectors throughout southern Africa are being adversely impacted by HIV/AIDS. The demands due to HIV/AIDS on already greatly overburdened and underfunded health care systems are manifold: "extending prevention and care for sexually transmitted infections, counseling and testing, prevention of mother to child transmission services, and HIV treatment and care." Moreover, just as the demand for care increases, so too does the toll on health care workers. "Malawi and Zambia, for example, are experiencing five to six-fold increases in health-worker related illness and death rates. To compensate, the training of doctors and nurses would have to increase by an estimated 25 to 40 percent in 2001–2010 in Southern Africa" (UNAIDS 2002a).

While much care is provided to family members in the home and the community, hospitals and clinics are also feeling the burden of the AIDS epidemic. Although care for AIDS patients in southern Africa is typically inadequate, AIDS threatens to swamp all other medical services, including hospital space. In 2001 it was estimated that half of all beds in some health care centers in Swaziland were occupied by people living with AIDS. Similarly, in Zimbabwe half of all inpatients at health care centers studied were people living with AIDS. In Swaziland and Namibia it is expected that the number of hospital beds needed for AIDS patients will exceed the total number of beds available by 2004 and 2005, respectively (UNAIDS 2002d). In South Africa, the health care system is said to be "reeling under the impact of the epidemic" (Delius and Marks 2002, 10). There is also immense pressure on health care budgets and health insurance schemes as a result of the epidemic.

■ *Agriculture*

Agriculture, the source of livelihood for about 70 percent of southern Africans, is also being hard hit by the HIV/AIDS crisis, with serious implications for food security in the region. As farmers fall ill or die, their labor and that of family members assigned to care for them is lost. In Namibia in 2001, 60 percent of commercial and smallholder farmers reported that they had suffered labor losses due to HIV/AIDS (UNAIDS/WHO 2002, 27). Labor losses mean that households are not able to produce enough food for their own consumption, or for sale, with implications for household nutrition and household income. In some instances, farmers have reported switching to less labor-intensive but also less nutritious food crops. In the quest to pay for much needed medicines and to meet household expenses in the face of income loss, farm equipment and other household assets may be sold off, thereby rendering household recovery more difficult. Similarly, in the face of lost labor power and lost income, farm infrastructure may fall into disrepair and agricultural inputs such as pesticides may become too expensive. The situation is all the more dire when, as in recent years, drought threatens the region.

Indeed, according to Alex de Waal and Joseph Tumushabe (2003), recent evidence suggests that "the HIV epidemic is disproportionately affecting agriculture relative to other sectors." This is not because HIV infection rates are higher among agricultural workers than other workers, but because "the structure of the agriculture sector, especially the small-holder subsector, is such that it is much less able to absorb the impacts of the human resource losses associated with the pandemic." The impact of the epidemic on the agricultural sector, according to the authors, will be to intensify labor bottlenecks, increase widespread malnutrition, add to the problems of rural women, and reduce agricultural exports. The reasons that the impact is likely to be so severe include "the pre-existing fragility of most African farming systems . . . and the role of the agrarian sector in most African countries as an unacknowledged social safety net." The authors conclude that, "under the strain of the HIV/AIDS epidemic, the more vulnerable farming systems are simply breaking down, threatening a social calamity on a scale not witnessed before on the continent."

At the end of 2002 about 15 million people were at risk of starvation in six famine-affected countries in southern Africa—Lesotho, Malawi, Mozambique, Swaziland, Zambia, and Zimbabwe (UNAIDS/WHO 2002, 26). According to many sources, the HIV/AIDS epidemic in the region was one of a number of factors clearly contributing to the most recent food crisis in southern Africa. Basically, the HIV/AIDS epidemic has eroded the few coping mechanisms that households have at their disposal. "It reduces households' capacities to produce and purchase food, depletes their assets, and exhausts social safety nets" (UNAIDS/WHO 2002, 27). A study conducted in Malawi in 2002 found a range of links between the HIV/AIDS epidemic and the onset of household food insecurity. "These include the loss of able bodied labour in the households, the loss of remittances from working family members, the additional challenge of caring for orphans, child-headed families, and increased expenditures on health care and funerals" (UNAIDS/WHO 2002, 27).

National Security

National security is also at risk in countries throughout southern Africa. Just as farmers and teachers are being hard hit by HIV/AIDS, so too are soldiers. According to UNAIDS (2002e), in African countries where HIV/AIDS has been present for more than a decade, the HIV prevalence rate among soldiers is as high as 50 to 60 percent; in other of the hard-hit countries the rate is about 20 to 40 percent. More specifically, the USIP (2001, 5) reports that 40 percent of the military in South Africa and up to 60 percent in Angola and the Democratic Republic of Congo are HIV-positive. According to the U.S. National Intelligence Council (2000), this is, in part, because of "risky lifestyles and deployment away from home." Further, according to UNAIDS (2002e), "the military cost of AIDS is likely to be highest among the more modernized armed forces in Africa, and especially in their officer ranks."[8] As armed forces lose soldiers and officers, their combat readiness and overall capability diminishes, thereby compromising countries' national security. Moreover, a compromised national defense capability also bodes ill for the social and political stability so integral to growth and development.

■ The Industrial Sector

A number of countries in southern Africa, in particular Zambia and Zimbabwe, have already experienced substantial deindustrialization as a result of years of structural adjustment programs. Still, industry in southern Africa stands to be further crippled by HIV/AIDS, and perhaps for that reason some of the most progressive responses to the disease are to be found in industry, in particular in Botswana and South Africa. Of course the vast majority of those affected by HIV/AIDS—fifteen- to forty-nine-year-olds—are precisely a country's economically active population and the most productive segment of that population. Already a host of factors are combining to reduce labor productivity and industry profits—and act as a disincentive to investment, especially foreign investment—throughout the region. Namibia's bulk water supplier, NamWater, reports that HIV/AIDS is hindering its operation as worker absenteeism rates rise and labor productivity rates fall. In Zambia, dozens of businesses report dramatic increases in annual mortality rates of their employees as well as marked increases in absenteeism among workers. The increased absenteeism is due to the declining health of HIV-infected workers, but also to time off spent at the funerals of other workers. High employee turnover rates mean increased training costs for businesses. Additional new costs to businesses include more medical care, salary compensation for the families of deceased workers, and funeral grants (Poku and Cheru 2001, 42). According to one study of several southern African countries, undertaken by UNAIDS (2002d), "the combined impact of AIDS-related absenteeism, productivity declines, health-care expenditures, and recruitment and training expenses [to replace lost workers] could cut [company] profits by at least six to eight percent." The situation may be even more critical in the informal sector, which provides a source of livelihood for so many in the developing world. In informal enterprises, "when the lead entrepreneur is no longer able to work, there is a high risk that the entire enterprise will collapse." With the collapse of the enterprise, the incomes of others are in turn lost, as are the goods or services produced.

In South Africa, business leaders worry that if present trends continue, they might well be training three people for every one job, thereby incurring significant additional costs and expenditure of resources. For example, it is estimated that anywhere from 5 to 45 percent of workers in South Africa's essential mining industry may be infected with HIV, thereby threatening the economic viability of the industry. As a result, a number of companies, such as South Africa's largest, the mining giant Anglo-American Corporation, have joined together to make available to their workers the antiretroviral drugs that have prolonged the lives of people living with AIDS in many other parts of the world. Even at greatly reduced prices, these drugs are prohibitively expensive to the average South African worker, and so company decisions to provide them to their workers are highly significant. Such a move has not been made in the public sector in South Africa. Still, the step does raise certain ethical, financial, and medical questions, such as whether the wives and children of affected miners should also be provided with the drugs (Hunter-Gault 2001). In Botswana, the mining company Debswana has moved to provide antiretrovirals to its workers and their families. Debswana's policy is in keeping with national policy in Botswana, the first country in Africa to make antiretrovirals available to the entire populace (Rollnick 2002).

Taken together, the interrelated effects of HIV/AIDS on all of these sectors portend a bleak future for southern African economies and polities. Why is the HIV/AIDS crisis so severe in Africa in general and southern Africa in particular? Many of the factors are common to all the states of the region.

■ An Epidemic Waiting to Happen?

Marks (2002, 17) suggests that in South Africa HIV has spread with such alarming speed because, "in many ways, HIV/AIDS was a pandemic waiting to happen." Marks cites A. B. Zwi and A. J. Cabral (1991) and their definition of a "high-risk situation"—a new term that describes "the range of social, economic, and political forces that place groups at particularly high risk of HIV infection." According to Zwi and Cabral, a number of features—impoverishment and disenfranchisement, rapid urbanization, the anonymity of urban life, labor migration, widespread population movements and displacements, social disruption, and wars, especially counterinsurgency wars—characterize these high-risk situations. According to Marks (2002, 17), in the 1980s South Africa's black population experienced nearly every one of these features. "Given its underlying health conditions and its levels of social dislocation in that decade," she continues, "it took no great prescience to predict that AIDS would wreak havoc in South, indeed Southern, Africa if and when it entered the region." Indeed, most of these attributes are widely shared throughout the region.

The set of factors that account for the rapid spread of the virus in Botswana, which lacked the conflict and the entrenched poverty of South Africa, nonetheless bear some similarities. According to Hwedie (2001a, 56), these include "the extreme mobility of the population and good communication systems; a high rate of sexually transmitted diseases [STDs]; the accepted norm of sexual behaviour that allows multiple partners and frequent change of partners prevalent in both rural and urban areas; the breakdown of traditional ways of regulating sexual behaviour due to rapid urbanization which currently stands at 45 percent; poverty, which, among other factors, forces women to engage in risky sexual behaviour; and gender relations which are biased in favour of males who dominate social and sexual relations leaving females powerless."

John Caldwell (2000, 120) describes another set of factors that seem to distinguish Africa from other parts of the world. For example, "uniquely in the world," in sub-Saharan Africa the virus is transmitted almost exclusively through heterosexual intercourse. Moreover, this heterosexual transmission of the virus is facilitated by "a higher level of sex outside marriage than occurs in Old World agrarian societies; a high level of prostitution, caused partly by the lack of wives or sexually accessible wives and partly by the mobility of the population and an excess of males in many urban areas; a resulting high level of STDs—the world's highest level according to a WHO study—which act as cofactors for infection . . . ; the persistence of ulcerating untreated and uncured STDs because of poverty and the world's poorest health facilities; a low level of condom use even in commercial sex." Further, according to Caldwell, the fact that "whole ethnic groups" in eastern and southern Africa do not practice male circumcision may contribute to the spread of the virus.

It is important to recognize that some of these variables are grounded in individual behaviors and cultural norms (agency). However, as evidenced from the country case studies in this volume, other factors, such as male living and migration patterns, are the result of historical and structural factors and thus cannot be divorced from apartheid and colonialism. Similarly, the condition of southern Africa's health care system can only be explained with reference to both international and domestic policies. Although the causes are equally diverse, Caldwell (2000) rightly notes that there has been a singular failure in Africa to control the spread of the virus, in strong contrast to other parts of the world.[9] Given the scope of the disease in southern Africa, the specific factors fueling the epidemic in that region warrant closer examination.

Mode of Transmission

The fact that in Africa the virus is transmitted primarily by heterosexual intercourse has meant, among other things, that many more women than men are infected in Africa (58 percent of adults infected in Africa are women) and that a much higher percentage of women are infected in Africa than anywhere else in the world.[10] A higher percentage of women infected with the virus leads directly to more children becoming infected with the virus. Indeed, 87 percent of the children infected with the virus worldwide live in Africa. This is because there are more women of childbearing age infected in Africa than elsewhere and because African women, on average, have more children than women elsewhere in the world.[11] According to the United Nations Development Fund for Women (UNIFEM) (n.d.), the UNDP estimates that more than 85 percent of the cases of pediatric infection in Africa have resulted from perinatal transmission. Moreover, nearly all children in Africa are breast-fed, and breast-feeding is another transmission route for the virus. Finally, the drugs, such as nevirapine, that are available in other parts of the world to prevent mother-to-child transmission—before, during, and after birth—are largely unavailable in Africa, though this is changing in some countries. The result is that 90 percent of mother-to-child transmissions of HIV occur in Africa (Marks 2002, 15).

The Status of Women

A lower status for women in most African societies also contributes to a higher HIV prevalence among African women. According to UNAIDS (n.d.), "A variety of factors increase the vulnerability of women and girls to HIV. They include social norms that deny women sexual health knowledge and practices that prevent them from controlling their bodies or deciding the terms on which they have sex. Compounding women's vulnerability is their limited access to economic opportunities and autonomy, and the multiple household and community roles they are saddled with." Women are often infected at a younger age than are men. As noted above, in many southern African countries, young women (in their teens and twenties) are many times more likely to be infected with the virus than are young men of the same age. This is due to several factors. In situations of poverty, for example, "relationships with men (casual or formalized through marriage) can serve as vital opportunities for financial and social security, or for satisfying material aspirations. Generally, older men are likely to be able to offer such security. But, in areas where HIV/AIDS is widespread, they are also more likely to have become infected with HIV" (UNAIDS/WHO 2002, 19). Moreover, in southern Africa and other parts of Africa, up to 80 percent of women aged fifteen to twenty-four have been shown to lack sufficient knowledge about HIV/AIDS. Finally, young women and girls are more biologically prone to HIV infection (UNAIDS/WHO 2002, 19).[12]

To make matters worse, HIV-positive women are typically discriminated against when they attempt to access care and support for themselves.

Men are more likely to be admitted to health care facilities than are women, and family resources, in the form of medicine and care, are more likely to be devoted to AIDS-infected men than to AIDS-infected women members of a household (UNAIDS 2001). Reflecting their lower status in society, women often have limited access to health care, meaning that their symptoms may also go unrecognized and untreated (UNIFEM, n.d.). HIV-positive women may be physically and emotionally abused when their status is revealed. In South Africa, a woman named Gugu Dlamini was brutally killed by young men in her community shortly after publicly announcing her HIV-positive status (Power 2003, 59). In Zimbabwe, AIDS widows have been accused of causing the deaths of their husbands (UNIFEM, n.d.).

Moreover, women are largely responsible for an invisible and unaccounted-for "care economy" that has emerged in many parts of the world, including southern Africa. This care economy is dominated by older women and young girls who sacrifice their lives to fill the HIV/AIDS care gap left by governments and the global community. This happens when young girls are pulled out of school to care for sick and dying parents or siblings, or when grandmothers take on the burden of caring for sick and dying family members or for orphaned children. With no information and training and few resources at their disposal, these female caregivers are looking after HIV-positive family members, often at great risk to themselves.[13]

In addition, according to UNAIDS (2001), there is growing evidence that a large share of new cases of HIV infection are due to gender-based violence in homes, schools, the workplace, and other social settings. Coerced sex, because of increased tearing, increases the likelihood of HIV transmission. Unwilling sex with an infected partner also increases the likelihood of HIV transmission, because a condom is not likely to be used (UNIFEM, n.d.). In situations of political strife, civil disorder, or war, women and girls are often systematically targeted for abuse, including sexual abuse, thereby dramatically increasing their chances of acquiring HIV or other sexually transmitted infections. In situations of political conflict and war one also finds poverty, famine, destruction of health and other infrastructure, large population movements, and the breakdown of families. All of this means a breakdown in the institutions and services that normally protect women and girls (USIP 2001, 8).

War and Conflict

Widespread conflict has certainly contributed to the HIV/AIDS epidemic in southern Africa. Soldiers, with their very high infection rates, are clearly a principal vector of the disease in southern Africa and other parts of Africa (USIP 2001, 8). They can be responsible for spreading HIV/AIDS not only within situations of conflict and war, but also once back in their home towns, villages, and communities upon demobilization. War and other conflicts contribute to persons being displaced from their homes internally and even becoming refugees across national borders. Displaced persons and refugees, the bulk of whom are women and children, are susceptible to harassment and exploitation by soldiers and others and usually have no recourse to any legal or social protections. In actual conflict situations, according to the USIP (2001, 8–9), "law enforcement, judicial, religious, and other state systems that protect individual rights break down. Within this set of circumstances the vulnerability of women to sexual intimidation is greatly increased." Indeed, the incidence of rape and other forms of sexual coercion skyrockets in conflict settings.

From 1998 to late 2002, several southern African countries, including Angola, Namibia, and Zimbabwe, were embroiled in a war in the Democratic Republic of Congo. Congolese soldiers are said to be heavily infected with HIV, as well as up to 70 percent of Zimbabwe's armed forces according to some estimates. In Angola, a long-standing war has only just barely ended, and civil strife certainly characterizes the climate in Zimbabwe at the moment. In South Africa, the province that has seen the highest levels of HIV infection is KwaZulu-Natal. This is also the part of South Africa that "witnessed the most prolonged, bloodiest and dirtiest of the conflicts that marked the last days of the apartheid government, as well as some of the most rapid and disorderly urbanization in the subcontinent" (Marks 2002, 19–20). Finally, as Joe Collins and Bill Rau (2000) note, "warfare presents major opportunity costs for Third World countries." In other words, money spent on military equipment and personnel is money not spent on HIV/AIDS treatment and prevention. In South Africa recently, a huge outcry followed an announced government decision to spend millions on arms and other military equipment, at the same time that the government refused to make antiretroviral drugs available to the public sector.

▓ *Labor Migration*

Southern Africa's migrant labor system—involving the internal migration of men from the rural areas to mines and other places of employment in Botswana, Namibia, South Africa, or Zambia, or the cross-border migration of men from any number of southern African countries into South Africa—has proved to be the perfect setting for a rampant HIV/AIDS epidemic. Already decades ago, according to Marks (2002, 17), South Africa's migrant labor system was implicated in the spread of another sexually transmitted infection, syphilis. According to health practitioners at the time, treatment of the disease could not be successful in the context of a widespread migrant labor system. In addition to depleting the rural areas of young men, with implications for food security and family stability, the migrant labor system had "vast repercussions on public health control as 'the process of continuous movement of large numbers of people spread a variety of communicable diseases'" (Marks 2002, 18).

In South Africa and Namibia, in the past decade or two, significant population movements accompanied the demise of apartheid, further facilitating the spread of infectious diseases. As influx controls were lifted, huge numbers of the rural poor and unemployed flocked to the urban areas seeking greater opportunities. Instead, according to Marks (2002, 19), many found themselves in "urban shacklands" where they were "easy prey to the diseases of poverty like malnutrition and tuberculosis, to parasitic infections and to sexually transmitted diseases. All of these diseases also lower resistance to HIV infection." Today, "the more disrupted informal settlements around South Africa's cities have the highest rates of STD and HIV infection."

The epidemiological relationship between labor mobility or migration and HIV has been established in study after study (Collins and Rau 2000). Male migrants typically leave impoverished rural areas that offer little or no hope of employment for lengthy stays at mines or other work sites far from home. Once there, removed from family and other support systems, men often spend hard-earned wages on alcohol and high-risk sex, sometimes even starting families at the work site.[14] When migrant workers return home to the rural areas, they act as another vector of HIV transmission (Collins and Rau 2000; Poku and Cheru 2001, 45). And as the male migrants themselves fall prey to the disease, their remittances home become less frequent, thereby adding to the hardships already facing women and children in the rural areas (Upton 2003, 317). Moreover, not only do women lose their husbands and their remittances, but they also often lose secure access to land, thereby jeopardizing their livelihoods and those of their children. In southern Africa today, the migrant labor system, in facilitating the spread of HIV/AIDS, contributes to a vicious cycle of poverty and need.[15]

■ The Constraints of Poverty

Another factor contributing to the HIV/AIDS epidemic in southern Africa today is high levels of poverty. While the South African economy is the most advanced on the African continent and countries such as Botswana and Namibia have relatively high per capita incomes by African standards, other countries such as Malawi, Zambia, Zimbabwe, Mozambique, and Angola are among the poorest countries in the world.[16] And poverty in the region has been exacerbated in recent decades by economic reform programs that have mandated large cutbacks to many social services. Indeed, poverty underlies a number of AIDS cofactors in the region. In general, poverty is associated with weak endowments of human and financial resources, such as low levels of education, including literacy and numeracy, few marketable skills, generally poor health, and low labor productivity (Poku 2001, 195). Poverty certainly contributes to higher levels of labor mobility and to women entering into commercial sex work.[17] Poverty in the rural areas means that households are much less able to cope with drought, famine, health emergencies, and other disasters.

One aspect of high poverty levels is overburdened and inadequate health care systems, which in turn facilitate the epidemic. Most health care systems in southern Africa are not able to cope with existing health care problems, let alone an epidemic of the magnitude of the HIV/AIDS crisis. Underfunded and understaffed health care systems mean that countries are not able to keep their blood supplies as clean as they might otherwise do, making available another transmission route for the virus. They also mean that countries are less able to diagnose the disease, allowing people to avoid knowing their HIV status.[18] Such health care systems also mean that people are less likely to be effectively treated for the opportunistic infections that accompany HIV/AIDS, thereby contributing to early deaths from HIV infection. Finally, countries with inadequate health care systems are less able to diagnose or treat the sexually transmitted infections that greatly amplify the chances of HIV transmission. Even already overstretched health care systems are not immune to turmoil and strife in southern Africa. According to UNAIDS/WHO (2002, 30–31), "hospitals and clinics, along with doctors and other medical personnel, have been deliberately targeted by warring parties" to conflicts in the region.

The Political Dimension

A final factor fueling the HIV/AIDS epidemic in southern Africa has been the failure of many governments to respond adequately to the epidemic, though this is slowly changing. In many ways, it comes as no surprise that governments have taken their time to respond appropriately. As Marks (2002, 16) notes, unlike other "plagues," because HIV "is transmitted sexually, it makes government and indeed public health intervention particularly fraught. Perhaps no other single human behaviour is as surrounded by cultural sensitivities." One early response to the crisis in many countries was simply to deny the existence of an HIV/AIDS crisis, or to refuse to acknowledge its magnitude and gravity.

South African president Thabo Mbeki's initial response to the crisis attracted widespread condemnation, both within South Africa and internationally. For some time Mbeki refused to acknowledge the link between HIV and AIDS; rather, in a public statement in mid-2000, Mbeki declared that extreme poverty rather than AIDS was "the world's biggest killer." "Since poverty also broke down people's immune systems, Mbeki said, 'We could not blame everything on a single virus'" (Power 2003, 63). As discussed above, poverty is clearly a cofactor for AIDS in southern Africa; in a very real sense, poverty can contribute to the spread of AIDS and the lack of resources to combat it. However, as observers note, "By attributing the AIDS epidemic to mass poverty and malnutrition, Mbeki sidestepped difficult questions about sex and responsibility" (Power 2003, 63). Mbeki has also refused to consider government sponsorship of antiretrovirals in the public sector, charging that the drugs were too dangerous and were being proposed for widespread use in an effort "to poison blacks" (Power 2003, 62). Indeed, it took a court ruling in mid-2001 to force the South African government to make available to pregnant women the drug nevirapine, which has proved so effective in other countries at reducing mother-to-child transmission of the virus. While private companies have begun to provide their HIV-infected workers with antiretrovirals, in mid-2003 the Mbeki government continued to refuse to make them available to HIV-positive people in the public sector.

Mbeki's stonewalling baffled both his critics and his allies alike. Helen Schneider (2002, 145) suggests that the seemingly bizarre response of Mbeki and some members of his government to HIV/AIDS and the making of AIDS policy in South Africa is symptomatic of a larger rivalry over state policymaking. "In a cycle established by early criticism of the new government by non-governmental AIDS players, public debate on AIDS has been dominated by a series of responses and counter-responses in which actors have competed to set the agenda for AIDS in South Africa. Many of the presidential and ministerial state interventions on AIDS can be seen as countering the attempts by activist and scientific communities to influence the policy terrain, despite the historical affiliation of the latter to the mass democratic movement of the pre-1994 period." The willingness or unwillingness of leaders to act forcefully in combating HIV/AIDS can be the difference in the life or death of thousands of their citizens, as the example of Yoweri Museveni in Uganda has shown.

Another response, although increasingly anachronistic, has been for leaders to stigmatize HIV and to punish those associated with it. As recently as late 2000 Malawi's then-president Bakili Muluzi reportedly called upon police to "intensify swoops on known brothels to slow down the spread of AIDS. So convinced was the president of the relationship between high prevalence and the sex industry that he proposed to give police greater powers to restrict the 'civil liberties' of known prostitutes and their clients" (Poku 2001, 199–200). In Swaziland, King Mswati III displayed both ignorance and a penchant for barbarism when, during a parliamentary debate, he called for HIV-positive citizens to be "sterilized and branded" (Poku 2001, 200). In Zimbabwe, according to Catherine Boone and Jake Batsell (2001, 10), AIDS remained a "closeted issue in Zimbabwean politics throughout the 1990s," despite a growing epidemic. According to the authors, *The Herald,* the government daily newspaper, consistently denied any government obligation to respond to the AIDS crisis and berated young people "who contract AIDS because they insist on indulging in risky sexual experimentation."

Caldwell (2000, 121) suggests that, in some respects, governments can not be condemned for not doing more. He argues that for many African leaders there is a "fear of alienating their followers by intruding into sexual matters and by speaking aloud on such subjects. There is [also] a fear of failure." Moreover, with some important exceptions today, such as South Africa, nowhere in southern Africa have citizens rioted or held demonstrations demanding that their governments do more to address the HIV/AIDS epidemic. In part this is due to the social stigma that still surrounds the disease in African cultures. Many governments, like their electorates, continues Caldwell, are content to leave the work of contending with HIV/AIDS to foreign-funded nongovernmental organizations (NGOs).

■ The Way Forward

Two issues dominate the discussion of combating HIV/AIDS in southern Africa: treatment and care for those already infected, and prevention for those not yet infected. Moreover, the roles of various actors— NGOs at all levels, national governments, the international community— must also be considered.

▨ *Treatment*

Treatment and care for those already infected with the virus has been a highly contentious issue, played out very publicly in South Africa. Antiretroviral drugs, which have done so much to prolong the lives of people living with AIDS in the West, are prohibitively expensive for all but a handful of Africans. Indeed, of the 28.2 million people living with AIDS in Africa today, only 30,000 have access to and are using the antiretroviral therapy (Rollnick 2002). In the developing world, two options have been open to countries seeking to reduce the cost of the antiretrovirals—producing generic versions of the drugs locally or importing them from third parties abroad.[19] In South Africa, the Treatment Action Campaign (TAC) took the lead in challenging the multinational pharmaceutical companies that produce the antiretroviral drugs and that sought to prevent South Africa from producing cheaper, generic versions of them. After initially filing a suit against the South African government, thirty-nine pharmaceutical companies withdrew the suit under intense local and international pressure (Akukwe and Foote 2001). Instead the companies pledged to facilitate the flow of lower-priced antiretrovirals (though likely still too expensive) to Africa. More recently, the TAC has challenged the South African government for its failure to make the anti-AIDS drugs widely available to the public sector as a whole. As noted, the South African government was finally forced, by court order, to begin making nevirapine available to pregnant women in mid-2001. But the TAC continues to lobby the government on antiretrovirals for the public sector. In the meantime, individual provincial governments, as in the Western Cape, have elected to defy the government and begin providing antiretrovirals, as well as nevirapine, to all of those people who need the drugs (Integrated Regional Information Networks [IRIN] 2003b).

In January 2002, Botswana became the first country in Africa to make antiretrovirals and other medicines available, through the public health system, to all Batswana who need them (Rollnick 2002). The government targeted 19,000 people (out of Botswana's total population of 330,000 HIV-positive adults) for enrollment in the first year of the program. Initial reports showed very high drug regimen adherence rates—90 to 100 percent—suggesting that the program is faring much better than anticipated (IRIN 2003a). Half of the cost of the program is being provided by the government of Botswana, with another quarter by the Bill and Melinda Gates Foundation and the rest by the Merck Foundation, supplier of the antiretrovirals. Free counseling and testing form another component of the treatment program, as well as increasing the number of health care professionals and facilities.

In June 2003 the government of Namibia announced that it would support the local production of generic anti-AIDS drugs. In making the announcement, Namibia's minister of health and social services noted that the local production of antiretrovirals in Namibia would make a "huge difference" in terms of access to affordable treatment for HIV-positive people in Namibia and throughout southern Africa (*The Namibian,* June 11, 2003). Already in 2002 the Namibian government had made nevirapine available to pregnant women, on a trial basis, in two large urban centers, Windhoek and Oshakati.

Initially, a number of arguments were made against the widespread use of antiretrovirals in Africa. One of the strongest was that Africa's generally very poor health infrastructures and high levels of poverty would make it very difficult for ordinary Africans, especially in the rural areas, to adhere to the strict regimens that are part and parcel of antiretroviral therapy.[20] So far, however, this has not proved to be the case—far from it. In the first public clinic in South Africa to begin offering antiretroviral therapy—in the

Cape Town township of Khayelitsha—380 men and women have adhered to the complex drug regimens, even more "fastidiously" than people in the United States, with the result that in 92 percent of cases "the virus had been suppressed to the point of being undetectable" (Power 2003, 56). Similarly, in Botswana in 2002, drug regimen adherence rates ranged between 90 and 100 percent (IRIN 2003a).

▓ Prevention

Several different prevention programs have been undertaken in Botswana. Prevention efforts have emphasized awareness campaigns targeted at all educational levels—primary, secondary, and tertiary—with the most conspicuous being the "ABC" campaign, successfully used in Uganda, which calls upon Batswana to "Abstain, Be Faithful, and Condomize." Widespread distribution of condoms is another part of overall prevention efforts (Hwedie 2001a, 59). The aim of Botswana's multisectoral approach to HIV/AIDS prevention is to have no new infections in the country by 2016 (IRIN 2003a).

A number of governments in southern Africa have recognized the advantages, if not the necessity, of working together with local and international NGOs. Zambia has proposed a multidonor debt relief program to enhance its national response to the HIV/AIDS crisis. For Zambia, this proposal provides a way for the government to address the crisis, despite the country's very high external debt. Under the plan, "scarce national funds which now go to service the debt would be set aside for investment into activities that will control the spread of HIV/AIDS" (Poku and Cheru 2001, 51). The funds are available to Zambian NGOs as well as to the government for use in implementing national programs that help to prevent HIV/AIDS transmission, manage existing cases, and address the country's growing population of AIDS orphans. The program is part of an overall national HIV/AIDS strategy developed by Zambia's HIV/AIDS Council and Secretariat (Poku and Cheru 2001, 51).

Botswana, with the second-highest HIV infection rate in the world in 2002, has had a national policy for fighting HIV/AIDS in place since 1993 (UNAIDS 2004). The policy, issued by presidential directive, is a comprehensive one: "stipulating roles for everyone involved; designing control strategies; facilitating ways of mobilizing resources to cover costs; developing structures for implementation, and mechanisms for coordination and evaluation; and promoting the rights of both the infected as well as those not infected to enable them to live healthy and responsible lives" (Hwedie 2001a, 57). Moreover, the policy includes roles for national leaders, government ministries, the private sector, NGOs, community-based organizations, and AIDS-infected people and their communities in the response to the epidemic. The policy, involving both prevention and care, aims to reduce the transmission of AIDS and its impact at all levels of society. "What is commendable about the policy," according to Hwedie (2001a, 58), is that it has been followed by successive national strategic plans that build upon, but also revise as necessary, previous policy.[21]

The solutions to southern Africa's AIDS crisis are evolving and still slow to emerge. Moreover, programs will not take root immediately, and progress will be tempered by the multiple and intersecting problems that confront the region; the HIV/AIDS crisis in southern Africa is life-threatening and all-encompassing. Clearly, AIDS in southern Africa is not just a health problem, but a development problem—indeed the "foremost threat to development in the region," according to the World Bank (Boone and Batsell 2001, 18). The AIDS crisis makes worse so many already difficult challenges in southern Africa—inequalities of wealth and income, slow rates of economic growth, lack of domestic and foreign investment, impoverished rural areas, harsh gender inequalities, struggling private sectors, recurring drought and famine, unconsolidated multiparty democracies—and the AIDS crisis is in turn made worse by these same challenges. The crisis is a particular challenge to nascent democracies in the region. At the same time, Boone and Batsell (2001, 13) suggest that those governments with the capacity to provide good governance will likely be the ones to do better in combating the AIDS crisis.

In addition, those governments that are able to work in partnership with NGOs and community groups will also fare better. Those governments that fail to act, meanwhile, do so at their own peril. Indeed, "experiences from the past 15 years show that where governments fail to act, the disease spreads faster, the eventual costs of dealing with it are higher, and the negative effects on development are more far-reaching and intractable" (Boone and Batsell 2001, 13). In this respect, political leadership may be something of a "supervariable" that helps explain national progress in combating AIDS. Unfortunately, few African leaders realized early in the epidemic the severity of the disease and the calamity of inaction. Southern Africa, with its myriad other contributing factors, had no leaders who initially aggressively championed an anti-AIDS platform. With the exceptions mentioned above, however, many leaders and former leaders have become actively engaged. Former South African president Nelson Mandela and former Zambian president Kenneth Kaunda have organized charitable foundations to address AIDS and AIDS-related problems. Former Mozambican president Joachim Chissano and his prime minister, Pascal Mocumbi, a medical doctor, have taken strong and public stands against HIV/AIDS. Even Zimbabwe's president, Robert Mugabe, noted reflectively that "there are few among us whose lives have not been impacted by AIDS."[22] National leadership, especially at the presidential level, is not only symbolic, but it also demonstrates that combating the disease is a part of the political agenda of African states.

■ Notes

1. Such HIV prevalence levels suggest an even higher lifetime probability of becoming infected with the virus. In Lesotho, for example, "it is estimated that a person who turned 15 in 2000 has a 74 percent chance of becoming infected with HIV by his or her 50th birthday" (UNAIDS 2002d).

2. Of these more than 5 million infected adults in South Africa, more than half are women; in addition, 250,000 children are living with HIV/AIDS.

3. "In Botswana, median HIV prevalence among pregnant women in urban areas already stood at 38.5 percent in 1997. In 2001 it had risen to 44.9 percent. . . . In Zimbabwe, HIV prevalence among pregnant women climbed from 29 percent in 1997 to 35 percent in 2000, while in Namibia it rose from 26 percent in 1998 to 29.6 percent in 2000, and in Swaziland from 30.3 percent to 32.3 percent in the same period" (UNAIDS 2002b).

4. Studies project that by 2015 the economies of Botswana and Swaziland will grow by 2.5 and 1.1 fewer percentage points, respectively, than they would have without the HIV/AIDS epidemic (UNAIDS 2002d). "Long-term scenarios developed for Mozambique indicate that AIDS would reduce gross domestic product and could discourage foreign and domestic investment." In South Africa it is expected that by 2010 the country will have a real GDP 17 percent lower than it would have been without AIDS (UNAIDS 2002d).

5. According to the U.S. National Intelligence Council (2000), "infant mortality is a good indicator of the overall quality of life, which correlates strongly with political instability . . . high infant mortality has a particularly strong correlation with the likelihood of state failure in partial democracies."

6. Assuming that teachers are infected at the same rate as the general adult population in southern Africa—between 20 and 30 percent—the outcome will be a tremendous drain on teaching staffs. This in a part of the world where half of the population is under the age of fifteen—in other words, of prime schooling age.

7. For example, according to UNAIDS (n.d.), "the cost of treatment for one AIDS patient for one year is about equal to the cost of providing education to 10 children for one year."

8. According to the U.S. National Intelligence Council (2000), the most modernized armed forces in Africa will be hardest hit by HIV/AIDS in part because of their mobility.

9. Uganda would be the main exception to Caldwell's assertion. There HIV infection rates were reduced from 30 percent in 1992 to 11 percent in 2000. Many attribute this stunning success to bold leadership on the part of President Yoweri Museveni, a successful campaign to change behavior and encourage fewer sexual partners, public acknowledgment of the threat of the disease, a destigmatization of HIV, and a decentralization of HIV education programs to the village level.

10. According to Caldwell (2000), in otherwise healthy persons, a woman is about three times as likely as a man to be infected through vaginal intercourse. According to UNAIDS/WHO (2002, 6), 55 percent of HIV-positive adults are women in North Africa and the Middle East, and 50 percent in the Caribbean. For all other regions of the world, the percentage is 36 percent (South and Southeast Asia) or lower.

11. The fertility rate for women in sub-Saharan Africa is 5.8 children per woman, the highest in the world. This compares to 4.1 for the Arab states, 3.6 for South Asia, and 2.7 for Latin America and the Caribbean (UNDP 2002, 165).

12. As noted, women are more susceptible to HIV infection than men during vaginal intercourse because of a larger mucosal surface and because microlesions that can occur during intercourse may be entry points for the virus. Very young women or girls, with immature genital tracts, are even more vulnerable in this respect. This risk is elevated by the common practice of early marriage for girls, often to older men, in parts of Africa. The problem has been further compounded by the belief in some places that intercourse with a virgin will cure HIV, meaning that younger girls are being forced into unsafe sex with HIV-positive men (UNIFEM, n.d.).

13. According to UNIFEM (n.d.), older women are sometimes looking after thirty to forty grandchildren orphaned by AIDS. UNIFEM studies in Zimbabwe show that girls are increasingly pulled out of school to take on the burden of health care and that there is a decrease in school enrollment of girls. The survey showed that 70 percent of the children pulled out of school were girls.

14. A number of authors, such as Peter Delius and Liz Walker (2002, 6) and Catherine Campbell and Brian Williams (2001, 138), note the link between constructions of masculine identity among migrant workers and risk-taking behaviors on the mines. Campbell and Williams assert that to help cope with harsh, potentially life-threatening conditions on the mines, "mineworkers constantly appeal to masculine identities reminding one another that as men they need to have the courage to deal with the stresses and dangers of underground work in order to fulfil their roles as breadwinners. While this concept of masculinity serves as a key coping mechanism at work, it also has other sexual associations: a rampant sexual desire driving men to seek out multiple casual partners; the representation of a biological male need for pleasures of 'flesh-to-flesh sex'; the desire to father many children; high levels of risk-taking which cause men to scorn the alleged dangers of a mysterious disease which may kill them in five to ten years time."

15. Delius and Walker (2002, 7), based upon the work of Mark Lurie (2000), suggest that the portrayal of migrant workers as transmitting HIV to the rural areas may be overdrawn. They write: "The idea that rural areas represent a haven from unsafe practices was also shown [in a recent conference] to be an illusion. Research presented at the conference suggests that people are having sex even younger in rural than in urban areas. . . . The image of returning workers being the main source of infection in rural communities was also called into question by data, which suggested that women in rural areas often have higher rates of HIV infection than their migrant husbands."

16. In 2000 South Africa, Namibia, and Botswana had per capita GDPs (adjusted for purchasing power parity) of U.S.$9,401, U.S.$6,431, and U.S.$7,184, respectively. Certainly in the case of South Africa and Namibia these figures mask great inequalities of wealth and therefore do not give an accurate indication of poverty levels in the two countries. Still, by contrast, adjusted per capita GDPs in Zambia, Malawi, and Mozambique were U.S.$780, U.S.$615, and U.S.$854, respectively (UNDP 2002, 151–152).

17. Not only does poverty drive women into commercial sex work, but it also "makes it difficult for women to refuse sex if a client refuses to use a condom and this is exacerbated by women's lack of confidence in a male-dominated community that accords them little social status or respect" (Campbell and Williams 2001, 138).

18. In many cases people are reluctant to know their HIV status anyway,

because of the stigmatization and even violence that often greet a known HIV-positive status. Moreover, in the absence of available antiretroviral drugs, the incentive for knowing one's status is greatly diminished.

19. Akukwe and Foote 2001. Otherwise known as "compulsory licensing"—an international trade mechanism by which countries can instruct a patent holder to license the right to use a patent to any national company or government agency—and "parallel importing"—whereby a country imports goods for resale without authorization from the original seller.

20. Rollnick 2002. The fear was that lack of proper adherence to such regimens, brought on by poor nutrition, lack of access to clean water, long distance to health clinics, and so on, would result in the development of drug-resistant strains of HIV. Another argument was that rather than "wasting" resources on those who were already ill and could likely not properly utilize the drugs, resources should be expended on preventing new infections.

21. In fact, already in 1985, when the first HIV-infected person in Botswana was diagnosed, the government of Botswana had developed programs to address HIV/AIDS. These included a national AIDS control program, a one-year emergency response, a short-term plan, and then a medium-term plan (Hwedie 2001a, 58).

22. Author interview, Harare, June 11, 2001.

11

Women and Politics
in Southern Africa

In many countries in southern Africa, women compose more than half the population. And yet they remain sorely underrepresented at nearly all levels of politics and decisionmaking, in many sectors of the formal economy, and in leadership positions throughout society. In a number of southern African countries where white minority rule continued into the 1980s and 1990s, women contend with the legacy of a triple oppression based on race, class, and gender. But even where independence was achieved sooner, women remain disadvantaged with regard to a variety of socioeconomic indicators, and they bear the burdens of an increasing feminization of poverty clearly exacerbated by decades of harsh economic reforms (see Table 11.1). Everywhere in the region women are subject to discrimination in the areas of land tenure and customary law. And throughout the region women face spiraling levels of violence and an HIV/AIDS crisis that is affecting them, in many diverse ways, even more harshly than it is men.

At the same time, southern African women have achieved some of the highest levels of parliamentary representation in the world, and they have organized vibrant women's movements across the region. In many countries they fought side by side with their male comrades in the struggle for independence, and in other countries they were part and parcel of efforts to end years of authoritarian, single-party rule in favor of a more democratic, multiparty rule. In a few countries in the region, women easily outnumber men at universities, and they are at the forefront of efforts to stem the tide of HIV/AIDS and to care for those already afflicted. For decades women have cared for families and communities in the rural areas while many men have migrated out in search of work.

In a region in which a resort to arms was necessary to win independence in more cases than not, in which local struggles were framed in larger Cold War terms, in which minority white settler populations ruled over

Table 11.1 Gender-Related Development Index and Other Indicators

	Gender-Related Development Index		Life Expectancy at Birth (2000)		Adult Literacy Rate (2000) (percentage age 15 and above)		Combined Primary, Secondary, and Tertiary Gross Enrollment Ratio (1999) (%)		Estimated Earned Income (2000) (PPP U.S.$)	
	Rank	Value	Female	Male	Female	Male	Female	Male	Female	Male
Angola	—	—	46.6	43.9	—	—	21	25	—	—
Botswana	104	0.566	40.1	40.2	79.8	74.5	70	70	5,418	9,025
Malawi	137	0.389	39.8	40.2	46.5	74.5	69	78	506	726
Mozambique	144	0.307	40.2	38.4	28.7	60.1	19	26	705	1,007
Namibia	101	0.604	44.7	44.6	81.2	82.8	80	77	4,413	8,498
South Africa	88	0.689	53.9	50.2	84.6	86.0	96	89	5,888	13,024
Zambia	129	0.424	40.9	41.8	71.5	85.2	46	52	562	995
Zimbabwe	107	0.545	42.5	43.2	84.7	92.8	63	67	1,946	3,324

Source: United Nations Development Program 2002, 224–225.

exploited and disenfranchised majority black populations, race and class oppression have received particular attention. But especially for the more than half the population in the region who are women, gender-based oppression has had a significance that cannot be ignored.

■ Women in the Precolonial and Colonial Periods in Southern Africa

As in all of Africa, the position of women in precolonial southern African societies varied considerably from one group to another and over place and time. Toward the end of the precolonial period, women fulfilled many important roles in their societies, as Iris Berger notes:

> During the nineteenth century, women in most societies remained central to production, trade, and other economic pursuits and had considerable autonomy in controlling the products of their labor. In centralized kingdoms, queen mothers and members of royal families wielded significant power and authority. As healers, priestesses, and spirit mediums, other women addressed individual and communal afflictions, while older women directed life-cycle rituals for girls that helped to create cohesion in values and institutions. Substantial variation remained, however, in the levels of women's political and legal authority and in the degree of submissiveness and deference demanded of them. (1999, 24)

For example, at one end of the spectrum, among the Tswana, "women remained legal minors all their lives. Access to land depended on the goodwill of their husband's family. Women were barred from the ward or chiefly court and thus rendered politically powerless. Severe beatings by husbands and fathers received no social censure. Although nominally protected by a web of obligations and dependencies, women who opposed male dominance lived in fear of abandonment and poverty" (Parpart 1988, 209). Xhosa women, like Tswana women, controlled the crops that they produced, but could not own cattle and also remained legal minors subject to male control throughout their lives. Zulu women "experienced similar forms of subordination, intensified by the development of a highly militaristic state in the early nineteenth century" (Berger 1999, 27). Among the Tonga of southern Zambia, by contrast, "although a woman's wealth was often in her brothers' custody, she had her own fields and granary as well as control over grain production. This control over land enabled women to command the labor and allegiance of sons and sons-in-law and facilitated a degree of access to political power. Some women even became village headwomen" (Parpart 1988, 209). Other women even held high political office—for example, among the Zulu (and other groups in Africa) as queen mothers; these positions could be inherited or elected. Yet the fact that most

Zulu women were mainly in subordinate roles reveals that there were clear limits to women's political power. Nonetheless, women who enjoyed relatively high status often "had important ritual roles, especially those concerned with fertility and social survival" (Parpart 1988, 210).

A number of factors likely account for such differences in women's access to political and economic power at the time. For example, when women controlled certain economic tasks or, as in the case of the Tonga, had security of tenure over land, they were more likely to wield some political authority or power within their group. So, in agricultural societies "where women controlled certain productive areas, such as farming, marketing or trading, their power and authority seem to have been largely based on this very control." Indeed where women were allowed to accumulate wealth they were most likely to have political institutions "which not only protected them but also enabled them to exert influence" (Parpart 1988, 209). Those societies that were matrilineal societies usually allowed greater land security for women thereby placing them in a more favorable position. In the case of the Tswana, the position of women "may have been connected with the society's great vulnerability to drought and economic scarcity" (Berger 1999, 27).[1] In general, according to Berger, many southern African societies combined cattle-keeping, state systems, and a greater domination of women. Age also played a significant role in determining women's access to power and authority.

Indeed, age was just as important as gender in many African societies, and as women aged they achieved positions of greater power and authority in the family and community.[2] All social relationships in a community reflected the idea that older members of the group (women and men) commanded the respect of younger members of the group. While this principle structured relations between rulers and family heads, patrons and clients, and husbands and wives, it also meant that "mothers-in-law held authority over wives, as did older over younger co-wives" (Berger 1999, 6). Thus women were able to wield public power and authority as members of older women's "age grades," in addition to positions as queen mothers, royal wives, priestesses, healers, and spirit mediums (Berger 1999, 6). So, for example, during the nineteenth century, "although Shona women exercised considerable influence in their households and lineages, only a few women, through their religious and political positions, occupied a status equivalent to that of men. . . . Women's status increased over the course of their life cycles, however, first as they married and bore children, and later as they exercised authority over co-wives and daughters-in-law" (Berger 1999, 25). According to Berger (1999, 6), women's access to greater power within the family and community as they aged makes it "hazardous to generalize about their status in society." As noted above, there was considerable variation in the level of women's political access and influence between, and in some instances within, societies. In any case, despite the critical role of women, the bulk of political power in southern Africa's precolonial societies was held by men.

With the onset of formal colonialism in the late nineteenth century in most of southern Africa, the peoples of the region became increasingly integrated into a European-dominated global economic and political system, and the relative positions of women and men were transformed in many ways. For women, most scholars suggest, colonialism brought about an overall decline in their position—particularly relative to that of men (Berger 1999; Parpart 1988; Staudt 1987). As Jane Parpart writes:

> For most African women (with the exception of some urban women) the colonial period was characterized by significant losses in both power and authority. Colonial officials accepted Western gender stereotypes which assigned women to the domestic domain, leaving economic and political matters to men. As a result, although many African men suffered under colonialism, new opportunities eventually appeared for them, while women's economic and political rights often diminished. Colonial officials ignored potential female candidates for chiefships, scholarships and other benefits. Many female institutions were destroyed, often more out of ignorance than malice. (1988, 210)

Women's loss of political power during this period was often associated with, if not a result of, losses in access to land and labor power. In the view of colonial officials, men were the farmers and producers of food in Africa, and when land rights were commercialized, men, considered to be the heads of households, received the titles to the land (Parpart 1988, 210–211). In Zimbabwe and South Africa, according to Parpart, women's land was often transferred to men as land was commercialized. Moreover, while women were considered mere subsistence farmers, men were identified as potential cash crop farmers and therefore were eligible for technical and other assistance. Indeed, new technologies, such as the plow, introduced in South Africa in the nineteeth century, often affected women negatively. "Both in the ethnically diverse northeastern Cape and among the Tswana, the plow increased men's work in food production, granting them rights to the crops they grew, and sometimes expanding their control over women's labor" (Berger 1999, 29). As a result, male farmers were better able to accumulate a surplus, and came increasingly to dominate the rural areas (Parpart 1988, 211).

Under such circumstances, some rural women were motivated to seek opportunities in emerging urban areas. But here again, women's efforts were often thwarted, for in the urban areas, "all but the most unskilled and irregular wage labor remained a male preserve," with the result that women moved largely into the informal sector (Parpart 1988, 211). Over time, colonial authorities attempted to close off that venue for women as well, passing laws that made it difficult for them to subsist independently in urban areas (Parpart 1988, 212). For example, such laws restricted women's ability to brew and sell homemade beer, one of the main informal income-generating opportunities for women in the urban areas. In some South African towns and cities at the turn of the century, many black women found employment as domestic workers. In Zambia around the same time some women were targeted to be trained as "children's nurses" or "girl domestic servants," thereby releasing men (who also worked as domestics) for the mining industry (Staudt 1987, 200). In Cape Town, as clothing production took hold by the onset of World War I, some women began working in factories, preferring this to domestic service in white households (Berger 1999, 34).

In controlling women's migration to the urban areas, colonial authorities were attempting to control the production and reproduction of labor, perhaps the critical ingredient in the emerging regionwide mineral economy. Indeed, a steady flow of low-wage male labor was essential to the exploitation of mines throughout southern Africa, as well as for building the associated infrastructure and for working the commercial farms and plantations. As many scholars have observed, rural women subsidized the regional mineral economy: "Women's continuing presence in the rural areas was necessary to subsidize the low wages of African men, to reproduce a new generation of laborers, and to provide the care to ill and aged workers that capital and parsimonious colonial states were equally unwilling to fund" (Berger 1999, 32). By continuing to produce food and provide care in the rural areas, women enabled male migrant workers to be paid less than a family, or living, wage.

Not only did rural women enable male out-migration from the rural areas during the colonial period, but they were also meant to encourage it, according to Kathleen Staudt (1987, 197): "The colonial state laid the foundation for societies to conform with its cultural notions of appropriate gender relations in industrializing class society, in which women enable and stimulate male work force productivity through home labor (which in Africa includes food production and water and fuel collection) and consumer demand as well as serve as a low skill reserve labor force. In this conception, women are also politically conservative and thus help maintain a given political order."[3]

Christian missionaries played a significant role in molding indigenous populations in the service of the colonial state. Certainly for most of the colonial period, mission schools provided the bulk of the education in African colonies.[4] And the Christian missionaries, like the colonial authorities, brought with them from overseas their own conceptions about gender roles and gender relations. Indeed, according to Staudt (1987, 197), the

Christian missionaries' "ideology and activities also prescribed an extreme dichotomization of gender along the lines of antiquated Victorian norms." For African women, the missionaries established home and marriage training programs, which set a standard for women as "helpmates, appendages, and financial dependents on men as well as moral guardians of the home, family, and children." As Otrude Moyo and Saliwe Kawewe (2002, 170) note, "missionaries believed that education was an opportunity to 'improve' the status of African women; also, African women themselves saw education as a route to better their life chances." Indeed, some African women were able to take advantage of the opportunities offered by mission educations and move into otherwise unattainable positions as teachers or nurses.

Over time, however, with some notable exceptions, the losses to women's position became more pronounced. In the late colonial period, following World War II, efforts to modernize African agriculture accelerated, again at the expense of women farmers. Continued greater access for men to credit, technology, extension services, and markets made many rural women increasingly dependent on their husbands. Likewise, a continued commercialization of land, with land titles invariably going to men, undermined women's autonomy in the economy and the family. Faced with hard times in the rural areas, men at least could usually leave in search of wage labor elsewhere. For example, in Malawi during the 1950s, "the failure of the peasant cotton economy, in which women and men had shared equally left women limited to precarious subsistence production, while men became increasingly involved in the cash economy, including migrant labor" (Berger 1999, 44).

But women, too, increasingly sought to leave the rural areas. Indeed, by the postwar period, according to Berger (1999, 45) the numbers of men and women in many urban areas began to equalize. Though most women continued to work in the informal sector, as petty traders, beer brewers, and prostitutes, some formal sector jobs were becoming increasingly available to women. Many urban women continued to be employed as domestic workers while others worked in factories processing food and tobacco and producing textiles. Some of the few women who had gained access to formal education entered "acceptably female professions" such as teaching, nursing, and social welfare. In many colonies, the authorities still balked at the increasing movement of women from the rural to urban areas, associating "urban women with prostitution, venereal disease, adultery, alcoholism, divorce, and high illegitimacy rates" (Berger 1999, 46). In an effort to stem the flow of women to the urban areas, South Africa took the most drastic step, extending pass laws to women in the 1950s and thereby severely curbing their freedom of movement (Berger 1999, 45). As the colonial state took over an increasing share of African education from the 1950s onward, colonial authorities imbued their educational efforts for girls and women with "a morally laden message emphasizing women's primary place in the home and family," combining academic subjects at school with a heavy emphasis on "domestic science" (Berger 1999, 46–47).[5]

■ Women in Nationalist Movements: The Struggle for Independence and Representation

In the 1950s in southern Africa (sometimes earlier), nationalist and labor movements emerged to challenge the colonial state and demand independence. In southern Africa and throughout the continent these movements "drew initially from educated, urbanized World War II veterans and from the wage-earning populace, most of whom were men" (Staudt 1987, 202). But women quickly became active participants in nationalist struggles as well, engaging in anticolonial protest activities in some cases, and in other cases in armed resistance and war. Independence came in three or four waves to the southern African region, and for the latter two waves, independence was achieved much later than on the rest of the continent. For countries such as Botswana, Malawi, and Zambia, however, independence was achieved relatively peacefully in the 1960s, following a trajectory similar to that of other sub-Saharan African countries. In those countries women typically participated in the independence struggle by joining the women's branches of newly organized nationalist parties. In Zambia, women joined women's wings of, first, the (Zambian) African National Congress and, later, the United National Independence Party (UNIP), organizing protests in the rural and urban areas. "The UNIP Women's Brigade participated in literacy drives to aid voter registration and helped organize town funerals, mass demonstrations, rallies and boycotts to prove UNIP's power" (Parpart 1988, 214). In Botswana, by contrast, "with no independence struggle to draw them into politics, women did not feature in political parties very much at all" (Geisler 1995, 549). Indeed, it was not until well after independence that the two main political parties in Botswana even organized women's wings. Immediately after independence, by contrast, the wife of the president established the Botswana Council of Women. This was an organization of "the wives of ministers, parliamentarians and tribal leaders, who engaged in activities related to social welfare and teaching African women the art of being a good housewife" (Geisler 1995, 550).

Once independence was attained in these countries, as elsewhere on the continent, women and their concerns were dealt with primarily through the women's wings of newly elected ruling political parties. Such organizations were often headed by the wives of national presidents and other prominent male politicians and their tasks were often ceremonial—celebrating the president and the ruling party and greeting visiting foreign dignitaries.[6] With the rapid consolidation of single-party rule, moreover, a separate female agenda outside of the women's wings of political parties became even more unlikely, as Gwendolyn Mikell observes:

> The new society was represented by the single political party—a symbol of the idealized classless African society, which was above ethnicity, traditional status distinctions, traditional political domination of one group over another, gross male dominance over women, and social exploitation in any form. The massive state commitment to social services—the guarantees of health provisions and universal education as well as water, sanitation, and roads—were seen as benefiting women as well as men. The post-independence national goals were portrayed as negating the necessity for a separate female agenda. (1997, 23)

In Malawi, for example, the League of Malawi Women and the National Council for Women in Development were two of several organizations affiliated to the ruling Malawi Congress Party and therefore precluded from articulating any positions independent of the ruling party. These two, like the other affiliated organizations, were "subjected to centralized presidential decision-making and they lacked meaningful influence in determining national development policies" (Kaunda 1992, 71). In Botswana, meanwhile, according to Judith van Allen (2001), the main gain for women from independence was the right to vote: independence had been achieved "through a generally peaceful, colonially-mediated process, with no particular commitment to the emancipation of women beyond the right of suffrage and the same ambiguities about women's status embedded in its constitution as could be found elsewhere in southern Africa."[7] After independence in Zambia, according to Parpart (1988, 215), "Women's Brigade organizers in UNIP [were] mainly backstage supporters for male politicians. The few women in high level politics . . . clustered in traditional female areas, such as welfare and health."

In Angola and Mozambique a resort to arms was necessary to oust the Portuguese colonial rulers and independence was not attained until the mid-1970s. In both countries, according to Mikell (1997, 24), "women staged their own demonstrations, fought alongside men to oppose colonial domination, and sustained the rural resistance that supported liberation fighters." In Mozambique women participated in the armed struggle as porters and occasionally even as combatants. As David Birmingham (1992, 62) recounts, they "headloaded ammunition, and occasionally perhaps even fired a gun, during the war of liberation." But once the Portuguese were defeated and independence attained, the results for women were mixed. On newly formed agricultural cooperatives they won for themselves "prestige posts," such as tractor drivers. They were outspoken members of community committees; in a way "they never had done in traditional society," and they even became magistrates at the local level with "unheard-of powers to order men to obey them." But at the same time that they established their own political organizations, "women were excluded from the real conclaves of power-broking and decision-making. The only government ministry given to a woman was in the caring field of education rather then in the mainstream of economics or national security." Stephanie Urdang (1989, 24–25) describes a similar paradox in Mozambique—women having been made equal before the law and in the constitution, and even taking on tasks previously confined to men, but at the same time being subject to an enduring subordination in the form of a rigid sexual division of labor within the household. Moreover, any suggestion that such subordination should be contested was seen as threatening "the male leadership, more than a little." Rather "women are actively called upon to leave aside such struggle, not to use women's liberation as a 'weapon,' and to wait."

Finally, in Zimbabwe, Namibia, and South Africa, independence came much later and only after a resort to arms. In those countries women's participation in nationalist struggles began long before armed struggle commenced. Indeed, women's resistance activities may not always have been linked directly to nationalist movement efforts, but nonetheless formed part of a broader protest against colonial rule. Often, women's actions were quite spontaneous, as in South Africa in the late 1950s. "Rural women, enraged at forced removals, stock control, and a new system of land allocation under which women no longer were guaranteed their own fields, smashed dipping trucks, burned fields, and attacked available symbols of the state. Women in Durban, responding to restrictions on domestic beer brewing and to government support for municipal beer halls, clashed with police, picketed, and engaged in ribald gestures" (Berger 1999, 48). In Namibia, Anna Mungunda is considered the first person to have died in the "modern period" of Namibia's anticolonial struggle—killed in December 1959 as she led a group of township residents protesting their forced removal from one location to another (Bauer 2004). Township women in Namibia had also earlier organized themselves to resist South African colonial policy that sought to deprive them of their primary income-generating opportunity, the brewing of beer. Female food and clothing workers in South Africa were among the early organizers of the Federation of South Africa Women, the group that led protests against passes for women in the late 1950s (Berger 1999, 47).[8] According to Gisela Geisler (2000, 608), the federation was distinctive during this period in that "it represented a broad based women's organization that was not conceived of as an auxiliary to a male-dominated body, such as other women's organizations at the time, and that is was thus 'a real and serious attempt to incorporate women into the political programme of the national liberation movement on an equal footing with men.'"

In all three countries, women participated in crucial ways in their national liberation struggles from both inside and outside the country. In Namibia, an armed struggle against South African colonial rule began with the first military incursion of the South West Africa People's Organization (SWAPO) into the country in 1965.[9] Over the years, women made up between 20 and 40 percent of Namibian exiles in neighboring countries, primarily Angola. From 1974 onward, at their insistence, young women exiles who were unmarried and had no children received the same military training as their male counterparts—and they participated in military combat. Moreover, young women in exile, in equal or greater numbers to men, also had access to many study and training opportunities at UN-sponsored institutions in Angola and Zambia, and at universities and polytechnics abroad. According to Heike Becker (1995, 149–150, 153), this participation on the part of women had a significant impact on men and women alike. On the one hand, "the participation of women in the armed fighting caused men to revise their perception of women and added much to women's self-confidence," while on the other hand, as a result of their various educational opportunities, by the time of independence "many educated young Namibian women were no longer prepared to be subordinate to male dominance but claimed equality and power-sharing, with men on all levels, including politics." In Zimbabwe, too, from 1972 onward women joined the armed struggle, "first as carriers of military equipment and later as front-line fighters" (Geisler 1995, 551). In the military camps, gender differences were suspended as men and women cooked, fought, and trained together. Those differences quickly resurfaced after independence, however, according to Geisler:

> Because women had lived side by side with men, they were now labeled "loose" women: parents would not allow their "clean sons" to marry an ex-combatant, thinking they would not make good wives. In "real" life the virtues of being an independent woman were again undesirable, to parents, to men and it seemed to the new government. Against expectations and hopes, very few women were brought into the new government. (1995, 552)

When not actually fighting for independence themselves, women often played supportive roles to those who were. In rural northern Namibia, which was the literal battleground in that country's war for independence, women joined the resistance effort by playing a supportive role to SWAPO combatants or those sought after by the police (Soiri 1996, 58–59). Iina Soiri (1996, 91) identifies these women as "radical mothers." According to her, the radical motherhood is marked by "family-mothers" taking an active part in political struggle based on their responsibilities and capabilities as members of a community under threat. The women "acted as mothers, daughters and sisters, utilizing the potential opportunities given by their traditional role. They were not aware of or even interested in feminism or its analysis of their situation, but were still empowered as women." Women in rural Zimbabwe—"mothers of the revolution," according to Irene Staunton (1990, xii)—repeatedly risked their lives to serve and protect the "freedom fighters," their common children, who were fighting to end minority white rule. "Without the women," Staunton concludes after interviewing dozens of them, "the war could not have been won." At the same time, according to Geisler (1995, 552), some rural women "used the change of gender ideologies that took place during the war to renegotiate relationships within the household." In South Africa as well, according to Geisler (2000, 608), "motherism" helped propel women into politics: "In South Africa, as elsewhere, women forced their way into political activism against male resistance on the basis of practical gender needs, namely as mothers who were to secure a better future for their children. . . . Motherhood served as a unifying factor across rural-urban, class and race boundaries . . . but also allowed for women's continued subordination to the broader nationalist project."

Indeed, while nationalist and liberation movements throughout the world often relied heavily on women and espoused laudable emancipatory goals with respect to them, they almost universally subordinated gender concerns to the larger nationalist struggle. This became especially evident once independence was achieved and the results for women were often found to be limited at best. The experience of women in nationalist movements in Botswana, Zambia, and Malawi largely confirms this observation. In other cases, it has been argued that violent conflict, which results in major disruptions to gender relations, can provide "new opportunities to articulate debate about gender politics as well as for individual women to live in a different way." This may be all the more true when "liberation movements" have been part of that conflict (Pankhurst 2002, 127). Zimbabwe, Namibia, and South Africa took this pathway to independence and the outcome for women appears, at least initially, to have been somewhat different as a result.

In Zimbabwe, although few women were brought into government at independence, major legal gains for women did follow independence, in the form of new laws to redress past discrimination and enhance women's status in society. The most significant of these was the Legal Age of Majority Act (LAMA) of 1982, which conferred legal adult status on both men and women at age eighteen, and provided women with a range of legal rights not recognized in customary law: to marry without parental consent or payment of bridewealth, inherit property, own a passport or business, open a bank account, enter into legal contracts, and vote (van Allen 2001). Other legislation containing provisions beneficial to women included a labor relations act, a matrimonial causes act, a maintenance act, and a finance act (Moyo and Kawewe 2002, 171). Interestingly, the LAMA was overturned in a 1999 Supreme Court ruling that found that "'the nature of African society' dictates that women are not equal to men, and that 'women should never be considered adults within the family, but only as a junior male, or teenager'" (van Allen 2001, 60). Of all of the provisions of the LAMA, only the right to vote was retained. According to van Allen (2001, 60), "the Court justified its ruling on the grounds that 'the majority of Africans in Zimbabwe still live in rural areas and still conduct their lives in terms of customary law.'" In addition, despite bitter protests from the Zimbabwean Women's Bureau, the government refused, in the course of introducing a land resettlement scheme, to change customary land-tenure practices that continue to discriminate against women (Parpart 1988, 219).[10]

In Zimbabwe, then, women proved unable to retain some of the early gains of independence. Sita Ranchod-Nilsson (1998, 274) attributes this to an increasing consolidation of power by a single-party state: "As access to state power has become more narrow and exclusive, the state's gender ideology has been transformed." Indeed, those with access to change power have changed. "Since independence," argues Ranchod-Nilsson, "the cast of state insiders and outsiders has drastically changed, as young, educated women and ex-combatants have been replaced by co-opted key women as regime insiders." Ranchod-Nilsson predicts that this will lead to a greater organization of women outside the parameters of the state. In the meantime, however, "the de-facto one party state's movements to exclude and even malign Zimbabwean women in recent years will likely lead to problems ranging from increased popular discontent with the state to economic development policies that overlook the important contributions of women."

Namibia and South Africa are different cases altogether, with independence and black majority rule attained only in the 1990s. In both cases, women's extensive participation in the liberation efforts from inside and outside the country has had significant implications for the postindependence gender dispensations, as is discussed in greater detail below. As Jo Beall (2001, 135) succinctly states, in the 1990s the African National Congress (ANC) in South Africa, "by taking gender seriously," appeared to "reverse the trend set by many liberation movements elsewhere: namely, women being mobilized as agents in struggle around class and race, yet denied the imperative of addressing gender subordination."

■ Women in Recent Political Transitions

The 1990s witnessed dramatic political transitions across the African continent, including in southern Africa as, in many countries, decades of authoritarian single-party rule gave way to a more democratic multiparty rule. In a number of countries, including Malawi and Zambia, it can be argued that initial democratic transitions have not been consolidated; indeed some backsliding may even have occurred. Nonetheless, as Aili Tripp (2001, 143) suggests, "it is important to note that the democratization efforts of the 1990s, despite their limitations, gave women the impetus to make bolder strides in the political arena." Indeed, women and their organizations, like student groups, trade unions, and human rights associations, were often at the forefront of such democratization efforts, openly opposing "corrupt and repressive regimes through public demonstrations and other militant actions" (Tripp 2001, 142). Moreover, the demise of single-party states and powerful ruling parties often freed women of their obligations to the women's wings of those parties and coincided with a rise in independent women's organizations "seeking to take advantage of the opening of new political space." Leaders of these new women's organizations moved beyond previous preoccupations with "development" and pushed for constitutional and legislative changes as well as greater access for women to political office at all levels (Tripp 2001, 143).

Women have been actively involved in Zambia's democratic transition. According to Tripp (2001, 148), "women from NGOs, churches, and political parties formed a nonpartisan National Women's Lobby Group (NWLG) in 1991, with the goal of increasing the representation of women in decision-making positions in government and the political parties. The NWLG encouraged women to compete in local elections, worked to repeal discriminatory legislation, and conducted human rights training and civic education seminars. By 1995, the organization had grown to 2,000 dues-paying members." Together with other nongovernmental organizations (NGOs), the NWLG also pressed to have a section on women's rights included in Zambia's new constitution. Despite heavy protest from a number of quarters, the groups were successful in including in the constitution sections on women's reproductive rights and equal opportunities for women in education (Tripp 2001, 149). More recently, the Nongovernmental Organization Coordinating Committee (NGOCC), an umbrella organization of women's lobby groups, played an instrumental role in national legal and political affairs. The NGOCC was a central player in the Oasis Forum, which in 2001 mobilized civil society to block President Frederick Chiluba's effort to seek an extraconstitutional third term in office.[11] The body also took a leading role in Zambia's 2003 constitutional review process. In Malawi since the transition, the National Commission on Women and Development has worked together with women's organizations for a greater representation of women in local and national political office. They have also pressed for the implementation of laws against domestic violence and for the protection of women's property in the event that their husbands die (Tripp 2001, 150–151).

Not surprisingly, perhaps, the results for women of the political openings offered by the region's democratic transitions have been mixed. For Zambia, Anne Ferguson and Beatrice Katundu (1994, 24–25) found 'continuities and change' with regard to women's participation in politics since the 1991 transition. On the one hand, as noted above, "the powerful gatekeeping role of women's wings of political parties" was found to be declining, "thus allowing for the representation of women with more diverse interests in politics and government." On the other hand, in the early years after the 1991 transition, Ferguson and Katundu (1994, 24–25) found that women involved in politics confronted a "persistent gender discrimination" reinforced by a constitution and legal code that "denies women equal rights with men in areas of family law, maintenance and inheritance rights, and thus contributes significantly to making participation in politics costly for many women."[12] In her examination of women's political participation in Botswana, Zambia, and Zimbabwe in the early 1990s, Geisler (1995, 566) found similar experiences: "Unless women keep to the prescribed spaces and roles in the political women's corner, they are considered to be out of bounds." Women in politics were watched more; treated as wives, mothers, and lovers; expected to work twice as hard as men; met with derision in meetings; received less campaign support; and lacked support from other women.

In Namibia and South Africa, meanwhile, a number of factors seem to have to come together to make for more enduring and more significant changes for women than elsewhere in the region in the posttransition period. Indeed, both countries adopted constitutions that are very progressive with respect to women and gender relations. For example, Namibia's constitution, written entirely in gender-neutral language, states that all people shall be equal before the law and prohibits discrimination based on sex, race, color, ethnic origin, and a number of other factors. It also notes that women have traditionally suffered special discrimination in Namibia and need to be encouraged and enabled, through affirmative action measures, to participate more fully in every aspect of life in Namibia. Finally, customary or common law (often discriminatory toward wives and women in general) is allowed to remain in effect in Namibia, but only to the extent that it does not conflict with the constitution or any other laws.

In addition, both countries have adopted a host of new laws that prohibit discrimination and harassment in the workplace on the basis of sex, marital status, family responsibilities, and sexual orientation; aim to ensure that women and other disadvantaged persons have equal access to employment opportunities; prescribe minimum sentences for rape and place more emphasis on the rights of rape victims; and treat women and men equally in the allocation of communal land and protect widows against dispossession, among other things. Finally, in both countries a number of offices and national policies—official "national machineries" for women[13]—have been established to monitor the progress of women and to ensure the representation of their interests. These include (but are not limited to), in Namibia, a ministry of women's affairs and child welfare, a women and law committee, and a national gender policy; and in South Africa, an office on the status of women, a women's empowerment unit, and a commission on gender equality.[14] And both countries have achieved among the highest representation of women in national legislatures in the world, to which we turn below.

In Namibia and South Africa significant legal and electoral gains have been recorded since the two countries' respective transitions in the early 1990s. Moreover, women activists in both countries appear to have avoided some of the reversals experienced in other parts of the region in postindependence periods. For South Africa, Gay Seidman (1999, 289) attributes some of these gains to an increasingly articulate women's movement that was able to challenge the antiapartheid movement's previous subordination of gender concerns to nationalist goals. This was accomplished in part, according to Seidman, through the discussion of how apartheid had actually treated black women and men differently and the realization that unless gender concerns were considered during the course of democratization, new political institutions would re-create and reinforce inequality. Moreover, in the years before the transition, antiapartheid activists began to develop separate women's groups in which women began to analyze their lives in terms of not only race and class oppression, but also gender oppression (Seidman 1999, 292).

Indeed, just as negotiations for a new South Africa were beginning, women from across the political spectrum came together to form one national organization. In April 1992, the Women's National Coalition (WNC)—comprising seventy organizations and eight regional coalitions—was launched. According to Shireen Hassim (2002), the WNC had the "single purpose of drafting a Women's Charter of Equality, which would gather the demands of individual women as well as women's organizations." The strategic impetus for the WNC, as an alliance between diverse and even competing women's organizations, was the failure of all the political parties to include women in their respective teams as the negotiations commenced in 1992. The Women's Charter was eventually completed in 1994, after an interim constitution had been finalized. But the WNC also played an important role in the negotiations process, according to Hassim (2002), identifying three key areas of intervention: "women's inclusion in negotiating teams, the inclusion of non-sexism in the constitutional principles, and the insertion of an equality clause in the constitution that would supersede the right to custom and tradition." In the end, according to Hassim, "the WNC gave organizational articulation to the awareness of the need for gender representation, and broadened it beyond the liberation movements to include political parties that either did not have democratic ideologies or saw democracy in narrow and formalistic terms. In doing this, it brought gender equality directly into the mainstream of public political discourse." By the time of the 1994 elections, most political parties in South Africa "expressed at least a rhetorical commitment to gender equality" (Seidman 1999, 294), although the commitment of the ANC's principal rivals was largely a last-minute attempt to answer the ANC's greater attention to gender issues.

Strongly influencing these developments, according to Seidman (1999, 295), were a new global discourse around gender issues that had emerged in the 1990s, and a global feminist movement. Global influences were brought to bear, for example, by international funding agencies that insisted on a focus on gender-specific aspects of democratization (Seidman 1999, 296). Such a dynamic was prominent in Mozambique, where, as Ruth Jacobson (1995, 31) notes, during the 1994 election women's organizations were a particularly important channel for foreign funding agencies engaged in civic education, as "their existing community-based structures provided a way of reaching the non-literate sectors of the urban and rural populations."[15]

Moreover, the global feminist movement and gender discourse were brought home to South Africa with the return of thousands of students and exiles following the suspension of armed struggle between the African National Congress and the white minority government. These activists returned home to take on leadership positions within antiapartheid organizations and were instrumental in starting new women's organizations and insisting that feminist concerns not be postponed until after the transition. In Namibia, a similar set of processes was at work—with women exiles exerting a significant influence on the postindependence gender dispensation and a global women's movement (manifest, among other ways, in the UN conferences on women) reinforcing the work of the women activists. Moreover, as the minister of women affairs in Namibia noted in an interview, the timing of Namibia's (and South Africa's) independence—"when gender issues were at a peak"—surely helped (Bauer 2004). The timing of independence for Namibia and South Africa—in the 1990s—may also explain some of the differences with Zimbabwe, which, like the other two countries, resorted to armed struggle in which women were actively involved and recorded initial gains for women, only to see them reversed within a fairly short period of time.

■ Increasing Women's Political Representation

One of the main areas of progress for women in Namibia and South Africa—and Mozambique—has been political representation. Indeed, these three countries are among the top worldwide in terms of representation of women in national legislatures, with women constituting nearly one-third of the members of parliament (MPs) in all three national assemblies (see Table 11.2).[16] This is a notable achievement given that 30 percent is widely considered to constitute the critical mass necessary to promote the recruitment of more women officeholders as well as to develop new legislation and institutions beneficial to women (Lovenduski and Karam 2002). In Namibia, moreover, more than 40 percent of members of local councils across the country are women, as are many mayors and deputy mayors.[17] In other branches of government women have not fared quite so well, although in many executives they have moved beyond some of the ministries typically reserved for women. So, in Namibia in 2004, the new minister of finance was a woman, as were the attorney general and the deputy ministers of labor and home affairs. In South Africa, the ministers of agriculture and land affairs, communications, foreign affairs, minerals and energy, and public works, among other positions, were women in 2004.[18]

In other countries in the region the representation of women in national legislatures remains close to the sub-Saharan African average—around 14 percent. In Botswana only four of fifty-seven MPs, or 7 percent, are women in 2005. In Botswana the president nominates four MPs and has used this

Table 11.2 Women's Political Participation

	Year Women Received Right to Vote and to Stand for Election	Year First Women Elected (E) or Appointed (A) to Parliament	Women in Government at Ministerial Level (2000) (as percentage of total)	Parliament Seats Held by Women—Lower House or Single House (2004) (as percentage of total)
Angola	1975	1980 E	14.7	15.5
Botswana	1965	1979 E	26.7	7.0
Malawi	1961	1964 E	11.8	17.0
Mozambique	1975	1977 E	—	30.0
Namibia	1989	1989 E	16.3	25.0
South Africa	1930, 1994a	1933 E	38.1	32.8
Zambia	1962	1964 E,A	6.2	12.0
Zimbabwe	1957, 1978a	1980 E,A	36.0	10.0

Sources: United Nations Development Programme 2002, 241–242; Interparliamentary Union 2004, "Women in National Parliaments," http://www.ipu.org/wmn-e/classif.htm.

Note: a. White women first received the right to vote in South Africa and Zimbabwe in 1930 and 1957, respectively, and the right to stand for election in 1994 and 1978, respectively.

prerogative to try to increase the number of women in parliament, but as Motsei Madisa (1999, 73) points out, this means that "only women from the ruling party are ever nominated, ignoring capable women from opposition parties."[19] In those countries where women have achieved the highest levels of political representation, a proportional representation electoral system and some form of gender electoral quota is used. In South Africa, the ruling African National Congress adopted a 30 percent gender quota for national elections beginning with the 1994 election, the first universal franchise election in the country. As a result, the representation of women jumped from 3 percent to 27 percent in the national legislature in one election. Following the 2004 election, the percentage increased to 32.8 percent. In Mozambique, the ruling party, Frente de Libertação de Moçambique (Frelimo), has also adopted a 30 percent quota for its party lists for national elections and for its party leadership. Frelimo has also called for a balanced distribution of men and women throughout its party lists.[20] In Namibia an informal quota of sorts has been adopted by political parties for national assembly elections and a 30 percent quota is required by law at the local level. Moreover, in Namibia strong efforts are being undertaken to ensure that party lists for each election are "zebra lists"—in other words, that men and women's names are alternated like the black and white stripes of a zebra, rather than grouping women at the bottom of the lists (Bauer 2004).

In southern Africa as a whole a number of regional initiatives exist to increase and support women's political representation. For example, in 1997, southern African heads of state and government signed a declaration on gender and development in the Southern African Development Community (SADC) that, among other things, calls very clearly for women to occupy 30 percent of positions of power and decisionmaking in national governments by 2005. This goal was repeated in an SADC gender action plan that was approved by the SADC Council of Ministers in 1998 (SADC Gender Unit 1999, 5). In making this demand, women activists and politicians in the region consider decisionmaking posts to include political offices at all levels of government, as well as positions in the public sector more generally, the private sector, and the professions (SADC Gender Unit, 6). In Namibia and South Africa, where nearly 30 percent representation of women at the national level has already been achieved, women's groups are being even more ambitious. In both countries, "fifty-fifty campaigns"—linked to a global effort by the same name—have been launched to achieve a 50 percent representation of women at all levels of politics and decisionmaking by 2005.

In 1998 the SADC Gender Unit was established in the SADC Secretariat in Gaborone, Botswana, with the mandate to coordinate the mainstreaming of gender issues throughout SADC programs and initiatives.

Another SADC initiative to support those women already elected to national office is the SADC Regional Women's Parliamentary Caucus, launched in Luanda, Angola, in April 2002. This organization brings together the members of parliamentary women's caucuses throughout the region (just over 300 of 1,800 MPs in the region are women) to provide an additional empowering strategy for women MPs. The SADC women's caucus will work with women MPs to identify important issue areas for women and to propose strategies for addressing them. Another aspect of the regional body will be skills development for women MPs, particularly in regard to introducing gender-sensitive legislation and ensuring a gender component to all laws and bills passing through parliaments.[21]

■ Women's Movements in the Region

The critical importance of women's movements to the success of women politicians and women's agendas is well documented (Bystydzienski 1992). Though a number of sources suggest that women in southern Africa have not historically been as "highly organized" (Berger 1999, 56; Mikell 1997, 28) as women in other parts of Africa, there is a diversity of experiences in the region. In some countries dynamic and powerful women's movements have emerged over the past two decades, often organized initially around a single issue or set of issues. In some countries a kind of synergy exists between a growing women's movement and increasing numbers of women in political office, while in others, one exists to the detriment of the other.

Van Allen (2001) describes the remarkable case of Botswana, where a vibrant women's equal rights movement emerged in the 1990s around the successful legal challenge to the nation's 1982–1984 citizenship law. At independence, citizenship in Botswana was determined by birth in the country; in the early 1980s, however, that was changed to birth by descent, and for married women, the citizenship of the father thereafter only determined the citizenship of a child. Thus a Botswanan woman married to a foreigner "could no longer pass her citizenship, with its significant educational and economic benefits, to her child" (van Allen 2001, 42). Within a few years of the new law's passage, a women's rights group, Emang Basadi, had emerged to challenge the law, first through education programs and second through legal means, in collaboration with a regional women lawyers' group. The challenge to the citizenship law was ultimately victorious and led to further challenges to discriminatory laws and practices. Other related developments in the 1990s were the establishment of a human rights center, a rape crisis center, and an NGO coalition of sixteen national women's organizations. Women activists in Botswana have also begun to focus on increasing the number of women in political office in the country.

In drawing lessons from the Botswana case, van Allen (2001, 57) highlights the importance of a "working liberal democratic system" and an autonomous women's movement—one that can "generate its own agenda and priorities." In Botswana today, the women's movement is seen as the strongest among civil society organizations and as contributing significantly (in a positive way) to the "changing character" of politics in the country (Good 1996, 57; Holm, Molutsi, and Somolekae 1996, 62–63).

In Namibia women have similarly been galvanized around a single issue—electing more women to political office—such that one might even identify a unified women's movement in the country for the first time ever (Bauer 2004). Since 1999 a number of women activists and women's organizations have joined together under the guise of the Namibian Women's Manifesto Network to demand the 50 percent representation of women at all levels of decisionmaking in the country.[22] In an unprecedented manner, this network has mobilized women across the country to attend workshops, visit schools and churches, meet with traditional leaders, local and regional councillors, and party leaders, and participate in marches demanding a greater representation of women in politics in Namibia. The campaign has garnered the support of major women's organizations and women politicians alike, as well as the support of much of the populace (Bauer 2004). It also seems to verify Mikell's observation (2003, 104) that "the pragmatics of political representation in the 1990s are shaping the emerging African women's movement."

In South Africa, where a long tradition of women's organizing exists, women's recent political successes are reported to have had a potentially deleterious impact on the women's movement there. Geisler (2000, 626) argues that women politicians' successes in South Africa—avoiding the mistakes of women elsewhere on the continent by being an integral part of the transition process from the beginning and in "numbers too large to be easily reversed"—may have come at a price. That price, according to Geisler (2000, 627) may be "the weakening [of] the mass-based movement that was the driving force behind South African women's move into parliament." In the new South Africa, according to Geisler (2000, 605), the women's movement has lost its strongest leaders to government, and women politicians lack the support of a strong women's movement. For example, Hassim (2002) notes that "the immediate decline of the WNC [discussed above] can be attributed to the movement of a significant number of leaders into government after 1994. Leadership fell onto the shoulders of less experienced women—and onto the tier of the coalition that had always been weaker and less able to make connections between national and women's politics." Since 1994 the WNC has been "virtually invisible." Such a trend could still be reversed. Hannah Britton (2001) reports that some women MPs are actually returning to their grassroots and women's organizations rather than continuing to work in an alienating environment at the pinnacle of power.

■ Women in Southern Africa: Present and Future Challenges

What have these political gains meant for the socioeconomic status of the majority of ordinary women in southern African countries today? What of the status of women in those countries where they remain largely excluded from positions of political power? These are vexing questions, as women in the whole of southern Africa continue to struggle for equality at the levels of the family, society, and state. For women in South Africa, Namibia, and Mozambique, the challenge lies in consolidating the gains of formal political representation; for women elsewhere in the region, it lies in creating an environment in which a higher degree of women's political participation is possible. Given the interconnectedness of the countries in the region, there may be some cause for optimism that the advances seen in these three countries may eventually take root in the whole of southern Africa.

Even in those countries that have achieved "juridical equality" for women, preventing reversals of those gains remains paramount. The seemingly intractable economic crises in the region, debilitating droughts, and the AIDS pandemic have a disproportionate impact on women's lives and livelihoods. For example, decades of economic reform measures have been especially harmful to the most vulnerable sections of the population, typically women and children (see Table 11.3). Whether structural adjustment programs implemented from outside or economic recovery programs adopted from within, the reforms of the past couple of decades have meant for women: longer work days, decreased access to basic resources such as land and labor, reduced opportunities in formal sector employment and education, increased costs of basic social services, greater family responsibilities often without the support of a male partner, increased rural to urban migration, and a growing number of female-headed households (SARDC-WIDSAA 2000, 32–33).

Women's struggles also take place against the background of the world's worst AIDS epidemic. Indeed, in southern Africa well over half of those infected with the virus are women. In the region and in Africa as a whole, women and children are particularly vulnerable to HIV infection, since the primary methods of transmission are through heterosexual intercourse and from mother to child. Women and girls are further vulnerable because of their lack of knowledge about and power over their sexuality and their reproductive functions, and because of limited access to economic opportunities and autonomy. Throughout the region, young and older women alike have became the primary actors in an emerging "care econo-

Table 11.3 Survival: Progress and Setbacks

	Life Expectancy at Birth (1995–2000) (years)	Infant Mortality Rate (2000) (per 1,000 live births)	Under 5 Mortality Rate (2000) (per 1,000 live births)	Maternal Mortality Ratio Reported (1985–1999) (per 100,000 live births)	Total Fertility Rate (1995–2000) (per woman)
Angola	44.6	172	295	—	7.2
Botswana	44.4	74	101	330	4.4
Malawi	40.7	117	188	1,100	6.8
Mozambique	40.6	126	200	1,100	6.3
Namibia	45.1	56	69	230	5.3
South Africa	56.7	55	70	—	3.1
Zambia	40.5	112	202	650	6.0
Zimbabwe	42.9	73	117	700	5.0
Sub-Saharan Africa	48.8	107	174	—	5.8
World	66.4	56	81	—	2.8

Source: United Nations Development Programme 2002, 176–177.

my" that has them caring for the AIDS-afflicted and dying, often at great risk to themselves. In the case of both economic reform and HIV/AIDS, women have taken over the tasks, now burdens, abandoned by states and governments.

These crises rob women and states of incentives and resources to deepen the commitment to gender equality. Moreover, they threaten democratic transitions and, ipso facto, the constitutional protections that these fragile polities might offer to women. Finally, even political advances such as those achieved by Mozambique, Namibia, and South Africa need to be cemented by corresponding changes at the grassroots level. In short, if it is to move beyond tokenism, greater representation at the state level must also be accompanied by measures to entrench gender equality at the societal level as well.

■ Notes

1. According to Berger (1999, 29): "In Tswana society, the ever present threat of drought helped to shape local forms of male domination and female submissiveness."

2. Meredith McKittrick (1998, 244) argues that it was actually seniority rather than age that mattered, and that "seniority is in fact more than age; it is a status which can be achieved only in certain circumstances." Especially as the colonial period progressed, not everyone was guaranteed senior status simply by becoming physically old. "Young people recognized this, and looked to new ideas and systems of authority that might hold a strong promise of increased status and economy power"—for example, migrant labor or Christianity.

3. Staudt (1987, 200) writes of a deliberate policy in colonial Kenya "to create competition and jealousy" in an effort to spur men to work. Wrote one colonial official of the rural woman in colonial Kenya: "She must be educated to want a better home, better furnishings, better food, better water supplies, etc. and if she wants them she will want them for her children. In short, the sustained effort from the male will only come when the woman is educated to the stage when her wants are never satisfied."

4. According to Staudt (1987, 197): "Early colonial governments put little or no energy into public education, especially for girls, but they did support and cooperate with mission education. As late as the 1950s, mission stations still controlled 80 to 90 percent of schools, with supplementary government grants-in-aid provided."

5. Gwendolyn Mikell (1997, 17) identifies four factors as significant in establishing a new form of gender bias during the colonial period: "1) Christianity, with its notions of monogamy and female domesticity and subordination; 2) Westernized education, which gave men advantages over women; 3) differential marriage systems, with Western marriage guaranteeing women access to property rights that women married under traditional rites could not claim; 4) alternative legal systems that supposedly acknowledged African women's independent rights, although colonial magistrates often treated women as jural minors needing male guardians."

6. Aili Tripp (2001, 146) writes: "Former dictator Hastings Banda of Malawi required members of the League of Malawi women to be present at all official functions, dress in party uniforms, singing and dancing in praise of him. Such women's

organizations were tied to the party's dictates and its overriding interest in securing women's votes. Similarly the women's leagues were unable to fight forcefully for women's interests if these were at odds with the priorities and goals of the ruling party."

7. According to James Zaffiro (1997, 20): "The Botswana constitution is silent regarding unfair or unequal treatment of citizens based on gender. Women still lack essential legal protections. Since patriarchy was a significant element of traditional Tswana society, nationalists who drafted key documents consciously omitted language outlining rights and protections of women."

8. According to Gisela Geisler (2000, 608) the formation of the Federation of South African Women was "premised on the observation that the existing male dominated political organizations were unlikely to meet women's specific needs . . . and although the organization claimed full gender equality . . . its membership 'wanted to expand the scope of women's work within nationalist liberation.'"

9. In Namibia, three women were among the first members of SWAPO to flee the country, found an exile base in Tanzania, and commence military training in the 1960s (Bauer 2004).

10. According to Berger (1999, 60): "When a rural woman in 1994 suggested that land permits in resettled areas be registered jointly in the names of both spouses, President Robert Mugabe retorted, 'If women want property, then they should not get married.'"

11. Author interview with the Oasis Forum Executive Committee, Lusaka, June 9, 2001.

12. "The legal framework in its current form perpetuates the disadvantaged and marginalized status of the women of Zambia. 1) Thirty nine years after independence the Zambian Constitution remains largely silent on issues of gender, women and children. Women remain subordinated, with limited access to resources and high levels of illiteracy. 2) Women suffer legalized discrimination as supported by the supreme law of the land, the Zambian Constitution in article 23 (4) (c), which allows discrimination in the area of personal laws. These are the areas such as marriage, property ownership, etc. which are of critical importance to women. 3) Zambia is party to a range of international instruments. Yet the women of this country can not enjoy the benefits of these because of lack of domestication of instruments such as the CEDAW, the SADC Declaration on Gender and Development and its Addendum." Press Conference by the Women's Movement on the State of the Nation and the Constitutional Review Process, Nakatindi Hall, Lusaka, June 25, 2003, http://www.ngocc.org.zm/press/press-releases/press%206-2003.htm.

13. Beall (2001, 137–138) writes that official national machineries for women, set up in more than 140 countries in recent decades, are a direct result of the United Nations Decade for Women (1975–1985). These include women's units, bureaus, desks, and ministries that, however, often lacked sufficient status, resources, and influence. Over time national machineries sought to focus more on linking gender issues and national policy and involving women's organizations from civil society.

14. Since the Beijing Conference in 1995 national machineries for women have been strengthened in a number of countries in the region. In Zambia a department of women was elevated to a gender-in-development division based in the cabinet office; in Botswana a women's affairs division has been elevated to a department; and in Zimbabwe in 1997 a small department under a minister responsible for gender was set up in the office of the president (SARDC-WIDSAA 2000, 30). Granted, these national machineries are dominated by the ruling parties of their respective governments and may well put party interests above those of women and children.

15. The leading organization in this regard was the Organizacão de Mulheres Moçambicanas, formerly the women's wing of the ruling party but by then a non-governmental organization.

16. Following elections in 2004, 32.8 percent of MPs in South Africa and 25 percent of MPs in Namibia were women. Just before Mozambique's 2004 election, 30 percent of MPs were women.

17. In 1999, according to the SADC Gender Unit, 3.1 percent of local councillors in Zimbabwe, 6.3 percent in Zambia, 15.0 percent in Botswana, and 18.0 percent in South Africa were women.

18. See http://www.gov.za/ministry/index.html; http://www.parliament.gov.na /default.asp.

19. In 1999 the Botswana Congress Party and the Botswana National Front both adopted 30 percent quotas for women on party lists, though neither party has met this target (http://www.idea.int/quota/displaycountry.cfm?countrycode=bw).

20. http://www.idea.int/quota/displaycountry.cfm?countrycode=bw. In South Africa the Municipal Structures Act of 1998 specifies that political parties should "seek to ensure" that 50 percent of candidates on party lists for local elections are women. However, there is no penalty if this recommendation is not followed.

21. Author interview with Rumbi Nhundu, SADC Parliamentary Forum gender officer, Windhoek, June 22, 2002.

22. In a clear sharing of resources and strategies across the region, Namibian women activists acknowledged that their manifesto is clearly modeled on the manifesto drawn up by women activists in Botswana.

12

Southern Africa's International Relations

Southern Africa is a land of enormous contradictions. Along major development indicators, it leads the continent. It has the wealthiest population per capita, the most urbanized population, the greatest industrial base, and the leading commercial agriculture output. It is also endowed with ample natural resources, including vast mineral deposits, natural gas, and petroleum; to aid in the exploitation of this natural and human capacity, the region boasts a vast transportation network and advanced communications systems that also work to boost trade and ensure the interconnectedness of the region. Yet southern Africa's promise is counterbalanced by numerous challenges, as described in the previous chapters of this book. The region has the highest HIV/AIDS infection rates in Africa and the world; it is home to four of the world's fifteen poorest countries; and it has millions of internally displaced persons from old conflicts, such as that now ebbing in Angola, and refugees fleeing new conflicts, such as the intractable crisis in Zimbabwe. Indeed, though the issues of trade, economic relations, and AIDS pose long-term challenges for the stability of the region, the Zimbabwe crisis, if unabated, threatens to undermine the positive developments in the region far more quickly. On both the long- and short-term horizon, then, the region's economic performance, investment opportunities, refugee flows, political instability, and high regional and international debt loads hang in the balance. There are, in short, many issues in the realm of international relations worthy of examination, as well as multiple perspectives through which to examine those issues in the southern Africa context.

This chapter emphasizes international concerns that can broadly be described as economic, rather than political, although they too are clearly important. In the absence of the war and interstate conflict that prevailed in the previous decades, the key to regional development lies in the region's ability to master international and intraregional economic relations.

Economic as well as political issues at the state and substate level have been addressed in the country chapters. The AIDS crisis, though clearly a transborder phenomenon with implications for regional development, was the subject of Chapter 10. This chapter speaks to the regional, continental, and "global" levels of analysis. There is also a growing tension, of sorts, between regionalism and internationalism—that is, between southern African states' identities as regional players and their identity and roles as global actors (Khadiagala and Lyons 2001, 2). As a result, at each level of analysis, there is not only a discernible tension between the role of structures and that of agents, but there are also forces at play that impact the coherence of southern Africa *as a region*.

The remainder of the chapter is divided into five sections. The first section examines southern Africa's principal regional institutions. The most prominent among these is the fourteen-member Southern African Development Community (SADC), although there are two other entities that warrant examination—the Southern African Customs Union (SACU) and Common Market for Eastern and Southern Africa (COMESA)—which at times complement SADC but often duplicate it. Despite the plethora of regional unions, the history of regional integration efforts in Africa is not very encouraging. Harmonizing trade and sectoral policies, a prerequisite for more comprehensive integration, has been difficult, as most of the states in the region have competing rather than complementary products and resources to offer the global marketplace. Moreover, with the exception of Botswana, Namibia, and South Africa, the countries in the region are weak states, lacking bureaucratic capacity and autonomy. As Gilbert Khadiagala (2001, 149) observes, "weak states furnish fragile bases for regionalism. . . . This is why the debilitating conflicts in Angola, the DRC [Democratic Republic of Congo], Lesotho, and Zimbabwe nullify institution building and postpone the creation of sturdy mechanisms for both economic development and security."[1] Nevertheless, it is also the case that greater promise for regional integration and development exists in southern Africa than in other regions on the continent.

The second section builds on this notion of regional strength, in terms of both economic clout and leadership, to address southern Africa's position within Africa as a whole. Southern Africa's relative economic development, its concentration of democratically elected governments, its regional hegemon South Africa (and President Thabo Mbeki's prominence in continental and international circles) all combine to give the region a leading profile on the continent. Indeed, led by Mbeki and South Africa, southern Africa has emerged as something of a focal point for recent pan-African initiatives, such as the African Union (AU) and the New Partnership for African Development (NEPAD). Few other countries, and few leaders, in Africa are in a position to lead such continental initiatives.

The third section of the chapter addresses the impact of globalization on southern Africa. In the 1980s, Africa's ties to the international community turned increasingly negative, as southern Africa became a hub of Cold War proxy battles, as the continent became increasingly marginalized, and as austerity programs in the form of structural adjustment programs (SAPs) were first imposed. In recent years, although Africa's structural dependency has not decreased, and in fact has worsened by many measures, the relationship with the outside world has become more complex than simplistic structuralist accounts allow. Moreover, neoliberal economic policies and the global free trade regime have created important opportunities for some states while severely undermining others. Some have suggested that this differential impact on the region's states could be eliminated through a collective, "new regionalist" strategy, enabling all southern African countries to derive benefits from globalization and relations with the global north.

Chapter 7 focused on Zimbabwe, but treated the crisis there as a domestic phenomenon, albeit one with both political and economic origins. In the fourth section of this chapter, we reexamine the crisis in Zimbabwe at the international level of analysis. Specifically, we consider the economic and political problems it poses for southern Africa, both within the region and for the region's relations with the developed world. By and large, African states, particularly in the south, have closed ranks around Zimbabwe, despite the fact that the devastation in that country, wrought mostly by the ruling party, will have profoundly negative regional and continental implications if it continues unchecked. Furthermore, it threatens to poison southern Africa's relations with the international community, by contributing to a view that the region is unstable, cannot enforce collective security concerns, and is not fully committed to transparent, democratic governance. The final section concludes with some perspectives on the direction of the region as a whole.

■ Southern African Regional Institutions and Issues

The region has three principal organizations that represent different levels of economic integration: the Southern African Customs Union, the Common Market for Eastern and Southern Africa, and the Southern African Development Community. This discussion focuses chiefly on SADC, which is the most comprehensive in scope and encompasses all of the states of the region, though it treats the other two organizations briefly.

▨ *SACU*

SACU has a narrow membership, which consists of only Botswana, Lesotho, South Africa, Swaziland, and Namibia. For these states, however,

SACU has fulfilled a number of positive functions. Established in the early twentieth century, SACU "serves as the best example of a customs union in sub-Saharan Africa. Except for agricultural products, the movement of goods within SACU countries is duty free, and member countries have a common external tariff" (Mshomba 2000, 177). SACU is a revenue-sharing arrangement. Given its origins in the colonial era, SACU overwhelmingly favored South Africa and created greater dependency on that country by its putative partners in the agreement. Some of these imbalances were subsequently addressed in renegotiations to the agreement in 1969 and in the 1990s (Sidaway and Gibb 1998, 173).

■ COMESA

The Common Market for Eastern and Southern Africa came into being in December 1994, but its origins lay in the Preferential Trade Area for Eastern and Southern Africa, which was established in 1981. By 1999, COMESA had seventeen members, including eight SADC states. Under apartheid, South Africa was excluded from both bodies. Prior to 1992, SADC and COMESA complemented one another: "SADC pursued a strategy of regional cooperation via sectoral development and the PTA/COMESA a strategy of trade integration" (Lee 2003, 88). After 1992, however, SADC decided to transform itself into a development community, thereby essentially duplicating COMESA's functions, including the removal of all non-tariff barriers and free movement of goods and services (Khadiagala 2001, 137).

The advent of majority rule in South Africa in 1994, therefore, was met with considerable anxiety by both SADC and COMESA adherents, as it was clear that the institution favored by South Africa, with an economy that dwarfs its neighbors, would be most likely to endure. South Africa's decision not to join COMESA severely undermined its prospects. Initially, SADC leaders wanted the trade functions claimed by COMESA to be incorporated into SADC, but this became unnecessary as SADC advised its members to quit COMESA in 1994 (Mshomba 2000, 186).[2] Among the problems plaguing COMESA is its unwieldiness. Whereas "SADC is massively heterogeneous in terms of economic and political conditions, most of its members are linked through a certain functional unity, derived from the (colonial) network of labour migration, trade and communications that was centered on the industrial, minerals-energy economy of South Africa. . . . COMESA does not enjoy even this asymmetric and uneven set of linkages" (Sidaway and Gibb 1998, 171). Margaret Lee (2003, 88–89) suggests that COMESA continues to claim members in southern Africa solely for political reasons; specifically, states resent South African domination within SADC.

■ *SADC*

The Southern African Development Community has a very different origin than its counterparts and an orientation that extends beyond the objective of economic integration to political and military cooperation and development functions. SADC's origins lie in the Frontline States, the regional political body established in 1975 to counteract apartheid South Africa. The hostile international and regional context in which the Frontline States emerged prompted its members to adopt something of a siege mentality, which also affected domestic institutions, such as the development of strong presidencies. "With the decolonization of Zimbabwe in 1980, the [Frontline States] moved to incorporate the more economically vulnerable regional states into an inclusive alliance, SADCC [the Southern African Development Coordination Conference], that sought economic integration and dependence reduction through sectoral coordination" (Khadiagala 2001, 133).

The original SADCC was established by the 1980 Lusaka Declaration, to which there were nine signatories: Angola, Botswana, Lesotho, Malawi, Mozambique, Swaziland, Tanzania, Zambia, and Zimbabwe. Namibia joined upon its independence in 1990. SADCC was a less "defensive" structure than the Frontline States, aiming chiefly to reduce economic dependence on South Africa, foster regional integration, and promote resource mobilization (Sidaway and Gibb 1998, 166). In none of these goals was SADCC particularly successful, however. When black majority rule appeared imminent in South Africa, SADCC was transformed into SADC (in 1992). When the African National Congress (ANC) was elected to power in 1994, South Africa joined SADC.

SADC seeks to move beyond the sectoral coordination efforts that preoccupied its predecessor organization, into deeper cooperation that would facilitate true regional integration, such as the creation of a common market including currency and labor integration, trade barrier elimination, and so on (Khadiagala 2001, 136). However, the failure of the SADDC generated great skepticism that the new organization would be able to deliver development or regional integration either. Even SADC's small secretariat in Gaborone, Botswana, was undersupported and the organization was highly dependent upon donors for project assistance (Sidaway and Gibb 1998, 166).

By the mid-1990s SADC included twelve member states: Angola, Botswana, Lesotho, Malawi, Mauritius, Mozambique, Namibia, South Africa, Swaziland, Tanzania, Zambia, and Zimbabwe; the Democratic Republic of Congo and Seychelles joined in 1997. South Africa, it was assumed, "would serve as the locomotive of recovery, growth and development for the region and the rest of [sub-Saharan Africa]" (Tsie 2001, 133). As Balefi Tsie (2001, 133) notes, South Africa "has the most sophisticated manufacturing industry in SSA, the best infrastructure, a highly developed mining industry, a relatively advanced agricultural sector . . . a robust service sector." South Africa's gross domestic product (GDP) is four times that of the other thirteen SADC countries combined, and its manufacturing value-added is five times that of the others combined, "and nearly 15 times that of the second biggest manufacturer," which was Zimbabwe prior to its collapse. South Africa exports finished manufactured goods to the region, imports raw materials from its neighbors, and exports four times as much as it imports from the region (Tsie 2001, 133).

In contrast to the other countries in the region, then, South Africa is a developed country, able to play the role of regional hegemon to foster development. But as Tsie (2001, 141) observes, South Africa has declined to play that role. "Unfortunately, available evidence suggests that South Africa is reluctant to assume the role of benign hegemon. . . . Instead, South Africa has increasingly displayed a neo-realist regional economic policy in which it uses its economic power to address domestic problems at the expense of the rest of the region. . . . As a result the previous neo-colonial pattern of regional economic relations [i.e., under apartheid] is being reinforced, this time more and more by South African corporate capital."[3] The consequences of South Africa's pursuit of a neorealist strategy vis-à-vis its neighbors rather than a more idealist "developmental regionalism" (Hettne 1990) are addressed below.

The inclusion of the war-torn DRC in SADC, at the insistence of South Africa, was clearly an error, analysts argue (Sidaway and Gibb 1998, 170; Khadiagala 2001, 145). According to James Sidaway and Richard Gibb (1998, 170), South Africa was anxious to include the DRC in SADC in part to access its resources, particularly its hydroelectric power. Yet the infrastructure of the Congo had been decimated by three decades of misrule and (then) two years of war; it lacked a functioning formal economy. Moreover, its connection to southern Africa was always tenuous, at best. Indeed, the DRC had almost none of the approved criteria for admission to the body, namely proximity to southern Africa, democratic government, and a sharing of SADC's ideals (Sidaway and Gibb 1998, 170). Of even greater concern, the DRC's membership in SADC provided SADC members Angola, Namibia, and Zimbabwe with a plausible excuse for their intervention in the Congo war in 1998: support of a regional ally (Nest 2001).

Stretching Southern Africa: SADC in the DRC

Even with its defensive origins in the Frontline States, SADC's principal function is as an economic body. Yet the emergence of security issues in the region, including in Lesotho in 1994, contributed to the establishment of the SADC Organ on Politics, Defense, and Security, which was launched at an extraordinary summit in Botswana on June 28, 1996. It was intended as a separate structure "to allow more flexibility and timely response, at the highest level, to sensitive and potentially explosive situations" (quoted in "SADC Puts on a New Face" 2001). According to Khadiagala (2001, 141), the organ was to function as the security arm of SADC, concerned with regional stability, political cooperation (including on issues of democracy and human rights), conflict prevention and resolution, and peacekeeping and collective security and defense.[4] However, the organ did not work as planned, especially as it was effectively captured by President Robert Mugabe of Zimbabwe.

Upon its launch, the organ was administered by Zimbabwe's Ministry of Foreign Affairs and headed by Mugabe, who was elected by his SADC counterparts. However, there was some debate in SADC as to the permanence and place of the organ. "It was eventually agreed that those SADC states that feel able to intervene to assist a member state at the request of its government, should do so" ("SADC Puts on a New Face" 2001). This resulted in an ad hoc practice in the interventions in both the DRC and Lesotho, when few if any collective controls were exercised (Khadiagala 2001, 143).

Mugabe, of course, used his position as head of the organ to rationalize Zimbabwe's intervention in the DRC in August 1998. Similarly, the September 1998 intervention by 900 South African and Botswanan troops in Lesotho (where they remained until April 1999) was also poorly conducted and revealed a lack of institutionalization of policies and procedures, although the action was immeasurably less violent and exploitative than the DRC intervention (Nest 2001). In fact, Angola's and Zimbabwe's involvement in the DRC was driven not by regional concerns and collective responsibility, but by far narrower *national* political and security interests, as well as economic opportunity. Mugabe in particular used the "SADC Organ as a unilateral instrument for his own aggressive foreign policy" (Khadiagala 2001, 145). A new Protocol on Politics, Defense, and Security Cooperation was enacted in 2001 in an attempt to rein in some of the functions of the organ (and perhaps of Mugabe, who then rotated out of the chairman's role). Not surprisingly, "the Organ has been a fault line in SADC" ("SADC Puts on a New Face" 2001).

In sum, with SADC's competing and duplicative structures, overexpansion, and diversion to the DRC, among other issues, it is not surprising that it has had scant success as a development body (Khadiagala 2001, 139). Partly to address these shortcomings, SADC underwent a restructuring in 2000–2001 to streamline a conflicting and redundant set of issues and institutions into four directorates: trade, industry, finance, and investment; infrastructure and services; food, agriculture, and natural resources; and social and human development and special programs ("SADC Puts on a

New Face" 2001). Nevertheless, it would appear that the regional institutions and their member states have yet to make regionalism benefit most southern Africans. Indeed, "southern African integration . . . still tends to have a plot from which the mass of the people are excluded" (Sidaway and Gibb 1998, 179). The African Union, in the launch of which South Africa played an instrumental role, has attracted similar criticism.

■ Southern Africa in Africa

▓ *The African Union*

In 2002 the African Union was officially launched in Durban, South Africa, replacing the nearly forty-year-old Organization of African Unity (OAU). Established at Addis Ababa in 1963, the OAU's charter "sought to establish a normative order that would permit the continent's sovereign states to live alongside one another in peace and amity" (Rothchild and Harbeson 2000, 13). Among the principal objectives of the OAU was to assert and protect the sovereignty of Africa's fragile new states; thus territorial integrity and the principle of noninterference were sacrosanct. Unable to project power themselves to defend their borders, weak states needed these assurances of security. However, the inviolability of national borders had disastrous consequences as well, as countless abuses were perpetrated against domestic populations by autocratic regimes that faced little sanction from OAU counterparts. Perhaps the most extreme example of this was the 1994 genocide in Rwanda. The slaughter of nearly 1 million ethnic Tutsis and Hutu sympathizers in just 100 days provided a stark illustration that the extant "institutions of interstate amity and cooperation were inadequate to cope with impending state and interstate dangers" (Rothchild and Harbeson 2000, 13).

Yet as long as the norms were mutually reinforcing and states respected each other's sovereignty, the OAU could persist. The war in the DRC, however, which eventually claimed over 3 million lives, and at one stage involved some eight countries—Angola, Chad, Namibia, Rwanda, Uganda, Zimbabwe, and briefly, Burundi and Sudan—marked an unprecedented degree of interstate conflict in Africa. "Africa's world war" in the Congo, then, decimated the noninterference norm and hastened the demise of the old order symbolized by the OAU (Khadiagala 2000, 98). It bears noting also that the OAU was largely incapable of fulfilling even its basic functions. Chronically underfunded, for example, the OAU was "unable to collect its dues and gripped with immobilism" as well as "unable to offer effective leadership on interstate matters envisaged in the Charter" (Rothchild and Harbeson 2000, 13).

In September 1999 the Sirte Declaration formally proposed that a new African Union should be established to foster continental unity and development and eventually integration along the European Union model. In this early period, Muammar Qaddafi, the controversial Libyan leader, played a leading role in financing and promoting the formation of a union (Huliaras 2001). Qaddafi was determined that the new parliament should be in the Libyan capital, Tripoli, and that he should serve as the initial president of the new body. Drawing on Libya's substantial oil wealth, Qaddafi was able to cultivate support among sub-Saharan African leaders, including by paying their countries' dues to the OAU. Qaddafi would have been a controversial and problematic choice to lead the new body, however, and strong resistance emerged from South African president Thabo Mbeki, among others. In contrast to others, especially Qaddafi, Mbeki enjoyed continental and international legitimacy. Moreover, his profile as a new leader and role in the development of the well-received development initiative the Millennium Africa Program (MAP) made him an attractive choice to serve as the AU's first chairperson (Hope 2002).

The AU replicates some of the OAU's more problematic structures, including that its chief representation remains at the presidential level. The main body of the AU is its assembly body, which is composed of the heads of state of the fifty-two AU members. Its executive council, which is responsible to the assembly, is a subordinate body composed of ministers designated by the governments of member states. In turn, there are eight commissioners, each of whom is responsible for a portfolio.[5] Where the AU attempts to depart from its predecessor organization is in its effort to better institutionalize governing structures, along the lines of the European Union model. Hence a pan-African parliament is in the works that will, AU officials believe, "ensure the full participation of African peoples in governance, development and economic integration of the Continent." Other administrative bodies, including a peace and security council, are in the process of ratification, and additional planned structures include an economic, social, and cultural council and a court of justice (http://www .africa-union.org/home/welcome.htm). As OAU adherents learned in the past, however, the problem is not the existence of such institutions. Rather it is that they are not endowed with appropriate resources and the legitimacy that would enable them to carry out their mandate. The paucity of resources on the continent for interstate institution building threatens the establishment and the autonomy of the AU.

◾ *NEPAD*

Those who championed the establishment of the AU argued that it marks the beginning of a mature pan-Africanism and a new era of collective identity, responsibility, and development on the African continent. In this vein, perhaps the biggest test of the AU's capacity to deliver is the New Partnership for African Development, which was launched in July 2001, endorsed by the outgoing OAU, and eventually adopted by the AU. NEPAD was the result of the merger between two competing visions of Africa's continental future. The first, articulated by Thabo Mbeki of South Africa, was the Millennium Africa Plan; the other was the Omega Plan, advocated by Senegalese president Abdoulaye Wade. Mbeki, who held the first AU chairmanship and whose MAP proposal became the principal basis for NEPAD, is perhaps most closely associated with "New Africa" globalization and the effort to promote an "African Renaissance."[6] Although NEPAD is a continental rather than exclusively southern African initiative, its origins—and some of its greatest obstacles to implementation—lie in southern Africa.

As its name implies, NEPAD is intended to herald a new era of partnership in Africa, both with the global North, symbolizing an end to exploitation and neocolonialism, and within the continent. The latter marks an unambiguous departure from the norm of noninterference that characterized the OAU; NEPAD insists that African countries should take interest in what goes on *inside* each others' borders. Toward this end, NEPAD contained among its goals: good governance; democracy, peace, and security; sound economic policy; "smart partnerships" with donors that will "reward achievers"; and domestic ownership of the programs enacted (Hope 2002). NEPAD embodied "a pledge by African leaders . . . that they have a pressing duty to eradicate poverty and place their countries, both individually and collectively, on a path of sustainable growth and development. . . . [Further] the Programme is anchored on the determination of *Africans to extricate themselves* and the continent from the malaise of underdevelopment and exclusion in a globalising world" (UNECA 2001, emphasis added).

In the developed world, therefore, NEPAD was greeted more favorably than previous initiatives because it adopted a new and seemingly aggressive framework that advances a uniquely intra-African collective responsibility. Similarly, its principal architects, particularly Mbeki, Wade, and Nigerian president Olusegun Obasanjo, each democratically elected, were hailed as exemplars of responsible leadership in Africa (Taylor and Nel 2002), and regarded by some as enlightened free marketeers and staunch advocates of democracy, good governance, human rights, and the rule of law (Hope 2002, 402).

NEPAD rejects withdrawal from the "world system" (Wallerstein 1974). Indeed, it fundamentally *opposes* exclusion and seeks greater integration into the global economy. Hence the envisioned integration embraces and affirms the dominant neoliberal paradigm. Critics of this approach argue that NEPAD's intention to "participate in the globalisation process" (UNECA 2001) amounts to business as usual (Taylor and Nel 2002). Problematically, as evidenced by its sponsors' appeals for financing to the Group of Eight (G8) countries, NEPAD relies substantially on the developed nations, and is not, practically speaking, a program of Africans solely extricating *themselves*. In this sense, NEPAD is not appreciably different from previous proposals, such as the African Alternative Framework, that also relied on donor states to get off the ground (Lancaster 2000).[7] At the same time, NEPAD's appeal to the global North is neither unrealistic nor unreasonable: whereas African agents bear great responsibility, the continent's malaise is hardly exclusively self-imposed; therefore, neither should its solutions be (Mkandawire and Soludo 1999). Yet because NEPAD duplicates many of the same donor dependencies of its predecessor strategies—a point sometimes obscured in the NEPAD policy documents—its proponents should expect similar problems ahead.[8]

Indeed, even as early as one year after its official launch, NEPAD appeared to be languishing. First was the 2002 G8 summit in Alberta, Canada. International terrorism dominated almost exclusively, despite the expectation that a substantial portion of the agenda would be dedicated to Africa and the developing world. Africa sought some U.S.$64 billion from the G8 for NEPAD, but only U.S.$6 billion was committed, sparking considerable outcry and disappointment ("G-8 Guilty" 2002). The 2003 G8 meeting, in Evian, France, yielded developed country support for fighting AIDS (a subject omitted, inexplicably, from NEPAD) but not through the NEPAD mechanism. These setbacks were anticipated by Ian Taylor and Philip Nel (2002, 164), who argued that the "New Africa" project of Mbeki and others "play[ed] into the hands of the [G8] strategists."

Where NEPAD does substantially depart from previous African-led approaches is in its "peer review mechanism," which insists, essentially, that Africa must police itself, particularly on issues of governance and democracy. At the launch of NEPAD, it appeared that this mechanism would give the AU power to impose various sanctions on errant member states. But the peer review system was only just beginning to materialize by the end of 2003, and in any event, participation—including a report on conditions in a given state done within six months of a visit by an "eminent persons" team—is to be on a voluntary basis. More problematic, the notion of peer review also reveals another major fault line in NEPAD. The persistence of conflict (including internal strife and political repression) anywhere on the continent poses tremendous legitimacy problems for NEPAD. The longer these continue unabated, the more NEPAD's credibility is eroded. This dilemma is particularly acute in southern Africa, which should be a centerpiece of Mbeki's "African Renaissance," but instead plays host to the Zimbabwe problem. In direct contradiction to the spirit, if not the letter, of

NEPAD, African countries like South Africa have opted for quiet, or passive, diplomacy in relation to Robert Mugabe. The elite stance on Zimbabwe, led by Mbeki and what has been disparagingly labeled as his "softly-softly" approach, forestalls any prospect of a deepening partnership with the West, at least via NEPAD and the AU.

■ Globalization and Southern Africa

▨ *The Neoliberal Prescription*

As each of the country chapters in this book reveals, the neoliberal model is as predominant in southern Africa as it is throughout the continent. Thus globalization, for our purposes, involves liberal or market-driven policies on trade, investment, employment, government spending, and so on. In theory, such policies are expected to undergird development; at worst, they may spark a "race to the bottom" with respect to labor, the environment, social spending, and poverty levels (Korten 2001). The vehicle for the neoliberal agenda is typically the structural adjustment program, although several countries in southern Africa, namely Botswana, Namibia, and South Africa, have avoided the SAPs prescribed by the International Monetary Fund and World Bank. None, however, has escaped the effects of globalization on economic life, and none is disconnected from the global economy; a complete delinking is not feasible.

South Africa's "Growth, Equity, and Redistribution" program (GEAR), for example, is a structural adjustment program that is as rigorous, if not more so, as one the international financial institutions (IFIs) might have drawn up themselves (I. Taylor 2002). Moreover, Botswana, with its diamond export–dominated economy, is highly dependent on global markets for this single commodity. Only Zimbabwe has turned its back on the international financial institutions and on its Western bilateral donors. Yet Zimbabwe is scarcely autarkic: it remains dependent on food aid, for example, as well as on its regional counterparts for energy and other essential imports, and on nontraditional sponsor states like Libya (Huliaris 2001; International Crisis Group [ICG] 2003c). Further, there is a widespread expectation that Zimbabwe will return to the global capitalist system, including, especially, IFI-sponsored adjustment, when the Mugabe regime is defeated or collapses (Economist Intelligence Unit 2002b). In short, although some states, notably South Africa, have embraced economic globalization to a greater degree than others, by and large globalization is not a *choice* for southern Africa. The countries of the region are embedded in the global political economy, albeit to highly variable degrees.

The connectedness of the global economy to southern Africa is revealed through trade relations, investment, the international debt regime, and international aid. Since aid is largely a bilateral function, we can dispense with that discussion here and instead refer the reader to the individual country chapters. The international finance regime, on the other hand, is multilateral and not only affects how individual states in the region deal with the IFIs, but also conditions the nature of their relationship with each other, such as through SADC, COMESA, or SACU. Moreover, with the exception of Zimbabwe, countries in the region are engaging more with the forces of globalization rather than delinking from it.

However, neoliberal SAPs, and the wider globalization of which they are a part, have had at best an uneven effect on southern Africa. Most states appear to have been harmed by the austerity measures that accompany SAPs, but what is not known—or knowable—is what the region would look like in the absence of such programs.[9] Privatization and attracting foreign investment, for example, are regarded as an essential corollary to SAPs. Yet critics have noted that under globalization, developing states tend to facilitate transnational investment with shallow and transient ties, leading them to become what James Mittelman (2000) calls "courtesan states." Fickle flows of foreign direct investment (FDI) in Zambia provide just one of many examples.

Indeed, it is clear that such concessions to global capitalism have consequences for states, not only externally, but in their internal relations as well. As Béatrice Hibou (1999, 97) observes, "the unending quest to satisfy the donors' financial requirements has particularly pernicious consequences. Since the survival of the government depends increasingly on its external resources, it is increasingly led to concern itself more with its exterior respectability than its interior legitimacy." Thus, as Pádraig Carmody and Scott Taylor (2003) note, this dependence on transnational forces impels the state to shift its priorities away from a domestic agenda. In southern Africa, the embrace of the market-led model of development has contributed to increased social dislocation, as states struggle to reduce government spending in line with donor prescriptions. Indeed, Malawi, South Africa, Zambia, and Zimbabwe, each of which has undergone an adjustment program, have experienced the consequences of these contradictory policies (Bond 2000; I. Taylor 2002; Carmody and Taylor 2003). Mozambique's experience may have been mitigated, in part, by debt relief provided through the PRSP process, although this too is not without social consequences (Hope 2002, 400).

Notwithstanding the discontent generated by globalization, however, as Jeremy Brecher, Tim Costello, and Brendan Smith point out, a strategy of "delinking" from the global economy, in which neoliberalism is hegemonic, is not one that is replicable, or even survivable for most states:

Imagine a single country withdrawing from the [World Trade Organization], refusing to service its debt, and putting a full array of progressive requirements on foreign investment. Aside from the obvious short-term consequences (e.g. inability to acquire parts, machinery or raw materials, except by barter), it would be cut off in the long run from modern technology, the Internet and everything else that is developed in the global economy. This is a formula for permanent underdevelopment. (2000, 135)

Nonetheless, this is effectively the path chosen by contemporary Zimbabwe, which has led to chronic shortages and near-total economic collapse (Carmody and Taylor 2003).

There may be a middle ground, however, between complete surrender to neoliberal hegemony and autarky, requiring a reinvigorated regional approach that scholars have labeled "mediated integration" or "new regionalism" (Hettne 2001; Carmody and Taylor 2003).

■ *New Regionalism: An Alternative in Southern Africa?*

"Regional trading blocs, it is argued, have the advantage of a larger market and as such become attractive to global operators." In this view, regional trading blocs are likely to be more successful in coping with the challenges of globalization than individual states (Ajulu 2001, 38). However, Balefi Tsie (2001, 136) rejects this benign "neoliberal regionalism"—which focuses on reducing tariffs to facilitate trade, financial market liberalization, and currency convertibility—because it "is premised on the contestable assumption that what is good for local and foreign capital is good for society as a whole or in this specific instance, for regional economies." Indeed, this type of regionalism offers no clues on the structural transformation of the region—plagued by uneven development and competitive, neocolonial production structures—and is likely to lead to political instability (Tsie 2001, 137). In contrast, developmental, or new, regionalism combines the economies of scale derived from regional integration with a call for the state to regulate capitalism at a regional level (Ajulu 2001, 38; Tsie 2001; Hettne 1990, 2001). It focuses on the economic, political, social, and cultural aspects of regionalism. Björn Hettne (1990, 25) defines new regionalism as "political co-operation on a regional level to promote the region as a viable economic, cultural, and ecological unit." In other words, it moves beyond mere economic integration in terms of trade relations and regards integration as a political and cultural matter.

Because of the historical ties between the countries in the region, a new regionalist project would appear to have more promise in southern Africa than in any other area of the continent. Unfortunately, as Carmody and Taylor (2003) note, "new regionalism is also problematic given the small size of Southern Africa's economy and the mobility and structural power of international finance capital. This power may mean that the forces of globalization may trump those of regionalization unless there is a fundamental rethinking of the macro-economic policy regime and current structures of production." Such a rethinking is not on the horizon; in fact, quite the contrary.

Led by South Africa, southern Africa instead appears bent on pursuit of full integration into the world economy (I. Taylor 2002; Taylor and Nel 2002). South Africa continues to deepen ties with the European Union (EU) and the United States at the expense of its neighbors' development. Moreover, although South Africa's exports to the region are largely finished goods, those to the developed world are predominantly raw materials. Thus, as Tsie argues (2001, 142), "in pursuing this line, both the ANC government and South African capital miss the fundamental point that South Africa cannot prosper while its neighbors are sinking deeper into the quagmire of poverty and dependence. Clearly, such a neo-realist policy regime is detrimental to structural transformation and equitable regional integration." Therefore, "it can be concluded that the prospects for balanced regional development in Southern Africa are dim."

In contrast, however, advocates of international free trade reject the neo-Marxist orientation of new regionalism. Further, observing that conditions in southern Africa in the near term are unpropitious even for the type of regional integration favored by neoliberals, such scholars applaud the trade pacts increasingly executed between Africa and the North (Mshomba 2000, 201–205). Finally, while accepting that a neorealist strategy may benefit South Africa disproportionately as the regional power, free trade advocates contend nonetheless that the introduction of liberalized trade agreements, whether with the United States, such as the Africa Growth and Opportunity Act (AGOA), or with the European Union, redound to the benefit of *each* of the countries of the region. This is not necessarily the case, as examination of two major recent trade agreements reveals.

■ The International Trade Regime

The Africa Growth and Opportunity Act. Signed into law by U.S. president Bill Clinton in May 2000, AGOA began as an eight-year pact designed to permit duty-free imports of certain African goods, particularly clothing and textiles, into the United States; the agreement was expanded to include a wider range of goods under the U.S. Trade Act of 2002.[10] In July 2004 it was extended to 2015 by the George W. Bush administration. The preferential trade agreement allows up to 3.5 percent of these imports to come from sub-Saharan Africa. As Eckhart Naumann (2003) notes, however, whereas AGOA has been touted "as the success story of US economic policy towards Africa, it has not increased aggregate African exports to the US. Instead, the value of total exports to the US from the 38 countries has shrunk by almost a quarter (in dollar terms) since AGOA's inception."[11] What has happened instead is that AGOA has supplanted non-AGOA exports to the United States from African countries. However, "a growing share of exports to the US from AGOA-eligible countries qualifies for duty-free access under this programme. [In 2002], this amounted to almost $9 billion, or roughly 65 percent of all exports" (Naumann 2003).

Many of the presumed benefits from AGOA are misleading because only a limited number of countries can actually take advantage of the program (Lee 2003, 183). Further, "more than 75 percent of exports under AGOA consist of relatively unprocessed products such as petroleum, which have low import tariff levels anyway. These are predominantly from Nigeria and Gabon."[12] Nonenergy exports are still dwarfed by petroleum, and the nonenergy sector that benefited most, clothing and textiles, accounted for only around 7 percent of the total in 2003 (U.S. International Trade Commission 2003). In southern Africa, the principal beneficiaries of AGOA's textile and clothing allotment are Mauritius and Lesotho.

AGOA contains numerous provisions and restrictions that make it an unreliable vehicle for the expansion of southern African export-oriented sectors. Strict restrictions on rules of origin (designed to thwart transshipment as a means of evading U.S. tariffs from Asian countries) were scheduled to enter into force in September 2004, although this was extended to 2007. Even with the longer grace period, however, the gains for African textile sectors may prove fragile. Moreover, according to the AGOA legislation, the U.S. president may designate sub-Saharan Africa countries eligible to receive the benefits of AGOA "if they are making progress in such areas as the establishment of market-based economies; development of political pluralism and the rule of law; elimination of barriers to US trade and investment; protection of intellectual property; efforts to combat corruption; policies to reduce poverty; increased availability of healthcare and educational opportunities; protection of human rights and worker rights; and elimination of certain practices of child labour" (du Toit 2003). The situation in Zimbabwe, therefore, bars that country's participation in AGOA.

As of March 2003, thirty-eight sub-Saharan African countries had been approved as AGOA-eligible, which admittedly is a significant percentage of sub-Saharan Africa's forty-seven states. Yet whereas recipient countries do not necessarily have to demonstrate equal progress in each area in order to be eligible, AGOA is clearly subject to the vagaries of U.S. domestic politics, as well as broader U.S. foreign policy concerns. As a result, critics question its capacity to facilitate long-term, sustainable development on the continent.

In sum, AGOA offers numerous opportunities for African states to export goods to the United States at no tariff. However, the structure of

AGOA favors petroleum-producing states and the handful of countries that have competitive or reasonably competitive textile sectors, including the southern African states of Mauritius, Lesotho, and South Africa.[13] For the remainder of sub-Saharan Africa and southern African countries, AGOA has not generated the degree of trade and investment envisioned by its early champions. Further, the existence of AGOA notwithstanding, the region is not all moving in the same direction regarding trade with the North; one of the initial criticisms of AGOA is that the poorest, least-developed nations in Africa would lack the industrial and export infrastructure to be able to take advantage of AGOA's provisions. Indeed, they certainly have not been able to benefit to the degree South Africa or Angola has.

South Africa has been a major beneficiary of the AGOA legislation, although the country ran trade surpluses with the United States over the past several years, even before AGOA. In general, "the US tends to export higher value-added products to SA, while export opportunities for SA products do exist in the fields of auto components, footwear and leather, wine, machinery, chemicals, jewelry and cut flowers" (du Toit 2003). In the area of textiles specifically (a major AGOA target), South Africa's own actions have hindered the ability of its regional partners to take advantage of AGOA. Notably, South Africa adheres to protectionist policies on yarns, textiles, and cotton produced by its regional counterparts; the result is higher-cost production in South Africa and the destruction of lower-cost producers in the region. Thus instead of using AGOA as a stepping-stone for the development of a globally competitive, *regionally based* textile industry, South Africa pursues a "go it alone," zero-sum strategy (Lee 2003, 191).

Since the end of apartheid, all of the southern African countries have increased their dependence on South Africa, notwithstanding this deepening one-way relationship. Yet whereas other countries run substantial trade deficits with South Africa and have experienced heavy investment and intervention by South African firms, South Africa instead looked increasingly to the European Union, as well as the United States. Richard Mshomba (2000, 197) suggests that free trade partnerships between Europe or the United States and Africa tend to "divert (rather than direct)" African attempts at regional economic cooperation, as the African states compete among themselves for attention and assistance from the developed "partners." This appears to have been the case with South Africa's October 1999 trade pact with the EU, which in fact "chagrined" other SADC members (Khadiagala 2001, 139).

Southern Africa and the European Union. In 1999, South Africa signed a trade, development, and cooperation agreement with the EU, its main trading partner, following three years of negotiations. The agreement stipulated the creation of a free trade area to be implemented over a twelve-year transition period in accordance with World Trade Organization rules ("South Africa Signs" 1999). Pursuant to the agreement, South Africa will offer duty-free access to 86 percent of its EU imports over the twelve-year period. Conversely, the EU is to grant duty-free status to 95 percent of South African exports. On paper, the EU was to open its market at a much faster pace, and was scheduled to complete most liberalization by 2002, but progress has been slower than expected. The EU is to eliminate all tariffs on exports of industrial goods from South Africa over time, as well as on 75 percent of agricultural products, including "sensitive products" like cut flowers and fruit. However, since the bulk of South African exports are primary goods, including metals and minerals, it is hard to see the major benefits accruing to South Africa as a result of this pact. Moreover, South Africa enjoyed greater access to EU markets than the EU did to South Africa prior to the trade agreement, thereby suggesting that South Africa gained more before its enactment (Lee 2003, 219). Margaret Lee (2003, 209) writes that "although the EU is a major trading partner for South Africa, South Africa is not a major trading partner for the EU." Hence, fully liberalized trade with South Africa scarcely threatens the EU, but in South Africa deindustrialization and unemployment are a possible result (Lee 2003, 219), although "sensitive products" (for South Africa, industrial goods) are supposed to take up to ten years (2012) to free up ("South Africa Signs" 1999).

In part stemming from South Africa's perceived neglect of the region and its protectionism, the agreement with the EU generated resistance in the region, as well as within South Africa itself.[14] South Africa's SACU partners, for example, were unenthusiastic about the agreement (Wadula and Maletsky 1999). Not only does the agreement threaten serious repercussions for Botswana, Lesotho, Namibia, and Swaziland, but these countries were not consulted about its establishment, even though their approval is required by SACU treaty (Lee 2003, 220). Moreover, as a de facto EU-*SACU* free trade area (Lee 2003, 220), the agreement effectively governed the trade policies of other SACU members, and these countries risked losing their own preferential, *nonreciprocal* benefits with the EU as a result.[15] According to Patrick Wadula and Christof Maletsky (1999), since "SACU has a common external tariff and all tariffs collected are surrendered to a common revenue pool and shared by all the member countries according to an agreed formula. . . . [T]he EU-SA agreement will mean reduced tariff revenue, which will reduce the revenue pool. Given that the EU accounts for a major portion of the [imports from Botswana, Lesotho, Namibia, and Swaziland], this revenue loss will be substantial." Lee puts the loss between U.S.$400 million and U.S.$800 million per year. Finally, all SADC countries must face greater competition from EU goods (including the EU's highly subsidized agriculture products) under the arrangement for access to the South African market (Lee 2003, 222). SACU countries, because of the common tariff, face EU competition within their own borders as well.

Whereas the long-term impact of the South Africa–EU trade deal remains unclear, it did promptly serve to reduce the competitiveness of U.S. imports to the country and region, which continued to attract higher tariffs. Thus, in 2003 the United States renewed a push for a new free trade agreement with SACU countries. If adopted, a free trade agreement would substantially replace the preferential access to U.S. markets that SACU countries currently enjoy under AGOA, but make such access more permanent. Yet while it would presumably open new markets in the United States for SACU countries, an SACU-U.S. free trade agreement potentially would also expose southern Africa to a far greater flow of U.S. imports, including U.S.-subsidized agricultural production and superior U.S. manufactured goods. These changes could reverse many of the benefits achieved thus far under AGOA. Moreover, it is worth reconsidering Mshomba's admonition (2000, 197) regarding a prospective free trade agreement with the United States: "If sub-Saharan African countries were honest with themselves and the United States [and by extension, the EU], they would have expressed their appreciation for the initiative and affirmed their belief in economic integration while explaining that it was too soon to discuss a free trade area with the United States." Regional subgroups like SACU or SADC have yet to achieve the level of integration and development necessary to establish a free trade agreement that would generate widely shared benefits. Yet in their headlong rush to consummate such deals, South Africa serves to undermine the region as a whole.

■ The Zimbabwe Dilemma

Zimbabwe has emerged as a fundamental obstacle to further economic and political integration in the region. Since Zimbabwe's decline accelerated beginning in 2000, the country has maintained its linkages to regional institutions such as SADC and, at a wider level, the AU; however, Zimbabwe plainly has become a liability for its erstwhile regional partners.

Zimbabwe's present condition is ironic. It was a key actor in the creation of SADCC in 1980, served as an anchor of stability in the region, especially in the tumult of the 1980s, and was regarded by some as a model for the successful transition from late settler rule (Herbst 1990).[16] Today, however, Zimbabwe is a laggard in a region that is generally marked by political stability, improving economic performance and some democratic promise. Indeed, some of the previous worst performers in the region are experiencing remarkable turnarounds. Peace and the prospect of civilian transition, once unimaginable, have come to Angola. Mozambique recently faced the prospect of democratic turnover. Zambia began to aggressively combat corruption (ICG 2002). Conversely, Zimbabwe's distinguishing features include an economy in free fall, unbridled political repression, and astronomical AIDS infection rates. Indeed, by these and other objective measures, Zimbabwe is in worse condition than ever. What is perhaps most striking about the Zimbabwe case is the rapidity of its collapse, and the fact that (as of this writing, at least), its fall has not precipitated the corresponding collapse—economic, political, social—of its better-performing but nonetheless fragile neighbors.

The structural similarities between Zimbabwe and its regional counterparts, particularly Namibia and South Africa, have been noted by numerous authors; indeed, we have emphasized them in this book. Both Namibia and South Africa have small but powerful white minorities who enjoy disproportionate economic privilege and land ownership vis-à-vis blacks, and race and class covary in highly destabilizing ways. It is less important that what precipitated Zimbabwe's collapse was not racial divisions per se; of prominence is the fact that President Mugabe could draw on those divisions in an attempt to score political points. If Zimbabwe is not a model for Namibia and South Africa, we should at least regard it as a cautionary tale for the future of the two other postsettler societies in the region.

Importantly, Mugabe himself has escaped widespread or sustained condemnation (certainly publicly) from his counterparts in the region for his destruction of the economy, subversion of the rule of law, and his persecution of the opposition, white and black. In fact, as early as May 2000 Mugabe urged his SADC neighbors in Namibia and South Africa to adopt the same approach, at least in regard to race relations: "It is a simple solution. If the other neighboring countries have problems similar to the ones we have encountered, why not apply the same solution as Zimbabwe. If the white commercial farmers are ready to discuss with you and give land then there is no need for a fight. But in Zimbabwe the British are not ready and we are making them ready now" (quoted in Khadiagala 2001, 152).

Mugabe's regional counterparts have come under repeated criticism from domestic activists and international observers for their inaction on Zimbabwe. Perhaps no one has attracted more attention than South Africa's Thabo Mbeki, whose position has been complicated by the high expectations that have accompanied his ambitious programs or his democratic legitimacy. Mbeki's behavior is all the more surprising considering that the fate of Zimbabwe will likely affect the prospects for the AU and NEPAD, two projects in which he has a major personal and political stake (ICG 2002). Indeed, Western critics, whose economic support is essential to the success of NEPAD and the AU, argue that "the unwillingness to confront the Mugabe policies more robustly has almost single-handedly destroyed the credibility of the nascent NEPAD" (ICG 2003b, 11).

Other members of SADC have been similarly muted in their criticism, as has the organization itself, despite the fact that Zimbabwe contravened various SADC directives before and during its March 2002 presidential election.[17] Some international observers of the Zimbabwe scene have advocated placing pressure on South Africa, which is responsible for 50 percent of Zimbabwe's imports and a significant portion of its electrical power, to use this economic leverage to compel Mugabe to reach a political solution with the opposition and to restore some semblance of democracy in the country (ICG 2002, 16).[18] Such pressure has repeatedly backfired, however, as SADC countries appear unwilling to take actions that will unleash even greater chaos in Zimbabwe. There is also a political loyalty issue at play that is admittedly difficult for analysts to dissect. In power since 1980, Mugabe is an elder statesman in the region and one of the few remaining leaders of the independence and antiapartheid eras. This legacy affords him a certain degree of deference in the region, especially among liberation movement leaders like Namibia's Sam Nujoma. Further, for their own domestic legitimacy and credibility, leaders like Mbeki are reluctant to be seen as carrying out a British or U.S. agenda with regard to Zimbabwe (ICG 2003b, 11). More concretely, Mugabe and Zimbabwe are part of a mutual defense pact with Angola and Namibia, whose presidents, Eduardo dos Santos and Sam Nujoma, are among Mugabe's staunchest supporters. Other SADC countries, chiefly South Africa, must be wary of taking any action that leans too hard on Mugabe—economic, political, or military— that would risk splitting the region (ICG 2002, 11).

In sum, the region is effectively paralyzed over Zimbabwe. Mugabe has deftly used the issues of race and regional solidarity to forestall any action against him, "the AU has largely deferred to SADC on Zimbabwe" (ICG 2003c, 13), and SADC has shown great reluctance to act, either jointly or individually. One thing that is abundantly clear is that Zimbabwe places the region under increasing strain, notwithstanding the damage already done to the institutions such as SADC and NEPAD, not to mention the unity of the Commonwealth. Refugees numbering more than 2 million have fled Zimbabwe, mostly to South Africa, straining fragile services there and elsewhere. The International Crisis Group estimates that the Zimbabwe crisis has cost South Africa some U.S.$1.9 billion between 2000–2003, claimed 30,000 jobs, and cut its GDP growth rate by 0.4 percent. As mentioned above, tens of millions of dollars are owed to South African public and private firms (ICG 2003b). At the end of the day, even if Zimbabwe's crisis has not been "externalized" to the degree feared by some observers, regional performance, growth, and advancement require stability in the region. Given Zimbabwe's geographic centrality, its large population, and its once significant wealth and economic output, genuine regional advancement cannot take place as long as the crisis continues.

■ Conclusion

Southern Africa appears to be headed in multiple directions at once. On the one hand, economic giant South Africa continues to anchor the region and lead in the development of trade initiatives with the developed countries that often place it on an equal footing with its new partners. Hence South Africa is generally regarded as having the capacity to act as regional hegemon in southern Africa, promoting and underwriting development and integration between itself and its neighbors. Notwithstanding the potentially detrimental impacts of free trade, other economies in the region are performing, although they remain quite poor. Further, norms of democracy and development and peaceful negotiation appear to have become entrenched throughout most of the region. Each of these factors augurs positively for efforts to develop a regional political economy.

On the other hand, South Africa's global aspirations may come at the *expense* of its neighbors, as it has shown disregard for the consequences of its own trade and investment strategies within the region or of the regional impact of its trade relations with the developed world. As numerous scholars have noted, such actions threaten to leave the region worse off; indeed, South Africa itself will not be well served by a moribund regional economy, regardless of its successes at the "international" level. The crisis in Zimbabwe also threatens economic integration within the region and capital flows from without, as FDI leaves the region or avoids it altogether (Lee 2003, 64).

In the end, even in the absence of an explicitly new regionalist agenda, these dilemmas suggest that southern Africa, and South Africa in particular, must reconsider its internal challenges and establish a cohesive foundation for development at the regional level before turning its attentions inexorably toward the global arena.

■ Notes

1. The Democratic Republic of Congo is a member of SADC; the addition of this (geographically) *central* African nation presents a number of problems for SADC, as discussed in this chapter.

2. Only three SADC countries—Lesotho, Mozambique, and Tanzania—later quit COMESA, and none as a result of the rivalry (Lee 2003, 89).

3. South African conglomerates are covering the continent in terms of investment, and these transcend the regional environment, from Egypt to Ghana. South African capital is increasingly mobile: "For instance from March 1995 until September 2000, the South African Reserve Bank approved 7.85 billion rand worth of direct investment in southern Africa while globally South African corporations received approval for 74.5 billion rand in foreign direct investment overseas" (Taylor and Nel 2002, 170).

4. The organ bore many similarities to the peacekeeping body established by

its West African counterpart, the Economic Community of West African States, whose peacekeeping and peace monitoring force, ECOMOG, was deployed in Liberia in the 1990s.

5. According to the homepage of the AU's official website, the African Union Commission is regarded as "the key organ playing a central role in the day-to-day management of the African Union. Among others, it represents the Union and defends its interests; elaborates draft common positions of the Union; prepares strategic plans and studies;" and so forth. Its eight portfolios are available at the AU homepage: http://www.africa-union.org/home/welcome.htm.

6. Mbeki's "voice has been among the loudest in promoting the New Africa project . . . in elite circles around the globe" (Taylor and Nel 2002, 164). The New Africa Initiative—resulting from the merger of the Omega Plan and MAP—was renamed NEPAD in October 2001.

7. The 1989 Africa Alternative Framework—an African proposal for a model of "independent" development meant to challenge SAPs—was dismissed, in large part because of its (paradoxical) overreliance on Western financing.

8. NEPAD "centres on African ownership and management" (UNECA 2001). The October 2001 NEPAD document does address the bilateral and multilateral role, but in a secondary way: see especially Section 6, "A New Global Partnership," and Section 7, "Implementation of the New Partnership for Africa's Development."

9. For conflicting interpretations of SAPs, compare, for example, adjustment critics Patrick Bond (2000) and John Saul (1999) to Nicolas van de Walle (2001) and Patrick Chabal and Jean Pascal Daloz (1999).

10. "AGOA builds on existing U.S. trade programs, and expands the benefits previously available only under the Generalised System of Preferences (GSP). . . . The number of products qualifying for duty-free access to U.S. market under AGOA presently stands at over 7,000, including the 4,600 GSP products, approximately 1800 products that have been added under AGOA (including footwear, wine, motor vehicle components etc.) and approximately 600 apparel products (subject to restrictions)" ("About AGOA" n.d.).

11. Total exports to the United States from sub-Saharan Africa declined by 18 percent, to $18.2 billion, between 2000 and 2003, although AGOA exports have increased (U.S. International Trade Commission 2003).

12. "Total non-energy exports under AGOA were $2.17 billion [in 2002], up 60% from $1.35 billion in 2001" (Naumann 2003).

13. In 2002, Lesotho accounted for 28 percent of all apparel imports under AGOA; the two next largest, South Africa and Mauritius, accounted for 18 percent and 23 percent, respectively. As "middle-income" countries, South Africa and Mauritius were subject to more stringent rules of origin requirements than Lesotho, hence the lower totals ("Apparel Trade Under AGOA" n.d.).

14. Licensing requirements instituted by the EU in 2000 for importers of dairy products, however, eliminated benefits on these goods to South African producers (Cook 2001).

15. The Lomé Accord, initiated in the 1970s and renegotiated in four rounds, gave certain trade preferences to African Caribbean and Pacific countries doing business with the EU. In the case of SACU countries, this meant duty-free manufactured exports to the EU and preferential treatment for agricultural goods.

16. Clearly the inclusive processes followed in Namibia and South Africa were far more comprehensive and resulted in liberal and democratic constitutions. Jeffrey Herbst's assessment (1990) preceded Namibian independence by a year.

17. Several provisions of SADC electoral norms and standards were violated,

including those governing the impartiality of the electoral commission, the role of security forces, and the presence of SADC observers (ICG 2002, 2).

18. The South African electrical power company ESKOM and Mozambique's Cahorra Bassa are reportedly owed U.S.$150 million by Zimbabwe's bankrupt state power authority, ZESCO (Cooke, Morrison, and Prendergast 2003, 4).

13

Conclusion: Meeting Regional Challenges

Perhaps it is telling that two recent, otherwise comprehensive political science texts on southern Africa, one empirical and the other theoretical, end without offering conclusions (Bradshaw and Ndegwa 2000; Vale, Swatuk, and Oden 2001). The point is not to impugn the scholarly merit of these works; on the contrary, this observation merely highlights the difficulty of "concluding" the region. York Bradshaw and Stephen Ndegwa (2000) suggest that the "promise" of southern Africa is "uncertain" and such an assessment is valid on its face. But how does the *region* fulfill its promise and transcend uncertainty? The chapters in this book have offered descriptive and analytical perspectives on the politics, society, and institutions of southern Africa. Each chapter ends, quite deliberately, with an investigation of the prospects for the twenty-first century. This chapter returns to that theme, but places it in a wider regional focus.

It is important to revisit the qualities that define southern Africa as a distinctive region, and reexamine the future prospects for the region. Indeed, southern Africa has many of the qualities that Sandra MacLean (1999) labeled "regionness," including a high level of economic interdependence, established communications, and a degree of cultural homogeneity—or at least cultural connectedness—and coherence. More important, however, to these qualities it is worth adding the many other parallels across states and societies. These include history, of course, but also political, social, and economic factors that increasingly bind southern African countries together to create a more encompassing notion of regionness.

The long-standing historical linkages are well established. In many respects, South Africa served as the launching point for the settlement and establishment of other colonies in the region. By the 1890s, each of today's Anglophone states was heavily penetrated by South African commercial interests. The British South Africa Company (BSAC) developed operations initially in Zimbabwe, Zambia, Malawi, and Botswana. Indeed, Peter Vale quotes Robert Rotberg on the powerful impact of the BSAC's Cecil Rhodes:

> Cecil Rhodes, the British imperialist, mining entrepreneur, and successful colonial politician forcefully gave the region its shape. By thrusting iron tentacles relentlessly northward from Cape Town into what is now Botswana, Zimbabwe, Zambia and Zaire, he tied the region's mining centres and population magnets together and bound them to ports of South Africa. His conquest of Zimbabwe, his attempted conquest of Zaire and Mozambique, his successful assertions of economic suzereignty over Zambia and Malawi also forged links . . . which endure in the administrative, legal and linguistic, educational, cultural, political and economic structures of the region. (Rotberg 1995, 9, quoted in Vale 2001, 20)

Later, when these became independent countries, their linkages to South Africa remained, albeit uncomfortably. Moreover, although Angola and Mozambique had a different relationship with South Africa, they were also inextricably linked to South Africa after their independence. Within the region today, only Angola, with its ties to the international petroleum industry, is not dependent on South Africa economically. Many of the states continue to define themselves in relation to South African markets and trade, business, and security.

The importance of South Africa notwithstanding, it is equally important to avoid analysis that is overly South Africa–centric, an approach that can be dismissive of the relevance of domestic-level politics in other states. As the organization of this book suggests, not only are the politics of the individual countries significant, but there is also a "multidirectionality" of politics and social forces that suggests an interaction between the "other countries" of the region and South Africa and among the countries, not including South Africa (see Chapter 12). Thus to suggest that the politics of the region somehow radiates from a South African center is to miss a number of key variables and issues. Indeed, through this interaction, formal and informal, bilateral and multilateral, the region is constructed.

The politics of identity and of race is one way in which the region is distinctive. The presence of settlers throughout most of southern Africa in the colonial period is a striking feature of the region: six of the eight states in this study—Angola, Mozambique, Namibia, South Africa, Zimbabwe, and Zambia—had measurable settler populations. From a long-term historical perspective, this had a profound influence on the prospects for the region; the settler territories of Namibia, South Africa, and Zimbabwe inherited a sophisticated political and economic infrastructure that had served white resident interests for a century or more. Equally significant, the resistance of the settler populations to black rule in all of the settler countries, save Zambia, suggests a critical variable in explaining the destructive conflicts that followed and their legacies, which continue to affect the region in complex ways today.

In addition to history, the concentration of executive power even in the posttransition period is also an important regional characteristic. For example, most of the countries in the region have fairly centralized presidential systems and unicameral legislatures. Moreover, parliaments tend to be weak and nonassertive vis-à-vis the executive, even where constitutional role permits greater involvement.[1] Competitive electoral systems exist in all countries but Zimbabwe, although ruling parties have manipulated the process, to varying degrees, in an effort to retain office or increase their margin of support. The cynical manipulation of politics, the deference of some parliaments to the president, and the inability to deliver constituency services have had a detrimental effect on popular participation in certain aspects of political life.[2] But we cannot reduce political outcomes solely to the actions of "big men." Indeed, people have not opted out of the process altogether, and the region has witnessed the strengthening of a number of nongovernmental organizations and of civil society activism.

This book has demonstrated that civil society is vibrant in southern Africa. From the Oasis Forum in Zambia, to the valiant fight of the endangered press in Zimbabwe, to AIDS activists from the Treatment Action Campaign in South Africa, civil society frequently finds avenues of expression. Moreover, civil society watchdog groups, although still often donor-dependent, are developing local capacity for such diverse activities as election monitoring, civic education, AIDS prevention, and so forth; these are essential in enhancing and undergirding fragile democracies.

In a related vein, we have witnessed something of a regional demonstration effect impacting both political and civil societies. Although Namibians acquiesced to the constitutional change that enabled President Sam Nujoma to stand for a previously illegal third term in office in 1999, it was not without controversy; in the end, as pledged, this was a one-term extension for President Nujoma only. Importantly, when Frederick Chiluba attempted the same thing in Zambia in 2001, he was blocked by a Zambian civil society that was in part influenced by the experience of Namibians, as well as their own domestic politics. Bakili Muluzi was also thwarted in his effort to enact a constitutional change for a third presidential term in Malawi. While it is difficult to determine precisely, it is likely that Mozambican president Joachim Chissano was influenced by these events in making his own decision not to run for a third term in 2004.[3] In each case, civil societies—and subsequently, political parties (and in Malawi and Zambia, parliaments)—reacted to their domestic situations in part by deriving lessons from the experiences of their neighbors.

A negative example of this regional solidarity and demonstration effect at the political level concerns the situation in Zimbabwe. The countries of southern Africa, particularly their leaders, have shown great support for Robert Mugabe and his ever-increasing authoritarianism. Despite presiding over considerably more democratic polities, the regional presidents have either openly or tacitly lent support to Mugabe's misrule.

Outside of Zimbabwe, however, a culture of constitutionalism appears to be emerging in the region, albeit imperfectly and in fits and starts. Led by the example of Namibia's and South Africa's comprehensive constitutions, other countries have endeavored to elevate the status of law in society. For example, in 2003, Zambia began yet another attempt at gathering popular input and support for a new, more inclusive and representative constitution, although the process was substantially flawed, as shown in Chapter 3. Conversely, while Zimbabwean civil society did engage in a comprehensive exercise to create a new national constitution, its efforts were summarily rejected by the ruling party, which had engaged in its own, far more politicized, constitution-drafting process. At the same time, however, the legal systems in every country, including South Africa, are overburdened and often weakly supported, thus revealing deeply embedded problems in institutionalizing a legal and constitutional culture. Legal and wider constitutional reform presents a formidable task.

The economies of southern Africa are increasingly convergent, at least at the mass level. Although several countries in the region enjoy "middle-income" status—Botswana, Namibia, and South Africa, with Angola experiencing rising national income as a result of its oil exploitation—the region nonetheless is characterized by poverty. Six of the eight countries examined in this book (including relatively wealthy South Africa) have implemented neoliberal reform programs mandated or simply inspired by the international financial institutions. As the chapters indicate, these have had, at best, mixed results, as countries struggle to compete in a globalized environment (Mkandawire and Soludo 1999; van de Walle 2001). Partly in response, the new methods of addressing economic decline seek to move away from the unfettered liberalism of the past decade to include, for example, a greater focus on poverty issues, local ownership, and so on, but these are as yet unproven. Moreover, even those countries in the region with the highest levels of development have among the widest income disparities in the world, suggesting looming social problems.

The region is also increasingly drawn together by its economic relations, although as noted, many of the countries have become de facto satellites of South Africa. As argued in Chapter 12, it will be antithetical to South Africa's long-term economic interests to create vassals instead of regional partners. Nevertheless, some form of accommodation, such as that expressed in the new regionalism, appears unlikely given South Africa's embrace of the globalization agenda, and even a wider pan-African one characterized by South Africa's ever-increasing investment in central

Africa and above. However, South Africa cannot be an island of stability in a region of economic chaos. Indeed, the porosity of southern Africa's borders, the intraregional labor movements, the international character of HIV/AIDS, the flow of refugees, not to mention the proximity of markets, all suggest that South Africa would benefit from a more significant developmental emphasis within the region.

Last, each of the issues discussed above returns us to the prospects for democratic stability in the region. All are critical to democracy's success or failure. The evolution of these processes—constitutional courts, constraints on executive power, electoral legitimacy, and the like—suggests that democratic "consolidation" (or something approximating it; see Carothers 2002) is only to be achieved slowly, and even then in occasionally violent fits and starts, as the Zimbabwe case discussed in Chapter 7 reveals. That country has undergone low-intensity conflict, severe economic degradation, and the unraveling of its once impressive political, legal, and social institutions. At the same time, however, although Zimbabwe is a "cautionary tale," Zimbabweans and their regional counterparts may also note that the seeds of a formidable opposition—if not the Movement for Democratic Change, then its successor—have been planted. Moreover, Zimbabwe highlights a regional precedent, of the unambiguously negative variety, to be avoided by other countries in the region.

Indeed, while Zimbabwe is trending negative, six of the eight countries examined in this book are proceeding—inching—in a more democratic direction. These modest democratic achievements cannot suggest that these states are moving inexorably toward deeper democracy, but the region as a whole may be more stable—more "promising"—than at any time in its recent history. Nonetheless, the region poses more questions than answers, and more challenges than ready solutions. The positive interaction of agents, structures, and ideas, as well as states and societies, will determine whether the region's trajectory continues.

◼ Notes

1. Examination of contemporary southern Africa suggests that there are a number of relatively new institutional restraints on the unbridled exercise of that power. Zimbabwe's Robert Mugabe is an important counterexample. However, the growth of a formidable opposition for the first time, even under threat, indicates pressure on the president (see Chapter 7).

2. For example, attitudes toward democracy in southern Africa were revealed to be quite weak in some *Afrobarometer* surveys, reflecting popular discontent (*Afrobarometer* 2003a, 2003b; Mattes 2002).

3. This was implied in an author interview with President Chissano, Maputo, June 2001.

Acronyms

ACN	Action Christian National (Namibia)
AFORD	Alliance for Democracy (Malawi)
AGOA	Africa Growth and Opportunity Act (United States)
AIDS	acquired immunodeficiency syndrome
AIPPA	Access to Privacy and Protection of Information Act (Zimbabwe)
ANC	African National Congress (South Africa)
AU	African Union
AZ	Agenda for Zambia
BAM	Botswana Alliance Movement
BCP	Botswana Congress Party
BDF	Botswana Defense Force
BDP	Bechuanaland Democratic Party
BDP	Botswana Democratic Party
BIP	Botswana Independence Party
BNF	Botswana National Front
BPP	Botswana People's Party
BSAC	British South Africa Company
CA	Conservative Alliance (Zimbabwe)
CCC	Committee for a Clean Campaign (Zambia)
CCN	Council of Churches of Namibia
CFU	Commercial Farmers Union (Zimbabwe)
CNE	National Electoral Commission (Mozambique)
COD	Congress of Democrats (Namibia)
COMESA	Common Market for Eastern and Southern Africa
COSATU	Congress of South African Trade Unions
CRC	constitutional review commission
CSO	civil society organization
DCN	Democratic Coalition of Namibia

DRC	Democratic Republic of Congo
DRK	Dutch Reformed Church
DTA	Democratic Turnhalle Alliance (Namibia)
ECOMOG	Economic Community of West African States Cease-Fire Monitoring Group
ECZ	Electoral Commission of Zambia
EIU	Economist Intelligence Unit
ESAP	economic structural adjustment program
EU	European Union
FAA	Angolan Armed Forces
FADM	Armed Forces for the Defense of Mozambique
FAM	Armed Forces of Mozambique
FCN	Federal Convention of Namibia
FDI	foreign direct investment
FESA	Eduardo dos Santos Foundation (Angola)
FNLA	National Front for the Liberation of Angola
Frelimo	Front for the Liberation of Mozambique
G8	Group of Eight
GDP	gross domestic product
GEAR	Growth, Employment, and Redistribution program (South Africa)
GNU	Government of National Unity (South Africa)
GPA	general peace agreement
GURN	government of national unity and reconciliation (Angola)
HIV	human immunodeficiency virus
HP	Heritage Party (Zambia)
IBA	International Bar Association
ICG	International Crisis Group
IFI	international financial institution
IFP	Inkatha Freedom Party (South Africa)
IMF	International Monetary Fund
IPADE	Institute for Peace and Democracy
IRIN	Integrated Regional Information Networks
ISI	import substitution industrialization
LAMA	Legal Age of Majority Act (Zimbabwe)
LPF	Liberal Progressive Front (Zambia)
MAG	Monitor Action Group (Namibia)
MAP	Millennium Africa Program
MBC	Malawi Broadcasting Corporation
MCP	Malawi Congress Party
MDC	Movement for Democratic Change (Zimbabwe)
MELS	The Marx, Engels, Lenin, and Stalin Movement of Botswana
MISA	Media Institute of Southern Africa

MMD	Movement for Multiparty Democracy (Zambia)
MNA	Mozambique News Agency
MNC	multinational corporation
MNR	Mozambique National Resistance (known as Renamo after 1981)
MP	member of parliament
MPLA	Popular Movement for the Liberation of Angola
NAC	Nyasaland African Congress
NANSO	Namibian National Student Organization
NCA	National Constitutional Assembly (Zimbabwe)
NCC	National Citizens' Coalition (Zambia)
NCOP	National Council of Provinces (South Africa)
NDA	National Democratic Alliance (Malawi)
NDF	Namibian Defense Force
NEPAD	New Partnership for African Development
NGO	nongovernmental organization
NGOCC	Nongovernmental Organization Coordinating Committee (Zambia)
NLD	National Leadership for Development (Zambia)
NNF	Namibia National Front
NNP	New National Party (South Africa)
NP	National Party (South Africa)
NPF	National Patriotic Front (Namibia)
NUNW	National Union of Namibian Workers
NWLG	National Women's Lobby Group (Zambia)
OAU	Organization of African Unity
OPO	Ovamboland People's Organization (Namibia)
PAC	Pan-Africanist Congress (South Africa)
PLAN	People's Liberation Army of Namibia
PMU	Police Mobile Unit (Botswana)
PRE	Economic Rehabilitation Program (Mozambique)
RDP	reconstruction and development program
Renamo	Mozambique National Resistance (known until 1981 as MNR)
RF	Rhodesia Front (Zimbabwe; known as the Conservative Alliance after 1983)
SABC	South African Broadcasting Corporation
SACC	South African Council of Churches
SACP	South African Communist Party
SACU	Southern African Customs Union
SADC	Southern African Development Community
SADCC	Southern African Development Coordination Conference
SADF	South African Defense Force

SAP	structural adjustment program
SDP	Social Democratic Party (Zambia)
SFF	Special Field Force (Namibia)
STD	sexually transmitted disease
SWANU	South West Africa National Union (Namibia)
SWAPO	South West Africa People's Organization (Namibia)
SWATF	South West Africa Territorial Force (Namibia)
TAC	Treatment Action Campaign (South Africa)
TRC	Truth and Reconciliation Commission (South Africa)
UANC	United African National Council (Zambia)
UDF	United Democratic Front (Malawi)
UDI	unilateral declaration of independence
UE	Electoral Union (Mozambique)
UK	United Kingdom
UN	United Nations
UNAIDS	United Nations AIDS Organization
UNDP	United Nations Development Programme
UNIFEM	United Nations Development Fund for Women
UNIP	United National Independence Party (Zambia)
UNITA	National Union for the Total Independence of Angola
UNSC	United Nations Security Council
UPND	United Party for National Development (Zambia)
UPP	United Progressive Party (Zambia)
USIP	U.S. Institute of Peace
WHO	World Health Organization
WNC	Women's National Coalition (South Africa)
ZANLA	Zimbabwe National Liberation Army
ZANU	Zimbabwe African National Union
ZANU-PF	Zimbabwe African National Union—Patriotic Front
ZAP	Zambia Alliance for Progress
ZAPU	Zimbabwe African People's Union
ZCCM	Zambian Consolidated Copper Mines
ZCTU	Zimbabwe Congress of Trade Unions
ZimRights	Zimbabwe Human Rights Association
ZIMT	Zambia Independent Monitoring Team
ZIPRA	Zimbabwe People's Revolutionary Army
ZPA	Zambia Privatization Agency
ZPP	Zambia Progressive Party
ZUDP	Zambia United Development Party

Bibliography

Adam, Kanya. 1997. "The Politics of Redress: South African Style Affirmative Action." *Journal of Modern African Studies.* 35: 231–249.

Afrobarometer. 2003a. "The Changing Public Agenda? South Africans' Assessments of the Country's Most Pressing Problems." Afrobarometer Briefing Paper no. 5. Cape Town: IDASA.

———. 2003b. "Trends in Political Party Support in South Africa." Afrobarometer Briefing Paper no. 6. Cape Town: IDASA.

Afronet. 1998. "The Dilemma of Local Courts in Zambia: A Question of Colonial Legal Continuity or Deliberate Customary Law Marginalisation?" http://afronet.org.za/reports/l_courts.htm.

Agadjanian, Victor, and Ndola Prata. 2001. "War and Reproduction: Angola's Fertility in Comparative Perspective." *Journal of Southern African Studies.* 27,2: 329–347.

AGOA.info. n.d. "About AGOA." http://www.agoa.info/index.php?view=about&story=about.

———. n.d. "Apparel Trade Under AGOA." http://www.agoa.info/index.php?view=trade_stats&story=apparel_trade.

"Aid Boycott Eases." 2004. *Angola Peace Monitor.* May 20.

Ajulu, Rok. 2001. "Thabo Mbeki's African Renaissance in a Globalising World Economy: The Struggle for the Soul of the Continent." *Review of African Political Economy.* 28,87: 27–42.

Akukwe, Chinua, and Melvin Foote. 2001. "HIV/AIDS in Africa: Time to Stop the Killing Fields." *Foreign Policy in Focus Policy Brief.* 6,15. April.

Alden, Chris. 2001. *Mozambique and the Construction of the New African State: From Negotiations to Nation Building.* Basingstoke: Palgrave.

Alexander, Peter. 2000. "Zimbabwean Workers, the MDC, and the 2000 Election." *Review of African Political Economy.* 27,85: 385–406.

Allen, Chris. 1995. "Understanding African Politics." *Review of African Political Economy.* 22,65: 301–320.

Anstee, Margaret Joan. 1996. *Orphan of the Cold War: The Inside Story of the Collapse of the Angolan Peace Process, 1992–93.* New York: St. Martin's.

Ayittey, George. 1998. *Africa in Chaos.* New York: St. Martin's.

Ba, Alice, and Matthew J. Hoffman. 2003. "Making and Remaking the World for IR 101: A Resource for Teaching Social Constructivism in Introductory Classes." *International Studies Perspectives.* 4,1: 15–33.

Ball, Nicole. 1988. *Security and Economy in the Third World*. Princeton: Princeton University Press.

Baloi, Obede. 1996. "Conflict Management and Democratic Transition." In Brazão Mazula, ed., *Mozambique: Elections, Democracy and Development*. Translated by Paul Fauvet. Maputo: Embassy of the Kingdom of the Netherlands.

Bates, Robert. 1981. *Markets and States in Tropical Africa*. Berkeley: University of California Press.

Bauer, Gretchen. 1998. *Labor and Democracy in Namibia, 1971–1996*. Athens: Ohio University Press.

———. 1999. "Challenges to Democratic Consolidation in Namibia." In Richard Joseph, ed., *State, Conflict, and Democracy in Africa*. Boulder: Lynne Rienner.

———. 2004. "'The Hand That Stirs the Pot Can Also Run the Country': Electing Women to Parliament in Namibia." *Journal of Modern African Studies*. 42,4: 479–509.

Bayart, Jean-François, Stephen Ellis, and Béatrice Hibou. 1999. *The Criminalization of the State in Africa*. Bloomington: Indiana University Press.

Baylies, Carolyn, and Morris Szeftel. 1984. "The Rise to Political Prominence of the Zambian Business Class." In Cherry Gertzel, ed., *The Dynamics of the One-Party State in Zambia*. Manchester: Manchester University Press.

———. 1992. "The Fall and Rise of Multiparty Politics in Zambia." *Review of African Political Economy*. 19,54: 75–91.

———. 1997. "The 1996 Zambian Elections: Still Awaiting Democratic Consolidation." *Review of African Political Economy*. 24,71: 113–128.

Beall, Jo. 2001. "Doing Gender from Top to Bottom? The South African Case." *Women: A Cultural Review*. 12,2: 136–146.

Becker, Heike. 1995. *Namibian Women's Movement 1980 to 1992: From Anti-Colonial Resistance to Reconstruction*. Frankfurt: IKO.

Berger, Iris. 1999. "Women in East and Southern Africa." In Iris Berger and Francis White, eds., *Women in Sub-Saharan Africa: Restoring Women to History*. Bloomington: Indiana University Press.

Berman, Eric. 1996. *Managing Arms in Peace Processes: Mozambique*. Geneva: United Nations Institute for Disarmament Research, Disarmament and Conflict Resolution Project.

Beveridge, Andrew, and Anthony Oberschall. 1979. *African Businessmen and Development in Zambia*. Princeton: Princeton University Press.

Birmingham, David. 1992. *Frontline Nationalism in Angola and Mozambique*. Trenton: Africa World Press.

———. 2002. "Angola." In Patrick Chabal, ed., *A History of Postcolonial Lusophone Africa*. Bloomington: Indiana University Press.

Blair, David. 2002. *Degrees in Violence: Robert Mugabe and the Struggle for Power in Zimbabwe*. London: Continuum.

Bond, Patrick. 1998. *Uneven Zimbabwe: A Study of Finance, Development, and Underdevelopment*. Trenton, N.J.: Africa World Press.

———. 2000. *Elite Transition: From Apartheid to Neoliberalism in South Africa*. London: Pluto Press.

Bond, Patrick, and Masimba Manyanya. 2002. *Zimbabwe's Plunge: Exhausted Nationalism, Neoliberalism, and the Struggle for Social Justice*. Trenton, N.J.: Africa World Press.

Boone, Catherine, and Jake Batsell. 2001. "Politics and AIDS in Africa: Research Agendas in Political Science and International Relations." *Africa Today*. 48,2: 3–33.

"Botswana Launches New Development Plan." 2003. Xinhua News Agency. July 23.

"Botswana Legislators Call for Tougher Stance on Mugabe." 2003. Africa News Service. April 28.

Bowen, Merle. 2000. *The State Against the Peasantry: Rural Struggles in Colonial and Postcolonial Mozambique*. Charlottesville: University Press of Virginia.

Bowyer-Bower, T. A. S., and Colin Stoneman, eds. 2000. *Land Reform in Zimbabwe: Constraints and Prospects*. Aldershot: Ashgate.

Bradshaw, York, and Stephen Ndegwa, eds. 2000. *The Uncertain Promise of Southern Africa*. Bloomington: Indiana University Press.

Brandt, A. M. 1998. "AIDS: From Social History to Social Policy." In E. Fee and D. M. Fox, eds., *AIDS: The Burdens of History*. Berkeley: University of California Press.

Bratton, Michael. 1989. "Beyond the State: Civil Society and Associational Life in Africa." *Comparative Politics*. 24,4: 407–430.

———. 1992. "Zambia Starts Over: The Rebirth of Political Pluralism." *Journal of Democracy*. 3,2: 81–94.

Bratton, Michael, and Daniel Posner. 1999. "A First Look at Second Elections in Africa, with Evidence from Zambia." In Richard Joseph, ed., *State, Conflict and Democracy in Africa*. Boulder: Lynne Rienner.

Bratton, Michael, and Nicolas van de Walle. 1997. *Democratic Experiments in Africa: Regime Transitions in Comparative Perspective*. Cambridge: Cambridge University Press.

Bräutigam, Deborah, Lise Rakner, and Scott Taylor. 2002. "Business Associations and Growth Coalitions in Sub-Saharan Africa." *Journal of Modern African Studies*. 40,4: 519–547.

Brecher, Jeremy, Tim Costello, and Brendan Smith. 2000. *Globalization for Below: The Power of Solidarity*. Boston: South End Press.

Brett, Tedy, and Simon Winter. 2003. "The Origins of the Zimbabwe Crisis." *Focus*. 30: 10–14. Johannesburg: Helen Suzman Foundation.

Britton, Hannah. 2001. "New Struggles, New Strategies: Emerging Patterns of Women's Political Participation in the South African Parliament." *International Politics*. 38: 173–200.

Burnell, Peter. 2001. "The Party System and Party Politics in Zambia: Continuities Past, Present, and Future." *African Affairs*. 100: 239–263.

———. 2002. "Parliamentary Committees in Zambia's Third Republic: Partial Reforms, Unfinished Agenda." *Journal of Southern African Studies*. 28,2: 291–323.

Busumtwi-Sam, James. 2002. "Sustainable Peace and Development in Angola." *Studies in Comparative International Development*. 37,3: 91–118.

Bwalya, Edgar, Maxton Tsoka, Lise Rakner, Arne Tostensen, and Lars Svåsand. 2003. "Poverty Reduction Strategy Processes in Malawi and Zambia." Unpublished Report to the Norwegian Agency for Development Cooperation (NORAD).

Bystydzienski, Jill. 1992. *Women Transforming Politics: Worldwide Strategies for Empowerment*. Bloomington: Indiana University Press.

Caldwell, John. 2000. "Rethinking the African AIDS Epidemic." *Population and Development Review*. 26,1: 117–135.

Callaghy, Thomas. 1990. "Lost Between State and Market: The Politics of Economic Adjustment in Ghana, Zambia, and Nigeria." In Joan Nelson, ed., *Economic Governance and Policy Choice: The Politics of Economic Adjustment*. Princeton: Princeton University Press.

Calland, Richard, ed. 1999. *The First Five Years: A Review of South Africa's Democratic Parliament*. Cape Town: IDASA.

Campbell, Catherine, and Brian Williams. 2001. "Briefing: Riding the Tiger: Contextualizing HIV Prevention in South Africa." *African Affairs*. 100: 135–140.

Carmody, Pádraig. 2001. *Tearing the Social Fabric: Neoliberalism, Deindustrialization, and the Crisis of Government in Zimbabwe*. Portsmouth: Heinemann.

Carmody, Pádraig, and Scott Taylor. 2003. "The Decline of the Industrial Sector in Zimbabwe." *African Studies Quarterly*. 7,2. http://www.ufl.edu/asq/v7/v7i2a3.htm.

Carothers, Thomas. 2002. "The End of the Transition Paradigm." *Journal of Democracy*. 13,1: 5–21.

Carrilho, Norberto. 1996. "The Electoral Legislation in Mozambique and the Political and Social Achievement." In Brazão Mazula, ed., *Mozambique: Elections, Democracy and Development*. Maputo: Embassy of the Kingdom of the Netherlands.

Carter, Gwendolen M. 1980. *Which Way Is South Africa Going?* Bloomington: Indiana University Press.

Carter Center. 2000. *Observing the 1999 Elections in Mozambique: Final Report*. Atlanta: Carter Center.

———. 2002. *Observing the 2001 Zambia Elections: Final Report*. Atlanta: Carter Center.

Chabal, Patrick, and Jean Pascal Daloz. 1999. *Africa Works: Disorder as Political Instrument*. Bloomington: Indiana University Press.

Chan, Stephen. 1999. "Troubled Pluralisms: Pondering an Indonesian Moment for Zimbabwe and Zambia." *Round Table*. 349: 61–76.

Chazan, Naomi, Peter Lewis, Robert Mortimer, Donald Rothchild, and Stephen John Stedman. 1999. *Politics and Society in Contemporary Africa*. 3rd ed. Boulder: Lynne Rienner.

Chinsinga, Blessings. 2002. "The Politics of Poverty Alleviation in Malawi: A Critical Review." In Harri Englund, ed., *A Democracy of Chameleons: Politics and Culture in the New Malawi*. Stockholm: Nordiska Afrikainstitutet.

Chirwa, Wiseman. 1994a. "Elections in Malawi: The Perils of Regionalism." *Southern Africa Report*. December: 17–20.

———. 1994b. "The Politics of Ethnicity and Regionalism in Contemporary Malawi." *African Rural and Urban Studies*. 1,2: 93–118.

"Chona Report." 1972. Report of the National Commission on the Establishment of a One-Party Participatory Democracy in Zambia. Lusaka: Government Printers, October.

Chua, Amy. 2003. *World on Fire: How Exporting Free Market Democracy Breeds Ethnic Hatred and Global Instability*. New York: Doubleday.

Cilliers, Jakkie. 2000. "Beyond the Stalemate." In Jakkie Cilliers and Christian Dietrich, eds., *Angola's War Economy: The Role of Oil and Diamonds*. Pretoria: ISS.

Clapham, Christopher. 1982. *Private Patronage and Public Power: Political Clientelism in the Modern State*. London: Pinter.

Cliffe, L., with R. Bush, J. Lindsay, B. Mokopakgosi, D. Pankhurst, and B. Tsie. 1993. *The Transition to Independence in Namibia*. Boulder: Lynne Rienner.

Collier, Paul, and Anke Hoeffler. 1999. "Justice-Seeking and Loot-Seeking in Civil War." Paper for the Conference on Economic Agendas in Civil Wars. London, April 26–27.

Collins, Joe, and Bill Rau. 2000. "HIV/AIDS and Failed Development." Africa Policy Information Center Working Paper. March.

Commonwealth Observer Group. 2000. "The Parliamentary Elections in Zimbabwe: 24–25 June 2000."

Cook, Louise. 2001. "European Union Trade Deal Brings Out Mixed Reaction." *Business Day* (South Africa). January 12.

Cooke, Jennifer, Steven Morrison, and John Prendergast. 2003. "Averting Chaos and Collapse in Zimbabwe: The Centrality of South African and US Leadership." *CSIS Africa Notes no. 15*. April.

Cowell, Alan. 2002. "Angry at Vote, Commonwealth Bars Zimbabwe." *New York Times*. March 20.

Crisis in Zimbabwe Coalition. 2003. http://www.kubatana.net/html/sectors/cri001.asp.

Crocker, Chester. 1992. *High Noon in Southern Africa: Making Peace in a Rough Neighborhood*. New York: W. W. Norton.

Culolo, Astrigildo João Pedro. 2001. "Combating Organised Crime in Angola." In Charles Goredema, ed., *Organised Crime in Southern Africa: Assessing Legislation*. Institute for Security Studies Monograph no. 56.http://www.iss.co.za/pubs/monographs/no56/chap9.html.

da Silva, Aida Gomes. 1996. "The Mozambican Press: A Historical Overview and a Political Analysis." Occasional Paper no. 54. Nijmegen, Netherlands: Catholic University of Nijmegen, Third World Center, July.

Davidow, Jeffrey. 1984. *A Peace in Southern Africa: The Lancaster House Conference on Rhodesia, 1979*. Boulder: Westview.

Davidson, Basil. 1994. *Modern Africa: A Social and Political History*. New York: Longman.

de Brito, Luis. 1996. "Voting Behaviour in Mozambique's First Multiparty Elections." In Brazão Mazula, ed., *Mozambique: Elections, Democracy, and Development*. Maputo: Embassy of the Netherlands.

de Klerk, F. W. 1999. *The Last Trek: A New Beginning—The Autobiography*. New York: St. Martin's.

Delius, Peter, and Liz Walker. 2002. "AIDS in Context." *African Studies*. 61,1: 5–12.

d'Engelbronner-Kolff, F. M. 1998. "The People as Law-Makers: The Juridical Foundation of the Legislative Power of Namibian Traditional Communities." In F. M. d'Engelbronner-Kolff, M. O. Hinz, and J. L. Sindano, eds., *Traditional Authority and Democracy in Southern Africa*. Windhoek: New Namibia Books.

de Waal, Alex, and Joseph Tumushabe. 2003. "HIV/AIDS and Food Security in Southern Africa." Pretoria: Southern African Regional Poverty Network/Human Sciences Research Council.

Diamond, Larry. 1999. *Developing Democracy: Toward Consolidation*. Baltimore: Johns Hopkins University Press.

"Did They Vote for This?" 2004. *Africa Confidential*. 45,12: 4. June 11.

Dietrich, Christian. 2000. "Power Struggles in the Diamond Fields." In Jakkie Cilliers and Christian Dietrich, eds., *Angola's War Economy: The Role of Oil and Diamonds*. Pretoria: Institute for Security Studies.

Dobell, Lauren. 1998. *SWAPO's Struggle for Namibia, 1960–1991: War by Other Means*. Basel Namibia Studies Series no. 3. Basel: P. Schlettwein.

Dubow, Saul. 1995. *Scientific Racism in Modern South Africa*. Cambridge: Cambridge University Press.

Dugard, John. 1998. "The New Constitution: A Triumph for Liberalism? A Positive View." In R. W. Johnson and David Welsh, eds., *Ironic Victory: Liberalism in Post-Liberation South Africa*. London: Oxford University Press.

Duncan, Jane. 2000. "Now on SABC: Ode to Thatcher." *Business Day* (South Africa). November 23.

du Toit, Jacques. 2003. "SA Enjoying Benefits of US Trade Largesse." *Business Day* (South Africa). September 1.

du Toit, Pierre. 1995. *State Building and Democracy in Southern Africa: Botswana, Zimbabwe, and South Africa.* Washington, D.C.: U.S. Institute of Peace.

———. 2001. *South Africa's Brittle Peace: The Problem of Post-Settlement Violence.* New York: Palgrave.

Economist Intelligence Unit (EIU). 2001a. *Country Profile 2001: Botswana Lesotho.* London: EIU.

———. 2001b. *Country Profile 2001: Zimbabwe.* London: EIU.

———. 2002a. *Country Report: Mozambique.* London: EIU, July.

———. 2002b. *Country Report: Zimbabwe.* London: EIU.

———. 2003a. "Angola: Economy: Outlook." *EIU Viewswire.* August 20.

———. 2003b. "Botswana: Politics: Political Structure." *EIU Viewswire.* July 3.

———. 2003c. *Country Profile: South Africa.* London: EIU, June.

———. 2003d. *Country Profile Angola.* London: EIU.

———. 2003e. *Country Profile Malawi.* London: EIU.

———. 2003f. *Country Profile Namibia Swaziland.* London: EIU.

———. 2003g. *Country Profile Zambia.* London: EIU.

———. 2003h. *Country Profile Zimbabwe.* London: EIU, October.

———. 2003i. *Country Report Malawi.* London: EIU.

———. 2003j. *Country Report Namibia.* London: EIU, July 14.

———. 2003k. *Country Report Zambia.* London: EIU, September.

———. 2003l. *Country Report Zimbabwe.* London: EIU.

"Edited Text of Communiqué on Commonwealth Ministers' Meeting on Zimbabwe's Land Crisis." 2001. Reuters. September 7.

Emmett, Tony. 1999. *Popular Resistance and the Roots of Nationalism in Namibia, 1915–1966.* Basel Namibia Studies Series no. 4. Basel: P. Schlettwein.

Englund, Harri. 2002. "Introduction: The Culture of Chameleon Politics." In Harri Englund, ed., *A Democracy of Chameleons: Politics and Culture in the New Malawi.* Stockholm: Nordiska Afrikainstitutet.

Erasmus, Gerhard. 2000. "The Constitution: Its Impact on Namibian Statehood and Politics." In Christiaan Keulder, ed., *State, Society, and Democracy: A Reader in Namibian Politics.* Windhoek: Gamsberg Macmillan.

European Union. 2001. *European Union Election Observation Mission: Zambian Elections 2001, Final Statement.* http://europa.eu.int/comm/external _relations/human_rights/eu_election_ass_observ/zambia.

"Fearing Extinction, Botswana Launches All-Out Assault on AIDS." 2003. *AIDS Vaccine Week.* July 28.

Ferguson, Anne, and Beatrice Liatto Katundu. 1994. "Women in Politics in Zambia: What Difference Has Democracy Made?" *African Rural and Urban Studies.* 1,2: 11–30.

Finnegan, William. 2001. "The Poison Keeper." *New Yorker.* January 15.

Finnemore, Martha, and Kathryn Sikkink. 2001. "Taking Stock: The Constructivist Research Program in International Relations and Comparative Politics." *Annual Review of Political Science.* 4: 391–416.

Forrest, Joshua. 1998. *Namibia's Post-Apartheid Regional Institutions: The Founding Year.* Rochester: University of Rochester Press.

Forster, Peter. 1994. "Culture, Nationalism, and the Invention of Tradition in Malawi." *Journal of Modern African Studies.* 32,3: 477–497.

Franklin, Harry. 1963. *Unholy Wedlock: The Failure of the Central African Federation*. London: Allen and Unwin.

Freedom House. 1999. "Freedom in the World Survey: 1998–99." http://www.freedomhouse.org/survey99/country/zambia.html.

———. 2002. "Mozambique." http://www.freedomhouse.org/research/africa2002/mozambique.doc.

"Frelimo Wins Huge Electoral Victory." 2004. Mozambique News Agency. AIM Report no. 289. December 22.

Friedman, Steven. 1999. "South Africa: Entering the Post-Mandela Era." *Journal of Democracy* 10,4: 3–18.

Gann, L. H. 1964. *A History of Northern Rhodesia, Early Days to 1953*. London: Chatto and Windus.

"G-8 Guilty of 'Moral Default,' Says UN Envoy on HIV/AIDS." 2002. *Africa News*. July 2.

Geisler, Gisela. 1995. "Troubled Sisterhood: Women and Politics in Southern Africa." *African Affairs*. 94: 545–578.

———. 2000. "Parliament Is Another Terrain of Struggle: Women, Men, and Politics in South Africa." *Journal of Modern African Studies*. 38,4: 605–630.

Gertzel, Cherry. 1984. Introduction to Cherry Gertzel, ed., *The Dynamics of the One-Party State in Zambia*. Manchester: Manchester University Press.

Giliomee, Hermann. 1983. "Constructing Afrikaner Nationalism." *Journal of Asian and African Studies*. 18,1–2: 83–98.

———. 1997. "Surrender Without Defeat: Afrikaners and the South African 'Miracle.'" *Daedalus*. 126,2: 113–146.

Global Witness. 2002a. *All the President's Men: The Devastating Story of Oil and Banking in Angola's Privatised War*. March. http://www.globalwitness.org/reports/download.php/00027.pdf.

———. 2002b. *Branching Out: Zimbabwe's Resource Colonialism in Democratic Republic of the Congo*. 2nd ed. London: Global Witness, February.

Godwin, Peter, and Ian Hancock. 1993. *Rhodesians Never Die: The Impact of War and Political Change on White Rhodesia*. Oxford: Oxford University Press.

Good, Kenneth. 1996. "Towards Popular Participation in Botswana." *Journal of Modern African Studies*. 34,1: 53–77.

Good, Kenneth, and Skye Hughes. 2002. "Globalization and Diversification: Two Cases in Southern Africa." *African Affairs*. 101: 39–59.

Gordon, April A., and Donald L. Gordon. 2001. *Understanding Contemporary Africa*. 3rd ed. Boulder: Lynne Rienner.

Graybill, Lyn. 2002. *Truth and Reconciliation in South Africa: Miracle or Model?* Boulder: Lynne Rienner.

Grunwald, Michael. 2002. "A Small Nation's Big Effort Against AIDS." Washington Post Foreign Service. December 2.

Gunning, Jan, and Remco Oostendorp. 2002. Introduction to Jan Willem Gunning and Remco Oostendorp, eds., *Industrial Change in Africa: Zimbabwean Firms Under Structural Adjustment*. Basingstoke: Palgrave.

Hadland, Adrian, and Jovial Rantao. 1998. *The Life and Times of Thabo Mbeki*. South Africa: New Holland Publishers.

Hall, Richard. 1966. *Zambia*. London: Pall Mall Press.

Hamilton, Carolyn. 1998. *Terrific Majesty: The Powers of Shaka Zulu and the Limits of Historical Invention*. Cambridge: Harvard University Press.

Harrison, Graham. 1996. "Democracy in Mozambique: The Significance of Multiparty Elections." *Review of African Political Economy*. 23,67: 19–35.

Hassim, Shireen. 2002. "'A Conspiracy of Women': The Women's Movement in South Africa's Transition to Democracy." *Social Research.* 69,3: 603–630.

Hayes, Patricia, Jeremy Silvester, Marion Wallace, and Wolfram Hartmann, eds. 1998. *Namibia Under South African Rule: Mobility and Containment, 1915–46.* Oxford: James Currey.

Herbst, Jeffrey. 1989. "Racial Reconciliation in Southern Africa." *International Affairs.* 65: 43–54.

———. 1990. *State Politics in Zimbabwe.* Harare: University of Zimbabwe Press.

———. 2000. *States and Power in Africa: Comparative Lessons in Authority and Control.* Princeton: Princeton University Press.

Hettne, Björn. 1990. *Development Theory and the Three Worlds.* Harlow: Longman.

———. 2001. "Regional Cooperation for Security and Development in Africa." In Peter Vale, Larry Swatuck, and Bertil Oden, eds., *Theory, Change, and Southern Africa's Future.* London: Palgrave.

Hibou, Béatrice. 1999. "The 'Social Capital' of the State as an Agent of Deception, or The Ruses of Economic Intelligence." In Jean-François Bayart, Stephen Ellis, and Béatrice Hibou, *The Criminalization of the State in Africa.* Bloomington: Indiana University Press.

Hinz, M. O. 1998. "The 'Traditional' of Traditional Government: Traditional Versus Democracy-Based Legitimacy." In F. M. d'Engelbronner-Kolff, M. O. Hinz, and J. L. Sindano, eds., *Traditional Authority and Democracy in Southern Africa.* Windhoek: New Namibia Books.

Hodges, Tony. 2004. *Angola: Anatomy of an Oil State.* Oxford: James Currey.

Holm, John. 1988. "Botswana: A Paternalistic Democracy." In Larry Diamond, Juan Linz, and Seymour Martin Lipset, eds., *Democracy in Developing Countries,* vol. 2, *Africa.* Boulder: Lynne Rienner.

Holm, John, and Staffan Darnolf. 2000. "Democratizing the Administrative State in Botswana." In York Bradshaw and Stephen Ndegwa, eds., *The Uncertain Promise of Southern Africa.* Bloomington: Indiana University Press.

Holm, John, Patrick Molutsi, and Gloria Somolekae. 1996. "The Development of Civil Society in a Democratic State: The Botswana Model." *African Studies Review.* 39,2: 43–69.

Hope, Kempe Ronald, Sr. 2002. "From Crisis to Renewal: Towards a Successful Implementation of the New Partnership for Africa's Development." *African Affairs.* 101: 387–402.

Horowitz, Donald. 1985. *Ethnic Groups in Conflict.* Berkeley: University of California Press.

Houser, George M. 1976. "Rhodesia to Zimbabwe: A Chronology, 1830 to 1976." New York: Africa Fund.

Howe, Herbert. 2001. *Ambiguous Order: Military Forces in African States.* Boulder: Lynne Rienner.

Huliaras, Asteris. 2001. "Qadhafi's Comeback: Libya and Sub-Saharan Africa in the 1990s." *African Affairs.* 398: 5–25.

Human Rights Watch. 2000. "South Africa: A Question of Principle—Arms Trade and Human Rights Report." http://www.hrw.org/reports/2000/safrica/index.htm.

———. 2002. "HIV/AIDS and Human Rights." *World Report 2002.* http://www.hrw.org/wr2k2/hivaids.html.

Hunter-Gault, Charlayne. 2001. "AIDS: 20 Years of an Epidemic: In South Africa, AIDS Sparks Fears of Devastation." http://www.cnn.com/specials/2001/aids/stories/hunter.html.

Hwedie, Osei. 2001a. "HIV/AIDS and the Politics of Domestic Response: The Case of Botswana." *International Relations.* 15,6: 55–68.

———. 2001b. "The State and Development in Southern Africa: A Comparative Analysis of Botswana and Mauritius with Angola, Malawi, and Zambia." *African Studies Quarterly.* 5,5.

Ignatius, David. 2002. "New Doubts Cast on Mugabe Victory: Fearing Defeat, Zimbabwe Aides Said to Have Inflated Vote Totals." *International Herald Tribune.* April 3.

Ihonvbere, Julius. 1995. *Economic Crisis, Civil Society, and Democratization: The Case of Zambia.* Trenton: Africa World Press.

———. 1997. "From Despotism to Democracy: The Rise of Multiparty Politics in Malawi." *International Studies.* 34,2: 193–219.

Independent Electoral Commission. 2003. *Atlas of Results.* http://www .elections.org.za/atlas.asp.

Institute for Justice and Reconciliation. 2003. "The SA Reconciliation Barometer." Rondebosch, South Africa. http://www.ijr.org.za/barometer/futraces.pdf.

Integrated Regional Information Networks (IRIN). 2003a. "Botswana: A Model for Combating HIV/AIDS." *Science in Africa.* http://www.scienceinafrica.co.za/ 2003/june/botswana.htm.

———. 2003b. "South Africa: Optimism over Possible ARV Rollout." http://www.irinnews.org.

International Bar Association. 2003. "Angola: Promoting Justice Post-Conflict." International Bar Association Human Rights Institute Report. July. http://www.ibanet.org/pdf/final_%20reportangolapostconflict2003july.pdf.

International Crisis Group (ICG). 2000. "Zimbabwe: At the Crossroads." *Africa Report* no. 22. July 10.

———. 2002. "Zimbabwe's Election: The Stakes for Southern Africa." January 11. http://www.crisisweb.org/projects/showreport.cfm?reportid=524.

———. 2003a. "Angola's Choice: Reform or Regress?" *Africa Report* no. 61. April 7.

———. 2003b. "Decision Time in Zimbabwe." Africa Briefing Paper. July 8.

———. 2003c. "Zimbabwe: Danger and Opportunity." *Africa Report* no. 60. March 10.

Jackson, Robert, and Carl Rosberg. 1982. *Personal Rule in Black Africa: Prince, Autocrat, Prophet, Tyrant.* Berkeley: University of California Press.

Jacobson, Ruth. 1995. "Women's Political Participation: Mozambique's Democratic Transition." *Gender and Development.* 3,3: 29–36.

Jeffery, Anthea. 1998. "The New Constitution: A Triumph for Liberalism?" In R. W. Johnson and David Welsh, eds., *Ironic Victory: Liberalism in Post-Liberation South Africa.* London: Oxford University Press.

Jenkins, Carolyn, and John Knight. 2002. *The Economic Decline of Zimbabwe: Neither Growth nor Equity.* New York: Palgrave.

Johnson, R. W. 2000. *Public Opinion and the Crisis of Zimbabwe.* Johannesburg: Helen Suzman Foundation, October.

———. 2003. "Botswana: Success Breeds Its Own Problems." *Focus.* 30. June. Helen Suzman Foundation. http://www.hsf.org.za/focus30/focus30 johnson.html.

Joseph, Richard. 1992. "Zambia: A Model for Democratic Change." *Current History.* 91,565. May: 199–203.

———. 1997. "Democratization in Africa After 1989: Comparative and Theoretical Perspectives." *Comparative Politics.* 29,3: 363–382.

Kalenga, Paul. 1999. "The Congress of Democrats." *Southern Africa Report.* 15,1: 25–27.

Kamwendo, Gregory. 2002. "Ethnic Revival and Language Associations in the New Malawi: The Case of Chitumbuka." In Harri Englund, ed., *A Democracy of Chameleons: Politics and Culture in the New Malawi.* Stockholm: Nordiska Afrikainstitutet.

Kaplan, Robert. 1994. "The Coming Anarchy." *Atlantic Monthly.* 273, 2. February: 44–76.

———. 2000. *The Coming Anarchy: Shattering the Dreams of the Post Cold War.* New York: Random House.

Kaspin, Deborah. 1995. "The Politics of Ethnicity in Malawi's Democratic Transition." *Journal of Modern African Studies.* 33,4: 595–620.

Katjavivi, Peter. 1990. *A History of Resistance in Namibia.* Trenton: Africa World Press.

Kaunda, Jonathan. 1992. "The Administrative Organisation and Processes of National Development Planning in Malawi." In Guy C. Z. Mhone, ed., *Malawi at the Crossroads: The Post-Colonial Political Economy.* Harare: SAPES Books.

Kayizzi-Mugerwa, Steve. 2003. "Privatization in Sub-Saharan Africa: On Factors Affecting Implementation." In S. Kayizzi-Mugerwa, ed., *Reforming Africa's Institutions: Ownership, Incentives and Capabilities.* New York: United Nations University Press.

Keulder, Christiaan. 1998. *Traditional Leaders and Local Government in Africa: Lessons for South Africa.* Pretoria: Human Sciences Research Council.

———. 1999a. "A Review of the Namibian Budget Process." Report Prepared for the National Democratic Institute (NDI). Windhoek: NDI.

———. 1999b. *Voting Behaviour in Namibia II: Regional Councils 1998.* Windhoek: Friedrich Ebert Stiftung.

———. 2000. "Traditional Leaders." In Christiaan Keulder, ed., *State, Society, and Democracy: A Reader in Namibian Politics.* Windhoek: Gamsberg Macmillan.

———. 2002. "Public Opinion and the Consolidation of Democracy in Namibia." Afrobarometer Paper no. 15. Cape Town: IDASA.

Khadiagala, Gilbert. 2000. "Europe in Africa's Renewal: Beyond Postcolonialism?" In John Harbeson and Donald Rothchild, eds., *Africa in World Politics: The African State System in Flux,* 3rd ed. Boulder: Westview.

———. 2001. "Foreign Policy Decisionmaking in Southern Africa's Fading Frontline." In Gilbert Khadiagala and Terrence Lyons, eds., *African Foreign Policies: Power and Process.* Boulder: Lynne Rienner.

Khadiagala, Gilbert, and Terrence Lyons. 2001. "Foreign Policy Making in Africa: An Introduction." In Gilbert Khadiagala and Terrence Lyons, eds., *African Foreign Policies: Power and Process.* Boulder: Lynne Rienner.

"Khama Win Eases Mogae's Concerns." 2003. Africa News Service. July 23.

Khapoya, Vincent B. 1998. *The African Experience: An Introduction.* 2nd ed. Saddle River, N.J.: Prentice Hall.

Kibble, Steve. 2002. "Options for Peace and Reconciliation." In Inge Tvedten, ed., *Angola 2001/2002: Key Development Issues and Aid in a Context of Peace.* Report R 2002: 8. Bergen: Christian Michelsen Institute.

Korten, David. 2001. *When Corporations Rule the World.* 2nd ed. San Francisco: Kumarian Press.

Kriger, Norma. 2000. "Zimbabwe Today: Hope Against Grim Realities." *Review of African Political Economy.* 27,85: 443–450.

——. 2003. *Guerrilla Veterans in Post-war Zimbabwe: Symbolic and Violent Politics, 1980–1987*. Cambridge: Cambridge University Press.

Krog, Antjie. 1999. *Country of My Skull: Guilt, Sorrow, and the Limits of Forgiveness in the New South Africa*. New York: Times Books.

Lancaster, Carol. 2000. "Africa in World Affairs." In John Harbeson and Donald Rothchild, eds., *Africa in World Politics: The African State System in Flux*, 3rd ed. Boulder: Westview.

le Billon, Philippe. 2001. "Angola's Political Economy of War: The Role of Oil and Diamonds, 1975–2000." *African Affairs*. 100: 55–80.

Lee, Margaret. 2003. *The Political Economy of Regionalism in Southern Africa*. Boulder: Lynne Rienner.

Legum, Colin. 2000. "The Balance of Power in Southern Africa." In York Bradshaw and Stephen Ndegwa, eds., *The Uncertain Promise of Southern Africa*. Bloomington: Indiana University Press.

Lekorwe, Mogopodi, Mpho Molomo, Wilford Molefe, and Kabelo Moseki. 2001. "Public Attitudes Toward Democracy, Governance, and Economic Development in Botswana." Afrobarometer Paper no. 14. Cape Town: IDASA.

Leys, Colin. 1994. "Theoretical Perspectives." In Colin Leys and Bruce Berman, eds., *African Capitalists in African Development*. Boulder: Lynne Rienner.

Leys, Colin, and Cranford Pratt, eds. 1960. *A New Deal in Central Africa*. London: Heinemann.

Leys, Colin, and John Saul. 1995. Introduction to Colin Leys and John Saul, eds., *Namibia's Liberation Struggle: The Two-Edged Sword*. London: James Currey.

Lijphart, Arend. 1977. *Democracy in Plural Societies: A Comparative Exploration*. New Haven: Yale University Press.

Lodge, Tom. 1999. *Consolidating Democracy: South Africa's Second Popular Election*. Johannesburg: Witwatersrand University Press.

——. 2000. "Heavy-Handed Democracy: SWAPO's Victory in Namibia." *Southern Africa Report*. 15,2: 26–29.

Lovenduski, Jone, and Azza Karam. 2002. "Women in Parliament." In International IDEA, *Women in Parliament*. Stockholm. http://www.idea.int.

Luric, Mark. 2000. "Migration and AIDS in Southern Africa: A Review." *South African Journal of Science*. 96,6: 343–346.

Luthuli, Albert. 1962. *Let My People Go*. New York: McGraw Hill.

Lwanda, John. 2002. "Tikutha: The Political Culture of the HIV/AIDS Epidemic in Malawi." In Harri Englund, ed., *A Democracy of Chameleons: Politics and Culture in the New Malawi*. Stockholm: Nordiska Afrikainstitutet.

Machangana, Keboitse. 1998. "Emang Basadi Women's Association and the *Women's Manifesto*: Advocating for Women's Rights in Botswana." In Phiroshaw Camay and Anne Gordon, eds., *Advocacy in Southern Africa: Lessons for the Future*. Johannesburg: CORE.

MacLean, Sandra J. 1999. "Peacebuilding and the New Regionalism in Southern Africa." *Third World Quarterly*. 20,5: 943–956.

Madisa, Motsei. 1999. "A Voluntary Party-Based Quota in a Constituency System: The Case of Botswana." In SADC Gender Unit, *Women in Politics and Decision Making in SADC: Beyond 30 Percent in 2005*. Conference proceedings. Gaborone: SADC Gender Unit.

Magnusson, Bruce. 2002. "Transnational Flows, Legitimacy, and Syncretic Democracy in Benin." In Daniel M. Green, ed., *Constructivism and Comparative Politics*. Armonk, N.Y.: M. E. Sharpe.

Malaquias, Assis. 2000. "Ethnicity and Conflict in Angola: Prospects for

Reconciliation." In Jakkie Cilliers and Christian Dietrich, eds., *Angola's War Economy: The Role of Oil and Diamonds*. Pretoria: Institute for Security Studies.

———. 2001. "Diamonds Are a Guerrilla's Best Friend: The Impact of Illicit Wealth on Insurgency Strategy." *Third World Quarterly*. 22,3: 311–325.

"Malawi President Gains Majority." 2004. June 18. http://news.bbc.co.uk.

Malherbe, Rassie. 1998. "The Legal System and the Judiciary." In Albert Venter, ed., *Government and Politics in the New South Africa*. Pretoria: Van Schaik.

Mandela, Nelson. 1995. *Long Walk to Freedom*. Boston: Little, Brown.

Manning, Carrie. 2001. "Competition and Accommodation in Post-Conflict Democracy: The Case of Mozambique." *Democratization*. 8,2: 140–168.

Marks, Shula. 2002. "An Epidemic Waiting to Happen? The Spread of HIV/AIDS in South Africa in Social and Historical Perspective." *African Studies*. 61,1: 13–26.

Maroleng, Chris. 2003. "Zimbabwe: Smoke Screens and Mirrors." African Security Analysis Programme, Situation Report. Pretoria: Institute for Security Studies.

Marshall, Monty G., and Keith Jaggers. 2001. "Polity IV Country Report 2001: Mozambique." CIDCM. http://www.cidcm.umd.edu/inscr/polity/mzm1.htm.

Martin, Matthew. 1993. "Neither Phoenix nor Icarus: Negotiating Economic Reform in Ghana and Zambia, 1983–92." In Thomas Callaghy and John Ravenhill, eds., *Hemmed In: Responses to Africa's Economic Decline*. New York: Columbia University Press.

Maseko, Sipho. 1995. "The Namibian Student Movement: Its Role and Effects." In Colin Leys and John Saul, eds., *Namibia's Liberation Struggle: The Two-Edged Sword*. London: James Currey.

Mattes, Robert. 2002. "South Africa: Democracy Without the People?" *Journal of Democracy*. 13,1: 22–36.

McCarthy, Colin 1999. "Regional Integration in Sub-Saharan Africa: Past, Present, and Future." In T. Ademola Oyijide, B. Ndulu, and D. Greenaway, eds., *Regional Integration and Trade Liberalization in Sub-Saharan Africa*, vol. 4, *Synthesis and Review*. London: Macmillan.

Mchombo, Sam. 1998. "Democratization in Malawi: Its Roots and Prospects." In Jean-Germain Gros, ed., *Democratization in Late Twentieth Century Africa*. Westport, Conn.: Greenwood Press.

McKittrick, Meredith. 1998. "Generational Struggles and Social Mobility in Western Ovambo Communities, 1915–1954." In Patricia Hayes et al., *Namibia Under South African Rule: Mobility and Containment 1915–46*. Oxford: James Currey.

Media Institute of Southern Africa (MISA). 2000. *So This Is Democracy? State of the Media in Southern Africa*. Windhoek: MISA.

Melber, Henning. 2003. "From Anti-Colonial Resistance to Government: A Sociology of Former Liberation Movements as Political Parties." Paper presented at the Institute of African Affairs. University of Hamburg, Germany.

Meldrum, Andrew. 2003. "The Observer." *Guardian Special Report*. March 30.

Meredith, Martin. 2003. *Our Votes, Our Guns: Robert Mugabe and the Tragedy of Zimbabwe*. New York: PublicAffairs.

Messiant, Christine. 2001. "The Eduardo Dos Santos Foundation, or How Angola's Regime Is Taking Over Civil Society." *African Affairs*. 100: 287–309.

Mikell, Gwendolyn. 1997. Introduction to Gwendolyn Mikell, ed., *African Feminism: The Politics of Survival in Sub-Saharan Africa*. Philadelphia: University of Pennsylvania Press.

———. 2003. "African Feminism: Toward a New Politics of Representation." In Carole McCann and Seung-Kyung Kim, eds., *Feminist Theory Reader: Local and Global Perspectives*. New York: Routledge.

Minow, Martha. 1998. *Between Vengeance and Forgiveness: Facing History After Genocide and Mass Violence*. Boston: Beacon Press.

Minter, William. 1994. *Apartheid Contras: An Inquiry into the Roots of War in Angola and Mozambique*. London: Zed Books.

Mittelmann, James. 2000. *The Globalization Syndrome: Transformation and Resistance*. Princeton: Princeton University Press.

Mkalipi, Zanethemba, Collette Herzenberg, Pumzo Mbana, and Masibonge Mzwakali. 2003. "Zimbabwe: Moving Towards a Negotiated Transition?" Pretoria: IDASA Political Information and Monitoring Service.

Mkandawire, Thandika, and Charles Soludo. 1999. *Our Continent, Our Future: African Perspectives on Structural Adjustment*. Trenton: Africa World Press.

Mogotsi, Vance. 1995. "Is the Centre Willing to Share Power? The Importance of Regional and Local Government." In Carrie Marais, Peter Katjavivi, and Arnold Wehmhoerner, eds., *Southern Africa After Elections: Towards a Culture of Democracy*. Windhoek: Friedrich Ebert Stiftung.

Molomo, Mpho. 2001. "Civil Military Relations in Botswana's Developmental State." *African Studies Quarterly*. 5,2.

Moyo, Otrude, and Saliwe Kawewe. 2002. "The Dynamics of a Racialized, Gendered, Ethnicized, and Economically Stratified Society: Understanding the Socioeconomic Status of Women in Zimbabwe." *Feminist Economics*. 8,2: 163–181.

Moyo, Sam. 1995. *The Land Question in Zimbabwe*. Harare: SAPES Books.

———. 2000. "The Political Economy of Land Acquisition and Redistribution in Zimbabwe, 1990–1999." *Journal of Southern African Studies*. 26,1: 5–28.

Mozambique News Agency (MNA). 2001. "President Chissano to Step Down in 2004." AIM Report no. 207. May 15. http://www.poptel.org.uk/mozambique news/newsletter/aim207.html#story1.

Mozambique Political Process Bulletin. 2004. Issue 26. December 15.

"Mozambique's Former Rebel Peace Negotiator Forms Political Party." 2003. South African Press Agency (SAPA). June 27. http://www.anc.org.za/anc/newsbrief /2003/news0630.txt.

Mshomba, Richard E. 2000. *Africa in the Global Economy*. Boulder: Lynne Rienner.

Mulemba, Humphrey. 1992. Speech delivered at the conference "Democracy and Economic Recovery in Africa: Lessons from Zambia." Reprinted in *Proceedings of the Zambia Consultation, June 11–12, 1992*. Atlanta: Carter Center.

Munslow, Barry. 1999. "Angola: The Politics of Unsustainable Development." *Third World Quarterly*. 20,3: 551–568.

Mutharika, A. Peter. 1996. "The 1995 Democratic Constitution of Malawi." *Journal of African Law*. 40,2: 205–220.

Myburgh, James. 2003. "Floor Crossing Adds New Muscle to ANC." *Focus*. 30. Helen Suzman Foundation. http://www.hsf.org.za/focus30/focus30johnson .html.

Nattrass, Nicoli. 1997. "Business and Employer Organisations in South Africa." Occasional Report no. 5. Geneva: International Labour Office.

———. 1999. "The Truth and Reconciliation Commission on Business and Apartheid: A Critical Evaluation." *African Affairs*. 98: 373–391.

Naumann, Eckhart. 2003. "A Stitch in Time: U.S. Deal Will Open New Markets for SACU but There Are Pitfalls." *Financial Mail* (South Africa). August 1.

Nest, Michael. 2001. "Ambitions, Profit, and Loss: Zimbabwean Economic Involvement in the Democratic Republic of the Congo." *African Affairs.* 400: 469–490.

"New Opposition Grouping Demands 2005 Election." 2004. *Angola Peace Monitor.* March 19. http://www.actsa.org/Angola/apm/apm1018.htm.

Ngavirue, Zedekia. 1997. *Political Parties and Interest Groups in South West Africa (Namibia): A Study of a Plural Society.* Basel Namibia Studies Series no. 1. Basel: P. Schlettwein.

Nhema, Alfred. 2002. *Democracy in Zimbabwe: From Liberation to Liberalization.* Harare: University of Zimbabwe.

Nordas, Hildegunn, and Leon Pretorius. 2000. "Mozambique: A Sub-Saharan African NIC?" CMI Working Paper no. 10. Bergen: Christian Michelsen Institute.

Northern Rhodesia Constitutional Conference. 1961. "Northern Rhodesia: Proposals for Constitutional Change." Presented to Parliament by the Secretary of State for the Colonies by Command of Her Majesty. London: HM Stationery Office.

Oasis Forum. 2001. "The Oasis Declaration." Lusaka, Zambia. February 21.

Oden, Bertil. 2001. "South African Benevolent Hegemony in Southern Africa: Impasse or Highway?" In Peter Vale, Larry Swatuk, and Bertil Oden, eds., *Theory, Change, and Southern Africa's Future.* Hampshire: Palgrave.

Ohlson, Thomas, and Stephen John Stedman. 1994. *The New Is Not Yet Born: Conflict Resolution in Southern Africa.* Washington, D.C.: Brookings Institution.

O'Meara, Dan. 1983. *Volkskapitalisme: Class, Capital, and Ideology in the Development of Afrikaner Nationalism.* Johannesburg: Ravan Press.

———. 1996. *Forty Lost Years: The Apartheid State and the Politics of the National Party, 1948–1994.* Athens: Ohio University Press.

Omer-Cooper, J. D. 1994. *A History of Southern Africa.* 2nd ed. Portsmouth, N.H.: Heinemann.

"Opposing Chiluba's Encore: Pressure Mounts in Zambia to Prevent an Unconstitutional Bid for Power." 2001. *Africa Analysis.* January 26.

Orre, Aslak. 2001. "Local Government Reform in Mozambique: Does It Matter?" M.A. thesis. Department of Comparative Politics, University of Bergen, Norway.

Pachai, B. 1973. *Malawi: The History of the Nation.* London: Longman Group.

Pachecho, Fernando. 2002. "The Role of Civil Society in the Social Reconstruction of Angola." In Inge Tvedten, ed., *Angola 2001/2002: Key Development Issues and Aid in a Context of Peace.* Report R 2002: 8. Bergen: Christian Michelsen Institute.

Padayachee, Vishnu. 1997. "The Evolution of South Africa's International Economic Relations." In Jonathan Michie and V. Padayachee, eds., *The Political Economy of South Africa's Transitions.* London: Dryden Press.

Pankhurst, Donna. 2002. "Women and Politics in Africa: The Case of Uganda." In Karen Ross, ed., *Women, Politics, and Change.* Oxford: Oxford University Press.

Parliament of South Africa. 2001. "Joint Investigation Report into the Strategic Defence Procurement Packages." November 14. http://www.parliament.gov.za/committees/sdp/index.asp.

Parpart, Jane. 1988. "Women and the State in Africa." In Donald Rothchild and Naomi Chazan, eds., *The Precarious Balance: State and Society in Africa.* Boulder: Westview.

Parsons, Neil. 1985. "The Evolution of Modern Botswana: Historical Revisions." In Louis Picard, ed., *The Evolution of Modern Botswana.* London: Rex Collings.

Picard, Louis. 1985. "From Bechuanaland to Botswana: An Overview." In Louis Picard, ed., *The Evolution of Modern Botswana.* London: Rex Collings.

Pitcher, M. Anne. 2003. *Transforming Mozambique: The Politics of Privatization, 1975–2001.* Cambridge: Cambridge University Press.

Poku, Nana. 2001. "Africa's AIDS Crisis in Context: 'How the Poor Are Dying.'" *Third World Quarterly.* 22,2: 191–204.

Poku, Nana, and Fantu Cheru. 2001. "The Politics of Poverty and Debt in Africa's AIDS Crisis." *International Relations.* 15,6: 37–54.

"Political Manoeuvres over Elections." 2004. *Angola Peace Monitor.* May 20. http://www.actsa.org/angola/apm/apm1020.htm.

Posner, Daniel. 1995. "Malawi's New Dawn." *Journal of Democracy.* 6,1: 131–145.

Power, Samantha. 2003. "Letter from South Africa: The AIDS Rebel." *New Yorker.* May 19.

"Presidential Candidate's Adoption Is an Act of Desperation." 2001. *The Post* (Zambia). August 27.

Pycroft, Christopher. 1994. "Angola: The Forgotten Tragedy." *Journal of Southern African Studies.* 20,2: 241–262.

Raftopoulos, Brian. 2001. "The Labour Movement and the Emergence of Opposition Politics in Zimbabwe." In Brian Raftopoulos and Lloyd Sachikonye, eds., *Striking Back: The Labour Movement and the Post-Colonial State in Zimbabwe.* Harare: Weaver Press.

Rakner, Lise. 1998. "Reform as a Matter of Political Survival: Political and Economic Liberalisation in Zambia, 1991–96." PhD diss. University of Bergen, Norway.

———. 2001. "The Pluralist Paradox: The Decline of Economic Interest Groups in Zambia." *Development and Change.* 32,3: 521–543.

Rakner, Lise, Nicolas van de Walle, and Dominic Mulaisho. 2001. "Zambia." In S. Devarajan, David Dollar, and T. Holmgren, eds., *Aid and Reform in Africa.* Washington, D.C.: World Bank.

Ranchod-Nilsson, Sita. 1998. "Zimbabwe: Women, Cultural Crisis, and the Reconfiguration of the One-Party State." In Leonardo Villalon and Phillip Huxtable, eds., *The African State at a Critical Juncture: Between Disintegration and Reconfiguration.* Boulder: Lynne Rienner.

"Recent Moves Welcomed by IMF." 2004. *Angola Peace Monitor.* May 20. http://www.actsa.org/Angola/apm/apm1020.htm.

Reed, John. 2004. "Black Elite Faces a Backlash over South Africa Wealth Reform." *Financial Times* (London). October 14.

"Renamo Boycotts and Marginalization." 2000. http://www.mozambique.mz/awepa/eawepa25/corpo.htm.

Reno, William. 1999. *Warlord Politics and African States.* Boulder: Lynne Rienner.

———. 2000. "The Real (War) Economy of Angola." In Jakkie Cilliers and Christian Dietrich, eds., *Angola's War Economy: The Role of Oil and Diamonds.* Pretoria: ISS.

"Report of the Committee on Economic Affairs and Labour on the Privatisation of Zambia Consolidated Copper Mines Limited for the Fourth Session of the Eighth National Assembly. Appointed on 10th February 2000." Lusaka.

Richburg, Keith. 1997. *Out of America: A Black Man Confronts Africa.* New York: Basic Books.

Roberts, Andrew. 1976. *A History of Zambia.* New York: Africana Publishing.

Rodney, Walter. 1974. *How Europe Underdeveloped Africa.* Washington, D.C.: Howard University Press.

Rollnick, Roman. 2002. "An African Test Case for Wide Distribution of Life-Prolonging Medicines." *Africa Recovery.* September 1. http://allafrica.com /sustainable/stories/200210230001.html.

Rotberg, Robert. 1995. "Centripetal Forces: Regional Convergence in Southern Africa." *Harvard International Review.* 17,8–9: 78–79.

———. 2000. "Africa's Mess: Mugabe's Mayhem." *Foreign Affairs.* 79,5: 47–61.

Rothchild, Donald, and John Harbeson. 2000. "The African State and State System in Flux." In John Harbeson and Donald Rothchild, eds., *Africa in World Politics: The African State System in Flux,* 3rd ed. Boulder: Westview.

Rugalema, Gabriel. 2000. "Coping or Struggling? A Journey into the Impact of HIV/AIDS in Southern Africa." *Review of African Political Economy.* 27,86: 537–545.

Rupiya, Martin. 1998. "Historical Context: War and Peace in Mozambique." In Alex Vines and Dylan Hendrickson, eds., *The Mozambican Peace Process in Perspective.* London: Conciliation Resources.

"SADC Puts on a New Face." 2001. *Review of African Political Economy* (Briefings). 28,87: 105–108.

Samatar, Abdi Ismail. 1999. *An African Miracle: State and Class Leadership and Colonial Legacy in Botswana Development.* Portsmouth, N.H.: Heinemann.

SARDC-WIDSAA. 2000. *Beyond Inequalities: Women in Southern Africa.* Harare: SARDC.

Saul, John. 1999. "Cry for the Beloved Country: The Post-Apartheid Denouement." *Monthly Review* 52,8: 1–51.

Saul, John, and Colin Leys. 1995. "SWAPO: The Politics of Exile." In Colin Leys and John Saul, eds., *Namibia's Liberation Struggle: The Two-Edged Sword.* London: James Currey.

———. 2003. "Lubango and After: 'Forgotten History' as Politics in Contemporary Namibia." *Journal of Southern African Studies.* 29,2: 333–353.

Schneider, Helen. 2002. "On the Fault-Line: The Politics of AIDS Policy in Contemporary South Africa." *African Studies.* 61,1: 145–167.

Schraeder, Peter J. 2000. *African Politics and Society: A Mosaic in Transformation.* New York: Bedford/St. Martins Press.

Seidman, Gay. 1999. "Gendered Citizenship: South Africa's Democratic Transition and the Construction of a Gendered State." *Gender and Society.* 13,3: 287–307.

Shafer, D. Michael. 1994. *Winners and Losers: How Sectors Shape the Developmental Prospects of States.* Ithaca: Cornell University Press.

Shaw, Timothy. 1989. "Corporatism in Zimbabwe." In Timothy Shaw and Julius Nyangoro, eds., *Corporatism in Africa: Comparative Analysis and Practice.* Boulder: Westview.

Sherbourne, Robin. 2004. "After the Dust Has Settled: Continuity or Stagnation?" IPPR Opinion no. 16. Windhoek: Institute for Public Policy Research.

Sidaway, James, and Richard Gibb. 1998. "SADC, COMESA, SACU: Contradictory Formats for Regional Integration in Southern Africa?" In David Simon, ed., *South Africa in Southern Africa: Reconfiguring the Region.* Athens: Ohio University Press.

Simpson, Mark. 1993. "Foreign and Domestic Factors in the Transformation of Frelimo." *Journal of Modern African Studies.* 31,2: 309–337.

Sindima, Harvey. 2002. *Malawi's First Republic: An Economic and Political Analysis.* Lanham, Md.: University Press of America.

Sisk, Timothy. 1995. *Democratization in South Africa: The Elusive Social Contract.* Princeton: Princeton University Press.

Sithole, Masipula. 1988. "Zimbabwe: In Search of a Stable Democracy." In Larry Diamond, Juan Linz, and Seymour Martin Lipset, eds., *Democracy in Developing Countries,* vol. 2, *Africa.* Boulder: Lynne Rienner.

———. 2000. "Zimbabwe: The Erosion of Authoritarianism and Prospects for Democracy." In York Bradshaw and Stephen Ndegwa, eds., *The Uncertain Promise of Southern Africa.* Bloomington: Indiana University Press.

———. 2001. "Fighting Authoritarianism in Zimbabwe." *Journal of Democracy.* 12,1: 160–169.

Skalnes, Tor. 1995. *The Political Economy of Economic Reform in Zimbabwe: Continuity and Change in Development.* New York: St. Martin's.

Sklar, Richard. 1975. *Corporate Power in an African State.* Los Angeles: University of California Press.

Smith, Ian Douglas. 2002. *Bitter Harvest: The Great Betrayal and the Dreadful Aftermath.* London: Blake.

Soiri, Iina. 1996. *The Radical Motherhood: Namibian Women's Independence Struggle.* Research Report no. 99. Uppsala: Nordiska Afrikainstitutet.

"South Africa Signs Historic Trade Deal with EU." 1999. *African Review of Business and Technology.* December 31.

South Scan. 2004. "Mbeki Stresses 'Developmental State' in Further Economic Swing." *South Scan.* 19,4. February 20.

Southern African Development Community (SADC) Gender Unit. 1999. *Women in Politics and Decision Making in SADC: Beyond 30 Percent in 2005.* Conference proceedings. Gaborone: SADC Gender Unit.

Staudt, Kathleen. 1987. "Women's Politics, the State, and Capitalist Transformation in Africa." In Irving Leonard Markovitz, ed., *Studies in Power and Class in Africa.* Oxford: Oxford University Press.

Staunton, Irene, ed. 1990. *Mothers of the Revolution.* Harare: Baobab Books.

Stedman, Stephen John. 1991. *Peacemaking in Civil War: International Mediation in Zimbabwe, 1974–1980.* Boulder: Lynne Rienner.

———. 1997. "Spoiler Problems in Peace Processes." *International Security.* 22,2: 5–53.

Steenkamp, Philip. 1995. "The Churches." In Colin Leys and John Saul, eds., *Namibia's Liberation Struggle: The Two-Edged Sword.* London: James Currey.

Stoneman, Colin. 1998. "Lessons Unlearned: South Africa's One-Way Relationship with Zimbabwe." In David Simon, ed., *South Africa in Southern Africa: Reconfiguring the Region.* Cape Town: David Philip.

Stoneman, Colin, ed. 1988. *Zimbabwe's Prospects.* London: Macmillan.

Stoneman, Colin, and Lionel Cliffe. 1989. *Zimbabwe: Politics, Economics and Society.* London: Pinter.

Stoneman, Colin, and Rob Davies. 1981. "The Economy: An Overview." In Colin Stoneman, ed., *Zimbabwe's Inheritance.* New York: St. Martin's.

Strachan, Brigid. 1986. "Report on Job Creation and Black Advancement, Part II: Black Advancement." Confederation of Zimbabwe Industries Job Creation/Black Advancement Subcommittee of the Labour and Manpower Committee. Harare.

————. 1989. "Black Managerial Advancement in a Sample of CZI Member Companies." Unpublished internal report for the Confederation of Zimbabwe Industries. Harare.

Sylvester, Christine. 1995. "Whither Democracy in Zimbabwe?" *Journal of Modern African Studies.* 33,3: 403–423.

Taljaard, Raenette, and Albert Venter. 1998. "Parliament." In Albert Venter, ed., *Government and Politics in the New South Africa.* Pretoria: Van Schaik.

Taylor, Ian. 2002. *Stuck in Middle GEAR: South Africa's Post-Apartheid Foreign Policy.* New York: St. Martin's.

Taylor, Ian, and Gladys Mokhawa. 2003. "Not Forever: Botswana, Conflict Diamonds, and the Bushmen." *African Affairs.* 102: 261–283.

Taylor, Ian, and Philip Nel. 2002. "'New Africa' Globalisation and the Confines of Elite Reformism: 'Getting the Rhetoric Right, Getting the Strategy Wrong.'" *Third World Quarterly.* 23,1: 163–180.

Taylor, Scott. 1999a. "Business and Politics in Zimbabwe's Commercial Agriculture Sector." *African Economic History.* 27: 177–215.

————. 1999b. "Race, Class, and Neopatrimonialism in Zimbabwe." In Richard Joseph, ed., *State, Conflict, and Democracy in Africa.* Boulder: Lynne Rienner.

————. 2002. "The Challenge of Indigenization, Affirmative Action, and Black Empowerment in Zimbabwe and South Africa." In Alusine Jalloh and Toyin Falola, eds., *Black Business and Economic Power.* Rochester: University of Rochester Press.

————. 2003. "Resource Networks, Political Movements, and the MDC in Zimbabwe: Opposition Prospects and a Framework for Analysis." CMI Working Paper. Bergen: Christian Michelsen Institute.

————. 2004. "Politics and Business in Southern Africa: Zambia, Zimbabwe, and South Africa." Unpublished book manuscript.

Thompson, Alex. 2001. *An Introduction to African Politics.* New York: Routledge.

Tingle, Rachel. 1998. "What Role for the Churches in the New South Africa?" In R. W. Johnson and David Welsh, eds., *Ironic Victory: Liberalism in Post-Liberation South Africa.* London: Oxford University Press.

Toetemeyer, Gerhard. 2000. "Decentralisation and State-Building at the Local Level." In Christiaan Keulder, ed., *State, Society, and Democracy: A Reader in Namibian Politics.* Windhoek: Gamsberg Macmillan.

Tordoff, William. 1980. Introduction to William Tordoff, ed., *Administration in Zambia.* Madison: University of Wisconsin Press.

————. 1996. *Government and Politics in Africa.* 3rd ed. Bloomington: Indiana University Press.

Tripp, Aili Mari. 2001. "The New Political Activism in Africa." *Journal of Democracy.* 12,3: 141–155.

Truth and Reconciliation Commission (TRC). 1999. *Truth and Reconciliation Commission of South Africa Report.* New York. Distributed by Grove's Dictionaries.

Tsie, Balefi. 1996. "The Political Context of Botswana's Development Performance." *Journal of Southern African Studies.* 22,4: 599–616.

————. 2001. "International Political Economy and Southern Africa." In Peter Vale, Larry A. Swatuk, and Bertil Oden, eds., *Theory, Change, and Southern Africa's Future.* London: Palgrave.

Tutu, Desmond. 1999. *No Future Without Forgiveness.* New York: Doubleday.

Tvedten, Inge. 1997. *Angola: Struggle for Peace and Reconstruction.* Boulder: Westview.

————. ed. 2002. *Angola 2001/2002: Key Development Issues and Aid in a Context of Peace.* Report R 2002: 8. Bergen: Christian Michelsen Institute.

UNAIDS. 2001. *Special Session Fact Sheets: Gender and HIV/AIDS.* http://www.unaids.org/fact_sheets/ungass/html/fsgender_en.htm.

————. 2002a. *Epidemiological Fact Sheets on HIV/AIDS and Sexually Transmitted Infections: South Africa.* http://www.unaids.org/hivaidsinfo/statistics/fact_sheets/pdfs/southafrica_en.pdf.

————. 2002b. "A Global Overview of the Epidemic." *Report on the Global HIV/AIDS Epidemic 2002.* http://www.unaids.org/barcelona/presskit/barcelona%20report/chapter2.html.

————. 2002c. "Join the Fight Against AIDS in Zambia." Menu of Partnership Options. Geneva: UNAIDS.

————. 2002d. "The Mounting Impact." *Report on the Global HIV/AIDS Epidemic 2002.* http://www.unaids.org/barcelona/presskit/barcelona%20report/chapter3.html.

————. 2002e. "UNAIDS Releases New Data Highlighting the Devastating Impact of AIDS in Africa." Press release. http://www.unaids.org/whatsnew/press/eng/pressarc02/g8_250602.html.

————. 2004. *AIDS Epidemic Update: December 2004.* http://www.unaids.org/wad2004/EPIupdate2004_html_en/epi04_00_en.htm.

————. N.d. *Gender and AIDS Fact Sheets.* http://www.unaids.org/gender/docs/gender%20package/factsheettableofcontents.pdf.

UNAIDS/WHO. 2002. *AIDS Epidemic Update: December 2002.* http://www.unaids.org/worldaidsday/2002/press/update/epiupdate_en.pdf.

————. 2003. *AIDS Epidemic Update: December 2003.* http://www.unaids.org/unaids/en/resources/publications/corporate+publications/aids+epidemic+update+-+december+2003.asp.

UNIFEM. N.d. *Women's Human Rights: Gender and AIDS.* http://www.unifem.undp.org/human_rights/facts.html.

United Nations Development Programme (UNDP). 2000. *Namibia: Human Development Report.* Windhoek: UNDP.

————. 2002. *Human Development Report 2002.* New York: Oxford University Press.

————. 2003. *Human Development Report 2003.* "Human Development Indicators." http://www.undp.org/hdr2003/pdf/hdr03_hdi.pdf.

United Nations Economic Commission for Africa (UNECA). 2001. "The New Partnership for African Development" (NEPAD). http://www.uneca.org/eca_resources/conference_reports_and_other_documents/nepad/nepad.htm.

United Nations Security Council. 2002. *Final Report of the Panel of Experts on the Illegal Exploitation of Natural Resources and Other Forms of Wealth of the Democratic Republic of Congo* (S/2002/1146). New York: United Nations Security Council.

U.S. Department of State. 2003a. *Background Note: Angola.* http://www.state.gov/r/pa/ei/bgn/6619.htm.

————. 2003b. *Country Reports on Human Rights Practices 2002: Angola.* http://www.state.gov/g/drl/rls/hrrpt/2002/18167.htm.

————. 2003c. *Country Reports on Human Rights Practices 2002: Botswana.* http://www.state.gov/g/drl/rls/hrrpt/2002/18169.htm.

————. 2003d. *Country Reports on Human Rights Practices 2002: Namibia.* http://www.state.gov/g/drl/rls/hrrpt/2002/18218.htm.

————. 2003e. *Malawi Country Reports on Human Rights Practices 2002.* http://www.state.gov/g/drl/rls/hrrpt/2002/18213.htm.

U.S. Institute of Peace (USIP). 2000. "Zimbabwe and the Politics of Torture." Special Report no. 92. Washington, D.C.: USIP, August.

———. 2001. "AIDS and Violent Conflict in Africa." Special report. Washington, D.C.: USIP, October.

U.S. International Trade Commission. 2003. "Sub-Saharan Africa: U.S. Exports, Imports, GSP Imports, and AGOA Imports, by Major Commodity Sectors, Annual and Year to Date Jan.–Jun." http://reportweb.usitc.gov/africa/by_country_all.jsp.

U.S. National Intelligence Council. 2000. *The Global Infectious Disease Threat and Its Implications for the United States.* January. http://www.cia.gov/nic/pubs/index.htm.

"U.S. Says Zim Election Fundamentally Flawed." 2002. *Financial Gazette* (Harare). Reuters, March 14.

Upton, Rebecca. 2003. "'Women Have No Tribe': Connecting Carework, Gender, and Migration in an Era of HIV/AIDS in Botswana." *Gender and Society.* 17,2: 314–322.

Urdang, Stephanie. 1989. *And Still They Dance: Women, War and the Struggle for Change in Mozambique.* New York: Monthly Review Press.

Vail, Leroy, ed. 1991. *The Creation of Tribalism in Southern Africa.* Berkeley: University of California Press.

Vale, Peter. 2001. "Dissenting Tale: Southern Africa's Search for Theory." In Peter Vale, Larry Swatuk, and Bertil Oden, eds., *Theory, Change, and Southern Africa's Future.* Hampshire: Palgrave.

Vale, Peter, Larry Swatuk, and Bertil Oden, eds. 2001. *Theory, Change, and Southern Africa's Future.* Hampshire: Palgrave.

van Allen, Judith. 2001. "Women's Rights Movements as a Measure of African Democracy." *Journal of Asian and African Studies.* 36,1: 39–64.

van de Walle, Nicolas. 2001. *African Economies and the Politics of Permanent Crisis, 1979–1999.* Cambridge: Cambridge University Press.

van Donge, Jon Kees. 1995. "Kamuzu's Legacy: The Democratization of Malawi." *African Affairs.* 94: 227–257.

Venter, Albert, ed. 1998. *Government and Politics in the New South Africa.* Pretoria: Van Schaik.

Vines, Alex. 1996. *Renamo: From Terrorism to Democracy in Mozambique?* Rev. ed. London: James Currey.

———. 2000. "Angola: 40 Years of War." Track Two Occasional Paper no. 9. Cape Town: Centre for Conflict Resolution.

von Doepp, Peter. 2001a. "Patterns of Judicial Activism in Malawi and Zambia: A Comparison and Initial Exploration." Paper presented at the annual meeting of the African Studies Association. Houston, Texas.

———. 2001b. "The Survival of Malawi's Enfeebled Democracy." *Current History.* 100,646: 232–237.

———. 2002. "Malawi's Local Clergy as Civil Society Activists? The Limiting Impact of Creed, Context, and Class." *Commonwealth and Comparative Politics.* 40,2: 21–46.

Wadula, Patrick, and Christof Maletsky. 1999. "SA's Neighbours Lose Out." *Business Day* (South Africa). October 15.

Wallerstein, Immanuel. 1974. *The Modern World System.* New York: Academic Press.

Weiland, H., and M. Braham, eds. 1994. *The Namibian Peace Process: Implications and Lessons for the Future.* Freiburg: Arnold-Bergstraesser-Institut.

Weinstein, Jeremy. 2002. "Mozambique: A Fading UN Success Story." *Journal of Democracy.* 13,1: 141–156.

Weiss, Ruth. 1994. *Zimbabwe and the New Elite.* London: St. Martin's.

Wendt, Alexander. 1999. *Social Theory of International Politics.* Cambridge: Cambridge University Press.

Widner, Jennifer A. 2001. *Building the Rule of Law: Francis Nyalali and the Road to Judicial Independence in Africa.* New York: W. W. Norton.

Williams, David. 1978. *Malawi: The Politics of Despair.* Ithaca: Cornell University Press.

Williams, Martin. 1998. "The Press Since 1994." In R. W. Johnson and David Welsh, eds., *Ironic Victory: Liberalism in Post-Liberation South Africa.* Oxford: Oxford University Press.

Wills, A. J. 1964. *An Introduction to the History of Central Africa.* Oxford: Oxford University Press.

Wilson, Richard. 2001. *The Politics of Truth and Reconciliation in South Africa: Legitimizing the Post-Apartheid State.* Cambridge: Cambridge University Press.

Wiseman, John. 1998. "The Slow Evolution of the Party System in Botswana." *Journal of Asian and African Studies.* 33,3: 241–265.

———. 2000. "Presidential and Parliamentary Elections in Malawi, 1999." *Electoral Studies.* 19,4: 615–646.

World Bank. 1981. *Accelerated Development in Sub-Saharan Africa.* Washington, D.C.: The World Bank.

———. 1995. *Zimbabwe: Achieving Shared Growth.* Country Economic Memorandum, 2 vols. Washington, D.C.: World Bank.

———. 2000. *Can Africa Claim the 21st Century?* Washington, D.C.: World Bank.

———. 2003a. *Sustainable Development in a Dynamic World: Transforming Institutions, Growth, and Quality of Life.* New York: Oxford University Press.

———. 2003b. *World Development Report 2003.* New York: Oxford University Press.

Zaffiro, James. 1997. "Women and Democratization of Politics in Botswana." Paper presented at the fortieth annual African Studies Association meeting. Columbus, Ohio.

"Zambia's Ruling Party Approves Third Term for Chiluba." 2001. Agence France Presse. April 30.

Zartman, I. William, ed. 1989. *Ripe for Resolution.* 2nd ed. New York: Oxford University Press.

Zartman, I. William, ed. 1995. *Collapsed States: The Disintegration and Restoration of Legitimate Authority.* Boulder: Lynne Rienner.

"Zim Cattle Spread FMD in Botswana." 2004. Africa News Service. May 20.

"Zim Parliament Passes Media Bill." 2002. Reuters. January 31.

Zimbabwe Alert. 2002. "Army General Warns Independent Media and Foreign Journalists." Windhoek: Media Institute of Southern Africa, January 10.

Zimbabwe Congress of Trade Unions (ZCTU). 1996. *Beyond ESAP.* Harare: ZCTU.

Zimbabwe Human Rights Association (ZimRights). 1996. "1996 Presidential Election Monitoring Report." Harare: Zimbabwe Human Rights Association.

———. 2002. Home page. http://www.kubatana.net/html/sectors/zim038.asp.

Zwi, A. B., and A. J. Cabral. 1991. "Identifying 'High Risk Situations' for Preventing AIDS." *British Medical Journal.* 303: 1527–1529.

Index

About the Book

Making a case for the regional distinctiveness of southern Africa, this new text systematically examines politics and society in the region.

The authors first introduce the themes and concepts that guide their analysis. Then, in each of eight country studies, they trace the country's political history (beginning with the precolonial period) and analyze state structures, political and social actors, fundamentals of the political economy, and the major challenges faced by state and society. The final section of the book investigates issues that transcend borders: gender and politics, the HIV/AIDS crisis, and southern Africa's role on the continent and in the world.

Gretchen Bauer is associate professor of political science and associate dean for social sciences and history at the University of Delaware. Her publications include *Labor and Democracy in Namibia, 1971–1996*. **Scott D. Taylor** is assistant professor of African politics and political economy in the School of Foreign Service at Georgetown University.